MW01036625

"This tour de force challenges the destr structures of our local and global socie tianity. Beginning with the discourse a lonial mentality has invaded many other forms of Christian..., European Christians and indigenous peoples of the Americas, caste and race in India, and Asian Americans and affirmative action. This is a topic which Christians today—especially evangelicals—can no longer ignore."

Alexander Chow, senior lecturer in theology and world Christianity, School of Divinity, University of Edinburgh

"As I read through this book (a compilation of papers from an important academic conference) my first response was, Why couldn't I have been there! For those of us who could not attend this dynamic and important gathering, we have the tremendous opportunity to interact with the significant findings from a meeting of some of the best scholars on this topic. The problem of race and its intersection with missiology continues to elude many in the American church. Told from multiple perspectives and voices arising from a myriad of experiences and expertise, this text will serve as a vital primer for those who seek a more profound understanding of race, theology, and mission."

Soong-Chan Rah, Milton B. Engebretson Professor of Church Growth and Evangelism, North Park Theological Seminary, author of *The Next Evangelicalism* and *Prophetic Lament*

"This book brilliantly captures and elucidates one of the gravest and long-standing threats to Christianity: a theology fashioned in the idolatrous images of race, power, gender, ability, or nationalism. Zeroing in on whiteness as a concrete example of this kind of treacherous theology, the book teaches us how to smash such idols and let radical love, equality for all of God's children, and shared human dignity shine forth from our theologies and practices."

Nimi Wariboko, Walter G. Muelder Professor of Social Ethics, Boston University

"The emphatically Christian voices in this important book explore the damage done to Christian witness by the tight bond between Western missionary activity and unreflective racist assumptions. While some particularly helpful contributors record parallel difficulties arising in other cultures, all pose a biblically based challenge to the aggressive nationalism, manipulative colonialism, and unthinking Enlightenment assumptions that long tainted Western missions activity. It is a sobering and thought-provoking book."

Mark Noll, coauthor, *Clouds of Witnesses: Christian Voices from Africa and Asia*

"In a growing corpus of work on antiracism, *Can 'White' People Be Saved?: Triangulating Race, Theology, and Mission* stands out at many levels. To begin with, it overcomes the tendency to engage the topic of racism as a black and white binary. The book includes a variety of outstanding scholars from various ethnic and cultural backgrounds, including evangelical or evangélic@ perspectives such as Drs. Love Sechrest, Willie James Jennings, Andrea Smith, Elizabeth Conde-Frazier, and Amos Yong. Second, the book is distinctive from other books on antiracism in that it is profoundly theological, intentionally scriptural, and eminently praxeological. Third, given the recent climate of stridency and intolerance, it is refreshing to read a book that seeks not to demonize any one constituency but rather to bring fresh knowledge and understanding to key concepts (racism, white supremacy, whiteness, postcolonialism, etc.). It enables the reader to see how racism is above all a structural problem that impoverishes the church and the world it is called to serve. Finally, the book is unique in that its constructive dialogue about overcoming the deforming dis-ease of racism and white supremacy leads to a missiological paradigm shift, allowing missions to become truly life giving and Spirit filled. It is an important book that everyone who is committed to the biblical notions of justice and the reign of God should read and own."

Loida I. Martell, vice president of academic affairs, dean and professor of constructive theology, Lexington Theological Seminary, Lexington, Kentucky

"In the series of essays found in *Can 'White' People Be Saved?* an all-star lineup of Christian scholars thoroughly challenge many of the notions of nobility that have always accompanied modern mission and its racist entanglement with white supremacy. The issue is complex but not complicated. Seamlessly, the authors out the premise of current and past systemic racism enmeshed with Christian mission, and then disentangle the practices associated with whiteness and mission. The exposure of whiteness as normal, embedded in modern mission, is competently examined and exposed in *Can 'White' People Be Saved?* How the church responds will answer the question."

Randy S. Woodley, author of *Shalom and the Community of Creation*

"*Can 'White' People Be Saved?: Triangulating Race, Theology, and Mission* is informed by a narrative historical timeline that traces and analyzes the study of race and racism. In an era where the relevance of church is increasingly called into question, this compilation of interdisciplinary essays is essential reading."

Angela D. Sims, author of *Lynched: The Power of Memory in a Culture of Terror*

"It is obvious from this volume's chapters that the past quarter decade of 'reconciliation miracles' in and among evangelical and Pentecostal denominations and movements were hopeful gestures. The authors lay down clear signposts of the rocky paths Christians have trod, of the troubled crossroads evangelicals inhabit, and of the way of straightening still to be done in search of a beloved community. *Can 'White' People Be Saved?* challenges readers to undertake a difficult but ultimately rewarding journey of introspection."

Daniel Ramírez, author, *Migrating Faith: Pentecostalism in the United States and Mexico in the Twentieth Century*

"For those of us whose skin pigmentation has been labeled black, we shall be delighted that finally the question is asked bluntly, Can 'White' People Be Saved? These essays demand, however (without stating it explicitly), that we ask the corollary, Can 'Black' People Be Saved? Both whiteness and blackness are 'demons' that ought to be exorcised for us to embrace God's salvation because as the essays articulate, any racial categorization renders some people outside of the category of human. I commend this volume in its entirety, not because it is infallible on matters of race and theology (for we know it is not) but because it models for us how as a people of God in this historical moment, in our diverse social locations, we may boldly confront, in love and with integrity, the distortions and deformations of the gospel inherent in the partiality and particularity of any location—historical, cultural, racial, or otherwise."

D. Zac Niringiye, bishop emeritus of Kampala Diocese, Anglican Church of Uganda, senior fellow, Institute of Religion, Faith and Culture in Public Life

CAN "WHITE" PEOPLE BE SAVED?

Triangulating Race, Theology, and Mission

Edited by
LOVE L. SECHREST,
JOHNNY RAMÍREZ-JOHNSON,
and AMOS YONG

IVP Academic
An imprint of InterVarsity Press
Downers Grove, Illinois

InterVarsity Press
P.O. Box 1400, Downers Grove, IL 60515-1426
ivpress.com
email@ivpress.com

InterVarsity Press® is the book-publishing division of InterVarsity Christian Fellowship/USA®, a movement of students and faculty active on campus at hundreds of universities, colleges, and schools of nursing in the United States of America, and a member movement of the International Fellowship of Evangelical Students. For information about local and regional activities, visit intervarsity.org.

Scripture quotations, unless otherwise noted, are from the New Revised Standard Version of the Bible, copyright 1989 by the Division of Christian Education of the National Council of the Churches of Christ in the USA. Used by permission. All rights reserved.

While any stories in this book are true, some names and identifying information may have been changed to protect the privacy of individuals.

Cover design and image composite: David Fassett
Interior design: Beth McGill
Images: white paint on red: © Lauren Burke / Digital Vision / Getty Images
       old engraved map: © bauhaus1000 / DigitalVision Vectors / Getty Images

ISBN 978-0-8308-5104-1 (print)
ISBN 978-0-8308-7375-3 (digital)

Printed in the United States of America ∞

InterVarsity Press is committed to ecological stewardship and to the conservation of natural resources in all our operations. This book was printed using sustainably sourced paper.

Library of Congress Cataloging-in-Publication Data

A catalog record for this book is available from the Library of Congress.

P	23	22	21	20	19	18	17	16	15	14	13	12	11	10	9	8	7	6	5	4	3	2
Y	37	36	35	34	33	32	31	30	29	28	27	26	25	24	23	22	21	20	19			

We dedicate this book
to the visionary founding leaders of the
multilingual and multicultural academic programs
at Fuller Theological Seminary:

William E. Pannell

George Gay (in memoriam)

Seyoon Kim

Timothy Park

Jehu Hanciles

Daniel D. Lee

Contents

Preface

This book has at least three geneses: the personal lives of the editors and contributors; the 2017 Missiology Lectures with the theme "Race, Theology, and Mission," at Fuller Theological Seminary's School of Intercultural Studies (SIS); and the life experiences of the conference participants and attendees. We all have seen the struggles of the church and its institutions to muster gospel-based initiatives to fight racism and discrimination emerging from the Western whiteness project. The combined distilled life experiences, institutional knowledge, and rigorous academic research come to you in this book.

We, the editors, acknowledge our incomplete work in that many experiences were ignored, including the experiences of Australian Aborigines with British colonial whiteness, the lives of Pilipino natives with Spanish and American whiteness colonial enterprises, and the myriad other native peoples from Greenland Inuit to Pitcairn Island natives, from the Sámi peoples of Lapland in northern Finland to Patagonia's Mapuche, from Taloyoak's Inuit to Lesotho's Bantu-speaking people. From all around the world as well as in our backyards, so many disenfranchised peoples affected by the Western whiteness project will remain unaddressed in these pages. This undertaking has accounted for just a few examples of the worldwide experiences with racist ideologies of the West. Though racism has been tackled here primarily as a Western phenomenon, we also acknowledge that racism is bigger and wider than the English-speaking West, much bigger than any one book project. While we are indebted to the many before us who have written excellent books on these issues, we hope that the focus in this book on missiology is one that makes a contribution to the study of race and racism.

We are grateful as well to Mark Labberton, president of Fuller Theological Seminary, for embracing the missiology conference's aims, for participating in the conference as a respondent, and especially for initiating an ongoing conversation at Fuller about dismantling racism in our institutional context. Our gratitude goes as well to all who dealt with a myriad of conference details and especially to Randa Hinton and Caitlyn Ference from Fuller's events office. The SIS dean's office was truly engaged and very helpful, specifically Acting Dean Bryant Myers, Dean Scott Sunquist, Wendy Walker, and Silvia Gutierrez. We are also grateful for the work of SIS doctoral student Dwight Radcliff, who coordinated all musical appearances with magnificent Christian artists Eric Sarwar, Redd Alder, David Kong, Mark Chase, Derrick Engoy, Tanya DeCuir, Danyol Jaye, Brooke Coxon, and Prince Purposed—we thank you all.

We thank Julie Tai, director of the Fuller Chapel, who led our opening session. We thank our Fuller race-warrior veteran William E. Pannell, professor emeritus of preaching, for his inspiring opening words. We could not have joined Fuller nor thrived once arrived if not for his labor as the first Fuller professor of Color and founder of Fuller's earliest race initiatives. We thank for their support all of Fuller's ethnic studies center leaders: Oscar García-Johnson, associate dean and director of Centro Latino; Clifton Clarke, associate dean and director of the William E. Pannell Center for African American Church Studies; Daniel D. Lee, director of the Center for Asian American Theology and Ministry; and Sebastian Kim, executive director of the Korean Studies Center. Their participation was critical to the success of the conference, including and especially García-Johnson, Clarke, and Lee, who each responded to one of the seven plenary lectures.

Those of us who were present at the conference witnessed the energy and craft of the conference presenters delivering their messages. The fully annotated academic versions of the papers presented at the conference and included in this volume are by Akintunde Akinade with Clifton Clarke, Elizabeth Conde-Frazier, Andrew Draper, Willie Jennings, Daniel Jeyaraj, Angel Santiago-Vendrell, Andrea Smith, and Jonathan Tran. We are deeply indebted to them for their scholarship, their warm and grace-filled spirits, and the way that their very presence blessed our entire community for those three rich conference days. Also included are essays not presented at the conference but offered here by each of the three coeditors (by Sechrest and Ramírez-Johnson, with Yong's concluding remarks) as well as one authored by colleague Hak Joon Lee from Fuller's School of Theology (SOT). We express our sincere appreciation to other colleagues at Fuller who did an excellent job responding to the presentations: Lisseth Rojas-Flores (School of Psychology), Kirsteen Kim (SIS), Juan F. Martínez (SOT), and Erin Dufault-Hunter (SOT). The last named also receives our gratitude for allowing us to include her unusual conference response here as an epilogue.

A chapel sermon initiated the proceedings, and the preacher who challenged us and set the tone for the conference was Fuller SIS alumnus Daniel White Hodge—thank you for your labor of love. Conference panel participants also gave their hearts to the audience: Grace Dyrness, David Leong, Duane T. Loynes Sr., Daniel Ramírez, and Gabe Veas—thank you all. These and other lunchtime seminar leaders opened doors to practical applications of the principles shared and were invaluable to the success of the conference: Chris Beard, lead pastor, People's Church, Cincinnati; Alexia Salvatierra, Lutheran pastor and a national leader in the arena of immigration rights and immigration reform; David Leong, Seattle Pacific University; Albert Tate, lead pastor, Fellowship Monrovia, California; Duane Loynes Sr., William Randolph Hearst Fellow, Rhodes College, Memphis, Tennessee; Daniel Ramírez, Claremont Graduate University; Gabe Veas, founder of LA Urban Educators Collaborative; Grace Dyrness, Institute for Transnational Research and Development; Daniel White Hodge, North Park University; Mathew John, creator of the Mosaic Course, an online platform for exploring world religions from a Christian perspective; D. Zac Niringiye, bishop emeritus of Kampala Diocese in the Anglican Church of Uganda, representing the African Christianity Scholars Network; and Janna Louie, co-area director of InterVarsity Christian Fellowship's Graduate and Faculty Ministries in Southern California. To all of them we express our humble gratitude for their invaluable contributions. All major presentations, including conference versions of the papers published here, responses and question-and-answer periods following, panel discussions, and the day-one chapel sermon are now available on the Fuller Studio website (Fuller.edu/Studio/RaceandIdentity).

We express our gratitude to the InterVarsity Press team who has helped with our Missiological Engagements series as well as with this volume.

Finally, we return thanks to the individuals and families who reached out to us after the conference and to the conference attendee who sent us a thank-you card saying that God had used the lectures to minister to her and to build on what God had already begun in her life. Similarly, we pray for each reader of this volume that God would begin a similar process of affirmation and edification in you.

We dedicate this book to the individuals shown on the dedication page and below, who are the visionary leaders of the multilingual and multicultural centers and academic programs at Fuller Theological Seminary. These programs and centers were the forerunners of today's conversations that promote the decolonization of race and language and the deconstruction of the whiteness project, making room for inclusiveness and equity in Fuller's theological curriculum and community today, to the glory of God and for the sake of the church's witness. We realize that there were many others involved in the founding and growth of these important initiatives—too many to name here—but we want to honor the following individuals for their vision and commitment to advancing theological and missiological conversations about race, ethnicity, and the glocal church in connection with efforts to establish their respective centers.

- William E. Pannell: Pannell Center for African American Church Studies, founded in 1974

- George Gay: Hispanic Church Studies program (now Centro Latino), founded in 1975 (in memoriam)

- Seyoon Kim: Korean DMin program (now the Korean Studies Center), founded in 1995

- Timothy Park: SIS Korean Studies program (now the Korean Studies Center), founded in 1996

- Jehu Hanciles: Center for Missiological Research, welcomed first cohort of PhD ICS students in 2010

- Daniel D. Lee: Asian American Theology and Ministry Initiative (now the Center for Asian American Theology and Ministry), founded in 2010

To God alone be the glory.
May 2018

Introduction

Race and Missiology in Glocal Perspective

Johnny Ramírez-Johnson
and Love L. Sechrest

The Interdependent Nature of Race and Missions

On December 13, 2017, US Senator Kamala Harris, Democrat from the state of California and the only Black woman in the Senate, tweeted:

> Black Women helped elect a Democrat to the US Senate in AL [Alabama] for the first time in more than 20 years. But we need to do more than congratulate them. Let's address issues that disproportionately affect Black women—like pay disparity, housing & under-representation in elected office.[1]

How would someone from Mars make sense of this tweet? If Martians are somehow well informed on data and events but lack the cultural nuances of earthlings, we might help them take note of several things. First, we might fill them in on the political background regarding the election Harris references. Alabama is a state that had not elected a Democrat in over twenty years but had just done so due to a 50 percent increase in Black voter turnout, in combination with high support from Black women, White millennials, and college-educated White women. Next, we might inform them that Black women like Senator Harris are underrepresented in the US Senate by over 80 percent given their share of the population. We might encourage our Martian friends to ask why Black women receive only 65 percent of the pay

---

[1]Kamala Harris (@SenKamalaHarris), "Black Women helped elect a Democrat," December 13, 2017, https://twitter.com/KamalaHarris/status/940992476441206785.

of White men and why Latinas receive only 58 percent of the pay of White men.[2] Why are there frequent and persistent disparities in the United States between Whites and people of Color with respect to unemployment rates,[3] incarceration rates,[4] home ownership rates,[5] and infant mortality rates?[6]

All of these questions revolve around race, and the topic dominates the national discourse in a myriad of forms: from debates about banning immigrants from majority-Muslim nations to those about border fence construction to keep out immigrants from Mexico and South America to controversies about police shootings of unarmed Black men, women, and children in Ferguson, Missouri, and Baltimore, Maryland. Other recent developments have catalyzed the Black Lives Matter movement, including the current Republican administration's affirmation of so-called alt-right white supremacist groups by tacitly endorsing these groups in the wake of a deadly demonstration in Charlottesville, Virginia.[7]

Yet these issues are not unique to the United States. Ecclesially, Sunday morning demarcates racially divided space and time across the United States, a fact known since Martin Luther King Jr. brought it to the forefront of the American psyche: "We must face the sad fact that at eleven o'clock

---

[2]Eileen Patten, "Racial, Gender Wage Gaps Persist in U.S. Depite Some Progress," Fact Tank, Pew Research Center, July 1, 2016, www.pewresearch.org/fact-tank/2016/07/01/racial-gender-wage-gaps-persist-in-u-s-despite-some-progress.

[3]The US Census reported that in the third quarter of 2017, the unemployment rate for Whites was 3.8%. Black unemployment was nearly double the White rate at 7.5%, and Latina/o unemployment was nearly 35% higher than Whites at 5.1%. Though Asian American unemployment generally tracks with White unemployment, 20- to 24-year-old Asians had an unemployment rate that was 25% higher than Whites in the same age group. See "Labor Force Statistics from the Current Population Survey," Bureau of Labor Statistics, www.bls.gov/web/empsit/cpsee_e16 .htm for current quarter comparisons.

[4]Michelle Alexander, *The New Jim Crow: Mass Incarceration in the Age of Colorblindness* (New York: New Press, 2012).

[5]Wealth creation for working-class and middle-class families in the United States is generally tied to home ownership according to Laura Sullivan et al. in "The Racial Wealth Gap: Why Policy Matters," a joint report from Demos and the Brandeis Institute for Assets and Social Policy (2015), www.demos.org/sites/default/files/publications/RacialWealthGap_1.pdf. Hence, wealth gaps are largely a product of vast differences in rates of home ownership: Whites at 71%, Blacks at 41%, and Latina/o families at 45% as of 2014.

[6]Number of infant deaths per 1,000 in 2014: Whites (4.89); Blacks (10.93); Latina/os (5.0); Native Americans (7.66); Asians/Pacific Islanders (3.68). See National Center for Health Statistics, *Health, United States, 2016: With Chartbook on Long-Term Trends in Health* (Hyattsville, MD: U.S. Department of Health and Human Services, 2017), 17.

[7]Liam Stack, "Alt-Right, Alt-Left, Antifa: A Glossary of Extremist Language," *New York Times*, August 15, 2017, www.nytimes.com/2017/08/15/us/politics/alt-left-alt-right-glossary.html.

on Sunday morning when we stand to sing 'In Christ there is no East or West,' we stand in the most segregated hour of America."[8] The same is true as well in the United Kingdom. Bishop Dr. Joe Aldred makes this point in poignant terms:

> All the signs are that the reason for White disinterest [in church attendance] was quite simply the dark pigmentation of the new migrants. Still today, colour prejudice feeds and informs the worldview of many. From early on, Black people in the post Windrush era, graphically describe from personal experience the context they found in Britain: for example, their experience on the bus, when looking for rooms to rent, on the job, in education, in fact anywhere they cared to look, their reception was as cold as the winter weather they had to get accustomed to. Io Smith complains, "I was looking for love and warmth and encouragement. I believed that the first place I would find that was in the Church, but it wasn't there."[9]

Likewise, racial animus is on the rise across the globe as nativism sweeps across democracies in Europe as well as the United States, from Brexit to the rise of Donald Trump. Anti-immigrant sentiment is nowhere better manifested than in the shameful reluctance of most nations in the European Union and the United States to absorb refugees from the Syrian civil war.[10] With over 70 percent of the world's millionaires living in the United States and majority-White Western European countries[11] and global missionary activity significantly shaped by the flow of people and wealth from these countries to the Global South and East, if it were ever possible to think that the racial dynamics in one corner of the world are of local import only, that naiveté is no longer practical. Our increasingly tightly woven domestic communities are profoundly interconnected with villages and towns on the other side of the world.

---

[8]Joseph Barndt, *Becoming an Anti-racist Church: Journeying Toward Wholeness* (Minneapolis: Fortress, 2011), 1.

[9]Joe Aldred, "Black Churches Contributing to Cohesion or Polarising Christians and Other Faith Groups?," Pentecostal and Multicultural Relations, Churches Together in England, June 15, 2007, www.cte.org.uk/Groups/236173/Home/Resources/Pentecostal_and_Multicultural/Black_Church_in/Black_Church_in.aspx.

[10]Max Fisher and Amanda Taub, "The Refugee Crisis: 9 Questions You Were Too Embarrassed to Ask," Vox, September 9, 2015, www.vox.com/2015/9/9/9290985/refugee-crisis-europe-syrian.

[11]"Global Inequality," Inequality.org, Institute for Policy Studies, https://inequality.org/facts/global-inequality/.

In theological education, evangelical institutions in particular remain challenged in navigating these issues, as the 2015–2016 events involving Dr. Larycia Hawkins and Wheaton College remind us. A political scientist, Hawkins was Wheaton's first tenured African American female professor, and in December 2015 she authored a Facebook posting that described her decision to wear the hijab, a distinctive head covering worn by traditional Muslim women, during the season of Lent, attaching with the posting a picture of herself in the hijab. In an act of "embodied solidarity" Hawkins wanted to demonstrate support for American Muslims at a time when they were being subjected to hostile discourse and further marginalization—this just after then–presidential candidate Donald Trump first called for a "a total and complete ban on Muslims entering the United States" in the aftermath of a terrorist attack in San Bernardino, California.[12] Alarm exploded in the media and among donors, parents, students, and alumni of Wheaton, and within days Hawkins had been placed on administrative leave pending closer examination of the orthodoxy of her theology and whether it aligned with Wheaton's Statement of Faith. Ostensibly, the center of the controversy concerned Hawkins's favorable allusion to Pope Francis's statement that Christians and Muslims worship the same God. Over the course of months of debate, several prominent Christian theologians and missiologists inside and outside of evangelicalism wrote essays regarding this central idea in the controversy.[13]

It was not lost on those watching that White males, including leaders at Wheaton, had expressed similar sentiments about the "same God" over the

---

[12]Jenna Johnson, "Trump Calls for 'Total and Complete Shutdown of Muslims Entering the United States,'" *Washington Post*, December 7, 2015, www.washingtonpost.com/news/post -politics/wp/2015/12/07/donald-trump-calls-for-total-and-complete-shutdown-of-muslims -entering-the-united-states/.

[13]See the essays in the 2016 special edition of the *Occasional Bulletin*, a publication of the Evangelical Missiological Society, www.emsweb.org/images/occasional-bulletin/special-editions /OB_SpecialEdition_2016.pdf. Hawkins herself linked a subsequent Facebook posting to Miroslav Volf, "Do Christians and Muslims Worship the Same God?," *The Blog, Huffington Post*, updated May 25, 2011, www.huffingtonpost.com/miroslav-volf/god-versus-allah_b_829955.html. Hawkins's written statement clarifying her remarks also included citations of prominent evangelicals such as Timothy George, John Stackhouse, and Scot McKnight (this document no longer available online). For a thoughtful description of the controversy, including extensive interviews with Hawkins, see Wheaton alumna Ruth Graham's article "The Professor Wore a Hijab in Solidarity—Then Lost Her Job," *New York Times*, October 13, 2016, www.nytimes .com/2016/10/16/magazine/the-professor-wore-a-hijab-in-solidarity-then-lost-her-job.html.

years without the threat of expulsion from their evangelical institutions.[14] Prominent evangelical theologian Miroslav Volf of Yale minced no words when he declared in a *Washington Post* opinion piece that Hawkins's suspension from the Wheaton faculty was "not about theology and orthodoxy. It is about enmity toward Muslims."[15] *Time* magazine released the contents of an email from a faculty diversity committee at Wheaton that described the university's process in adjudicating this controversy surrounding its first African American female tenured professor as "discriminatory": "We believe that the college has demonstrated a pattern of differential over-scrutiny about Dr. Hawkins's beliefs in ways often tied to race, gender, and marital status." Despite the fact that Wheaton administrators explicitly claimed that "Dr. Hawkins' administrative leave resulted from theological statements that seemed inconsistent with Wheaton College's doctrinal convictions, and is in no way related to her race, gender or commitment to wear a hijab during Advent," the diversity committee believed that "the scope or formality of the inquiry—along with the failure to calm down over-wrought alumni and donors seems to have been an absorption of raced, gendered, and fear-based over-reaction from outside audiences."[16] Larycia Hawkins's identity and social location seemingly touched a number of nerves in the White evangelical psyche: she was a Black woman at the center of controversy, and thus "angry"; she was unmarried, which animated fears regarding her sexual identity; and she was pictured wearing Muslim garb, which rendered her suspect theologically, fears that were reinforced when she cited the Catholic pontiff as support for her decision.

The controversy involved threats of termination and accusations of insubordination as well as counteraccusations of racism, sexism, and anti-Muslim

---

[14]According to Graham, "Hawkins's defenders pointed out that Jones [Wheaton's provost] and Wheaton's previous president had signed an interfaith statement in 2007 implying that same thing. Each later removed his signature, but the president said at the time that no one had pressured him to do so—a fact that suggests the 'same God' language might not bother Wheaton's constituents when it comes from the college's white male leaders." Graham, "Professor Wore a Hijab in Solidarity."

[15]Miroslav Volf, "Wheaton Professor's Suspension Is About Anti-Muslim Bigotry, Not Theology," *Washington Post*, December 17, 2015, www.washingtonpost.com/news/acts-of-faith/wp /2015/12/17/wheaton-professors-suspension-is-about-anti-muslim-bigotry-not-theology /?utm_term=.1f8aff7af059.

[16]Elizabeth Dias, "Exclusive: Wheaton College Faculty Say School 'Discriminatory' in Treatment of Tenured Black Professor," *Time*, February 4, 2016, http://time.com/4208102/wheaton-college-larycia-hawkins-discrimination/.

bigotry. It was resolved months later when Wheaton withdrew the threat of termination while Hawkins simultaneously agreed to resign voluntarily, but this painful tangle of events demonstrates the urgency of examining missiological and theological concepts in a way that is informed by scholarship and deep reflection on race and ethnicity. This episode at a premier evangelical institution of higher education served to discredit evangelical institutions and contributed to painting the evangelical movement in racialized overtones. As a leading missiologist put it, "Wheaton [belongs] not merely to the Wheaton board, faculty, administration, and alumni—but to the worldwide evangelical community. What Wheaton does affects us all."[17] The incident undoubtedly impeached evangelical witness to the Muslim world and to US communities of Color.[18]

However, it is important to realize that the Hawkins incident transpired in the context of larger US trends impacting race relations. Political events in these opening years of the twenty-first century are quite possibly new inflection points across the broad sweep of race relations in US history. Advances in civil rights in this country are often met with a White backlash, as for instance when the Jim Crow codes rolled back Black advancement after the Civil War and Reconstruction.[19] Passage of the Voting Rights Act gave rise to the decades-long persistence of the so-called Southern Strategy, which first introduced coded racist appeals in political debate (i.e., "dog-whistle racism") and transformed the South from a rock-solid Democratic stronghold to an equally dependable Republican bastion. We are convinced that the current moment of demographic change, manifest concretely in the election of the first African American president in 2008 and 2012, represents a similar moment of rising White fear and backlash against what is perceived as an

[17]Robert J. Priest, "Wheaton and the Controversy over Whether Muslims and Christians Worship the Same God," *Occasional Bulletin: A Publication of the Evangelical Missiological Society*, Special Edition 2016, 1. Priest, who was then serving as the president of the Evangelical Missiological Society (EMS), invited twenty-two missiologists to discuss the controversy at the heart of the Hawkins controversy—Do Christians and Muslims worship the same God?—but without directly engaging or assigning validity to any of the participants in the events at Wheaton.
[18]For more on the latest thinking on evangelical witness to the Muslim world, see Evelyne Reisacher, ed., *Dynamics of Muslim Worlds: Regional, Theological, and Missiological Perspectives*, Missiological Engagements (Downers Grove, IL: InterVarsity Press, 2017).
[19]For a scholarly treatment of this argument, see Carol Anderson's provocative and critically acclaimed book *White Rage: The Unspoken Truth of Our Racial Divide* (New York: Bloomsbury, 2016).

imminent loss of White social dominance.[20] In other words, the open bigotry of "Trumpism" is not so much a disease that is resurrecting xenophobia's dark and bitter past; rather, it is a symptom of the disease pathology of racism.

Thus, evangelical fear of Larycia Hawkins and broad evangelical support for the present Republican administration—whether consciously or unconsciously animated by Hawkins's social location and the president's openly racist rhetoric and governing agenda[21]—can both be seen as of a piece. Both responses are congruent with the ebb and flow of civil rights advances and reactive bias retreat, and both function to discredit evangelical witness among people of Color and other outsiders.[22] This is not to label all evangelicals so implicated as bigots or racists, but it is to worry aloud about how fear of living in a radically multiethnic country is strong enough to drive members of the body of Christ to embrace profoundly un-Christian behaviors and actors. It is to worry that racism is tightening its grip on the evangelical psyche, resulting in idolatry of the first order.[23] It is our hope that this book can help inoculate our beloved evangelical church from such viral strains of fear of the other.

---

[20]Recent psychological studies have demonstrated a link among Whites between responses to demographic change and negative perceptions of people of Color. See Maureen A. Craig and Jennifer A. Richeson, "More Diverse Yet Less Tolerant? How the Increasingly Diverse Racial Landscape Affects White Americans' Racial Attitudes," *Personality and Social Psychology Bulletin* 40, no. 6 (2014): 750-61. Similarly, this research team found a correlation between responses to demographic change and political alignment among Whites: Maureen A. Craig and Jennifer A. Richeson, "On the Precipice of a 'Majority-Minority' America: Perceived Status Threat from the Racial Demographic Shift Affects White Americans' Political Ideology," *Psychological Science* 25, no. 6 (2014): 1189-97.

[21]For more on Trump's racism, see Duke professor Jay A. Pearson's op-ed article "Donald Trump Is a Textbook Racist," *Los Angeles Times*, October 4, 2017, www.latimes.com/opinion/op-ed /la-oe-pearson-trumps-textbook-racism-20171004-story.html. In this article Pearson introduces various categories of racism (e.g., institutional, structural, interpersonal) and aligns them with several widely known Trump campaign statements and policy prescriptions.

[22]See for example the op-ed essay by *Christianity Today* editor in chief Mark Galli about the damage done to evangelical witness in view of broad support of immoral candidates like Roy Moore: "The Biggest Loser in the Alabama Election: It's Not Republicans or Democrats, but Christian Witness," *Christianity Today*, December 12, 2017, at www.christianitytoday.com/ct/2017/december -web-only/roy-moore-doug-jones-alabama-editorial.html.

[23]Michael O. Emerson and Christian Smith's widely read book documents the long-standing nature of the way that evangelicals manifest particular blind spots with respect to understanding race and racism, *Divided by Faith: Evangelical Religion and the Problem of Race in America* (New York: Oxford University Press, 2000). Strikingly, Jason E. Shelton and Michael O. Emerson show in *Blacks and Whites in Christian America: How Racial Discrimination Shapes Religious Convictions* (New York: New York University Press, 2012) that White evangelicals manifest more racial aversion than any other sector of the US religious landscape.

STUDYING RACISM AND RACE IN MISSIOLOGICAL CONTEXT

Psychologically, racism inflicts a profound pain of rejection born of prejudice against one's very personhood—personhood attached to a bodily appearance at birth that cannot be substantively changed. As hinted above, the issue of skin pigmentation is one that profoundly influences human relations in often subtle and perhaps unconscious ways. Contemporary psychological research into the phenomenon of implicit bias tries to measure the degree to which our communication, decision making, and social interactions may be influenced by negative and positive stereotypical associations with particular racial groups.[24] There is no lineal logic to justify dividing humans based on the color of their skin, but it works in concert with logics embedded in national origins, ethnicity, and culture, particularly when colonization and economic exploitation are the motivations. Thus, race is not only an emblem of classification that associates someone with past slavery, but it also operates in present-day prejudice and ongoing exploitation. A racialized society is one that uses race for maintaining the power and economic advantage for some while others are permanently disadvantaged and subjugated. Categorization for economic exploitation is a universal issue for people of Color around the whole English-speaking world. For instance, Aboriginal Australians suffer the consequences of economic exploitation even today:

> In 1788, the First Fleet transported not just convicts but also a new social system: a class society based on the accumulation of capital, the exploitation of wage labour, acquisitive individualism, hierarchy and inequality. In contrast, Aboriginal society was egalitarian. Conflict between two such radically different social systems was inevitable. Blacks did not lack the intelligence or skills to fit into white society. As G. A. Robinson, the Victorian "Protector" of Aborigines, noted, "they have been found faithful guides, able bullock drivers, efficient shepherds, stockkeepers and whalers."[25]

This testimony tells something about what the whiteness project looks like for Aboriginal Australians. Left only with passive resistance and surrender

---

[24]See Johnny Ramírez-Johnson's essay in this volume for more on the concept of implicit biases in intercultural communication.

[25]Mick Armstrong, "Aborigines: Problems of Race and Class," *Class and Struggle in Australia Seminar Series* (Canberra: Australian National University, 2004), 2, https://openresearch-repository .anu.edu.au/bitstream/1885/42696/2/Aborigines.pdf.

as survival tactics, Aboriginal Australians found the ideologies behind their forceful oppression repulsive. Although Robinson was hailed as a "Protector" of Aborigines, it is clear that he could only conceive of these Black natives as common laborers, and this notion prevails even today. The Australian case illustrates the conflict between two cultural paradigms and the European tendency to scientism and categorization that classified, throughout the world, native peoples from Australia, the Americas, Africa, and Asia as ignorant and incapable. On the contrary, hunter gatherers in particular and many indigenous societies in general had egalitarian systems that gave equal power to females, elected their leaders in some tribal consensus fashion, or had no leaders at all:[26]

> The equality of unequals, on the other hand, describes the pattern which was typical of many First Nations, and of other egalitarian peoples throughout the world. Here the inequalities in talents and abilities which people naturally have are accepted as given, yet every effort is made to bring about *equal distribution of property*, and of the essential support of life.[27]

Many of these native cultures around the world did not have notions of private property, which naturalizes the notion of human ownership generally and land ownership specifically; instead, they experienced the land owning them.[28]

Religious ideology has been central to the maintenance and origins of racialization and whiteness embedded in the European project inasmuch as gradations in skin pigmentation coincide with religious, geographical, and

---

[26]For more on this subject, see the accessible introduction by Boston College psychologist Peter Gray in the blog posting "How Hunter-Gatherers Maintained Their Egalitarian Ways: The Important Lessons from Hunter-Gatherers Are About culture, Not Genes," *Freedom to Learn* (blog), *Psychology Today*, May 16, 2011, www.psychologytoday.com/blog/freedom-learn/201105/how-hunter-gatherers-maintained-their-egalitarian-ways.

[27]Roy C. Dudgeon, *Common Ground: Eco-Holism and Native American Philosophy* (Winnipeg, Manitoba: Pitch Black, 2008), 86 (emphasis original).

[28]Dudgeon, *Common Ground*, 133: "These differences in the way in which the land was valued were also connected to the way in which it was owned. Consistent with liberal individualism, the Western world owned the land privately; as individuals. . . . Among First Nations such private ownership of the Earth itself was very rare—if not unknown. Even in agricultural societies such as those of the Pueblos, where families claimed access to plots and the products which they grew upon them, if the land went unused it became available for the use of others—it could not be sold. Consistent with egalitarian ideals, the land was considered to be a common inheritance which was accessible to all, so that even the poorest still had access to that which they required for subsistence."

cultural divisions that segment the world into colonizers and the colonized.[29] In constructing handles to engage race and racism, this volume builds on the previous scholarly work of many but fills a missiological lacuna. Here we describe the missiological implications regarding constructions of race and the influence of racism in a variety of interlocking domestic and international contexts, offering practical guidelines for developing new habits of mind and body toward the development of an intercultural missiology that is sensitive to matters of race.[30] In this volume, the authors advance the current prevailing academic dialogue of race and whiteness beyond a mere focus on past ills of the seventeenth to twentieth centuries of European colonialism, toward a positive intercultural missiology. Though the essays do not hesitate to situate contemporary race relations in their proper historical context in terms of global and local social forces, the authors do not stop there or prioritize deconstructing, excusing, or simply explaining how the church, its orthodox theology, and its kingdom building missiology contributed to the abuses, racism, and prejudices against women, Blacks, and non-European cultural values. Each essay presses forward by offering a positive vision toward building a new intercultural missiological imagination and practice. The interdisciplinary dialogue we offer in this collection incorporates an interweaving of theological, historical, womanist/feminist, postmodern, and cultural psychological as well as sociological analyses of racism and the whiteness enterprise.

Hence, in tackling the nexus of race, theology, and mission, the essays in this volume deftly deploy cutting-edge theory in racial and ethnic studies while putting this reflection to the service of scholarship in theology and missiology for the global church. For example, these days it is not uncommon to hear multiethnic criticisms of discourse about race and racism

[29]Colin Kidd, *The Forging of Races: Race and Scripture in the Protestant Atlantic World, 1600–2000* (Cambridge, UK: Cambridge University Press, 2006); Willie James Jennings, *The Christian Imagination: Theology and the Origins of Race* (New Haven, CT: Yale University Press, 2010).

[30]Christopher M. Driscoll, *White Lies: Race and Uncertainty in the Twilight of American Religion* (New York: Routledge, Taylor and Francis, 2016); Kidd, *Forging of Races*; Craig R. Prentiss, ed., *Religion and the Creation of Race and Ethnicity: An Introduction* (New York: New York University Press, 2003); J. Kameron Carter, *Race: A Theological Account* (New York: Oxford University Press, 2008); and John B. Cobb Jr., *Postmodernism and Public Policy: Reframing Religion, Culture, Education, Sexuality, Class, Race, Politics, and the Economy*, Constructive Postmodern Thought (Albany: State University of New York Press, 2002).

that fails to go beyond the "Black/White binary."[31] Among other things, these critical theorists advocate for analyses of racism that explore how other communities of Color experience the effects of racialization, though some populist or postracialist versions of this demand can be decried as a desire to ignore or avoid anti-Black bias, which thus operates to deepen it.[32] We heartily agree with the sentiment that Christian analysis of race relations must explore the myriad of ways that racism deforms *all peoples* as image bearers, and we think it is important that conversations about racism examine the way that the phenomenon of whiteness establishes a racial logic that categorizes peoples from White to Black and functions to elide the pluriformity of social, cultural, and economic diversity *within* the phenomena of global African, Asian, Amerindian, and Latina/o diasporas.[33]

Thus, the volume serves the church by introducing key concepts in ethnic and racial studies—among them racism in its various forms (institutional, cultural, internalized, passive, active, etc.), whiteness, white supremacy, and race—and analyzing how they relate to theological and missiological reflection.[34] Over the years, theorists have debated the wisdom of defining *racism* in terms of the way it provides unequal access to social privilege or the levers of social power for those in the group at the top of the racial hierarchy.[35] The authors in this volume who discuss the contours of racism all opt in favor of seeing *privilege* as the critical resource mediated in racist societies, defining racism as the ideology that operationalizes race in social institutions involving belief (whether conscious or unconsciously held) in the congenital superiority of one race over others, resulting in privilege for those atop the racial hierarchy and unequal treatment, exclusion from legal protections, exploitation, and violence for those lower on the hierarchy.[36]

---

[31]Juan F. Perea, "The Black/White Binary Paradigm of Race: The 'Normal Science' of American Racial Thought," *La Raza Law Journal* 10 (1998): 127-72.

[32]E.g., Linda Martín Alcoff, *Visible Identities: Race, Gender, and the Self*, Studies in Feminist Philosophy (New York: Oxford University Press, 2006).

[33]Kathryn T. Gines, "A Critique of Postracialism: Conserving Race and Complicating Blackness Beyond the Black-White Binary," *Du Bois Review* 11, no. 1 (2014): 75-86, at 82-83.

[34]See the Sechrest essay in this volume for more on these subcategories within the broader category of racism.

[35]Beverly Daniel Tatum, *Why Are All the Black Kids Sitting Together in the Cafeteria?*, fully revised and updated (New York: Basic Books, 2017), 87-89.

[36]See essays by Hak Joon Lee, Jonathan Tran, and Love Sechrest in this volume.

The volume connects the discussion of racism in ancient times to contemporary forms of the phenomenon by describing the similarities between modern racism and ancient ideologies that similarly function to order peoples hierarchically (i.e., *protoracism*). Both ancient racism and modern racism proceed via the mechanism of determinism; that is, they both involve ideologies that assign negative psychosocial characteristics to people via immutable qualities like ancestry or place of birth.[37] On the other hand, the volume also extends a conversation about race into the future by examining the concept of *postracialism*, various forms of which represent the goals and mechanisms to which and by which a society grappling with racism should move. As one of our contributors notes, intriguingly, these goals can actually function as a way of perpetuating the racializing effects of inequalities embedded in society.[38] Indeed, some accounts of postracialism are synonymous with *colorblindness* as a response to racism, a commonly held value among evangelicals that rejects attention to race in society as a way of eliminating racial discrimination. Yet, in calling for an end to racial categorizations without first recognizing and eradicating historical, persistent, and ongoing differentials between racial groups in terms of access to housing, employment, education, wealth, health care, political representation, and more is to render racial inequities permanent—in effect, it perpetuates "racism without racists."[39] As with some forms of postracialism, colorblindness allows people to espouse egalitarian values while continuing to enjoy the benefits of unequally ordered social arrangements that advantage Whites and disadvantage people of Color.

The volume opens with an essay that examines the phenomenon of *whiteness*, which orders global systems of dominance that favor Whites and that have in turn nurtured racism, white supremacy, and patriarchy.[40] Critically, several of these essays distinguish whiteness from white skin color and European ancestry, describing it as an idolatrous way of being in the

---

[37]For instance, see in this volume Sechrest's discussion about whether a controversial passage in the Gospel of Matthew can be called racist.

[38]See in this volume Jonathan Tran's discussion of postracialism, where he divides the concepts into three major variations of simple, biological, and aspirant postracialism.

[39]This oft-cited phrase comes from Eduardo Bonilla-Silva's widely read book *Racism Without Racists: Color-Blind Racism and the Persistence of Racial Inequality in America*, 5th ed. (Lanham, MD: Rowman & Littlefield, 2017).

[40]See Willie Jennings's chapter in this volume.

world at its core and thus activating a question that any reader needs to confront about the degree to which one's own praxis and worldview yearns for or participates in whiteness.[41] For those curious about differentiating whiteness from the concept of white supremacy, one might say that white supremacy is a specific and historically particular form of racism, which in turn refers to a general set of practices and beliefs embedded in institutions that promote a hierarchical ordering of racial groups from best to worst.[42] Hence, *white supremacy* can be defined as the ideology that centers whiteness, and we can note how it creates and sustains institutions and practices that promote the social, political, and economic dominance of Whites and the oppression of people of Color. Accordingly, several of our authors reflect on racism as an ideology that operates in conjunction with white supremacy.

Having differentiated the concept of *whiteness* from *white skin color* above, and having defined whiteness as an idolatrous mode of being in the world that participates in white supremacy—whether actively or passively, explicitly or implicitly—we think it is important to address questions raised by the title of this book, which is drawn in part from Jennings's essay: "Can White People Be Saved?" Biblically, of course, this question can be answered only one way, the same way that Peter responded to a question about the healing miracle at the Beautiful Gate when questioned by the authorities: "By what power or by what name did you do this [healing]?" (Acts 4:7). Filled with the Holy Spirit, Peter gave an answer that speaks to the multivalent nature of salvation in the Bible:

> "Let it be known to all of you, and to all the people of Israel, that this man is standing before you in *good health* by the name of Jesus Christ of Nazareth, whom you crucified, whom God raised from the dead. This Jesus is
>
>   'the stone that was rejected by you, the builders;
>   it has become the cornerstone.'
>
> There is *salvation* in no one else, for there is no other name under heaven given among mortals by which we must be *saved*."

---

[41]On this point, see in this volume the essays by Willie Jennings, Andrew Draper, and also Erin Dufault-Hunter.

[42]See especially Elizabeth Conde-Frazier's chapter in this volume for a definition of *white supremacy*, while Hak Joon Lee's chapter provides a helpful definition of *racism*.

> Now when they saw the boldness of Peter and John and realized that they
> were uneducated and ordinary men, they were amazed and recognized them
> as companions of Jesus. (Acts 4:10-13, emphases ours)

Peter's answer identifies Jesus as the source of the physical healing, which
provides good health, and also identifies Jesus as the only source to fill the
people's spiritual need to be saved. Yet it is not an accident that both material
and spiritual needs are addressed under the unified category of salvation.
Only Jesus can give salvation—there is no other vehicle, avenue, source, or
process by which one can obtain deliverance. And as was true for Peter,
those working in Jesus' name today are the conduits of the blessings of salvation among human communities. Therefore, yes, of course, all people,
including those who have white skin, can be saved by the name of Jesus—
with respect to both a physical or material need for healing and a spiritual
need to obtain mercy from God.

If this is so, why do we pose this provocative question in the first place? We
do so in order to highlight the distinction between people with *white skin
color* as those who can all be saved by Jesus like all other humans and the
culture of *whiteness* predicated on the *material* value of white supremacy, a
value that can also be promoted—whether explicitly or implicitly—by people
of any color. The culture of whiteness, as explained by Willie Jennings in
chapter one, refers to a sociopolitical enterprise that promotes European
white supremacy along with the Western project of expansion, conquest, and
colonization that subjugated Natives, enslaved Africans, and exploited Asians
as well as Pacific Islanders. Whiteness is unmarked in the West as the histories,
doctrines, and cultural identification of Whites are assumed as standard,
while those of people of Color are noted and particular (i.e., Black theology
vs. theology). In other words, though it is true that Western society makes it
easy for Whites to remain blind to the pervasive nature of white supremacy,[43]
White people and the whiteness project are not necessarily one and the same.

The Acts passage does not parse or differentiate the power to heal a man
lame from birth from the power to save from perdition (Acts 3:1–4:21),
though today it is common to bifurcate a vertical component of salvation

---

[43]For more on this theme see Charles Mills, *The Racial Contract* (Ithaca, NY: Cornell University
Press, 1997), which maintains that Western society is *designed* to render white supremacy invisible for the sake of White advantage.

from God's judgment from a horizontal deliverance from physical privation. When the church preaches salvation of souls while matters of physical and social well-being are ceded to outside institutions such as government and dedicated charities, the result divides *salvation* into two separate spheres—physical and spiritual—that subvert the original multilayered concept exhibited in Peter's explanation to the socioreligious authorities in Acts 4. This bifurcated ideology creates, nourishes, and maintains fertile soil for the whiteness project to prosper, and we maintain that this whiteness project (signified by our use of the phrase *"White" People* in the title) *cannot be saved!* We who have benefited from the whiteness project, whether by the color of our skin or by our unconscious biases in favor of white norms, white institutions, and white culture, are like that man lame from birth in need of walking again. Having benefitted economically, politically, and socially, we are lame because of the weight of the sins of the system that have accrued to us. We need the healing of Jesus to make us whole.

Thus, each of the essayists discusses *race* as a socially constructed category that has been used to divide humanity based on physical, cultural, and socioeconomic realities. Two chapters trace the origins of the modern concept of race to the Enlightenment-era epistemological fascination with so-called scientifically derived biological delineations of racial groups based on biased measurements of physical features that invariably favored English-speaking Europeans atop a racial hierarchy and non-English-speaking Whites and non-Whites below. This *scientific racism* was influential especially in the context of the modern colonial period in both Europe and Africa, but systems that privilege lighter skin and European ancestry spread apace in the Americas as well through the proliferation of laws and values about blood purity from the so-called Old World.[44] Though these concepts spread alongside European and US imperialism, among the Indian people in South Asia completely different modes of racial organization prevailed, associating genealogy, skin color, family, bloodlines, and religion to mark permanent and discriminatory divisions among peoples.[45] Yet, wherever racial categorizations are rooted in

---

[44]See in this volume the chapters by Akintunde Akinade, Johnny Ramírez-Johnson, and Angel Santiago-Vendrell.

[45]See the chapter by Daniel Jeyaraj in this volume. The conceptualization of race in India as described in Professor Jeyaraj's essay hints at another issue that, sadly, this book overlooked—the fact that racism has a millennia of sophistication in older societies outside of the West.

society, they function to render some peoples outside of the category of human. As one of our authors puts it: "*Racialization* is the process by which the marker between human and nonhuman is biologized."[46] As we collectively maintain herein, race, racism, and white supremacy together define a spiritual condition that shapes and orders our lives and worship, consciously and unconsciously, much more than many of us know.[47]

But these discourses are undertaken not simply for the purpose of indulging in navel gazing or intellectual gymnastics but for the purpose of building a new missiology for race relations in the twenty-first century—an intercultural, interconnected missiology of race relations grounded in mutuality. Instead of making the locus the past, our eyes are on the future, a future that belongs to the Holy Spirit. This intercultural missiology of race is grounded on Holy Spirit kingdom building, a kingdom of the Spirit that upsets a "bullock-cart" type of missiology as named by the Indian theologian Sttīphan.[48] Sttīphan defines bullock-cart practice as that which involves an everyday person's enterprise. The missiology toward which we aim is neither the enterprise of empires nor the work of the everyday person; it is the work of the Holy Ghost, done with, from, and through the common person. We are aiming toward a missiology that goes beyond a focus on the postcolonial past and instead sets its eyes on an apocalyptic future of mutuality that only the Holy Spirit can bring to the church. We are building toward a cohesive global church, indivisible and united though never uniform. This is the dream expressed by Jesus in his high priestly prayer in John 17; this is the chaotic church that emerged from Pentecost. This book dreams of a church that bears witness to the exponential creativity and profound pluriformity of a united church. It bears witness to every power on the earth and in the cosmos that the power of God in Christ is sufficient for creating unity out of dissension and brokenness (Eph 2–3). This book seeks to model how such unity can be manifest in our day.

RACE AND MISSIONS IN GLOCAL PERSPECTIVE

There were several questions that drove our desire to convene a conference

---

[46]See in this volume the essay by Andrea Smith, "Decolonizing Salvation."

[47]For more on racism as spiritual stratagem, see Erin Dufault-Hunter's epilogue in this volume.

[48]Em Sttīphan, *A Christian Theology in the Indian Context* (Delhi, India: ISPCK, 2001), 88.

and produce a subsequent book on the intersection of race, theology, and mission. Among them were the following:

1. How do we develop a language with categories to describe and understand the current realities and challenges regarding race—for example, with respect to phenotype racism (colorism) versus ethnic conflict or communal-relational reconciliation versus structural-institutional decolonization?

2. How might historical and contemporary perspectives about Black-White relations from African, African diaspora, and North American historical contexts prompt fresh theological and missiological questions about race and racism in relationship to white supremacy?

3. How could Native, Hispanic, and Latino/a experiences of colonialism, migration, and hybridity inspire evangelical theologies and practices of racial justice and shalom?

4. How will Asian, Asian diaspora, and Asian American experiences of race, ethnicity, and class contribute to discussions in North America and generate transnational resources for responding to the challenge of injustices around these systemic realities?

5. How might evangelical Christianity in particular and the North American church in general think more critically, theoretically, and constructively about race, ethnicity, and migration, and how might such historical and theological perspectives impact the church's practice and witness regarding intercultural relations globally and its engagement of structural and systemic injustices?

All but one of the authors in this volume were also participants in the Race, Theology, and Mission lectures at Fuller Theological Seminary in Pasadena, California, on November 1-3, 2017, and we are pleased with the way that their essays substantively address these issues. Conference attendees were overwhelmingly appreciative of the breadth and diversity of viewpoints selected. Even so, though we were successful in identifying persons whose scholarship and research interests examine many of these questions, limitations of resources did constrain our ability to address all of them. For example, we regret the absence in this volume of critical scholarship engaging race relations and ethnic conflict in East Asia, South America, or central Africa.

That said, while it is unusual to find treatments of domestic concerns in a missiological text, we are yet unapologetic about the need to situate a missiology on race relations in both global and local contexts. The word *glocal* is a hybrid theoretical term that attempts to capture the ways that dynamics that are parochial and limited to a particular context may also be connected to trends that touch multiple peoples distributed across geographic and political locations. Missiologists are increasingly talking about the church as both local and global, a perspective that captures contemporary reality at the same time that it describes a New Testament vision of the church as both a collection of local congregations and a supernatural entity that connects peoples into the holy, catholic, and cosmic body of Christ (e.g., Acts 16:4-5; cf. Eph 1:3-23).[49] Today, churches can no longer afford to be inwardly focused on internal affairs; they must also develop a global vision. As missiologist Charles Van Engen put it:

> A truly catholic local group of believers is in fact the local manifestation of the universal glocal church. . . . These glocal believers—no matter where they are in the world—are therefore commissioned to be "witnesses in Jerusalem, and in all Judea and in Samaria, and to the ends of the earth" (Acts 1:8) simultaneously. Thus, a healthy glocal group of believers in this new century must be involved, at the same time, in God's mission locally and globally, that is glocally.[50]

And what is true generally with respect to contemporary mission acquires even greater significance in the context of a discussion about race, a phenomenon birthed in the mists of antiquity but coming of age in the context of a global encounter between empire and mission. Given the flow of money and missionaries from west to east and north to south as a part of the nineteenth-century colonial project, it should come as no surprise that racialized worldviews flowed alongside the movement of capital and doctrine. The transfer of implicit biases and unconscious stereotypes is only more complicated in the present moment, as racialization processes take

---

[49]E.g., Tormod Engelsviken, Erling Lundeby, and Dagfinn Solheim, eds., *The Church Going Glocal: Mission and Globalisation*, Proceedings of the Fjellhaug Symposium 2010 (Oxford: Regnum Books, 2011).

[50]Charles E. Van Engen, "The Glocal Church: Locality and Catholicity in a Globalizing World," in *Globalizing Theology: Belief and Practice in an Era of World Christianity*, ed. Craig Ott and Harold A. Netland (Grand Rapids: Baker Academic, 2006), 179.

place in the form of dialogical exchanges rather than hegemonic monologues. Thus, along with a constructive conclusion and an epistolary epilogue, this collection attempts to capture discourse about race in ways that reflect our own glocal horizons, with eleven essays divided among the following five contextual realities: (1) race and place at the dawn of modernity, (2) race and the colonial enterprise, (3) race and mission to Latin America, (4) race in North America—between and beyond Black-and-White, and (5) scriptural reconsiderations and ethnoracial hermeneutics.

"Can White People Be Saved? Reflections on the Relationship of Missions and Whiteness" by Willie Jennings is the first essay in part 1, which is on race and place at the dawn of modernity. Jennings describes the missionary enterprise as the result of a tragic fusion between whiteness and Christianity, a fusion that acts as a constraining factor on Christian faith and, yet, paradoxically draws its energy from Christianity. The challenge that Christianity faces in this new century is to overturn white subjectivity in all its modalities since whiteness acts as the yardstick for maturity in terms of our politics, our ways of inhabiting space, and our ways of building communities. This chapter offers a way to uncouple Christian faith from whiteness by means of a theology of place, an uncoupling that is critical to Christian witness in the twenty-first century.

The second chapter in this section is "Decolonizing Salvation" by Andrea Smith. This chapter notes that the history of mission to Indigenous peoples in the United States has been simultaneously the history of Indigenous genocide. Drawing on a broad swath of scholarship by Indigenous scholars, Smith proposes that the goal of mission among Indigenous peoples was not their salvation. Western Christianity, deeming as human only those suitable for salvation and thus under the protection of Christendom, has never defined native peoples within the category of the human. Smith briefly explores how we might challenge structures of oppression, reenvisioning peoplehood and labor in a radical reorientation toward land in an expansive vision of indigeneity. Rather than dismissing the missionary enterprise altogether as hopelessly corrupted, Smith instead wrestles with the idea of decolonizing the mission enterprise by ordering our affections such that we see all our interlocutors as humans, as kin, whether or not we share the bonds of blood or spirit.

Smith's essay thus leads seamlessly into the two essays in part 2, on race and the colonial enterprise. "Christian Debates on Race, Theology, and Mission in India" by Daniel Jeyaraj is the first chapter in this section. Jeyaraj focuses his attention on excavating the multilayered notions of race among the Tamil people of India. While briefly addressing how early Jesuit, Lutheran, and Anglican missionaries attempted to make sense of and interact with the segregating and complex dynamics of race (*iṉam*), skin-color (*varṇa*), and blood-based birth group (*jāti*), the essay centers on Indian society, providing a thick description of the marginalized in that context. This background sets the stage for a final discussion that interacts appreciatively and critically with Christian Dalit theopolitical liberation activities, an analysis that both models and reflects theological discourse about race vis-à-vis other social contexts.

"Ambivalent Modalities: Mission, Race, and the African Factor" by Akintunde Akinade with Clifton Clarke is the last essay in this section on the colonial enterprise. This paper examines constructs of race in colonial modernity (i.e., scientific racism) and briefly brings African projects that theorize and theologize race (Appiah, Gyekye, Walls, Bediako, and Mofokeng) into conversation with those of African American scholars (Jennings and Carter). Yet the focal point of this essay is its examination of various African responses to the colonial past and the way that race has shaped the ebb and flow of the Christian faith in Africa in *resistance* to Eurocentric narratives, briefly surveying movements among the Zulu and Xhosa while centering on the heroic stories of Kimpa Vita (a.k.a. Donna Beatrice) and especially Bishop Ajayi Crowther. Constructively, this essay proposes an Ubuntu kenosis missiology that combines Ubuntu, the philosophical worldview of African societies as an interconnected, contingent, and collective whole, with the biblical concept of kenosis from the Christian tradition.

Shifting gears to consider race and mission to Latin America, part 3 offers chapters that discuss Latinx experience broadly and the Puerto Rico–American context specifically. Elizabeth Conde-Frazier begins from her own particular location as a Puerto Rican professor of practical theology, pastor, and leader before moving to a discussion of the broad contours of the Latinx experience within evangelicalism in "*Siempre Lo Mismo*: Theology, Rhetoric and Broken Praxis." Conde-Frazier begins with an explicitly evangelical and theological description of racism as sin before synthesizing this perspective with concepts from ethnic and racial studies, including white supremacy, colorblind racism, and the racist roots of the colonization of Latin America and the Caribbean. Conde-Frazier shows how the idea of manifest destiny underwrites territorial conflict between the United States and Mexico but also makes its way into economic and theological discourse as well as ecclesial practice. After considering the Disciples of Christ in Texas as well as Christian missions in Latin America, Conde-Frazier ends by offering a Latinx-inspired Christian spirituality of perichoresis that attends to and transforms structures through an incarnational preaching of the Word enfleshed through Christian disciples.

Angel Santiago-Vendrell writes the last chapter in this section, "Constructing Race in Puerto Rico: The Colonial Legacy of Christianity and Empires, 1510–1910." Santiago-Vendrell begins by unpacking the influence of the medieval Spanish blood-purity laws. A tool of religious exclusion, these laws originally served to discriminate against Jews in fifteenth-century Spain. Yet, in Puerto Rico the desirability of White Spanish heritage continued to create hierarchies of exclusion against a backdrop of centuries of profuse racial mixing among African slaves, the Native Amerindian population, and European conquistadors. Thus, the population's apparent hybridity masks centuries of white privilege exacerbated by the missionaries' own white supremacy–embedded theology. Santiago-Vendrell concludes by exposing the way that the myth of a *Mestizaje* Puerto Rican identity erases the real and continuing disadvantages faced by those of African or Amerindian descent. Santiago-Vendrell positions himself among those Latinx theologians and scholars who appeal to a prophetic vision of evangelism that calls new disciples simultaneously to a conversion to God and a conversion to neighbor.

There are three essays in part 4 of the book on the subject of race in North America: between and beyond Black-and-White. An essay by Andrew Draper, "The End of 'Mission': Christian Witness and the Decentering of White Identity," begins this section. Draper explores the vulnerability necessary for the White body to be joined with others in ways that decenter false claims to a universal subjectivity and proceeds by describing a set of five spiritual disciplines that Whites may use in building an antiracist identity. Whites must (1) repent of complicity in systemic sin, (2) learn from cultural and theological resources not their own, (3) choose to locate their lives in places and structures in which they are necessarily guests, (4) manifest tangible submission to leadership by people of Color, and (5) immerse themselves in contexts in which they will hear the glory of God spoken in unfamiliar cadences. For Draper, faithful Christian witness can no longer operate in modalities of control, power, or "hosting"; it must instead learn the practice of "guesting."

In the next chapter, ethicist and Martin Luther King Jr. scholar Hak Joon Lee shows that moving beyond the Black-White binary does not entail leaving behind the perspectives and legacy of the Black church. In "Community, Mission, and Race: A Missiological Meaning of Martin Luther King Jr.'s Beloved Community for Racial Relationships and Identity Politics," Lee studies Martin Luther King Jr.'s wisdom and legacy for leverage in addressing the complexity and tumult of race relations in a post-civil-rights-era United States complicated by white identity politics in the mold of Donald Trump. He explores the role of King's construction of the beloved community in building a holistic vision of Christian mission. Using King's thought, Lee proposes that the beloved community, an inclusive, interdependent, and egalitarian moral community, should function as the goal of the *missio Dei* in history. Lee maintains that King's missional life models the theopolitical and social contours of Christian mission in community and constructs uniquely Christian identity politics that make communal-political activity and social witness an integral—not optional—part of Christian mission.

In the last chapter of this section, Jonathan Tran examines Asian American experience in an essay titled "'The Spirit of God Was Hovering over the Waters': Pressing Past Racialization in the Decolonial Missionary Context; or, Why Asian American Christians Should Give Up Their Spots at Harvard." By taking up the affirmative-action debate, Tran questions the ethics of various modes of postracialism, that is, the concept that US society is already or should soon be free from the effects of racism. Tran critiques postracialism in the way that it tries to imagine a future that is disconnected from the past, a characteristic shared with many accounts of Christian racial reconciliation. Decrying the way that one framing of the affirmative-action debate essentially pits Asian Americans against other communities of Color, he locates affirmative action as a site for gospel-centered missional reasoning that joins the past to a Spirit-empowered eschatological future. Tran challenges Asian American Christians to think about affirmative action from a missional perspective, done in a way that challenges all Christians to seek kingdom futures instead of reaching for the chimera of whiteness and white privilege.

The focus on ethics and practice in part 4 segues into a discussion of mission practice that is shaped by New Testament narratives about encounters with the other in part 5: scriptural reconsiderations and ethnoracial hermeneutics. The first of two essays in this section is "Intercultural Communication Skills for a Missiology of Interdependent Mutuality" by Johnny Ramírez-Johnson. This chapter describes human anthropology from two critical perspectives before developing a model of intercultural communication. Ramírez-Johnson excavates the tortured history of cultural anthropology to outline the evolution of race as a biological construct in the racial hierarchies in the West, contrasting this deformed vision of humanity with a biblically based and God-centered model of anthropology from the Genesis creation accounts. In the heart of the chapter, he develops a model of intercultural communication from the narratives about Gentile incorporation in the church in Acts 10–11 and the narrative about intercultural conflict resolution in Acts 15. These texts form the backdrop for Ramírez-Johnson's discussion of interracial cognitive-emotion skills exposed by questions in his Image-IQ intercultural skills inventory assessment tool.[51]

In "'Humbled Among the Nations': Matthew 15:21-28 in Antiracist Womanist Missiological Engagement," Love Sechrest reads the scene between Jesus and the Canaanite woman back into its historical milieu by describing the active oppression and sectarian conflict at the time of its composition. In Matthew 15:27, Sechrest sees the Canaanite's humble posture as an implicit critique of the social hegemony of modern Christian culture, one that reminds Gentile Christians of all colors that, like the Canaanite, they too have been accepted into a group from which they were excluded by birth. Hence, subsequent missionary activity should be done in light of this optic. The

---

[51]The Image-IQ Survey (www.image-iq.org) is available as a free assessment tool for discovering personal levels of incorporation of four mostly unconscious cognitive-emotional skills that define intercultural communication.

Jesus of Matthew 15:24 is also a model for contemporary mission, not as the exalted one who stoops to dispense healing to the pitiful woman but as the humble leader of a broken and humiliated people who recognizes his calling to serve the broken, defeated, humbled, and marginalized at home before turning and reaching out to more remote others among the nations.

In the conclusion, "Mission After Colonialism and Whiteness: The Pentecost Witness of the 'Perpetual Foreigner' for the Third Millennium," Amos Yong surveys the theological and missiological implications of each essay in the book. His reflections additionally sketch a missional theology of race and ethnicity that is informed by his own Malaysian American Pentecostal social location. Yong leverages the "forever foreign" experience of continual liminality to describe a diasporic, exilic, and counterimperial perspective that is consistent with biblical traditions.

Originally delivered as a response to Andrew Draper's essay at the Missiology Lectures that convened the contributors herein, Erin Dufault-Hunter provides a final word for the book in an epilogue, an imaginative essay that is a reprise of C. S. Lewis's classic *The Screwtape Letters*.[52] Her essay is titled "A Letter from the Demon of Racialization to Her Angels in the United States" and examines the spirituality of racism by describing it and whiteness as weapons in demonic warfare designed to obstruct union in the body of Christ across all kinds of racial, ethnic, cultural, and gender difference. It is a fitting end to a book offered in service to the global evangelical movement, in the hope that the ideas and practices herein may redound to the glory of God, to the advancement of God's mission on earth, and for the sake of the church.

---

[52]C. S. Lewis, *The Screwtape Letters: Letters from a Senior to a Junior Devil* (London: Bles, 1942; repr., London: Collins, 2016). Dufault-Hunter's essay in this volume is also reminiscent of a posthumously published book by Mark Twain titled *Letters from the Earth* (1942; repr., New York: Classical Books, 2010). Twain's manuscript describes a set of letters and conversation where God, angels, and Satan engage each other.

PART I

Race and Place at the
Dawn of Modernity

1
· ·

Can White People Be Saved?

Reflections on the Relationship
of Missions and Whiteness

Willie James Jennings

Can White people be saved? For some, the question that titles this essay is deeply offensive. It suggests that there is a category of people whose existence raises the question of the efficacy of salvation. The efficacy of salvation is a very complicated theological idea, involving not just one's status in eternity (as many great evangelists have put it) but also the quality and character of one's Christian commitment—and not only these matters but also the nature of the redemptive dynamic of a life, that is, the level or depth of one's deliverance from captivity or bondage. At this moment, I am less concerned about the efficacy of salvation with this question and more interested in the status of two keywords in the question: *salvation* and *whiteness*. These terms point to a history that we yet live within, a history where whiteness as a way of being in the world has been parasitically joined to a Christianity that is also a way of being in the world. It was the fusion of these two realities that gave tragic shape to Christian faith in the New World at the dawn of what we now call the modern colonialist era, or colonial modernity.[1]

---

[1]I am not sure who first coined the term *colonial modernity*, but a good definition of it can be found in Walter Mignolo's *The Darker Side of Western Modernity: Global Futures, Decolonial Options* (Durham, NC: Duke University Press, 2011). Colonial modernity is the moment of ascendancy (from the 1500s forward) when those who inhabited the geographic and cultural sites designated the West and the Global North gained dominant control over the peoples who inhabited places of colonial conquest and forced them into temporal and spatial schemas that defined and determined every aspect of their existence.

It is precisely this fusing together of Christianity with whiteness that constitutes the ground of many of our struggles today. The struggle against aggressive nationalism is the struggle against the fusion of Christianity and whiteness. The struggle against racism and white supremacy and some aspects of sexism and patriarchy is the struggle against this fusion. The struggle against the exploitation of the planet is bound up in the struggle against this joining. So many people today see these problems—of planetary exploitation, of racism, of sexism, of nationalism, and so forth—but they do not see the deeper problem of this fusion, which means they have not yet grasped the energy that drives many of our problems.

We have always had difficulty in seeing the deeper problem of this fusion. On the one hand, many people have not been able to see this as a fusion, a joining that should never have happened. Many people collapse Christianity and whiteness into one thing, loved or hated. They cannot see two things, two mutual interpenetrating realities, the one always performing itself inside the other. On the other hand, there are just as many people who do not see this as a deep problem or even as a problem. They have made whiteness an irreversible accident of history or even an attribute of creation. That whiteness is a problem remains an elusive point to get across because too many people have no idea what to do with such a concept. Beside bewilderment, the typical response I get to the idea that whiteness is a problem is a mixture of guilt and anger, and of course the inevitable pushback. (I will return to these important emotional responses later.)

It is an ironic truth of Christian life that most people perform a faith, embody a faith, far more complex than they articulate. There is a vastness to our lives in faith that we cannot adequately capture with our words. The difficulty with racial existence, and with whiteness in particular, is that it has woven itself into that vastness, making seeing the fusion and seeing our way beyond the fusion very difficult work. This essay aims to aid us in the work of ending the fusion of whiteness and Christianity.

To speak of whiteness is not to speak of particular people but of people caught up in a deformed building project aimed at bringing the world to its full maturity. What does maturity look like, maturity of mind and body, land and animal (use), landscape and building, family and government? Whiteness is a horrific answer to this question formed exactly at the site of

Christian missions. So in this essay I want to explore whiteness as a deformed formation toward maturity, along the way to consider some of its affective (emotional) dimensions, and finally to suggest how we might begin to separate whiteness from Christianity by forming places that offer a different building project toward maturity. But before we turn to these matters, let me raise a couple of questions that some will want addressed.

Have I already made whiteness too important, made matters of racial identity too decisive? This is a fair question if it is asked from a position where the history and the continuing influence of the West and of Christianity have only been and continue to be tangential at best. But if I am inside the story of modern Christianity, then I am inside the story of racial identity, and if I am inside a faith confessed or a social and economic order performed that echoes down the centuries from the colonial shores or homes of the masters of the Old World of Europe, then I am inside the story of whiteness, whether I see it that way or not.

Another related question often asked at this moment is whether a focus on whiteness obscures the voices and visions of all those peoples designated non-White, especially those designated Black?[2] Does focusing on whiteness continue the tragic history of making the minds, actions, and decisions of Europeans and their descendants central to our imaginations and our actions? In short, does this focus continue to undermine non-White agency both historically and existentially? This too is a fair question if it is asked with a view toward the struggle of so many peoples in the world to be heard and taken seriously. But if we want to understand what finding voice and forming life-sustaining vision mean at this moment, then we have to understand how whiteness informs the intellectual, artistic, economic, and geographic stage on which vision and voice are realized and performed.

Moreover, both of these questions have not yet reckoned with the reality of creaturely entanglement. We have always lived in an enmeshed world

---

[2]I am using the term *non-White* rather than *people of Color* to highlight the historical trajectory from which came racial designations as well as the continuing energy that drives forward racial designation. Without the emergence of whiteness there would be no people of Color, that is, no racial designation in its current forms. Racial designation lives through the originating energy of whiteness as a powerful and attractive form of self-designation that continues to this moment. So by preferring the clunky designation *non-White* I am pointing not to the people so designated but to the colonial matrix of designation itself.

where lives are intertwined and constantly and continuously interweaving. It was and is a mistake to ever imagine a separate but equal existence. It is one thing to imagine the voice and vision of a people being heard and seen. It is an entirely different matter to imagine voice and vision existing alone, singularly or in competition with other voices. Even if it could be imagined in the past, it certainly cannot and should not be imagined now. Yet even in the past, separate existence was never realized as sequestered existence. We are joined at the site of the dirt, and the dirt is our undeniable kin. Even geographic distance and the difference of strange tongues cannot thwart this truth—we are creatures bound together. It was precisely this recognition and the historic resistance to it that showed itself so powerfully in the emergence of whiteness.

WHITENESS AS A FORMATION TOWARD MATURITY

Imagine people who recognize our creaturely connection and deny it at the exact moment they recognize it. Whiteness as we now know it and experience it emerged at a moment in human history when the world in all its epistemological density was opening up to those we would later call Europeans.[3] It began simply as an impulse. Early Europeans entered worlds overwhelming in every way, not just in majestic beauty but also in stunning landscapes, not just with inexplicable animals in their mind-bending variety but with a vast array of differing languages carried by different peoples. Different peoples—similar but different. These early Europeans in these new places asked themselves the question, who am I in this strange new place? This is the right question, the holy and good question. The newness of place should provoke from us such questions. The question is never the root of selfishness. Selfishness grows from its answer.

---

[3]To speak of Europeans at the emergence of colonial modernity is an anachronism that most scholars working in these matters acknowledge. *European* is a placeholder for peoples, some of whom formed themselves into sovereign states or transatlantic corporations and positioned themselves at the sites of difference in the New World and from those sites formed settler colonialism as a crucial precursor to the formation of a shared imperialist vision of superiority, oversight, authority, and control over Indigenous peoples and their lands. In this regard, Indigenous and European share in the same history of geographic struggle over control of lands and the formation of bordered and racial existence. See Anthony Pagden, *The Idea of Europe: From Antiquity to the European Union* (Cambridge, UK: Woodrow Wilson Center Press; Cambridge University Press, 2002); and Brendan Simms, *Europe: The Struggle for Supremacy, from 1453 to the Present* (New York: Basic Books, 2013).

These early Europeans answered the question without the voice or vision of the peoples of the New World.[4] They self-designated. This was bad enough, but the horror continued as they designated vast numbers of remarkably different peoples. As they did this, they quickly began to suture different peoples, clans, and tribes into racial categories. They, the Europeans, were White, and the others were almost White, not quite White, or non-White, or almost Black, not quite Black, or Black. They also created a viral world of designation between White and Black, capable of capturing all people in racial identity. What began, we should say, as harmless designating soon took its place in a matrix of harm. In that matrix of harm, these categories took on an aggressive life of their own. As I have noted elsewhere in print, the work of proto-Europeans naming themselves White and others not White was only one side of what constituted racial identity.[5] The other crucial part of that constitution was the formation of modern private property and the destruction of place-centered identities.

For the first time in human history, peoples (especially in the colonized world) would be forced to think of themselves in disorienting ways, to think of themselves away from land and away from animals and into racial encasement, that is, into races. They were forced to reduce their identities down to their bodies and the activities of the body. Why? Because the land was being taken, the animals were being captured and killed at a monstrous rate, and the plants and the landscape were being altered irreversibly. These Christian settlers understood themselves to be present in the new worlds only by the hand of God, only through God's ineffable providence. They were there for one central purpose—to bring the New World into

---

[4]Take for example, a comment by Pedro de Cieza de León, from his important text, *The Discovery and Conquest of Peru: Chronicles of the New World Encounter*, ed. and trans. Alexandra Parma Cook and Noble David Cook (Durham, NC: Duke University Press, 1998), which offers us an indispensable account of the conquest of Peru and also a window into the logics of a Spanish colonialist. He states, "And that God could have permitted something so great [Peru] would be hidden from the world for so many years and such a long time, and not known by men, yet that it would be found and discovered and won, all in the time of Emperor Charles, who had such need of its help because of the wars that had taken place in Germany against the Lutherans and [because of] other most important expeditions" (Cieza de León, *Discovery and Conquest of Peru*, 37). Cieza de León imagines the New World as a resource for the emperor, a resource with no relevant past but only a useful future.

[5]Willie James Jennings, *The Christian Imagination: Theology and the Origins of Race* (New Haven, CT: Yale University Press, 2010), chap. 1.

maturity, mature use, mature development, and of course a mature perception of the world.

As the taking of land and animals was being done, European Christians challenged to its core the vision shared by many Native peoples that both their identities and their sense of well-being formed and flourished through constant interaction with specific places and animals. They were not simply in a place and with animals. They were not simply on land. The place was in them, and they were within the animals, sharing life and vision, joined together as family. Such a vision for most missionaries was demonically inspired confusion, later in time to be called by others animism, and still later to be called cultural primitivism. In place of this vision, these Christians installed the conceptual building we live in to this day. That is, the vision of a world that revolves around a centered White self, a body that projects meaning onto the world, onto land and animals, through reductive forms of naming, designating, classifying, analyzing, and summarizing the nature of being and the beings of nature. There was a central reason for the emergence of this new self. It was necessary in order to bring nature and human beings to maturity, to the full realization of their purpose and their use.[6]

The pedagogical goal of missionaries and others was not simply to bring New World peoples into the reality of salvation, but it was fundamental to that salvation to change their ways of seeing the world so that they too would see themselves rightly as centered selves who project meaning onto the world and who may bring nature to its full purpose and use. This crucial educational hope was to disabuse Native peoples of any idea that lands and animals, landscapes and seasons carried any communicative or animate density, and therefore any ethical or moral direction in how to live in the world. Instead, they offered peoples a relationship with the world that was basically one dimensional—we interpret and manipulate the world as we see fit, taking from it what we need, and caring for it within the logics of making it more productive for us; that is, we draw the world to its proper fulfillment. This is crudely put, but it captures the trajectory

---

[6]Father Bernabe Cobo in his crucial text, *History of the Inca Empire: An Account of the Indians' Customs and Their Origin Together with a Treatise on Inca Legends, History and Social Institution*, ed. and trans. Roland Hamilton (Austin: University of Texas Press, 1979), 46, gives us an example of someone who offers categorization of the various kinds of Natives in order to help establish the best way to convert them and bring them into a rightly ordered New World.

of how humanity's imperial position as stewards of the creation was most often interpreted in colonial contexts.

The whole world in this way of thinking was framed temporally, always in need of being moved from its potential to its full realization, potentiality to actuality. This way of perceiving the world, as the great Native American religious scholar, Vine Deloria Jr. reminds us, drained the spatial realities of life of any real significance. Native peoples, he says, were forced to think of their lives temporally and not spatially.[7] The Western Christianity they received taught them this crucial lesson: where you are (temporally), that is, where you are going, moving, developing toward is far more important than where you are (spatially)—that is, where you live, where you live now or with what people, animals, plants, and landscape you share habitation. In fact, the latter is utterly inconsequential.

The most important thing in the world, in this Christianized way of thinking, is to allow yourself to be moved toward maturity. It is precisely this commitment to a life aimed at maturity that joined visions of salvation to ideas of the transformation of lands and peoples and together formed visions of Christian missions. Whiteness formed at this joining. From the beginning of colonialism, salvation and the transformation of land and peoples have been coupled together, and that coupling turned Christianity's creative powers against itself. Christian faith is about new life in Christ and forming life inside that newness. The new situation of colonial power enfolded the newness that is Christian faith within the newness that was the transformation of land and people, earth and animal.

We need precision here to see the problem. The problem is not that things change. Things do change. We could even say things evolve. Nor is the problem the impulse to transform. Transformation is not inherently evil. The horror here is the colonialist's denial of the voice and vision of peoples who inhabit a place, denial that defies the logic of life together in a place as the basic wisdom that should shape change and transformation. The horror here is the emergence of a form of creating that destroys creation. This is not the logic of breaking eggs to make omelets, recognizing that some destruction

---

[7]Vine Deloria Jr., *God Is Red: A Native View of Religion*, 30th anniv. ed. (Golden, CO: Fulcrum, 2003), 61-76, 113-32. Also see Barbara Alice Mann, *Spirits of Blood, Spirits of Breath: The Twinned Cosmos of Indigenous America* (New York: Oxford University Press, 2016), 15-40.

is always inherent in creation. This logic destroys the life of chickens by distorting their bodies to maximize egg production. This logic drives creation toward death.

Death began with denying the voice of peoples and the voice of the earth, that is, the earth's own semiotic reality, and in doing this rendered inconsequential peoples' identities as bound to places.[8] Death expanded its reach by designating peoples and the earth in reductive categories, isolating lives and life itself into fragments in order to make them useful, turning everything into commodities. We were then taught to project meaning onto our lives and to life itself, which was now formed in fragments. We learned to reassemble life as interchangeable, exchangeable, and connectible bodies, buildings, goods, and services.[9] We have remained on this trajectory, and it set in place the processes of transformation that captured the energy and logic of Christian conversion and placed it inside whiteness as a formation toward maturity.

If you have not followed this, let me state it clearly. No one is born white. There is no white biology, but whiteness is real. Whiteness is a working, a forming toward a maturity that destroys. Whiteness is an invitation to a form of agency and a subjectivity that imagines life progressing toward what is in fact a diseased understanding of maturity, a maturity that invites us to evaluate the entire world by how far along it is toward this goal. Most people have a sense of what agency is—to be the source of one's own actions and decisions and to claim immediate control over one's body. Subjectivity is a more recent addition to our thinking about a self, and in this regard what I mean by subjectivity is the narrative form one gives to one's life.[10] Subjectivity is the way people imagine their negotiating of the positions and roles they occupy, the circumstances and situations they must traverse, the pleasures they seek, and the pain they wish to avoid. Subjectivity is created both

---

[8] Eduardo Kohn, *How Forests Think: Toward an Anthropology Beyond the Human* (Berkeley: University of California Press, 2013), 27-100. In this groundbreaking book, Kohn articulates a vision of semiotic reality (semiosis) that cannot be reduced to the symbolic as that which is the sole reality of human communicability or representation. He argues that more than humans operate in representation, and thereby more than humans constitute the semiotic nature of the world.

[9] Jason W. Moore, *Capitalism in the Web of Life: Ecology and the Accumulation of Capital* (London: Verso, 2015), 141-92.

[10] Kelly Oliver, *Colonization of Psychic Space: A Psychoanalytic Social Theory of Oppression* (Minneapolis: University of Minnesota Press, 2004).

by that which is placed upon us and by the drama we form to make sense of the world we inhabit.

White agency and subjectivity form as people imagine themselves being transformed in three fundamental ways: (1) from being owned to being an owner, (2) from being a stranger to being a citizen, and (3) from being identified with darkness to being seen as White. It should also be clear at this point that anyone can enter White agency and subjectivity. In the limited space of this essay, I will only briefly outline these three ways.

From owned to ownership. "You were bought with a price; do not become slaves of human masters." So says 1 Corinthians 7:23. It is the purchase of a life, the taking back of it from enslavement that signals a powerful motif of our salvation. Someone gave what is necessary for us to be freed from slavery. What was necessary for freedom in the new colonial world was labor that led to ownership. There were two questions people had to wrestle with when it came to labor and work in the new colonial world. First, what would you do in order to work in a way that would bring you to ownership? Second, what would you do if you were forced to work as if you were owned? Both questions are really the one question of New World labor—what would you do to survive? What would you do to hold death at bay? "If you don't work, you don't eat, and if you don't eat . . ." It all comes back to the land. From the sixteenth century forward, as more and more land is seized, enclosed, and turned into private property, labor is fundamentally transformed—people are placed on a trajectory that is inescapable—you must see your own body as raw material just like the land.

The body stood at the center of this powerful commodification of the New World, and no one escaped. Two kinds of workers become paradigmatic for labor, the indentured servant and the slave. Indentured servitude is an old practice by which workers offer themselves in service (sometimes edging toward slavery) for a specific length of time in exchange for something, normally a skill only obtained through apprenticeship or, in the case of the New World, for passage to it and land on it once the time of indentured servitude ends. In the New World of colonial modernity, indentured servitude would become more than just a discrete practice. It pointed to the very character of hired labor in the New World. Indentured servitude suggested a trajectory of identity whereby poor Old World people could become like wealthy landed people, become like the landed class, if they agreed with the work of transformation, transforming themselves from Old World people to owners of the New World. There has always been a level of submission or subservience that has characterized American labor, even with the rise of unions, protest movements, and labor negotiations. That submission has been in large measure energized by the imagined fraternity of whiteness and especially of white masculinity.[11]

The second kind of paradigmatic labor was of course the slave. Slavery is also an ancient practice, but in the New World and with colonial modernity, the slave was most intensely raw material. All bodies in the New World were captured in narratives of development and processes of commodification. It is crucial that we hold these things together. If the slave was property, then the indentured servant was temporary property, and between them labor and work formed in the New World. This meant that labor formed in the New World as first a sacrifice of the body, an offering up of the body. The well-being of the body was never a central part of the calculus of work. Work as survival, yes—work bound to well-being and to flourishing, no.

Flourishing life was reserved for ownership. Ownership of property and of one's own labor meant freedom. Advancement from being raw material to owning property and labor was very serious business. It meant you would move from vulnerability to invulnerability, from being one without voice to one with some measure of voice in society. Historically, owning land not only connected one to the land but also connected one to the growing nationalist ideologies of land ownership being the prerequisite for freedom, which brings me to the next transformation.

From stranger to citizen. "So then you are no longer strangers and aliens, but you are citizens with the saints and also members of the household of God." So says Ephesians 2:19. To be a stranger is to live in vulnerability, subject to isolation and violence, and clothed in suspicion. No immigrant ever wanted to be a stranger. Immigrants transform, not always quickly, almost never uniformly, but all aim at the "no longer" of being never again

---

[11]Dana Nelson, *National Manhood: Capitalist Citizenship and the Imagined Fraternity of White Men* (Durham, NC: Duke University Press, 1998). Also see David R. Roediger and Elizabeth D. Esch, *The Production of Difference: Race and the Management of Labor in U.S. History* (New York: Oxford University Press, 2012).

in the position of stranger. Coming to the New World as an immigrant, especially to the place that would come to be called the United States, meant you were willing to tame the wilderness. Taming the wilderness meant much more than clearing land. It meant that you were willing to place your bodies in the unfolding drama of destroying the Native inhabitants. Participating in the destruction of Indigenous peoples was one of the primary ways immigrants signaled to the world and to themselves that they were part of the American landscape, the formation of a White nation in contrast to the "Indians." Yet taming the wilderness was also an analogy for stripping away their immigrant past—that is, those cultural artifacts that signaled indebtedness to the old country, the old cultural ways, and the primitive mentalities of lower classes of the Old World.[12]

To look like a Native, of the New World or the Old World or of a different world, was to be deemed inappropriate to the new order emerging in America. Barbarians existed, and they were those who by their appearance signaled they were not ready to participate in the formation of this new nation. They showed immaturity. This meant that transformation was the order of the day. To transform requires creation not only out of destruction, the stripping away of the foreign worlds inappropriate to this new national space, but also by the concealment of those worlds. Immigrants conceal, not always quickly, almost never uniformly, but all aim at dismissing that for which they might be dismissed or determined to be, barbarians inside the gate. Nationalism formed between the twin energies of immigrant angst and the privatization of property where old logics of boundaries and borders transformed inside the new logic of the commodification of space. That is, boundaries and borders matured.

Nationalism was a new way to reassemble life with land. Nationalism was never life inside the land, never life lived in serious reciprocity with plant and animal, sky and season, dirt and water, listening, learning, and finding a way to know oneself as deep partner in the world through a particular place. Nationalism was ownership, property ownership made plural and made the universal right of a people to their space. Yes, there was attachment

---

[12]Nell Irvin Painter, *The History of White People* (New York: Norton & Norton, 2010). Also see Matthew Frye Jacobson, *Barbarian Virtues: The United States Encounters Foreign Peoples at Home and Abroad, 1876–1917* (New York: Hill & Wang, 2000).

to the land; yes, there was blood bound to soil; and yes, there were deep
sentiment and sensibilities born of living in a land, but this was different.
This was owning the land, not being owned by the land. This was speaking
for the land as one who controls it, not having land and animal speak
through you, as though you extended their lives through your life. Nationalism places people inside borders, and borders inside people; place-
centered identity removes the borders between people and the actual world
and points to the artificiality of all borders. Yet few people see the artificiality
of borders because the transformation toward citizens has distorted our
view of the world. It creates a sense of sovereignty that Christian conversion
has been forced to serve.[13] Conversion to the faith has been brought inside
the cultivating work of turning immigrants into citizens. Christianity indeed
makes good citizens. This brings me to the third transformation.

From darkness to White. "Work out your own salvation with fear and
trembling; for it is God who is at work in you, enabling you both to will and
to work for his good pleasure." This is the famous passage from Philippians
2:12-13. Salvation is not our work. It is God working on us and in us, enabling
us in and through our work to show God's own work. Work transforms and
labor ennobles—this is what colonial settlers in many ways imagined for
themselves and their Native subjects. They imagined a moral transformation
at work in the transformation of the New World. That moral transformation
captured both body and labor, drawing all workers toward an idealized
vision of the morality of work.

In order to understand this moral transformation, we have to return to
the formation of labor in the New World. Central to that formation was the
juxtaposing of two racialized body types energized through the mechanisms
of modern slavery and indentured servitude. Between these two body types
the entire world of bodies and labor would be judged, gauged, and articulated.[14] There was the White body—the civilized, honorable, and beautiful
prototype—and the non-White body, most centrally the Black body—the
uncivilized, primitive, dangerous, and ugly body. In the New World of

---

[13]Reviel Netz, *Barbed Wire: An Ecology of Modernity* (Middletown, CT: Wesleyan University Press, 2004).

[14]David R. Roediger, *The Wages of Whiteness: Race and the Making of the American Working Class* (London: Verso, 2007). Also see George Lipsitz, *The Possessive Investment in Whiteness: How White People Profit from Identity Politics* (Philadelphia: Temple University Press, 2006).

Indigenous peoples, Native bodies were perceived as closer to nature and its raw condition of unproductivity, of potentiality, yet to be realized.

Long before the shadow colonialism covered the New World, peoples worked, but under its transformational regimes, their work was framed inside a project of morality that meant very different things for racialized bodies. No matter how hard the Black slave worked, her work was read through the prism of a primitive and uncivilized body, one that was inefficient, lazy, and in need of constant supervision. These dark bodies must be drawn through work from their raw condition of potentiality. White workers and their work have always been read differently as the bearers of an inherent moral integrity. This does not mean that White workers were never accused of being lazy or inefficient, but this was never assumed as their natural state, a state out of which they must be disciplined.

The labor of White workers *revealed* their honor, the honor inherent to the White body. The labor of Black workers (and all whose bodies were associated with the Black body) *proved* that they were worthy of honor; through working they were moving away from the primitive and uncivilized Black body. That is, Black workers *held at bay* dishonor by their work. This racial anthropology has always flowed through work and workers in the West, shaping how the energy and efforts of people are read. From factory floors to playing fields, from shops and corner stores to corporate offices, non-White workers work to prove their honor; the work of White workers simply reveals their honor. So labor has been framed inside a movement toward a morality bound up in whiteness, which means there is a double burden for people without work shaped in this vision, both the burden of a lack of income and the burden of a lack of honor. This is the tormented search for honor—honor that is yet to be revealed for the White worker or honor that is yet to be created for the Black worker. For so many people the latter burden weighs heavier than the former.

The association of honor with work did not begin with colonialism, and the double burden of losing honor with the loss of work is not new. This, however, is a double burden framed inside the racialization of bodies and the long history of racial hierarchies that played with Black and White, dark and light, forming them into signs of the deep connection of appearance and behavior. It is precisely this framing that remains untouched by a Christianity that helped to give it life and continues to breathe life into it. This idealized morality of work has helped to conceal the immorality of the kinds of work we are often pressed to do, work that destroys the earth, animals, and our own bodies. No one disputes the value of work or the importance of being a worker, but not enough of us dispute what work is calibrated to a flourishing life. No one imagined that those slaves working from sunup to sundown and then by candlelight and then late into the night should gain from their labor the fruits of a good life. As far as the master class was concerned, these workers were property. However, the slave masters did imagine that slavery was good for them. And in a tragic way, being formed to be a worker today continues along that same path.

These three imagined transformations, from raw material to owner, from stranger to citizen, and from darkness to whiteness, formed at the site of hope for these Christian settlers who did not simply want to make the New World their world but wished to make them the way the world ought to be. "Do not be conformed to this world, but be transformed by the renewing of your minds, so that you may discern what is the will of God—what is good and acceptable and perfect." So says Romans 12:2. Transforming the world, drawing it toward maturity is exactly what they imagined it meant to not be conformed to a world still in its adolescence or even in its embryonic form. They bequeathed to us whiteness and formed Christian mission inside it. I am certainly not saying that all European Christian settlers in the New World from generation to generation understood that this is what they were doing. They did in fact understand themselves to be doing exactly what was normal and natural, a normal planting and a natural harvesting, a normal tearing down and a natural building up.

THE FEELING OF WHITENESS

The difficulty we face at this moment is the success of that work. Whiteness feels normal and natural. It feels normal and natural because it is woven into how we imagine moving toward maturity. Whiteness feels. It has an affective structure. So, like extremely comfortable clothing that moves with the body, whiteness becomes what Anne Anlin Cheng calls a second skin.[15] Whiteness

---

[15]Anne Anlin Cheng, *Second Skin: Josephine Baker and the Modern Surface* (New York: Oxford University Press, 2011). What I mean by second skin is not a direct application of Cheng's brilliant meditation on Josephine Baker's deployment of a "second skin" to challenge and make

is being questioned at this moment like never before, and it feels terrible to so many people. We have to talk about whiteness in relation to affect and feeling because how whiteness feels is how whiteness thinks. Agency and subjectivity form in how we feel and think as one single reality of personhood. So the questioning of whiteness feels terrible in two ways to many people. First, it feels as if we are abandoning the goal of progress, and, second, it feels as if we have become obsessed with matters of identity and have lost a sense of common purpose.

It feels as if we are abandoning the goal of progress because we have been led to believe that the way life has formed over the colonial centuries is the only viable way that remains open to us. Some argue strongly that the denial of Indigenous ways summarized as primitivisms; the necessary reductionism inherent in scientific investigation; and the commodification, fragmentation, and reassembling of life into products for exchange necessary for modern economies may have had some bad consequences and collateral damage, but look at all that has been produced and continues to be produced thanks to the transforming of the new worlds. Ownership and nations and productive labor are all good and necessary things. The way things have formed is a sign of maturity, they contend. Yet what is at stake here for so many people is defense of a maturity that is not maturity at all but defense of a vision that has left them with no other path that can look backward or forward. They are forced to minimize the horrors of the past, maximize the accomplishments of the present, and live with a highly constrained imagination for what is possible. For many Christians the tragedy here is even greater. We have often baptized this progress as a blessing of God. We have too quickly blessed this sick vision of maturity as consistent with faithful growth, and we have failed to remember what was lost, not simply ways of life but the ways of many peoples for living and moving forward in and with the world.

Those who are uncomfortable with the questioning of whiteness also feel as though we have become obsessed with matters of identity and have lost a sense of common purpose. There is a sense in which whiteness is invisible, not because it cannot be seen but because the point was never to see it.

---

productive counteruse of the gaze of whiteness. My use of the idea of second skin refers to the loss of sight of authentic creatureliness beneath or below the formation of whiteness.

Rather, the point was to live life and perform life toward it. It is only when you resist that performance can you actually start to see it. People have resisted from the very beginning—resisted the loss of life in a place; resisted being designated racially; resisted their lives being commodified; resisted being forced to live inside global systems of exchange, debt, and money; and resisted as long as they could the relentless systems of education and evaluation that supported these things. They sought to perform a different life than the life demanded by whiteness and to suggest for consideration a different path to a common purpose. The issue was never having a common purpose. The issue has always been who gets to define the common purpose and what energies and instruments have been used to force people into a common purpose that destroys life. So, from the beginning of the workings of whiteness, people have used the only weapon consistently at their disposal to challenge that common purpose—their bodies, their stories, their memories, and their hopes, all found in their identities.

For Christians, the struggle for us here has been exquisitely painful because we have been of two minds from the very beginning of colonialism. We have been those who have accepted and sometimes promoted a death-dealing common purpose aimed at eradicating all differences that we imagined would undermine a uniform efficiency in the creation of the good life. But we have also remembered our difference. We remembered from time to time that we were not of this world and of its common purposes. And many who became Christian whose identities were formed in the New World resisted the plans and purposes of Europeans who feverishly wanted to transform their world. Christianity is about identities woven together in Christ to transform the world and not about a common purpose that transforms identities.

FORMING A PLACE TO BE

We need at this moment a Christian faith that can start to break our deep connection to whiteness by resisting its vision of maturity. Suggesting a first step is all I have space for in this essay, but the first step is decisively the most important. The paths that have been formed by whiteness, carved on the earth and in bodies, cannot be undone, but they can be redirected, drawn into new paths that lead away from death and into life. It all begins again with the land, with dirt, air, water, cities, towns, neighborhoods, and homes. It begins with new kinds of intentional communities that challenge where people live and how people live in places. As I close, I am doubling down on what some people know and feel but are afraid to say—it all comes to rest in geography and living spaces. Whiteness comes to rest in space. The maturity whiteness aims at always forms segregated spaces. It forms lives lived in parallel, whether separated by miles or inches. It constructs bordered life, life lived in separate endeavors of wish fulfillment.

Segregated spaces must be turned toward living places where people construct together an everyday that turns life in health-giving directions. Overcoming whiteness begins by reconfiguring life geographically so that all the flows work differently; the flows of money, education, support, and attention move across people who have been separated by the processes that have formed us racially, economically, and nationally. We start with the communities that have been left behind in the movement toward maturity, those no longer imagined through the goals of ownership, citizenship, or productive labor, and we join them, we move to them, or we stay in them, or we form them, or we advocate for them, or we protect them. The *we* here are we Christians and all those willing to live toward a different formation of places. We fight against the segregation that shapes our worlds, and we work to weave lives together. Remember, this is only the first step; there are many more to follow. But the point not to be missed is that we should feel compelled to form what Gerhard Lohfink many years ago called a contrast society, by forming contrast communities.[16] But that contrast must be formed on the actual ground, in neighborhoods and living spaces.

Indeed, this is what Christian mission at its best was always aiming at—following Jesus into new places to form new life, life together. So am I advocating compelling people to live together across all the lines of formation that divide us and have habituated us to be comfortable with those divides? Yes, because I want to turn us from a formation that is yet compelling people to aim their lives toward a vision of maturity that is bound in death. I want to save us from becoming or being White people.

---

[16]Gerhard Lohfink, *Jesus and Community* (Philadelphia: Fortress, 1984).

2

Decolonizing Salvation

Andrea Smith

The history of missionization to Indigenous peoples in the United States has been simultaneously the history of Indigenous genocide. This is true because the goal of the missionization of Indigenous peoples was not their salvation; rather, the project of missionization was essentially a racial project that divided humans from nonhumans. Only humans are suitable for salvation, and Native peoples have been defined outside the category of the human. Consequently, Native peoples' conversion to Christianity has never protected them from violence. I will explore how this theological abandonment of Native peoples fundamentally structures US law today as well as the contemporary treatment of Native peoples. In light of this theological abandonment, this article will assess evangelical and nonevangelical Indigenous responses. Based on these Indigenous theological resources, I will further explore alternative possibilities for reconstructing the "human" and thus challenging the logic of disposability within Western Christianity.

As scholars such as Sylvia Wynter, Denise da Silva, Alexander Weheliye, and other critical race theorists have argued, raciality is not simply a result of unfortunate stereotypes from peoples of different cultural backgrounds but the fundamental logic by which certain peoples are placed outside the category of the human.[1] Or to quote Ruth Wilson Gilmore: "Racism, specifically,

---

[1] Sylvia Wynter, "Columbus, the Ocean Blue, and Fables That Stir the Mind: To Reinvent the Study of Letters," in *Poetics of the Americas: Race, Founding, Textuality*, ed. Bainard Cowan and Jefferson Humphries (Baton Rouge: Louisiana State University Press, 1997); Denise Ferreira da Silva, *Toward a Global Idea of Race*, Barrows Lectures (Minneapolis: University of Minnesota Press, 2007); and Alexander G. Weheliye, *Habeas Viscus: Racializing Assemblages, Biopolitics, and Black Feminist Theories of the Human* (Durham: NC: Duke University Press, 2014).

is the state-sanctioned or extralegal production and exploitation of group-differentiated vulnerability to premature death."[2] These understandings move us away from thinking about *race* as a noun in terms of set people groups such as African Americans, Latinos, Native peoples, Asian Americans, and so on to *racialize* as a verb that can impact different peoples across time and space. *Racialization* is a process by which the marker between human and non-human is biologized even as who gets racialized and the markers of racialization may change over time and space.

The racialization of Indigenous peoples is complex because racialization does not operate uniformly. As I have argued elsewhere, there are multiple logics of white supremacy.[3] Indigenous peoples have often been marked by a proximity to whiteness. That is, Native peoples have been subjected to a variety of civilization strategies, from land allotment to boarding schools, designed to assimilate them into whiteness. However, this assimilation process is not a pathway to liberation but a pathway to genocide because Native peoples are supposed to lose their indigeneity and disappear into whiteness. Settler colonialism requires the ongoing disappearance of Native peoples that allows whiteness to, in the words of Maile Arvin, possess indigeneity so that it can lay claim to it and hence maintain rightful claim to indigenous lands.[4] Essentially, then, Native peoples are structurally defined as nonhuman because to be "human" is to be White. Native peoples can only attain humanity by no longer being Native.

INDIGENOUS COLONIZATION AND CHRISTIAN MISSIONIZATION

Even today, Native people are legally defined outside the category of human. In Johnson v. McIntosh (1823), the Supreme Court held that, while Indigenous people had a right to occupancy, they could not hold title to land on the basis of the doctrine of discovery. The European nation that "discovered" land had the right to legal title. Native peoples were disqualified from being

---

[2]Ruth Wilson Gilmore, *Golden Gulag: Prisons, Surplus, Crisis, and Opposition in Globalizing California* (Berkeley: University of California Press, 2007), 28.

[3]Andrea Smith, "Indigeneity, Settler Colonialism, White Supremacy," in *Racial Formations in the Twenty-First Century*, ed. David Martinez HoSang, Oneka LaBennett, and Laura Pulido (Berkeley: University of California Press, 2012), 66-89.

[4]Maile Arvin, "Pacifically Possessed: Scientific Production and Native Hawaiian Critique of the 'Almost White' Polynesian Race" (PhD diss., University of California, San Diego, Ethnic Studies, 2013).

"discoverers" because they did not properly work. "The tribes of Indians in-habiting this country were fierce savages, whose occupation was war, and whose subsistence was drawn chiefly from the forest. To leave them in pos-session of their country, was to leave the country a wilderness."[5] As the labor performed by Native peoples was never considered to be work, Native peoples had the ontological status of things to be discovered—the status of nature. Work is that which transforms nature into property. Native peoples as nature can only create more nature rather than property.

The presumed inability of Native peoples to work thus rendered them in a perpetual state of childhood (childhood being marked by the period of life in which one cannot be a proper worker). The colonial project then consisted of forcing Native peoples to mature into adulthood through work as defined by capitalism. For instance, the Dawes Allotment Act, which divided indigenous lands into individual allotments, was deemed necessary because only through individual property ownership could Native peoples have a need to work. In the 1887 Indian Commissioner's Report, J. D. C. Atkins explains how allotment will free Native peoples into the status of workers.

> It must be apparent . . . that the system of gathering the Indians in bands or tribes on reservations . . . thus relieving them of the necessity of labor, never will and never can civilize them. Labor is an essential element in producing civilization. . . . The greatest kindness the government can bestow upon the Indian is to teach him to labor for his own support, thus developing his true manhood, and, as a consequence, making him self-relying and self-supporting.

The report warns that allotment will not work overnight: "Idleness, improv-idence, ignorance, and superstition cannot by law be transformed into in-dustry, thrift, intelligence, and Christianity speedily."[6] Nonetheless, the pathway toward civilization requires Native peoples to adapt to a capitalist work model. Of course, as I have argued elsewhere, when Native peoples began to work, they still never achieved full adulthood (i.e., whiteness).[7] For

---

[5]*Johnson v. McIntosh*, 21 U.S. 543, 590, 5 L. Ed. 681 (1823).

[6]Secretary of Interior, "Report of the Secretary of the Interior" (Washington, DC: Washington Government Printing Office, 1887), 4.

[7]Andrea Smith, "Voting and Indigenous Disappearance," *Settler Colonial Studies* 2, nos. 3-4 (2013): 352-68.

instance Native peoples were not actually trained to be successful in the capitalist system. And when they have been successful, this has created problems regarding capital (i.e., the controversies around Native American gaming) because capitalism is supposed to be White.[8]

The problem then with Christian missionization to Indigenous peoples is that only humans can be saved. As a result, as George Tinker notes, Puritans in particular often did not bother missionizing Native peoples unless it was politically expedient because they did not see Native peoples as peoples at all.[9] Rather, as many Native scholars have noted, Native peoples were seen as biblical Canaanites. Albert Cave and others have demonstrated that Christian colonizers often envisioned Native peoples as Canaanites, worthy of mass destruction.[10] As an example, George Henry Lokei wrote in 1794: "The human behavior of the governor at Pittsburgh greatly incensed those people, who according to the account given in the former Part of this history, represented the Indians as Canaanites, who without mercy ought to be destroyed from the face of the earth, and considered America as the land of promise given to the Christians."[11] As Canaanites, Native peoples had a one-way destination to destruction to allow for the "New Israel" of whiteness in what would become the United States. The only people worth saving were Europeans.

Eventually, however, those who came to be called "friends of Indians" organized to save Native peoples. But how to save nonhumans? That was impossible, so Native peoples had to first become human, which is to say— to cease to be Native. This can be exemplified in the US boarding school system. During the nineteenth century and into the twentieth century, Native American children were forcibly abducted from their homes to attend Christian and US-government-run boarding schools as state policy.

---

[8]Jessica Cattelino, *High Stakes: Florida Seminole Gaming and Sovereignty* (Durham, NC: Duke University Press, 2008).

[9]George E. Tinker, *Missionary Conquest: The Gospel and Native American Cultural Genocide* (Minneapolis: Fortress, 1993).

[10]Albert Cave, "Canaanites in a Promised Land," *American Indian Quarterly* (Fall 1988): 277-97. Also see Djelai Kadir, *Columbus and the Ends of the Earth: Europe's Prophetic Rhetoric as Conquering Ideology* (Berkeley: University of California Press, 1992); and Ronald Sanders, *Lost Tribes and Promised Lands: The Origins of American Racism* (Boston: Little, Brown, 1978).

[11]Quoted in David R. Wrone and Russel S. Nelson Jr., eds., *Who's the Savage? A Documentary History of the Mistreatment of the Native North Americans* (Malabar, FL: Krieger, 1982), 68.

The boarding-school system became more formalized under Grant's Peace Policy of 1869–1870, which turned over the administration of Native American reservations to Christian denominations. As part of this policy, Congress set aside funds to erect school facilities to be run by churches and missionary societies.[12] These facilities were a combination of day and boarding schools erected on Native American reservations.

Then, in 1879, the first off-reservation boarding school, Carlisle, was founded by Richard Pratt.[13] He argued that as long as boarding schools were primarily situated on reservations, then (1) it was too easy for children to run away from school, and (2) the efforts to assimilate Native children into boarding schools would be reversed when children went back home to their families during the summer. He proposed a system in which children would be taken far from their homes at an early age and not returned to their homes until they were young adults. By 1909, there were over 25 off-reservation boarding schools, 157 on-reservation boarding schools, and 307 day schools in operation.[14] Thousands of Native children were forced into attending these schools. Interestingly, Richard Pratt was actually one of the "friends of the Indians." That is, US colonists, in their attempt to end Native control over their land bases, generally came up with two policies to address the "Indian problem." Some sectors advocated outright physical extermination of Native peoples. Meanwhile, the "friends of the Indians," such as Pratt, advocated cultural rather than physical genocide. Carl Schurz, at that time a former Commissioner of Indian Affairs, concluded that Native peoples had "this stern alternative: extermination or civilization."[15] Henry Pancoast, a Philadelphia lawyer, advocated a similar policy in 1882: "We must either butcher them or civilize them, and what we do we must do quickly."[16]

---

[12]Jorje Noriega, "American Indian Education in the United States: Indoctrination for Subordination to Colonialism," in *State of Native America: Genocide, Colonization, and Resistance*, ed. M. Annette Jaimes (Boston: South End Press, 1992), 380.

[13]For more information on boarding schools, including material cited in this paragraph and essay, see Andrea Smith, "Indigenous Peoples and Boarding Schools" (New York: United Nations Report, January 26, 2009), www.un.org/esa/socdev/unpfii/documents/E_C19_2009_CRP_1.doc.

[14]David Wallace Adams, *Education for Extinction: American Indians and the Boarding School Experience, 1875–1928* (Lawrence: University Press of Kansas, 1995), 57-58.

[15]Adams, *Education for Extinction*, 15.

[16]Adams, *Education for Extinction*, 12.

Thus, when Pratt founded off-reservation boarding schools, his rationale was "Kill the Indian in order to save the Man."[17] Essentially, Native peoples could be saved only if they were no longer Native. Unfortunately for Native peoples, this policy put them in the position of being subjected to systemic physical, emotional, and sexual abuse. Children died in mass numbers through torture, neglect, disease, and starvation. Most of the dysfunctionality in Native communities today can be traced to the first generation that was forced to attend boarding schools.[18] Thus, Christian missionization, rather than conveying the gospel of life to Native peoples, enacted policies of physical and cultural genocide.

EVANGELICALS/PENTECOSTALS AND CHRISTIAN COLONIZATION

Many evangelical and Pentecostal denominations were not involved in the Christian boarding-school process and argue as a result that they are less complicit in Indigenous genocide. However, this claim fails to account for the *current* racist rhetoric utilized by evangelicals and Pentecostals against Native peoples. While I have explored this more in depth in other work, here are some examples to illustrate.[19]

Moody Monthly ran an article that describes Native Americans as "savages."[20] According to Dick Bernal of Jubilee Christian Center, Native spirituality is "a clever scheme of Satan to seduce the naive."[21] Native peoples who have attempted to integrate Native culture into evangelical worship have often met with resistance. Indicative is Art Begay (Assemblies of God) saying that his use of Native dance in worship contributed to "one pastor's wife ask[ing] if she could cast an Indian spirit out of him."[22] *Charisma* reports that at one Native Christian conference in Branson, Missouri, the

---

[17]Richard H. Pratt, "The Advantages of Mingling Indians with Whites," in *Americanizing the American Indians: Writings by the "Friends of the Indian" 1880-1900*, ed. Francis Paul Prucha (Cambridge, MA: Harvard University Press, 1973), 260-71.

[18]Andrea Smith, *Conquest: Sexual Violence and American Indian Genocide* (Cambridge, MA: South End Press, 2005).

[19]See Andrea Smith, *Native Americans and the Christian Right: The Gendered Politics of Unlikely Alliances* (Durham, NC: Duke University Press, 2008); and "'The One Who Did Not Break His Promises': Native Americans in the Evangelical Race Reconciliation Movement," *American Behavioral Scientist* 50, no. 4 (2006): 478-509.

[20]Daniel Scalberg and Joy Cordell, "A Savage with the Savages," *Moody Monthly* 70 (April 1987): 55.

[21]Dick Bernal, *America's Spirituality Mapped* (San Jose, CA: Jubilee Christian Center, n.d.), 94.

[22]J. Lee Grady, "Native Americans Use Culture for Christ," *Charisma* 28 (July 2000): 22.

brochure announced "no drums or feathers."[23] This rhetoric has genocidal consequences for Native peoples. For instance, Pat Robertson provided material support to former Guatemalan President Rios Mott's war against indigenous peoples. The rationale of this war was, "The Army doesn't massacre the Indians. It massacres demons, and the Indians are demon possessed; they are communists."[24] Pat Robertson further justified his support:

> These tribes are . . . in an arrested state of social development. They are not less valuable as human beings because of that, but they offer scant wisdom or learning or philosophical vision that can be instructive to a society that can feed the entire population of the earth in a single harvest and send spacecraft to the moon. . . . Except for our crimes, our wars and our frantic pace of life, what we have is superior to the ways of primitive peoples. . . . Which life do you think people would prefer: freedom in an enlightened Christian civilization or the suffering of subsistence living and superstition in a jungle? You choose.[25]

Echoing a similar sentiment was this joke published in *New Man* magazine: "After 43 years of working in the Amazon jungle, the Right Reverend Thornton Standish retires to pen a book titled *Traumatic Lessons from the Mission Field: I Wish Someone Would Have Told Me That 'Indigenous People' Is Just a Fancy Term for 'Naked People.'*"[26]

This being said, it should be noted that charismatics and Pentecostals in particular have also challenged the presumption that all native traditional practices are satanic and promoted the visibility of Native Christians with the advent of the race reconciliation movement.[27] *Charisma*, for instance regularly featured articles from prominent Indigenous evangelical leader Richard Twiss. And as Angela Tarango's germinal text demonstrates, Native peoples within Pentecostal traditions have challenged racism from within in order to promote a gospel that reflects God's love of Native people.[28]

---

[23]Grady, "Native Americans," 22.

[24]Sara Diamond, *Roads to Dominion: Right-Wing Movements and Political Power in the United States* (New York: Guilford Press, 1995), 238.

[25]Pat Robertson, *The Turning Tide: The Fall of Liberalism and the Rise of Common Sense* (Dallas: Word Books, 1993), 153.

[26]Dave Meurer, "Great Moments in Guy History," *New Man* 11 (July/August 2004): 42.

[27]Smith, *Native Americans and the Christian Right*; Smith "Native Evangelicals and Scriptural Ethnologies," in *MisReading America: Scriptures and Difference*, ed. Vincent Wimbush (Oxford: Oxford University Press, 2013), 23-85.

[28]Angela Tarango, *Choosing the Jesus Way: American Indian Pentecostals and the Fight for the Indigenous Principle* (Durham: University of North Carolina Press, 2014).

The question arises, then; is the missionization of Native peoples possible without the genocide with which it has been inextricably linked? Many Native scholars and theologians have struggled with this question, as will be discussed in the next section.

NATIVE THEOLOGIES

One of the first scholars to systematically wrestle with the colonial legacies of missionization was Vine Deloria Jr., who was previously involved in Christian denominations but later left.[29] He eventually came to argue that even Christian theologies that claim to be liberative could not escape their colonial legacies. While the premise of liberation theology is that Christianity can be redeemed if articulated from a liberation paradigm, Deloria argues that Christianity is inextricably linked to imperialism. Consequently, Deloria questions if, in attempting to redeem Christianity, liberation theology is essentially a colonial discourse disguised within the language of liberation. He contends that liberation theology is grounded on a Western European epistemological framework that is no less oppressive to Native communities than is mainstream theology. "Liberation theology," Deloria cynically argues, "was an absolute necessity if the establishment was going to continue to control the minds of minorities. If a person of a minority group had not invented it, the liberal establishment most certainly would have created it."[30] According to Deloria, Native liberation must be grounded in indigenous epistemologies —epistemologies that are inconsistent with Western epistemologies, of which liberation theology is a part. "If we are then to talk seriously about the necessity of liberation, we are talking about the destruction of the whole complex of Western theories of knowledge and the construction of a new and more comprehensive synthesis of human knowledge and experience."[31] The challenge posed by Native scholars/activists to other liberation theologians would be, even if we distinguish the liberation church from mainstream churches, can any church escape complicity in Christian imperialism? Deloria in particular argues that Christianity, because it is a temporally rather

---

[29]The following is expanded on in Andrea Smith, "Decolonizing Theology," *USQR* 59, nos. 1-2 (2005): 65-66.

[30]Vine Deloria Jr., *For This Land: Writings on Religion in America* (New York: Routledge, 1999), 100.

[31]Deloria, *For This Land*, 106.

than a spatially based tradition (that is, it is not tied to a particular land base but can seek converts from any land base), it is necessarily a religion tied to imperialism because it will never be content to remain within a particular place or community. Rather, adherents of temporal-based religions will try to convince other peoples of the veracity of their religious truth claims. "Once religion becomes specific to a group, its nature also appears to change, being directed to the internal mechanics of the group, not to grandiose schemes of world conquest."[32] Hence, Deloria is essentially arguing that missiological work is necessarily colonial. Further, from Deloria's perspective, all Christian theology, even liberation theology, remains complicit in the missionization and genocide of Native peoples in the Americas. Deloria poses important challenges to liberation theology. Can a Christian theology ever really liberate? Or are Christianity and the Bible hopelessly implicated in colonialism and genocide?

Justine Smith's work, by contrast, demonstrates that Indigenous peoples have engaged the biblical text in complicated ways that go beyond a simple paradigm of assimilation. She argues that when the Bible is translated into different languages (in her case study, Cherokee), the very meanings of the texts change.[33] Hence, the Cherokee Bible (which was translated directly from the Greek and Hebrew) can be read as a counternarrative to the English text rather than as a simple mimicry of it. We cannot assume that Indigenous peoples deploy the same reading strategies as do those of the dominant culture. She demonstrates how indigenous reading strategies and performances disrupt the colonial narrative of the Bible. As Dorinne Kondo notes, assimilation is always unfinished business. "Even when colonized peoples imitate the colonizer, the mimesis is never complete, for the specter of the 'not quite, not white' haunts the colonizer, a dis-ease that always contains an implicit threat to the colonizer's hegemony."[34] In other words, groups that seemingly attempt to replicate the dominant culture or religious practice never fully do so, and the very act of mimesis challenges the hegemonic claims of colonizers.

---

[32]Vine Deloria Jr., *God Is Red: A Native View of Religion* (New York: Delta, 1973), 296-97.

[33]Justine Smith, "Indigenous Performance and Aporetic Texts," *Union Seminary Quarterly Review* 59, nos. 1-2 (2005): 114-24.

[34]Dorinne Kondo, *About Face: Performing Race in Fashion and Theater* (New York: Routledge, 1997), 10.

Many native activists argue that Native peoples should reject Christianity completely and return to traditional spiritual practices. A common story told among Natives is, "When the missionaries came to the Indian, they had the Bible and we had the land. By the time they left, we had the Bible and they had the land." Christianity and America cannot be disentangled; together they represent the genocide of Native people. As George Tinker (Osage) notes in *Missionary Conquest*:

> Europe's colonial conquest of the Americas was largely fought on two separate but symbiotically related fronts. One front was relatively open and explicit; it involved the political and military strategy that drove Indian peoples from their land. . . . The second front, which was just as decisive in the conquest if more subtle and less explicitly apparent, was the religious strategy pursued by missionaries of all denominations. . . . In this conquest . . . theology becomes a crucial ingredient, and the missionaries become an important strategic phalanx.[35]

These articulations often depict Native spirituality as fundamentally distinct from Christianity, including its relationship to the written Word. As Ted Means stated at an American Indian Movement conference held at the Piscataway Nation on May 27, 1989, "The pages of our Bible are all of nature. Our church is the whole world. Our ten commandments are the natural law which is that everything is related."[36] Traditional spirituality is based on orality and kinship. Its practices are rooted in past traditions but unashamedly change as social contexts change. Christianity, by contrast, places more importance on faithfulness to the Word of God than on maintaining communal relationships. Christian spirituality, according to many Native people, is mediated through text; whereas, traditional spirituality is mediated through interpersonal relationships. This priority on the written text, and particularly adherence to textual inerrancy or infallibility, is responsible for the patriarchal and oppressive social structures found in Christian societies as compared to the relatively nonhierarchical and nonpatriarchal social

---

[35]Tinker, *Missionary Conquest*, 120.
[36]Ted Means, American Indian Movement Conference, Piscataway Nation, May 27, 1989, personal notes.

structures found in Indigenous communities prior to colonization.[37] As
Russell Means contends:

> I detest writing. The process itself epitomizes the European concept of "le-
> gitimate" thinking; what is written has an importance that is denied the
> spoken. My culture, the Lakota culture, has an oral tradition and so I ordi-
> narily reject writing. It is one of the white world's ways of destroying the
> cultures of non-European peoples, the imposing of an abstraction over the
> spoken relationship of a people.[38]

Deloria's analysis tends to presume that there is only one meaning from
the Bible, and that is the meaning as defined by Western Christianity.
However, while the biblical text may be inerrant or infallible, there is no
inerrant or infallible reader of the text. Often what we presume to be true of
the Bible is primarily the result of the history of European interpretation as
translated into European languages. As Justine Smith's work points out,
however, we would have a completely different understanding of the Bible
if we read it through Indigenous languages translated directly from Greek
and Hebrew. Thus, what many Native peoples identify as colonial in biblical
texts is not necessarily the text itself as it is the colonial translations from
the text. This is not to say that colonial interpretations of the Bible do not
also influence Native peoples. Indeed, Western Christianity has so successfully normalized the whiteness of biblical interpretation that even Native
peoples take this paradigm for granted.

NATIVE EVANGELICALS AND DECOLONIZATION

Until very recently, most studies of Native peoples and religion have focused
on either traditional spiritualities or more mainline forms of Christianity.
Very few have focused on Native peoples and evangelicalism, thus rendering
the critical work done by Native evangelicals invisible. And yet, not only
does Native evangelicalism exist, but it is as diverse as evangelicalism in
general, with many sharp divides and debates. For purposes of this essay,

---

[37]M. Annette Jaimes and Theresa Halsey, "American Indian Women: At the Center of Indigenous
Resistance in North America," in Jaimes, *State of Native America*, 311-44; and Paula Gunn Allen,
The Sacred Hoop: Recovering the Feminine in American Indian Traditions (Boston: Beacon, 1986).
[38]Russell Means, with Marvin Wolf, *Where White Men Fear to Tread: Autobiography of Russell
Means* (New York: St. Martin's Griffin, 1995), 545.

however, I wish to focus on the work of Native evangelicals who have argued that the politics of decolonization as articulated by Tinker and Deloria is consistent, albeit in tension, with Christian evangelicalism.[39]

My People International, a Native evangelical organization in Canada, published vacation Bible school (VBS) curriculum that addresses the tensions Native Christians face in engaging decolonization: "For many Native people nothing good came of colonization. For others, only one good thing came—the news about God's Son Jesus which came to us with the Bible. . . . We realized we are part of this plan of God from the beginning as all people everywhere."[40] Native evangelicals address the entanglement of colonization and Christianization in a number of complex ways. In the VBS curricula, we see an interesting departure from Robert Warrior's famous critique of the exodus narrative in "Canaanites, Cowboys, and Indians." In this essay, Warrior argues that the Bible is not a liberatory text for Native peoples, especially considering the fact that the liberation motif commonly adopted by liberation theologians—the exodus—is premised on the genocide of the indigenous people occupying the Promised Land—the Canaanites. Warrior does not argue for the historical veracity of the conquest of the Canaanites. Rather, the exodus operates as a *narrative* of conquest—a narrative that was foundational to the European conquest of the Americas. Warrior's essay points not only to problems with the exodus motif but also to liberation theology's conceptualization of a God of deliverance. He contends that "as long as people believe in the Yahweh of deliverance, the world will not be safe from Yahweh the conqueror." That is, by conceptualizing ourselves as oppressed peoples who are to be delivered at all costs, we necessarily become complicit in oppressing those who stand in the way of our deliverance. Instead, Warrior argues, we need to reconceptualize ourselves as "a society of people delivered from oppression who are not so afraid of becoming victims again that they become oppressors themselves."[41]

---

[39]See also Andrea Smith, "Decolonization in Unexpected Places: Native Evangelicalism and the Rearticulation of Mission," *American Quarterly* 62, no. 3 (2010): 569-90.

[40]*Vacation Bible School Curriculum*, year 1, book 1 (Evansburg, Alberta: My People International, 2000), 35.

[41]Robert Warrior, "Canaanites, Cowboys, and Indians," in *Natives and Christians: Indigenous Voices on Religious Identity in the United States and Canada*, ed. James Treat (New York: Routledge, 1996), 99.

The VBS curriculum, by contrast, seems to demonstrate a shifting in narrative sympathy. At first, this curriculum similarly likens Native peoples to the Canaanites about to be destroyed at Jericho. "Native North Americans, like many others, have been victims of war that came with colonization. . . . Like the people in the city of Jericho, our defenses were destroyed, our villages stripped and torn down. . . . This colonization of North and South America is an example of ungodly, selfish and sinful patterns of people." However, the narrative sympathy then switches to the Israelites who destroy Jericho because "Joshua had to fight with these people to take control of the land as God has asked."[42] In other words, the curriculum does not question the conquest of the Canaanites who had previously been likened to Native peoples because "the people of Israel trusted in God. That is why they received the new land and the city."[43]

At this point, the curriculum then tries to resolve this tension by likening Native peoples to Rahab. Rahab is described as a Canaanite/Indigenous believer who recognizes that God is on the side of Israelites—sides with them and hence earns God's protection. "As we trust in God he will take care of us, just like God took care of Rahab."[44] The Native student is then asked to ponder this question: "Would you be found in Rahab's house willing to get to know and to follow the God of the Bible or would you be found within the walls of the city of Jericho where the people chose not to believe in the power of God?"[45] So it is implied that the godly response of Native peoples to colonization was to side with Christian colonizers against Native communities.

Ironically, the text then points to four Black Seminole fighters who sided with the US army and won a medal of honor, only to find that their people would be relocated west of the Mississippi. This text is interesting in terms of making an intervention in anti-Black racism in Native communities by pointing to the joint histories of Native and African Americans. But it also demonstrates that when Native peoples assume the role of Rahab, they are in fact not protected from their colonizers by God. By contrast, the *NAIITS* [*North American Institute for Indigenous Theological Studies*] *Journal* ran an

---

[42] *Vacation Bible School Curriculum*, year 5, book 5 (Evansburg, Alberta: My People International, 2000), 35.
[43] *Vacation Bible*, 39.
[44] *Vacation Bible*, 39.
[45] *Vacation Bible*, n.p.

article by Jonathan Dyck and Cornelius Buller that calls into question the
notion of a promised land. They contend that the notion of a promised land
"is always also a vigorous ideological assertion of entitlement without regard
for other inhabitants. Land may be given by promise but it is taken by violence."[46]

Another approach to addressing these tensions is found in a leaflet for a
"Memorial Prayer for Reconciliation" developed by the Healing for the
Native Ministry. It says in part:

> For the policy of genocide and for the ongoing unjust policies of the United
> States government, we ask your forgiveness. . . .
>
> For the destruction of the Native family structure through the demoral-
> ization of Native American men, for placing your children in foster homes
> and boarding schools, and for the subservient positions forced on your
> women, we ask for your forgiveness.
>
> For over three-hundred broken treaties, for the myth of "Manifest Destiny,"
> and for the notion that Native people stood in the way of progress, we ask
> your forgiveness.
>
> For the sins of the church, for withholding the true gospel, for misrepre-
> senting Jesus Christ, and for using religion in an attempt to "civilize the Na-
> tives," we ask your forgiveness . . .
>
> We ask for . . .
>
> Forgiveness for taking your land at gunpoint and for forcing you on to
> barren reservations . . .
>
> Forgiveness for the policy of our government of genocide toward the
> Native Americans . . .
>
> Forgiveness for the broken treaties . . .
>
> Forgiveness for the ongoing policies of the government . . .
>
> Forgiveness for misrepresenting the gospel to our Native American forefa-
> thers. When your fathers asked us for truth we gave them white man's religions.
> When your fathers asked for God we withheld the true gospel of Jesus Christ.[47]

In Native studies, many scholars propose decolonization as a guiding
principle for Native scholarship and activism. This work generally presumes
a non-Christian framework for decolonization. But interestingly, some
Native evangelicals also support decolonization as a guiding principle for
biblical faith. At the 2007 NAIITS Conference, Robert Francis gave a

[46]Jonathan Dyck and Cornelius Buller, "Mapping the Land," *NAIITS Journal* 2 (2004): 66.
[47]"Memorial Prayer for Reconciliation," Healing for the Native Ministry, leaflet, n.d., cited in part
in Smith, *Native Americans and the Christian Right*, 102.

keynote address centering on the need for decolonization. According to
Francis, colonization can be defined as

> what happens when one people invades the territory of another people, ap-
> propriating the territory as their own, asserting control over and actually or
> essentially destroying the original inhabitants through outright murder, he-
> gemonic subjugation, enslavement, removal or absorption into the society
> and culture of the colonizers.... Colonization is violence and violation of the
> most extreme sort. Colonization is theft and rape and murder and canni-
> balism on the grandest scale. Colonization is genocide. There is nothing
> worse under the sun.[48]

He began his talk with an adaptation of Mark 5:1-20 in which Jesus and
his disciples get transported to a twenty-first-century Native reservation,
where they encounter a demon-possessed woman.

> The woman stood there, hesitating, a hideously twisted expression on her face,
> but her astonished silence did not last long. "Jesus! What are you doing here?"
> screamed a voice from within the woman. "You're the last person I'd expect
> to see here!" This statement was followed with maniacal laughter.
>
>   Looking deeply into the woman's eyes, Jesus asked, "What is your name?"
>
>   "My name?" asked the voice. "What is my name? My name is . . . Cavalry
> . . . Infantry . . . Military Mega-Complex. My name is Trading-Company . . .
> Border-Town Liquor Store . . . Multi-National Corporation. My name is Pros-
> elytizing Missionary . . . Religious Order . . . Denominational Mission Board.
> My name is White Man's School . . . Historical Misrepresentation . . . Hol-
> lywood Stereotype. We are many. We are organized. We are in control. Our
> intentions are always and only for the very best."
>
>   "Get out of her," Jesus said. . . .
>
>   With one last shriek, the evil spirits left the woman. . . . The woman who
> had been healed also stood. "Jesus," she said, "may I go with you? I want to
> become a Christian."
>
>   With a weary smile and a shake of his head, Jesus replied, "No child; this
> is not my intent for you. Stay here, with your own people, and tell them what
> Creator has done."[49]

---

[48]Robert Francis, "Colonization: Weapons, Gifts, Diseases and Medicine," plenary address, North
American Institute for Indigenous Theological Studies (NAIITS) Symposium, Sioux Falls, SD,
November 30, 2007, http://midamericanindianfellowships.org/PDF/DCRS%201%20Coloniza
tion%20Weapons%20Gifts%20Diseases%20Medicine.pdf.
[49]Francis, "Colonization."

Francis seems to take the most radical stance of suggesting that evangelicals may even need to leave the church to follow a truly decolonized Christianity. Others argue that decolonization can occur within the church. But to do so, churches must address the continuing injustices against Native peoples and support contemporary land struggles. On his television show aired on July 2, 2009, on the God's Learning Channel, I heard Negiel Bigpond assert that Native nations are "independent sovereign nations . . . just like China." The following week on the same show, he asserted, "You better get used to it; Native peoples have the authority over this land." His cohost Jay Swallow also argued that the ills of this land can be attributed to broken treaties. When the United States broke its treaties with Native peoples, the land was defiled and hence the name of God was defiled. Qaumaniq and Suuquinah contend:

> Because of a history of *manifest destiny*, most Euro-Americans have an understanding that says they have a right to go anywhere, anytime, unhindered, and settle anywhere without opposition. This so-called *manifest destiny* was and is a lie that has been used to create unspeakable hardships for indigenous people everywhere, and to dishonor them in the most egregious ways possible.[50]

Adrian Jacobs argues that God uses nations to judge other nations. So he suggests that colonization may have been a judgment against Native nations. For instance, he considers the possibility that the colonization of the Iroquois may be a judgment for their role in the destruction of the Huron. He also postulates that the destruction of the Aztec was a judgment against its human sacrifices.[51] He does not think all Native nations are equally guilty but thinks that Native nations that were less sinful may have escaped the harsher forms of genocide.

However, Jacobs does not place colonizers on the side of God. Rather, he contends that they too may face the same judgment. Jacobs evokes Saul's broken treaty with the Gibeonites to say, "God really does care about broken treaties and will bring judgment eventually."[52] He suggests that the billion-dollar damage to Hydro Quebec during an ice storm in January 1998 was

---

[50]Qaumaniq and Suuqiina, *Warfare by Honor: The Restoration of Honor; A Protocol Handbook* (Portland, TN: Indigenous Messengers International, 2007), 143.

[51]Adrian Jacobs, *Aboriginal Christianity: The Way It Was Meant to Be* (Rapid City, SD: Self-published, 1998), 64.

[52]Jacobs, *Aboriginal Christianity*, 64.

perhaps a consequence of its constructing a dam that flooded and destroyed Cree territory. Jacobs states that he is not a prophet and thus cannot "declare the state of affairs in the North America to be His judgment on broken treaties" but concludes that "when there is a recounting concerning broken treaties, I do not want to be on the side of the violators."[53]

Richard Twiss criticizes conquest in a joke: "An older Native man once asked a group of people if they knew why America is called a free country. 'Because they never paid us for it.'"[54] Randy Woodley asserts that race reconciliation with Native peoples must go "beyond 'Getting Along'" and include restitution in the form of "monetary payment, services and the return of lands."[55]

Meanwhile, Adrian Jacobs suggests an alternate model for both Indigenous and church governance that resonates with Taiaiake Alfred's critique of sovereignty. Mohawk scholar Taiaiake Alfred contends that while the term *sovereignty* is popular among Native scholars/activists, it is an inappropriate term to describe the political/spiritual/cultural aspirations of Native peoples. He contends that sovereignty is premised on the ability to exercise power through the state by means of coercion and domination. Traditional forms of indigenous governance by contrast are based on different understandings of power:

> The Native concept of governance is based on . . . the "primacy of conscience." There is no central or coercive authority, and decision-making is collective. Leaders rely on their persuasive abilities to achieve a consensus that respects the autonomy of individuals, each of whom is free to dissent from and remain unaffected by the collective decision. . . .
>
> A crucial feature of the indigenous concept of governance is its respect for individual autonomy. This respect precludes the notion of "sovereignty"—the idea that there can be a permanent transference of power or authority from the individual to an abstraction of the collective called "government." . . .
>
> In the indigenous tradition, . . . there is no coercion, only the compelling force of conscience based on those inherited and collectively refined principles that structure the society.[56]

[53]Jacobs, *Aboriginal Christianity*, 66.
[54]Richard Twiss, "Can I Call You Gringo?," *Charisma* 26 (December 2000): 44.
[55]Randy Woodley, *Living in Color: Embracing God's Passion for Ethnic Diversity* (Downers Grove, IL: InterVarsity Press, 2001), 176-77.
[56]Taiaiake Alfred, *Peace, Power, Righteousness: An Indigenous Manifesto* (New York: Oxford University Press, 1999), 25.

As long as Indigenous peoples frame their struggles in terms of sovereignty, Alfred argues, they inevitably find themselves coopted by the state-reproducing forms of governance based on oppressive, Western forms of governance. In addition, the concept of sovereignty continues to affirm the legitimacy of the state: "To frame the struggle to achieve justice in terms of indigenous 'claims' against the state is implicitly to accept the fiction of state sovereignty."[57] He generally juxtaposes *nationhood* and *nationalism*, preferring these terms to *sovereignty.*

> Sovereignty is an exclusionary concept rooted in an adversarial and coercive Western notion of power.[58]
>
> It is with indigenous notions of power such as these that contemporary Native nationalism seeks to replace the dividing, alienating, and exploitative notions, based on fear, that drive politics inside and outside Native communities today.[59]

Similarly, Adrian Jacob argues that both churches and society at large can model themselves on the principles of consensus and egalitarianism that Alfred outlines. He concurs that Iroquois leaders "derived their power from the people."[60] He then contends that this model is one that can be informative to all Christians.

> I am suggesting that one of the greatest contributions that Iroquoian people can make toward reformation among Aboriginal people is assisting the return to the value of consensus decision-making and the inherent respect of that process. Abusive people find it very hard to work in an environment of open heartedness, respect trust, and group sharing. Hierarchical systems maintain their structures through the careful control of information. Closed-door meetings and in-camera sessions abound in this system emphasizing privileged information. Dictators know the value of propaganda.[61]

Jacobs echoes the analysis of many Native organizers and scholars who state that decolonization requires a transformation of governance, not only for Native peoples but for the world. Such ideas may seem radical, but not if we

---

[57] Alfred, *Peace, Power, Righteousness,* 57.
[58] Alfred, *Peace, Power, Righteousness,* 59.
[59] Alfred, *Peace, Power, Righteousness,* 53.
[60] Jacobs, *Aboriginal Christianity,* 69.
[61] Adrian Jacobs, *Pagan Prophets and Heathen Believers* (Rapid City, SD: Self-published, 1999), 25.

remember that the Bible is set in a context of colonialism. Now, evangelicals read the Bible essentially from the perspective of Rome and thus domesticate the anticolonial ideas that are clearly articulated by Jesus. But if we reread the Bible in its colonial context, in which both the writers and audience are the colonized, then Jesus' call for a new heaven on earth can be read as a call for a transformation of the colonial world order.

DECOLONIZATION AND SALVATION

Deloria notes that neotraditionalist attempts to reclaim Native spirituality often draw upon an either/or logic system (i.e., Christian versus traditional, American versus Indian, oral versus written) foreign to Native cultures.[62] According to the European positivist grammar of truth, if proposition p is true, then not-p must be false. Indigenous epistemologies are not beholden to such logic systems. Beliefs, even systems of belief that seem contradictory to European and Euro-American culture—for example, Christianity and Indigenous religions—can coexist in Indigenous cultures. For example, at a conference several years ago I heard a story about an Indian man who gave a speech in which he claimed that the next speaker was going to say things that were completely wrong. When his turn came, the next speaker, also Indian, began not by attacking the preceding speaker but by announcing that everything the previous speaker had said was completely true. The event is notable because it struck no one present—not the speakers, not the Indian audience—as odd. Charles Eastman (Sioux) illustrates with the following story:

> A missionary once undertook to instruct a group of Indians in the truths of his holy religion. He told them of the creation of the earth in six days, and of the fall of our first parents by eating an apple. The courteous savages listened attentively, and after thanking him, one related in his turn a very ancient tradition concerning the origin of maize. But the missionary plainly showed his disgust and disbelief, indignantly saying: "What I delivered to you were sacred truths, but this that you tell me is mere fable and falsehood!" "My Brother," gravely replied the offended Indian, "it seems that you have not been well grounded in the rules of civility. You saw that we, who practice these rules, believed your stories; why, then, do you refuse to credit ours?"[63]

---

[62]Deloria, *For This Land*, 100-107.
[63]Deloria, *God Is Red*, 86.

Ironically, however, Deloria himself maintains an either/or approach: "We cannot reject the Christian religion piecemeal. . . . The whole religion has been misdirected from its inception."[64] Deloria's either/or framework is emblematic of some of the problems with how Native studies engage in theories about decolonization. That is, in order to decolonize, Native peoples must extract everything colonial from their lives. Consequently, this model, argues Kirisitina Sailiata, becomes a litmus test for authenticity: who is truly pure, and who is still engaging in colonial practices?[65] We end up in the same racializing trap of dividing the world into those who are decolonized humans and those who are colonized and less than human. Rather, she suggests, our vision should be forward looking: how do we *transform* the current conditions of colonialism to create a different world based on principles of peace, respect, and interrelatedness? These processes of transformation can then engage all the members of our communities however they are situated.

Part of building a new world involves not only challenging structures of oppression but transforming the way all of us have been shaped by these structures. As Rita Nakashima Brock notes, the "myth of innocence" is a colonial entrapment that prevents communities from engaging in internal self-critique.[66] That is, the logic of innocence says that suffering is only bad when it is inflicted upon those who are innocent. Those who are viewed as "less innocent" somehow deserve oppression. White people often flock to reservations to help "poor Indians," whom they romanticize as perfect victims. When they discover the amount of violence and dysfunctionality that exists in Native communities, they become disenchanted, no longer want to work with Native people, and decide Natives are getting what they deserve. The fact that there are no innocents does not justify oppression; rather, it means that oppression is unacceptable regardless of the innocence of its victims. Furthermore, when oppressed groups are liberated from constantly having to maintain the image that they are innocent and

---

[64]Quoted in Deloria, *God Is Red*, 265.

[65]Kirisitina Sailiata, "Decolonization," in *Native Studies Keywords*, ed. Stephanie Nohelani Teves, Andrea Smith, and Michelle H. Raheja (Tucson: University of Arizona Press, 2015), 301-8.

[66]Rita Nakashima Brock, "Ending Innocence and Nurturing Willfulness," in *Violence Against Women and Children: A Christian Theological Sourcebook*, ed. Carol J. Adams and Marie M. Fortune (New York: Continuum, 1995), 71-84.

perfect victims, they can take responsibility for the oppression that exists within their communities. We can finally be viewed as moral agents who will often make mistakes but who do not deserve oppression regardless of the mistakes we make. When we no longer have to prove ourselves innocent, we can engage all of our community in the struggles for justice without writing off some sectors as hopeless sell outs because we recognize that all of us are complicit to some degree within the logics of colonialism and white supremacy.

Essentially, decolonization often mirrors the same racializing logics in Western Christianity. Some can be saved and/or decolonized, and others never can. And now in a context where the majority of White evangelicals voted for Donald Trump, whose candidacy was based on the principle that people of Color, immigrants, Muslims, women, and people with disabilities are disposable, it becomes clear that it is necessary to decolonize missionization and decolonize Christianity. In fact, Jesus clearly preached a gospel of nondisposability. He associated with tax collectors, sinners, and people from all walks of life.

> When the Pharisees saw this, they asked his disciples, "Why does your teacher eat with tax collectors and sinners?" But when he heard this, [Jesus] said, "Those who are well have no need of a physician, but those who are sick. Go and learn what this means, 'I desire mercy, not sacrifice.' For I have come to call not the righteous but sinners." (Mt 9:11-13 ESV)

Jesus' approach mirrors indigenous principles of radical relationality in which we see ourselves as fundamentally connected and related with all of creation.

One such example would be the statements issued by Indigenous peoples' organizations at the 2008 World Social Forum. These groups contended that the goal of Indigenous struggle was not simply to fight for the survival of their particular peoples but to transform the world so that it is governed according to principles of participatory democracy rather than as colonial states. Their vision of nationhood required a radical reorientation toward land. All are welcome to live on the land, they asserted, but we must all live in a different relationship to the land. We must understand ourselves as peoples who must care for the land rather than control it. Because they articulate indigeneity within the context of global liberation, their understanding of indigeneity becomes expansive and inclusive. Their politics is not based on claims for special status to be recognized by the state; it is based on a commitment to liberation for all peoples.

BEYOND THE WHITE SAVIOR INDUSTRIAL COMPLEX

As many evangelicals of Color have pointed out, White evangelicals are often very invested in the White savior industrial complex. But Native Christians have noted that maybe it is White evangelicals who actually need to be saved. Craig Smith contends that US churches should stop seeing themselves as sending churches and recognize that they are themselves a mission field. Christianity originated in Jerusalem, after all, not the United States:

> I have often told Anglo churches that you can't get much farther from Jerusalem than the United States of America! In the biblical sense, we are actually the end of the earth, the boondocks, and the foreign field! I have also said to them, "Have you ever thought that you should be the ones on the slides, rather than the ones watching the slides of foreign fields when missionary conference time rolls around?"[67]

Similarly, when the Southern Baptist Convention developed a program with the International Mission Board to use Native peoples in the United States to evangelize in other Indigenous missions globally, Native evangelical Randy Woodley contended: "I don't think we should allow ourselves to be exploited for a Western approach to the gospel. . . . If we're going to leverage the fact that we're Native, we have to make sure that it actually is the Good News."[68] As Eugene Cho pointed out at the 2013 Justice Conference, we asked God to help us move mountains without considering the possibility that we may be the mountains that need to be moved.[69]

In addition, taking the colonial context of the Gospels seriously requires us to consider that the theology that has emerged from colonizers may not be the most accurate rendering of Scriptures that were written by and for the colonized. Jesus' call for us to become new people actually coincides with the work of postcolonial scholars such as Frantz Fanon, who argue that decolonization is not simply about a struggle for land and resources but the

---

[67]Craig Stephen Smith, *Whiteman's Gospel* (Winnipeg, Manitoba: Indian Life Books, 1999), 88.
[68]Kate Tracy, "Native Approach," *Christianity Today* 58 (March 2014): 16.
[69]Eugene Cho, plenary speaker, Justice Conference, Philadelphia, February 24, 2013, personal notes.

struggle to become new peoples who do not require relationships of colonization to define ourselves.[70] If racialization is the logic that defines the human from those who are not human, then antiracist work is not simply about changing personal beliefs or even making structural change. This work involves creating a new sense of humanity altogether. "So if anyone is in Christ, there is a new creation: everything old has passed away; see, everything has become new!" (2 Cor 5:17). This new creation is a new sense of humanity for which we currently do not have words.

That said, some would argue that decolonization requires the end of missionization altogether. But missionization is fundamentally structured around sharing beliefs one holds strongly with people who do not share those beliefs. Missionization is thus an inescapable part of life because we live in a world where not everyone agrees with us. The answer is not pretending we (whoever we are) do not have the convictions that we do. The answer is decolonizing missionization so that we fundamentally respect, and understand, that the people with whom we engage are our relatives—that they are fully human, even if they are never convinced by what we say. We need not require people to become human/White in order to hear the gospel. We must decolonize our perceptions of Christianity by recognizing how Western imperialism shapes what we think the gospel is. In doing so, we save not only others with whom we wish to share the gospel, but we save ourselves as well.

---

[70]Frantz Fanon, *Wretched of the Earth*, trans. Constance Farrington (New York: Grove Press, 1963).

PART II

Race and the
Colonial Enterprise

3

Christian Debates on Race, Theology, and Mission in India

Daniel Jeyaraj

INTRODUCTION

This essay examines the multilayered Tamil concepts of race (*iṉam*) and the inseparable association of race with skin color (*varṇa*), blood-based birth group (*jāti*), family (*kulam*), genealogy (*vaṃśa*), nation (*nāṭu*), religion (*matam*), and dispositions. Then it explores how Jesuit, Lutheran, and Anglican missionaries from Europe understood and handled these realities in India. At the end, it briefly discusses select aspects of contemporary *jāti*-based tensions, theologies, and mission practices among the Tamil Christians in South India.

The English noun *race* has different connotations for the Tamil people. Anthropologists, sociologists, and linguists of Dravidian, African, and Australian languages differ in their estimation of the exact origin of the Tamil people and their physiognomic appearances (e.g., lip size, shape, and hair or eye color). This essay examines some of the ways that European missionaries interacted with the Tamil understandings of race: several missionaries who interpreted race as a social category indispensable for Indian identity and existence tolerated racial distinctions within their Christian congregations. Other missionaries who supported the notion that race was a religious construct that contradicted the creation narrative of the Bible and the values of the gospel of Jesus Christ opposed it. This essay, however, places these arguments within the self-understanding of the Tamil people as Dravidians, who in the course of time had interacted with Sanskrit ideas of race.

TAMIL UNDERSTANDINGS OF CASTE AS RACE

The Tamil noun *iṉam* stands for a group of people according to race, clan, or tribe.[1] Its members are related to one another by marriage, by birth, or by other forms of blood relationship. They practice among themselves equality, friendship, and fellowship, and they support one another during times of joy and of sorrow. All these activities form and nourish their sense of bond (*iṉakkaṭṭu*), mutual belonging, loyalty, and character.[2] In order to keep their lineage and immovable properties intact, they practice endogamy, which means that they marry within their own *iṉam*. They consider and treat the members of each *iṉam* as mothers and fathers, sisters and brothers, aunts and uncles, nieces and nephews. Individuals can express their individuality as long as they relate to the other members of their own *iṉam*. As far as possible, they keep themselves away from another *iṉam*. They consciously transmit their customary beliefs and lifestyle to their children and young people.

If a person adopts the attitudes and behaviors of another *iṉam*, through either exogamy or religious conversion, the leaders of an *iṉam* may exclude this person from their group (*iṉampiral*). This disloyal person has already disrupted the life of other members (*iṉamuṟai*, "way of life," of each *jāti*) and harmed their ancestry (*iṉavaḻi*). Thus, noncompliance brings with it a deep sense of shame.

Each *iṉam*, like a tree, can spread its branches everywhere and occupy different *kuṭis* (families, villages, and areas). The members of each *kuṭi* have the duty to loyally safeguard the good reputation of their group and refrain from disruptive acts such as intermarriage, religious conversion, and social dislocation. They can organize their household affairs in their own way, but they should not look down on the Tamils belonging to another *iṉam* or *kuṭi* with distinct histories, social customs, rites of passage, and religious traditions. They should not disrupt the sociocultural, political, and economic equilibrium of another *iṉam* or *kuṭi* because, as Tamils, they are equals who maintain and cultivate parallel existences. The 972nd couplet of the

---

[1] *Tamil Lexicon*, vol. 1 (Madras: University of Madras, 1924; repr., Madras: University of Madras, 1982), 370.

[2] *Tirukkuṟaḷ*, couplet number 453: *maṉattāṉam māntark kuṇarcci iṉattāṉam iṉṉāṉ eṉappaṭuñ ceyal* ("naturally, all people use their mind to think; however, they develop their character through their interactions with others"; author's transportation).

Tirukkuṟaḷ, popularly known as the Tamil scripture (*tamiḻmaṟai*), articulates this self-understanding of the Tamils as follows: "all people are born equal; their work, however, distinguishes them from one another."[3]

After the increased impact of Sanskrit culture on the minds and lives of the Tamil people from about the sixth century CE, this pre-Vedic notion of equality of all people at birth disappeared. The Sanskrit notions of *varṇa* and *jāti* began to dominate the Tamil psyche. The first word, *varṇa*, can stand for skin complexion; outward appearance; internal and external properties, such as character, race, or species; and other characteristics. Canonical Sanskrit scriptures such as the Ṛgveda 10.7.90.1-16 recognize only four *varṇa*s in their hierarchical order: when the Primordial Being created the world, the Brahmins emerged from its head; the Kṣatriyas came through its arms. The Vaiśyas came out of its thighs, and the Sūdras came from its feet. Of these four groups, only the male members of the Brahmins, the Kṣatriyas, and the Vaiśyas are twice-born people. Their second birth takes place during their initiation ceremony. By contrast, the fourth group, the Sūdras, have only one physical birth. Since they should not undergo initiation, they do not have a second birth. No one can either abandon or convert into another *varṇa*; members must be born into it. No one can be initiated into it, and *varṇa*s do not permit upward mobility in this present life. Inter-*varṇa* and inter-*jāti* marriages incur bad karma, plunging the marriage partners and their offspring in their next birth into lower categories of (human and non-human) existence and making their chances for final release from the cycle of births and deaths difficult. These millennia-old presuppositions and practices have influenced Indian psyche to a great extent.

Each of these four groups has specific notions of ritual purity and pollution based on marriage alliances and worship practices. At the same time, each hierarchy can perform only six predetermined jobs. For example, the Brahmins can recite and teach the Vedas; they can perform sacrifices for themselves and others; they can accept offerings such as gold, cows, lands, and houses; and, finally, they can bless others, but only with the sacred ash or other invisible, intangible spiritual blessings. By this privileged position,

---

[3]The Tamil text of this couplet reads as follows: *piṟappokkum ellā uyirkkum ciṟappovvā ceytoḻil vēṟṟumai yāṉ.* Unless specified, all translations are my own.

they have secured for themselves permanent access to public acknowledgment and opportunities for education, wealth, and other benefits. The Kṣatriyas, as rulers, can recite the Vedas, offer sacrifices for themselves, give gifts, learn warfare, protect lives, and know the strength of their enemies. However, in the course of time, their power has diminished. Nowadays their influence is limited. The Vaiśyas can recite the Vedas, offer sacrifices for themselves, give gifts, cultivate fields, be generous, and engage in business. This group has monopolized access to lands, cultivation, economic wealth, and business. The Sūdras, who constitute the fourth *varṇa*, should protect the cows, earn material wealth, engage in agricultural work, recite the *purāṇas* (ancient stories), offer material and religious gifts to the above-mentioned three groups, and serve them. This fourfold social system excludes about one-fifth of the Indian population; traditionally, the *varṇa* people see these *avarṇa* people as not fully human. This view explains a major socioreligious reason for the exclusion and discrimination of the *avarṇa* people in all levels of their existence. The notion that within the creation of the cosmos, the Primordial Being placed human beings into an unequal system of socioreligious hierarchy finds another ideological support among the peoples of various birth-groups known as *jātis*.

The second Tamilized Sanskrit word *jāti* etymologically refers to a birth group and to blood relatives. The members of each *jāti* practice endogamy, perform a hereditary occupation, eat particular types of food, live in a specified place, and frequently worship their own protective (meat-eating) deities. Their existence depends on the geographical location where they are born, where they live, and perhaps where they might die. The word *jāti*, however, has acquired several meanings, and each meaning has its own socioeconomic and political consequence. For example, *jāti* often functions as a synonym to *varṇa*. As a result, the members of each *jāti* within a particular *varṇa* can recall their long lines of family lineages (*gotras*) and trace their origin to their own progenitor-ancestor. Families that are not as big as *gotras* constitute the *kulams*; each *kulam* has a patron deity (*kulateivam*), work (*jātitarumam*), rules (*jātikkaṭṭu*), and obligations (*jātikaṭamai*). This is a main reason why the members of a particular *jāti* are careful to honor their families. For example, they may not mix the *jātis* by cross-*jāti* marriages. They avoid religious conversions. These and other factors make the *jātis* resilient and hereditary. Within their own hierarchy and interrelated network, they repel strangers and outsiders. At the same time, they deepen their relationship with their own *jāti* peoples via mate selection, rites of passage, and performance of certain occupations. Thus, they preserve the purity and longevity of their *jātis* and their social position.

Other related sociocultural habits ensure the persistence of *jāti* among Indians. For example, when two total strangers meet for the first time, they normally want to know who they are and whether they can continue conversation and interaction. They will pose the question "Who are you?" Those who respond will reveal not their name but their *jāti*. If they are unsure, they will proceed to ask about their fathers or grandfathers and what occupation they had and where they lived. As soon as they have established their *jāti* identity, they exchange other information about themselves, their families, and the like. Thus, most Indians jealously guard what they have borrowed from Sanskrit culture.

Before the Tamils adopted the Sanskrit ideas and practices of *jāti* around the seventh century CE, they maintained their social distinctions based on the geographical locations of their domiciles. At that time, they divided the Tamil country into five tracts (*tiṇais*): hills, arid areas, forested areas for pastoral purposes, agricultural tracts, and maritime tracts (*kuṟiñci, pāllai, mullai, marutam,* and *neytal*). The native people of each tract exhibited professional expertise in those areas that enriched their lives and gave them meaning. The people of the hills, arid areas, the forests, and maritime areas ate meat and worshiped meat-eating deities. By contrast, the people living in the fertile agricultural areas were happy with their vegetarian diet, which satisfied their need for protein. Their deities too were vegetarians. It is true that the Buddhists and Jains, who had opposed harming animal life, lived along the deltas of the River Vaikai in Maturai or the River Kāvēri in Tañcāvūr. Likewise, many of the Tamils in these deltas, who were neither Buddhists nor Jains, also abstained from eating meat.

After the people of the five tracts had imbibed the Sanskrit notions of *jāti*, they began imitating the lifestyle of the Sanskrit-speakers involving the fourfold *varṇa*, ritual purity, and pollution of people based on their birth. Especially, this imitation included the much-hated practice of untouchability of the *avarṇa* peoples. Tamil Brahmins, Vaiśyas, and Śūdras (ab)used these *avarṇa* peoples mostly as bonded laborers (*kottaṭimaikaḷ*) to cultivate their agricultural fields and take care of their cattle. They did not encourage them to think for themselves and define their destiny. Instead, the *avarṇa* were forced to execute the works that their lords had designed for them. This unfortunate situation continued for a long time, until Muslim missionaries and Christian missionaries came to them. Consequently, some of these *avarṇa* peoples became Muslims or Christians and sought to shake off the shackles of the *varṇa* system. Nowadays, these peoples call themselves either Dalits (oppressed people) or Ādivāsis ("original, native inhabitants" of the land, meaning those tribes who live among the remote hills and forests).

Initially, the Portuguese who arrived in South India in successive waves after 1498 could not understand the complexities and intricacies of the *varṇās* and *jātis*. They observed how the people of these interrelated groups practiced endogamy and insisted on racial purity. Therefore, they named these Indian realities with their own notion of *casta* (race, pure breed). Consequently, European scholars adopted this single word to describe the multifaceted relationships of *varṇās* and *jātis*, and thus created much confusion. Indian administrators, revenue officers, politicians, and other policymakers continue to employ words such as *caste*, *high caste*, and *low caste* for various purposes. These words cover up their racial connotations. For example, when students apply for admission to a college or when job seekers apply for a government job, they have to submit their community certificate containing details of their religion, *jāti*, and place of living. Outwardly, these details amount to affirmation action, but in real terms, they discriminate and stigmatize the same people whom the system seeks to assist. For example, those who seek admission to schools and colleges or employment with the government should obtain a community certificate from the village administrative officer and attach it to their application. For this purpose, every professional college or government agency will publish a list of *jāti*. The Public Service Commission of Tamil Nadu, for an examination in 2016, asked its applicants to identify their caste from the list of 76 scheduled castes, 34 scheduled tribes (i.e., Ādivāsis), 139 backward classes, and 68 most backward classes.[4] The system of affirmative action has a good purpose, but it also perpetuates the *jāti* distinctions.

JESUIT EXPERIENCES WITH THE TAMIL
PEOPLES OF VARIOUS CASTES

Ever since the Portuguese established their naval power along the southeastern coast of Tamil country, the pearl fishers and other seafaring peoples, commonly known as Paravas, sought Portuguese protection against Muslim traders;[5] eventually, some of them embraced Roman Catholicism. Yet, they held onto their pre-Christian loyalties to their *jātis*.[6] They elected their own *jāti* leader (*jāti talaivaṉ*) to represent their concerns to local and regional authorities and maintained their *jāti*-related identities. The arrival of Francis Xavier among the Paravas (1542–1544), however, heralded a new era for Tamil Parava Christians of these regions. He is said to have baptized about 15,000 Paravas and become their "spiritual exemplar," "supernatural intercessor," and "the creator of their new caste lifestyle."[7] Mother Mary of the place Tūttukkuṭi began reflecting several aspects of the unmarried female guardian deities of the local people (e.g., warding off the evil spirits, healing from sicknesses, and protecting cattle, trade, and the like). Susan Bayley has shown that the conversion of the Paravas to Roman Catholicism did not eradicate their loyalty to their *jāti* identity; instead, it reshaped it with

---

[4]"Tamil Nadu Public Service Commission 'Instructions to Applicants' (Revised with effect from 07.11.2016)," www.tnpsc.gov.in/instructions%20to%20candiates.pdf. Pages 72-83 of this document contain the names and related details of 76 Scheduled Castes, 36 Scheduled Tribes, 139 Backward Classes, 7 Backward Classes (Muslims), 48 Most Backward Classes, and 68 Denotified Communities.

[5]Susan Bayly, *Saints, Goddesses and Kings: Muslims and Christians in South Indian Society 1700–1900* (Cambridge: Cambridge University Press, 1989), 325: "The Paravas' conversion to Christianity took place in the course of a savage maritime war fought between 1527 and 1539 by the Portuguese and the south Indian Muslim forces who were allied with the Zamorin of Calicut. In 1532 a delegation of seventy Paravas presented themselves at the Portuguese stronghold in Cochin and appealed for protection against the Tamil Muslim diving groups and the local rulers who supported them. These Paravas claimed that they were the victims of an age-old rivalry with the region's sea-going Muslims."

[6]Bayly, *Saints, Goddesses, and Kings*, 326: "Throughout the colonial period the Paravas maintained a hierarchy of notables and title-holders known as *sittāttis, adappam, moupam* and *pattangattis*. These notables collected fees known as *kānikkai* from all the lesser-ranking Paravas in their localities."

[7]Bayly, *Saints, Goddesses, and Kings*, 330-31.

additional meanings and institutional structures.[8] For example, they expressed
their pre-Christian *jāti* loyalties in many ways. Like their non-Christian religious neighbors, they claimed that their cultural, social, and ritual practices
entitled them to pull their own *capparam* or *tēr*, which is a decorated chariot-
like vehicle of the Śaivites. Its raised platform displayed the images of Virgin
Mary and other Christian saints. They drew these vehicles along the streets of
their villages or towns. When they passed by the houses or temples of non-
Christians, conflicts arose; they even faced each other in courts.[9]

In spite of their association with the Portuguese colonial power, increased
economic privileges with better tools for trade (e.g., owning fishing boats)
and trade networks across Tamil country, their work with fish, pearl oysters,
and conch shells rendered them ritually impure, at least in the eyes of the
worshipers of vegetarian goddesses and gods (e.g., Pārvatī and Śiva of
Maturai). Particularly, the sellers of dry fish (*karuvāṭu*) in the city of Maturai
were Parava Christians. Non-Parava communities were unwilling to join
their church and worship with them. Roberto de Nobili, an Italian aristocrat,
who had become a Jesuit missionary, came to Maturai in November 1606.
He immediately noticed that the Tamil congregation of the Roman Catholics did not include members of the higher *varṇas*. He wanted to know why
these custodians of professional knowledge and public administration did
not come to the Tamil congregation. Instead, it contained only one hundred
Parava traders.[10] Since 1595, Gonçalo Fernandes (1541–1619),[11] who had
earlier served as a soldier of the Portuguese army in the town of Maṉṉār and
met Henriques, had pastored this congregation.

---

[8]Bayly, *Saints, Goddesses, and Kings*, 332: "In effect Christianity became a caste lifestyle for the
group, and the *pattangatti*s and other notables became its guardians. The concept of a caste
lifestyle has usually been associated with Hindus for whom shared dress styles, eating habits,
marriage customs and traditions of worship have long helped to mark off one *jāti* from another.
Yet this is just what evolved amongst the Paravas."

[9]Bayly, *Saints, Goddesses, and Kings*, 375, 440: During the Assumption Festival of 1872, the Cāṉār,
Parayar, and Veḷḷāḷar Christians of the small town Vaṭakkaṇkulam waged bloody conflicts
against each other. Their *jāti* loyalty decisively weighed more than their Christian loyalty.

[10]S. Rajamanickam, *The First Oriental Scholar: Roberto de Nobili alias Tattuva Podagar—The Father
of Tamil Prose* (Tirunelveli: De Nobili Research Institute at St. Xavier's College, 1972), 18.

[11]Ines G. Županov, *Disputed Mission: Jesuit Experiments and Brahmanical Knowledge in Seventeenth-
Century India* (New Delhi: Oxford University Press, 1999), 4: Županov's view that Nobili considered Fernandes a devil seems to be exaggerated. Her writing correctly points out the differences between the two men in their origin, age, sociocultural orientation, theological and
linguistic competencies, professional and practical expressions, and the like.

Non-Christian Tamils looked down on Christians and called them *Paraṅkikārer,* a word that originally came from the Frankish crusaders and indicated those Europeans and Indian Christians who ate beef, consumed alcohol, were used to inter-*jāti* marriages, and led an immoral life. Rajamanickam, who had examined the notion of Paraṅki, asserted that this term referred to the European Christians, who, in the opinion of the Tamils in Maturai, were "devoid of culture, decency and honour."[12] Additionally, the non-Christian Tamils considered the Tamil Roman Catholic Christians as having embraced another *jāti.* In other words, Christians in Madurai belonged to a lower *jāti,* and they were social outcasts.

Most Tamils in Maturai worshiped the goddess Mīṉāṭci and her spouse Cuntarīcuvarar in their famous temple in the city center. They used Sanskrit for liturgical purposes, Telugu for administrative needs, and Tamil for local communication. Nobili learned these languages and discovered the residual monotheistic truths in their literature. He began to translate the teachings of the Council of Trent (1545–1563) into the Tamil, Telugu, and Sanskrit languages. For this purpose, he borrowed words from Tamil and Sanskrit and coined new terms for God, Jesus Christ, sin, salvation, and other Christian concepts. He was unable to find compatible words for the Holy Spirit, whom he called Isparintu Cāntu, transliterating from Portuguese (*Espírito Santo*). Likewise, he transliterated the Latin word *sacramentum* as *cākkiramantu.* His affinity to Sanskrit and the Brahmins reveals itself in the words that he chose either to transliterate or coin. For example, he borrowed the Vaiṣṇavite word *Parāparavastu* to name the unrevealed God of the Bible. He adopted a Sanskrit lifestyle because in his context it made sense. It came close to his aristocratic origin, education in Latin, and social interaction with the people of similar background.

Additionally, Nobili observed how ordinary Tamils and Telugus of his time revered and listened to the Sanskrit-speaking priests in Maturai. At that time, the rulers of Maturai were rebuilding the famous Mīṉāṭci temple according to Sanskrit religious and architectural principles. For example, King Tirumalai Nāyakkar, who ruled Maturai from 1623 to 1659, was Nobili's contemporary. As a patron of the Mīṉāṭci temple, he added to it lavishly

---

[12]Rajamanickam, *First Oriental Scholar,* 61.

decorated halls and entrance gateways. These edifices still display his passion
for Sanskrit expressions of religious faith and social organization. One can
easily assume that his subjects were also involved in this renewed dedication
to Sanskrit ideals. Some of Nobili's discussion partners, including converts,
must have been associated with this or other similar temples in Maturai.
Recognizing this sociopolitical and religious context of Nobili's Maturai
helps us to better understand his position on *jāti*.

Nobili insisted that he was from a royal background and was not a
Paraṅki. He began to eat vegetarian meals and wear the dress of Brahmin
priests. He taught his students while squatting on a piece of wooden plank.
He wore a sacred thread with three strands denoting Trinity and an empty
cross (denoting the risen and living Jesus Christ). He walked on wooden
sandals. When he went out, he wound up the sacred thread on a long staff
and carried it with him. He drank water from a clay pot known as a
kamaṇṭalam. He covered his head with a turban. He pierced his ears to
demonstrate his obedience to the Lord Jesus Christ. His outward appearance
resembled that of the Śaivite religious leaders of Brahmin *varṇa*. Županov
described Nobili's adaptation with a following statement: To Nobili, a

> Roman aristocrat, Brahmanism offered the closest analogue to the European
> culture of the literati. If somewhat extreme in details, Tamil purity and pol-
> lution rules were for Nobili equal to the separation of social orders in both
> contemporary Rome and even more so in its classical times. Therefore, he
> enthusiastically renounced polluting substances (meat and alcohol) and pol-
> luting relationships (low-caste people) in order to penetrate among those
> whom he considered his equals.[13]

Nobili was skilled in communicating the gospel of Jesus Christ to others.
After twenty days of persuasive discussions, he baptized his first convert and
called him Albert after the name of his Jesuit provincial Albert Laerzio. This
Albert was instrumental in persuading his Guru Dakṣiṇamūrti to embrace
Roman Catholicism. Soon other converts such as "Alexis Nāyak, Ignatius
Nāyak, Eustac Nāyak and others" from upper *jātis* followed suit.[14] However,
they were unable to survive for long. They were unable to find jobs to earn

---

[13]Županov, *Disputed Mission*, 26.
[14]Rajamanickam, *First Oriental Scholar*, 22.

their livelihood. They and their direct descendants had difficulties in finding fitting spouses and establishing families. Hence, the legacy of the upper-*jāti* converts was short-lived.

At the same time, the Tamils of other *varṇas* and lower *jātis* were uncomfortable with Nobili's mission methods and his converts. Realizing this important factor, he had wisely initiated a separate branch of mission with Jesuit priests known as Paṇṭāracuvāmis (i.e., similar to non-Brahmin religious leaders). These missionaries concentrated their efforts on Kaḷḷars and Maṟavars but failed to attract them in large numbers.[15] However, their number was larger and more widespread than that of the upper-*jāti* converts in Madurai.

Nobili's Madurai Mission and the work of the Jesuit Paṇṭāracuvāmis clearly illustrated the tenacity of the *varṇa* system and *jāti* categories of their times. Rajamanickam explained how Saint Thomas Christians living the lifestyle of the Brahmin Nāyars of Kerala maintained their *jāti* congregations, from which they had excluded the *avarṇā* groups such as the forest-dwelling Pulayars and the sea-faring Mukkuvars. Even during the times of Francis Xavier, the Mukkuvar Christians had prevented the Christian Karaiyars and Pulayars from entering their chapels.

In this context, Rajamanickam admired how Nobili succeeded in gathering Christians from different *jāti* groups under the same roof. They sat in separate places but received the same teaching and the same Eucharist (*naṟkaruṇai*, good grace).[16] True to Roman Catholic tradition, the people received only the sanctified wafer, and not the wine, during the Eucharist. Nobili considered the sociopolitical and economic aspects of the *varṇas* and

---

[15]Županov, *Disputed Mission*, 28: As "the militarized clans of Kaḷḷars and Maṟavars were in the process of regrouping and becoming more caste-like in the second half of the 17th century, Jesuit pantāracāmi missionaries were able to attract them to Christianity, precisely on the basis of a promise to promote their ritual status through spiritual intercession. However, in the long run they were not able to secure a permanent conversion because of the lack of missionary personnel and because these clans turned to other ritualists and their patronage networks."

[16]Rajamanickam, *First Oriental Scholar*, 63: "Christianity preaches the doctrine of the Mystical Body of Christ of which all including the low castes are members, but a few Christians could not dictate to the Hindu Society. They would have been ostracized, sent out of the caste, stripped of all their belongings and severely punished. That would have stopped all further propagation of the Gospel. So Nobili admitted caste as his predecessors had done, with mental reservations. What Chrysostom says of St. Paul may be applied to Nobli: 'Behold this, he circumcises in order to destroy circumcision.' Nobili condoned the caste system in order to destroy it."

jātis. He adopted and condoned a method that was incompatible with the values of the gospel of Jesus Christ, perhaps assuming that the Tamil Catholics would eventually give up the inequalities stemming from their adherence to the *varṇas* and the *jātis.* By following this method, he helped his followers to gain their rightful place in the main land, such as the Temple City of Maturai. Otherwise, Tamil Roman Catholicism would have remained in the faith of the seafaring people, who lived along the seacoast of the Tamil country. When Francis Xavier and his successors came to these coastal areas, these people embraced Roman Catholicism. Nobili's efforts enabled the traders of these seafaring peoples to practice their Christian faith in places like Maturai, where orthodox Śaivism ruled.

Nobili and his successors made a difficult moral choice and tolerated at least some aspects of racism inherent in *varṇas* and *jātis.* This adjustment opposed the biblical teachings of creation (that all human beings are created equal), salvation (that Jesus Christ died and rose to redeem them), and the presence of the Holy Spirit in the lives of all Christians (Gal 3:28).

LUTHERAN EXPERIENCES WITH THE TAMIL
PEOPLES OF VARIOUS CASTES

July 9, 1706, marked the beginning of a new chapter in the history of Christianity in India. On that day Bartholomäus Ziegenbalg and Heinrich Plütschau landed in Tranquebar; they brought with them German Lutheran pietism, which, like the Tamil *bhakti* religions, sought to influence human reason, emotions, devotions, and actions with reference to God and fellow human beings. The German Lutheran Pietists derived their understanding of the triune God from the Bible; they emphasized that people should place their trust in the God whom the Lord Jesus Christ has revealed in the Bible and then perform works that benefit fellow human beings in need. They believed that the world had only four religions, of which Christianity, Judaism, and Islam were monotheistic and Scripture-based and paganism was polytheistic and without any proper language, written Scripture, culture, or civil life. In their minds, the pagans were barbarians who lived under the sway of the devil, the archenemy of the God of the Bible. Their actions, however good they might have been, had no moral value because their doers did not believe in the Lord Jesus Christ. In other words, these non-Christians should be viewed as racially, culturally, intellectually, and humanly inferior to European Christians.

Ziegenbalg shared this unhealthy worldview and began to interact with the Tamils on this basis. As soon as he had learned to speak, read, and write the Tamil language and begun to appreciate the richness of Tamil literature, he changed his opinion about the Tamil people. Theologically, the Tamils remained not so much pagans as *aññāṇikaḷ* ("ignorant people," without the salvific knowledge of God of the Bible). They indeed belonged to Śivacamayam (religion of Śiva), to Viṣṇusamayam (religion of Viṣṇu), to the śakti cult of goddesses, or to a religion of the guardian deities of villages. They were simultaneously monotheistic and polytheistic. They believed that the One God had created countless female and male deputies and commanded human beings to worship them. Any worship rendered to them would ultimately reach this One God. Their belief in the endless cycle of births and deaths as a purification rite of the soul; their *jāti* as a tangible marker of their position within this cycle; and the almighty power of *karma* in determining one's fate and *jāti* during their next life compelled them to perform their *jāti* duties. This compulsion revealed itself in their moral life, which often, in Ziegenbalg's words, ashamed Christians, and their lifestyle. The Europeans in Tranquebar did not follow the social and religious etiquettes of the Tamil people. They suppressed the Tamils and exploited their labor. They even mistreated them as if they were "black dogs." The Europeans forced the Tamil women into prostitution.[17] The external lives of the Europeans indicated that they neither honored God nor thought about their life to come. For these and other sociocultural, religious, political, and economic reasons, the Tamils viewed the Europeans in Tranquebar as *atarmar* (irreligious, unrighteous, evil people) and *irāṭcatar* (demons).[18]

Ziegenbalg was not fully free from his racial thinking. On March 3, 1714, he visited a group of Tamils who were attending a temple festival and discussed with a few of them various themes, including the creation of Adam and Eve. A Tamil interrupted Ziegenbalg to ask why the Europeans

---

[17]Willem Caland, ed., *B. Ziegenbalg's Kleinere Schriften* (Amsterdam: Uitgave van de Koninklijke Akademie van Wetenschappen, 1930), 15.
[18]*Halle Reports*, i.e., *Der Königl: Missionarien aus Ost-Indien eingesandter Ausführlichen Berichten Erster Theil* (Halle: Verlegung des Wäysen-Hauses, 1735), vol. 1, continuation 1 (1710); continuation 7 (1714), 457.

were White and the Tamils were Black. Ziegenbalg's response to this question began with a correct answer and slipped into a racial prejudice that he clothed with his theology. The German text of his response is long, which I summarize as follows:

> Originally, God created a man and a woman as our ancestors. They were neither white nor black. White people cannot beget black children. Likewise, black people cannot beget white children, unless they intermarry. In the course of time, people intermarried; some of them moved to warmer countries and lived there. Gradually, they became black. Even though we Europeans live in your warm country, we remain white; the children whom we beget are also white. There is also another reason why you are black and always remain black. God has desired that, due to your paganism, your external appearance should stay a strong curse. Among all the inhabitants of the world, you are the last people to abandon your paganism and return to God. This is the reason that today all heathen peoples of Asia, Africa, and America are black, with the exception of the Chinese, Japanese, and a few others. Immediately, a Brahmin answered: if this was the reason for our black skin complexion, God must have been partial in creation. Ziegenbalg responded: God is common to all people just as the sun is common to all. Those who close their eyes cannot see its light. By contrast, if you accept Jesus Christ as your savior, God will accept you. God looks not at your skin color or external appearance but at the right condition of your heart.[19]

Ziegenbalg's racial prejudice equated human sin with skin color. For him the dark skin color of the Tamils gave evidence of their sin. I am unable to find any other source that would indicate that he ever changed his mind in this regard. Some of his successors (e.g., Hüttemann) too entertained traces of these racial and theological prejudices. Yet others had a different opinion. For example, Benjamin Schultze, who came to Tranquebar in 1719, briefly described the external appearances of the Tamil people. He insisted that the skin color of the Tamil people depended on their geographical location. The people of the northern Tamil country were no longer dark but were brown. The Brahmins and the Muslims were not dark. Only those Tamils who were exposed more to sunlight than others were black. The Pariahs, who were working for the whole day in hot sun, were blacker than others.

---

[19] *Halle Reports*, vol. 1, continuation 9 (1716), 736-37.

The white and black colors of the skin were inheritable.[20] Thus, Schultze's view was scientifically correct. His view lacked the racism evident in Ziegenbalg's narrative.

Eventually, toward the end of the eighteenth century, the Tamil Lutherans had different *jāti*-based church buildings. In the beginning, Ziegenbalg viewed the *jāti* as *Geschlecht*, which at that time referred not only to a species but also to a large blood-related family such as a clan or a tribe. It also referred to various social strata like the nobles and aristocrats at the top of any European society of that time.[21] The Jerusalem Church that he and his Tamil adherents erected in 1707 was a long rectangular hall. It accommodated the Tamils who had earlier belonged to various *jātis*. Ziegenbalg considered the *jāti* distinctions to be superstition (*Aberglaube*) and claimed that he did not permit it among the Tamil Lutherans. He taught that at creation all people were equal. Likewise, the death of Jesus Christ was applicable to all people without any distinction. Additionally, he quoted Tamil authors such as Civavākkiyar, Kapilar, and others, who had opposed *varṇa* and *jāti* distinctions. With this mindset, he also built the New Jerusalem Church and dedicated it on October 11, 1718. This cross-shaped church building still exists today and has become a hotbed for *jāti* controversies. After his death, few people of the higher *jātis*, mostly from the kingdom of Tañcāvūr, embraced Lutheranism, and they insisted on observing their *jāti* distinctions. In 1727, missionary Christoph Theodosius Walther permitted his catechists in the kingdom of Tañcāvūr to observe dignity based on *jāti*. When the Lutherans chose their first Tamil pastor in December 1733, they preferred Aaron from the Piḷḷai *jāti* to Diago from a lower *jāti*.

The ordination of Aaron to the full office of a Lutheran clergyperson unexpectedly led to a transnational racial problem. The German Lutheran pastor Conrad Daniel Kleinknecht (1691–1753) knew of this problem and addressed it effectively. He was a friend of the missionary Nikolaus Dahl (1690–1747), who was among those clergy persons who ordained Aaron in Tranquebar. Kleinknecht and Dahl studied in Jena, Germany. Later, Kleinknecht worked in the orphanage (i.e., the current Francke Foundations

---

[20]*Halle Reports*, vol. 2 (1729), continuation 22 (1728), 896-97.
[21]Jacob Grimm and Wilhelm Grimm, *Deutsches Wörterbuch*, vol. 5, cols. 3903-13, http://dwb .uni-trier.de/de/.

in Halle/Saale, Germany) that had been supporting the Lutheran missionaries in Tranquebar. In 1719 he moved to the city of Ulm in southern
Germany. Later in 1731 he became a pastor of the Lutheran Church in
Leipheim and remained there until his death. He regularly corresponded
with Dahl, and he read the missionary reports from Tranquebar. When he
realized that his clergy colleagues in Germany had not accepted Reverend
Aaron as their equal because of his race, Kleinknecht composed a book
that pleaded for Aaron's recognition.[22] He unhesitatingly called attention
to the "dark-brown" skin color of Aaron and other Tamil Lutherans to
highlight the nonracial application of Christ's salvation. He insisted that
the Lord Jesus Christ died and rose again not only for European Christians
but also for the dark-brown "sheep" in India. It seems that his German
clergy colleagues did not change their opinion drastically. Therefore, soon
after the death of Aaron in 1745 and his friend Dahl in 1747, Kleinknecht
published another book with a similar title.[23] It insisted that all German
Lutheran pastors should learn from Aaron's exemplary ministry, good
characteristics, and achievements. Kleinknecht's approach seems to have
had some impact on several Lutheran Pietists in Germany. Therefore,
when Aaron's successors were appointed not only for the church in
Māyāvaram but also to other places, the Lutheran pastors in Germany did
not raise any objections.

As Lutheran congregations branched out into the kingdom of Tañcāvūr,
jāti-related tensions became acute. For example, by the end of the eighteenth
century, Christian Friedrich Schwartz, the famous patriarch of all Lutheran
missionaries, worked in the capital city of the kingdom of Tañcāvūr. His
Tamil adherents adamantly upheld their *jāti* distinctions. The administration of Eucharist, which supposedly should promote unity and fellowship
among Christians, became a tool to affirm *jāti* distinctions. Schwartz had to
use two different chalices. The Tamil Lutherans hailing from a higher *jāti*

---

[22]Conrad Daniel Kleinknecht, *Zuverlässige Nachricht, von der, durch das Blut des erwürgten Lammes theuer-erkaufften schwarzen Schaaf- und Lämmer-Heerde; Das ist: Neu-bekehrten malabarischen Christen, in Ost-Indien [. . .]* (Ulm: Wagner, 1738).
[23]Conrad Daniel Kleinknecht, *Zuverlässige Nachricht, von der, durch das Blut des erwürgten Lammes theuer-erkauften schwarzen Schaaf- und Lämmer-Herde, oder von den neu-bekehrten malabarischen Christen in Ost-Indien [. . . .] Dem noch beygefügt: Nachrichten von den Englis[chen]. Colonisten Georgiens zu Eben-Ezer in America [. . .]* (Augsburg: Johann Jakob Lotters, 1749).

used one chalice, and others drank from the second chalice. Schwartz expressed his dismay about this practice, which he could not abolish. He hoped that the Pariah members of his congregations would enjoy more acceptance if they would not eat beef, and thus minimize the danger of ritual pollution. He also used local folk wisdom to remind the members of his congregation that in heaven a *Toṇṭaimāṉ* (i.e., the ruler of a land) and a *Tōṭṭi* (sweeper) would have the same status. Therefore, they should learn to give up their *jāti* distinctions at the earliest. Schwartz's efforts resembled that of Nobili more than 150 years earlier. He believed that a good knowledge of Christian theology and the practice of Christian virtues would persuade the Tamil Lutherans to give up their loyal observance of *jāti*. In this manner, they could fully demonstrate their new identity as God's people.

Lutheran and Anglican Debates About Caste Among the Tamil Christians

Toward the end of Schwartz's ministry in South India, decisive changes took place in Kolkata, the capital city of the English East India Company. In 1792, William Carey arrived there and brought Baptist Christianity to India. His dissenter background had no place for the hierarchal arrangement of the Church of England. Hence, he encouraged his convert Krishna Pal to renounce his *jāti* attachments. During this period, the British population experienced a kind of evangelical revival. They began to share their financial resources with newly emerging mission agencies (e.g., the London Missionary Society in 1795, the Church Mission Society in 1799, and others). They developed an interest in sending missionaries to their overseas colonies to share their version of Christianity with the colonized people. The commercial and political prospects of the English East India Company (EIC) also changed. After much debate in the English Parliament in London and with considerable hesitation, the EIC introduced into its charter the Pious Clause in 1813 and 1833. Soon after 1813, the Church Missionary Society, the London Missionary Society, and other British missionary societies sent their deputies to India. The change in 1833 permitted Protestant mission agencies from Europe, North America, and Australia to come to India. Thus, the nineteenth century provided a good opportunity for different Protestant missionaries to carry out their experiments with the thorny issue of *jāti* among Christians.

This is not the place to enumerate the number of works on caste. Representative references to the following works sufficiently illustrate the rich body of literature on the question of caste. Duncan Forrester's work provides a good overview of the *jāti* and its impact on Christians in India. Jürgen Stein examined the role of *jāti* in Indian society and Christian response to it. In particular, Geoffrey Oddie has illustrated how few British missionaries opposed the observance of *jāti* in their congregations and how other missionaries maintained an ambiguous approach to it. Similarly, Andreas Nehring documented how few Lutheran missionaries from the Leipzig Evangelical Lutheran Mission engaged with the issues of *jāti* in Tamil country from 1840 to 1940.[24] I do not want to repeat what these and other scholars have already examined. Instead, I wish to discuss briefly how three men construed the relationship between *jāti* and Christianity. Karl Graul (1814–1864), on behalf of the Tamil Lutherans and the Madras Missionary Conference (1850),[25] wanted to tolerate social aspects of *jāti*. By contrast, Bishop Daniel Wilson (1778–1858) and George U. Pope (1820–1908), on behalf of the Anglicans, vehemently opposed and rejected the observance of *jāti* among the Anglican Christians in India.[26] Their views crystallized the key issues.

The Lutherans, coming from their folk churches (*Volkskirche*), sought to retain everything that they considered essential to the dignity and identity of the people. Like the Jesuits in Tamil country, they interpreted the system of *jāti* as an integral element of the identity of the Tamil people. Therefore, they allowed it, just as God had permitted the twelve different tribes to form the one people of Israel. Each of these tribes had their geographical regions;

---

[24]Duncan B. Forrester, *Caste and Christianity: Attitudes and Policies on Caste of Anglo-Saxon Protestant Missions in India* (London: Curzon Press, 1980); also available as an ebook (London: Routledge, 2017). Jürgen Stein, *Christentum und Kastenwesen: Zum Verhältnis von Religion und Gesellschaft in Indien* (Frankfurt am Main: Verlag Otto Lembeck, 2002). Geoffrey A. Oddie, *Social Protest in India: Protestant Missionaries and Social Reforms 1850–1900* (New Delhi: Manohar, 1979); Oddie, *Imagined Hinduism: Protestant Missionary Construction of Hinduism, 1793–1900* (New Delhi: Sage, 2006); and Oddie, *Religious Conversion Movements in South Asia: Continuities and Change 1800–1990* (London: Routledge, 2016). Andreas Nehring, *Orientalismus und Mission: Die Repräsentation der tamilischen Gesellschaft und Religion durch Leipziger Missionare 1840–1940* (Wiesbaden: Harrassowitz, 2003).
[25]Karl Graul, *Explanations Concerning the Principles of the Leipzig Missionary Society, with Regard to the Caste Question* (Madras: Athenaeum, 1851). See also *Minutes of the Madras Missionary Conference and Other Documents on the Subject of Caste* (Madras: American Mission Press, 1850).
[26]George Uglow Pope, *The Lutheran Aggression: A Letter to the Tranquebar Missionaries Regarding "Their Position, Their Proceedings, and Their Doctrine"* (Madras: American Mission Press, 1853).

accordingly, they developed their characteristics. As far as the gospel of Jesus Christ was concerned, the *jāti* remained an *adiaphora* (neither required nor prohibited). However, since it shaped the Tamil identity in places like Tañcāvūr, where what the Lutherans called Hinduism was strong, Tamil Christians could tolerate it for a period, but they should not practice untouchability, particularly when they appointed catechists, pastors, and other functionaries of their congregations. The Lutherans hesitated to ban the practice of *jāti* altogether because it might stop the Tamils of higher *jātis* from embracing Lutheranism. Nehring states how the Veḷḷāḷar Christians of Tañcāvūr had welcomed this Lutheran position.[27]

At the same time, not all Lutheran missionaries among the Tamils endorsed this position. For example, Carl Ochs opposed this view.[28] He could not accept that Nallatampi, a Tamil Lutheran candidate for pastoral ordination, refused to eat food with the German Lutheran missionaries and thus to nullify his *jāti* identity. In his writing against the *jāti*, Ochs first cited the 45th poem of anti-*jāti* Tamil work titled *Civavakkiam*:

> *jātiyāvatu ētaṭā calam tiraṇṭa nīrallō*
> *pūtavācal oṉṟallō pūtam aintum oṉṟallō*
> *kātilvāḻi kāraikampi pāṭakam poṉ oṉṟalō*
> *jāti pētam ōtukiṉṟa taṉmai eṉṉa taṉmaiyō.*[29]
> What is *jāti*? Water that fills entire world;
> our body is one made of the five elements.
> Are not the earring, the nose ring, and the
> bangles made of the same gold? Then, why
> do you speak about *jāti* differences?

Then, Ochs quoted the 80th *Tirukkuṟaḷ*, which teaches that love is the highest virtue of life; a loveless life resembles the skeleton covered with flesh.[30] It is noteworthy that Ochs appealed to the Tamil poets, who stressed the equality of life. Regarding the question of *jāti*, Ochs and Graul disagreed. In their writings, both Ochs and Graul referred to the same passages from

---

[27]Nehring, *Orientalismus und Mission*, 113.

[28]Carl Ochs, *Die Kaste in Ostindien und die Geschichte derselben in der alten lutherischen Mission* (Rostock: Leopold, 1860).

[29]Just before the beginning of the first chapter of *Kaste in Ostindien*, Ochs translates this poem.

[30]*Aṉpiṉ vaḻiyatu uyirnilai aḥtilārkku / eṉputōl pōrtta uṭampu.* Ochs's German rendering can be translated as follows: "Love is the most important aspect of life. Those who do not have it are nothing but skeletons covered with skin."

the records of the older Lutheran missionaries in Tamil country but interpreted them differently.[31] Ochs obtained the help of the newly founded
Danish Mission and formed a *jāti*-less church (1861), which evolved into the
contemporary Arcot Lutheran Church. Over the course of time, the Tamil
Lutherans tolerated *jāti* identities in marriage practices, appointment of
pastors, and selection of church officers.

The Anglicans took an opposite view. Most of them looked down on the
select aspects (e.g., image worship, *devadāsī*, system) of what they called
Hinduism. In this manner, they completely rejected the system of *jāti* because they perceived *jāti* to be a religious institution that was incompatible
with the gospel of Jesus Christ. The *jāti*, for them, perpetuated prejudices,
inequalities, and socioeconomic injustices. It hindered people's social mobility and became an abomination for Christianity. It hampered Christian
witnesses among their non-Christian neighbors. Nehring documented that
after Bishop Wilson had asked all Anglicans in India to ban the tolerance of
jāti among them, 1,700 Tamil Christians in Tañcāvūr and 1,846 Tamil Christians in Vepery in Chennai left their Anglican congregations.[32] Several
former Anglicans joined the Lutheran congregations, and *jāti* earned the
wrath of G. U. Pope, who opposed the Lutheran tolerance of it in their congregations. This love-hate relationship between Christians and their *jāti*
continued well into the twentieth century.

Issues of Caste Among the Tamil Christians After the Nineteenth Century

The World Wars had a dramatic impact on the Protestant churches in Tamil
country. British, American, and Australian missionaries fared better than
missionaries from continental Europe. Particularly, German missionaries
had to renounce their leadership roles and transfer them either to the missionaries from neutral countries such as Sweden or to Indian Christians.
Thus, for example, the Tamil Evangelical Lutheran Church attained its independence with its own constitution (1919). Ernst Heuman became its
first Swedish bishop (1921–1926). During this time, all the Lutheran

---

[31]Karl Graul, *Die Stellung der Evangelisch-Lutherischen Mission in Leipzig zur ostindischen Kasten-frage* (Leipzig: Evangelisch-Lutherische Mission, 1861).
[32]Nehring, *Orientalismus und Mission*, 107.

churches in India experienced a similar transition of power, and they formed the Federation of Evangelical Lutheran Churches in India (1926–1927). A few years later, on April 30, 1936, Buckingham Palace in London passed the Government of India (Scheduled Castes) Order. Its section 3 (a) stated: "No Indian Christian shall be deemed a member of the Scheduled Caste."[33] The British government attempted to safeguard the interests of the ruling *varṇas* and *jātis*, and failed to consider the economic and political situation of those converts from the scheduled castes who had embraced Christianity. This exclusion would haunt Indian Christian converts from scheduled caste backgrounds; the majority of Indian Christians hailed from such backgrounds, especially after the Peoples Movement from the latter part of the nineteenth century into the early part of the twentieth century.[34] Christians were aware of this prohibition, but they could not persuade the government of India to change it. Even the formation of the powerful Church of South India (1947) did not have any impact on this provision. This united body inherited several Lutheran congregations in Tranquebar, Tañcāvūr, Tiruccy, Chennai, and Kolkata. It also incorporated Anglican, Presbyterian, and Congregational traditions. The Presidential Order of Scheduled Castes and Scheduled Tribes Order (1950) and the Constitution of India (1950, especially article 341) provided legal safeguards for the scheduled castes. Untouchability became a crime in 1955. Members of these lower *jātis* gained access to temples, common wells, roads, and eateries. They could acquire, possess, or dispose of their own properties. They could apply for government scholarships. After they completed their studies, they were eligible to apply for government jobs. Special commissioners and police officers looked after the welfare of these scheduled castes. However, Christian converts from these scheduled castes could not automatically claim these privileges. In order to address this unequal treatment, Christians started many protest movements. They learned from the activities of leaders like Mahatma Jyotirao Phule (d. 1890) and B. R. Ambedkar

---

[33]Scheduled Caste Orders were issued at various times. See "The Government of India (Scheduled Castes) Order, 1936, at the Court at Buckingham Palace, the 30th day of April, 1936, the King's Most Excellent Majesty, in Council," *The Gazette of India*, June 6, 1936, http://socialjustice.nic .in/writereaddata/UploadFile/GOI-SC-ORDER-1936.pdf.

[34]Jarrell Waskom Pickett, *Christian Mass Movements in India: A Study with Recommendations* (New York: Abingdon, 1933).

(d. 1956) and derived insights from the experiences of the Dalit Panther Movement (1970s).[35]

The *avarṇa* peoples, who had no place within the fourfold *varṇa* system and were considered to be at the lowest social position, were variously called depressed classes, exterior castes, Harijans (Hari's People), Untouchables, and other designations. By contrast, they themselves adopted the name *Dalit* (split, meaning multiple oppressions, atrocities, and exploitations) for themselves. This name does not merely refer to their plight; instead, it stands for their dignity, fight against atrocities (e.g., humiliation, rape of Dalit women, murder of Dalit youths), and demand for constitutional safeguards. Most of them do not own either land or house. Therefore, they depend on their employers, who could arbitrarily abuse their labor. They perform the hard jobs (e.g., tilling the ground, removing and burying dead animals, skinning animals slaughtered for meat) that others do not wish to perform. They struggle against the social stigma and ritual pollution that the *varṇa* peoples and the upper *jātis* have ascribed to them. They consciously reject the Sanskrit language, its culture, and its proponents (especially the political Brahmins, who still dominate the Indian administrative machinery, business, education, and politics). They seek to end the pathos that has characterized their history.

Most Indian Christians in all branches and denominations have Dalit backgrounds. Like their non-Christian counterparts, they began reinterpreting their history, religion, and position within and outside of their congregations. They received their interpretive tools from different sources. Some of them included the liberation theology of Latin America, the Black theology of North America, Marxist ideology, Dalit movements, anti-Hindi agitations in Tamil Nadu in the 1960s, and anticonversion laws promulgated by various states in India.

First, the Dalit Christians were not satisfied with reshaping the Indian Christian theology that had earlier oriented itself toward Sanskrit and the ideals of the upper *jātis*. They rejected Sanskrit ways of being human:

---

[35]G. P. Deshpande, ed., *Selected Writings of Jotirao Phule* (New Delhi: Leftword, 2002). B. R. Ambedkar, *Annihilation of Caste with a Reply to Mahatma Gandhi and Castes in India, Their Mechanism, Genesis, and Development* (Jullundar City: Bheem Patrika Publications, 1968). Lata Murugkar, *Dalit Panther Movement in Maharashtra* (Bombay: Sangham, 1991).

describing God as *parāparavastu* (the Supreme Being) or *deva* (a shining being in the heavens) and human actions as *karma* (deed, with its merit or demerit influencing one's rebirths and redeaths), *mokṣa* (liberation, release from the cycle of rebirths and redeaths), *papa* (sin, mistake, transgression, failure), and the like. Likewise, they rejected Sanskrit teachings on human origin (*varṇa* and *avarṇa*), original sin, purity, and pollution. They believed that certain words and concepts found in the Sanskrit religious literature, such as the menial servants (*dasa*), nonheroes (*asura*), accursed people (*chandālās*), aliens (*mlecchās*), demons (*rākṣasa*), and monkey (*anumar*), actually referred to the Dalits. By rejecting the Sanskrit traditions and religious scriptures, they constructed their own legends, stories, songs, customs, and sayings, and thus emphasized their superiority. rejection of translation model?

Second, the Dalit Christians have taken their suffering as a norm by which to interpret the Bible. Their understanding of being "created in the image of God" has enabled them to have better self-respect. Their life in this world is not a punishment for the sins in their past lives. Instead, God has willingly and lovingly created them and seeks to remain in fellowship with them. This notion of God's love and purpose for their lives transforms them. Their God is not merely a disinterested ruler; rather, their God is interested in their affairs and enables them to get out of oppression. With eagerness and dedication they expound the exodus narratives of the Pentateuch, Christ's teachings on suffering and liberation in the Gospels, and the Pauline view on equality. The passion, death, resurrection, and current lordship of Jesus Christ powerfully influence the Dalits to persevere against all odds. They feel that Jesus Christ sympathizes with their pain and suffering. He touched and healed the sick. The Dalits understand this human touch as a welcome blow to the untouchability inherent in the systems of *varṇa*, *avarṇa*, and *jāti*. The Dalits rightly believe that sin is not hereditary; instead, it is the result of unjust systems, which could have been prevented. This systemic evil includes millennia-old prejudices regarding purity and pollution; deliberate exclusion from access to knowledge, power, and privileges; prolonged poor nutrition; unjust wages; inhuman living conditions; and lack of health care. The Dalits view the *varṇa* and *avarṇa* systems as the embodiment of the most vicious systemic evils. Therefore, salvation, granted by the Lord Jesus Christ, is their freedom from the clutches of these systems and assurance for a better, more humane future.

Third, the Dalit Christians are the main targets of the Hindu fundamentalist groups, who deny fellow Indians the freedom of conscience and religious choice. They attack or pressure these Christians to give up their Christian faith and return to their "father's home," namely Hinduism. In this context, the Dalit Christians seek their rights and privileges provided in the Constitution of India, but they have to face another hurdle. When they embrace Christianity, they automatically lose their previous scheduled caste status and do not enjoy the same levels of protections and privileges that their non-Christian counterparts have.

Fourth, Dalit Christians were unwilling to accept the presence and power of *jāti* in Christian congregations. They fought for Dalit pastors and bishops; nowadays, most bishops of the Lutheran churches, the Church of South India, and the Church of North India are from Dalit backgrounds. Their leadership does not automatically mean stability in these churches. Many of the leaders are new to power, and the power has a tendency to corrupt them. They often forget their own peoples and get embroiled in court cases pertaining to the sale of immovable properties, accepting bribes for appointments, and the like. Dalit pastors and bishops maintain strong hatred toward Christian leaders from Nāṭār and Veḷḷāḷar communities because they assume that their predecessors had little or no understanding for the Dalits.[36] This blanket prejudice prevents access to the history of Christianity in a balanced manner. For example, Bishop V. S. Azariah, himself a Nāṭār, empowered the Dalit Christians of the Dornakal Diocese in Andhra Pradesh. This and other contributions by non-Dalit leaders to the betterment of the Dalits should be included in the courses on Dalit theology taught at undergraduate and postgraduate levels in several institutions of higher learning.

Fifth, Dalit Christians should pay particular attention to those non-Dalits who have worked for human dignity. Every Tamil school child knows the dictum of the ancient Tamil poet Kaṇiyaṉ Pūṅkuṉṟaṉ (at the dawn of the

---

[36]Nowadays, Dalit bishops administer most of the dioceses of the Church of South India and the Church of North India. Similarly, Indian Dalit Christian leaders govern most of the theological seminaries. These leaders do not have any sympathy for non-Dalit theological students or teachers. For example, the dioceses of the Church of South India in northern Tamil Nadu hesitate to appoint Nāṭār pastors from Tirunelvēli.

first millennium), as recorded in the 192nd song of the collection of poems *Puṟanāūṟu* (400 poems on worldly life): "my native place is everywhere; all people are kith and kin" (*yātum ūrē, yāvarum kēḷīr*). This poem reiterates the truth that in this world all human beings have a common origin. Therefore, they are related to one another. Later, poets like Kapilar and Civavākkiyar have forcefully rejected the division of people along *jāti* lines.[37] During modern times, poet Pāratiyār (1882–1928), himself a Brahmin, worked for the abolishment of *jāti* distinctions. In his song titled "Ōṭi viḷaiyāṭu pāppā" (run around and play, oh girl child), he encourages the children to learn well, to oppose all evils, and to look for a better future. One of the evils, which he advises them to give up, is the *jāti* distinction:

> *Cātikaḷ illaiyaṭi pāppā;—kulat,*
> *tāḻcci uyarcci collal pāvam;*
> *nīti, uyarntamati, kalvi—aṉpu*
> *niṟaiya uṭaiyavarkaḷ mēlōr.*
> Oh, Girl Child, there are no *jātis*;
> it is a sin to speak about the higher or lower *jāti*.
> Those, who have in abundance justice, higher wisdom, learning, and love,
> are the noble ones.

Likewise, Pāratiyār's other song, titled "Muracu" (war drum),[38] deserves our attention. It advocates an old idea that *jāti* identity should be measured not by one's birth but by one's character and good deeds that benefit the society. It chides those who promote *jāti* distinctions because they destroy justice and indulge in permanent violence. It forcefully rejects the violence done on the basis of *jāti* and pleads for mutual support in all professions. It explains its teaching through a parable about a white queen who gave birth to kittens. One kitten was as black as a clay. The other was fair; yet another one had the color of a snake. The fourth kitten was as white as milk. Though they had different colors, they were all kittens. None of them was either superior or inferior to the other. This song also explains the meaning of this parable: the skin color of the people may vary, but, in essence, all of them

---

[37]For further details on these poets, see Daniel Jeyaraj, *A German Exploration of Indian Society: Ziegenbalg's "Malabarian Heathenism"; An Annotated English Translation with an Introduction and a Glossary* (Chennai: Mylapore Institute for Indigenous Studies, 2006), 100-114.

[38]*Pāratiyār kavitaikaḷ* (Ceṉṉai: Māṇikkavācakar Patippakam, 1990), 302-6.

are similar. If they think and work together, they can destroy *jāti* differences. They should uphold love because it is creative and it can remove human misery. All people should realize the fundamental fact that like these siblings they are equals. Like Pāratiyār, there are other good-hearted Tamils in Hinduism, Buddhism, and other religions. The more the Dalit Christians identify these people and obtain their cooperation, the more they can create a humane society for all peoples.

Conclusion

Most Indians derive their identity from concepts such as *iṇam*, *varṇa*, *jāti*, *kula*, and *gotra*. Yet these concepts harbor within themselves inward-looking racial aspects that draw boundaries to keep outsiders out. They nourish prejudices, mistreatment, and conflicts against those whom they consider as either rivals or inferiors. Christians in Tamil country had to deal with the inclusive and exclusive sides of Indian ways of thinking and linking. During more recent times, the Jesuits interacted with the Tamils; their followers viewed the realities of *iṇam*, *varṇa*, and *jāti* in certain ways, and they dealt with the resultant conflicts in their own way. The Protestant missionaries, especially the Lutherans, followed these Jesuits in eighteenth-century Tamil country. Their theological outlook enabled them to integrate certain elements of the Tamil ideas of *iṇam*, *varṇa*, and *jāti*. By the middle of the nineteenth century, however, their monopoly in Tamil country diminished; the Anglican missionaries of different persuasions worked among the Tamils. They firmly rejected the hierarchical views of *varṇa* and *jāti*, aspired for egalitarian Christian congregations, and obtained partial success. The twentieth century was different. Due to the World Wars and their aftermath, many Protestant church bodies obtained their independent identity. Since most of their members hailed from the Dalit background, they had to fight for their recognition as Christian Dalits who need the safeguards and provisions that the government of India makes available to non-Christian Dalits through its constitution and several administrative mechanisms.

As discussed above, race in India is inseparably rooted in the systems of *varṇa* and *jāti*, which epitomize and reinforce inequalities and injustices. Particularly the people of the *avarṇa* and lower *jāti* categories suffer discriminations and atrocities. For Dalit Christians the pathos of their people forms the basis for Dalit theology. They question and reinterpret the teachings of the Sanskrit religious literature. They struggle for liberation from the clutches of *varṇa* and *jāti* systems. They are aware of the *jāti*-related activities of the Jesuits, the Lutherans, the Anglicans, and other European Christian leaders. On the whole, they judge these activities inadequate. These European Christian leaders viewed the *jāti* systems as either a social institution required for one's dignity or a religious institution incompatible with the gospel message of Jesus Christ. Depending on their choice, they treated the Christians of various *jātis* differently. In part, this treatment reflected the attitudes of the European colonizers, in whose territories they were working.[39] *rejection of trans and anthro*

Additionally, the Dalit Christians find the previous attempts of Indian Christian leaders regarding the *jāti* to be less convincing. They reject Christian theologies of enculturation that are based on Sanskrit ideas, philosophies, and ways of life. Instead, they derive inspiration from their own non-Sanskrit heroines and heroes, cultures and traditions. As they struggle to liberate themselves and their contemporaries from the chains of *varṇa* and *jāti*, they opt for the values of the rule of God (e.g., Jesus' Nazareth Manifesto in Luke 4:18-21). Christian debates on race, mission, and theology in India, particularly Dalit attempts to create authentic Indian Christian expressions and theologies, continue unabated. Their attempts portray a complex reality in which their ardent efforts for enculturation, liberation, and transformation find their place. None of these efforts is perfect, final, and closed. They are in a state of being and becoming.

---

[39]Contemporary debates between African American (Black) theologians and White theologians highlight whiteness as a category of willful suppression, discrimination, and humiliation. For further details, see Willie James Jennings, *The Christian Imagination: Theology and the Origins of Race* (New Haven, CT: Yale University Press, 2015).

4

....

Ambivalent Modalities

Mission, Race, and the African Factor

Akintunde E. Akinade
with Clifton R. Clarke

If Christianity seeks to be anything more than a vast
effort to swindle a mass of mystified blacks, the churches of Africa
must all join to come to terms with this question.

JEAN-MARC ÉLA

The schools have been integrated, the courts have been
integrated, the workplaces have been integrated,
but the churches have not been integrated.

JIMMY CARTER

Now there were devout Jews from every nation under heaven living in
Jerusalem. And at this sound the crowd gathered and was bewildered,
because each one heard them speaking the native language of each.
Amazed and astonished, they asked, "Are not all these who are speaking
Galileans? And how is it that we hear, each of us, in our own native
language? . . . In our own languages we hear them speaking about God's
deeds of power." All were amazed and perplexed, saying to one another,
"What does this mean?"

ACTS 2:5-12

INTRODUCTION: REVIEWING THE LAY OF THE LAND

The historical legacy of missionary agents and agencies in Africa is varied and complex. It is full of narratives about domination, resistance, autonomy, and nationalism. Mission and evangelism are central to the Christian faith; however, the intersection between race and mission in Africa is a subject that is often ignored or glossed over by theologians, missiologists, and church practitioners. Beyond emotive and sensational responses to Christian mission in Africa, it is imperative to understand the layout of a complex terrain and tease out the paradoxes of missionary engagement in Africa. The pattern that emanates from discussion on race and mission is not monochrome. It evokes several dimensions and colors. The veritable linkages between mission and race in this paper are situated within some key developments, events, and circumstances in African Christianity.

African Christianity has evolved out of a dynamic encounter between the biblical revelation of Jesus Christ and African culture, which has given expression to various African Christian traditions from the African Indigenous church to African Pentecostalism. Although the vestiges of colonialism and Western imperialism continues to bleed through African governmental systems and political structures, the church has managed to maintain a firm grip on the shape of African Christianity. African Christians have demonstrated tremendous innovation in interpreting biblical Christianity in such a way that it speaks to the African heart and soul through such hermeneutical methods as inculturation and translation of the biblical faith.[1]

The understanding of religion as a cultural system enunciated by Clifford Geertz provides a useful lens for grasping the enduring nature of religious identities and norms in African societies.[2] Religious identities and affirmations have cultural significance in many African societies. Religion is always an embedded phenomenon that cannot be divorced from peoples' social, cultural, and historical setting. In African societies, devotion and spirituality are bolstered by many cultural precepts and sensibilities. However, the yardstick of theological orthodoxy remains relevant and useful. It was used as

---

[1]For further information about this dynamic process, see Akintunde E. Akinade, "Musings on the Ebb and Flow of World Christianity," in *Creativity and Change in Nigerian Christianity*, ed. David Ogungbile and Akintunde E. Akinade (Lagos: Malthouse Press, 2010), xvi-xxiii.
[2]Clifford Geertz, *The Interpretation of Cultures: Selected Essays* (New York: Basic Books, 1973).

the ultimate barometer to judge certain cultural practices and beliefs. Indigenous creativity on the other hand provided the antidote to prefabricated theologies and doctrines. Beyond the dictates of functionalism and other materialistic understanding of religion, African Christians understand that religious experience and expressions are real. They take religion seriously and have embarked on different projects and initiatives to express the Christian faith in ways that are meaningful to both individuals and societies. After all, isn't faith about the existential queries of its *dramatis personae*?

ENGAGING AND ENCOUNTERING THE
CRUCIBLE OF MISSION AND RACE

The missionary enterprise has engendered many issues, modalities, and controversies since its global inception. In an effort to seek contextual relevance, missionary agents have endeavored to develop meaningful paradigms that will reconcile both faith and practice. The Great Commission never operates in a vacuum; it must connect with various social, cultural, political, and economic realities. Christian mission has been tested in different contexts and periods, each of which has demanded new methodologies and models. It has been enhanced and supported by colonial trappings and indigenous initiatives. It has also been shaped by several societal conditions and circumstances, always enduring the test of time and producing many movements and organizations. These are some of the nonnegotiable facts about Christian mission.

The six elements of mission include witness and proclamation; liturgy, prayer, and contemplation; justice, peace, and the integrity of creation; interreligious dialogue; inculturation; and reconciliation. All are in one way or another related to the theme of this conference: mission and race. These six elements continue to engender various theological and missiological constructs. The tension between the ideal and the real has been a perennial issue in the transmission of the Christian faith. The process of resolving this dilemma has given the impetus to creative and contextual ideas in mission and theology. Like the woman in a desperate search for her lost coin, missiologists continue to search for meaningful methodologies for engaging the six elements of mission.

This process is invigorated by a continuing search for the fullness of the truth of God made known in Jesus Christ. However, the line that runs through their various perspectives like a crimson thread is the bold rejection of a metanarrative that glosses over individual voices and sensibilities.[3] For instance, it is especially imperative to come to terms with the task of mission among the dispossessed and marginalized communities. The mission of the church must be reevaluated in a context characterized by poverty and injustice. An antimetanarrative impulse has contributed to the diversity and polycentrism within world Christianity today. According to Lamin Sanneh,

> Christianity is not a garment made to specifications of a bygone golden age, nor is it an add-on whimsical patchwork rigged up without regard to the overall design. Rather, Christianity is a multicolored fabric where each thread, chosen and refined at the Designer's hand, adds luster and strength to the whole.[4]

This has always been an integral part of the ebb and flow of world Christianity. The universality of the gospel calls for multiple voices and perspectives. From its inception, Christianity has flourished because of its universal character. In light of its innate polycentrism, Christianity cannot develop a phobia for such a subject as controversial and vast as race. Christianity is not a religion of cultural conformity. In its expansion, it has vigorously demonstrated that it belongs to all races and cultures.

Race remains a contested issue in Africa as well as in many parts of the world. In his BBC Reith Lectures, "Mistaken Identities," Kwame Anthony Appiah, a Ghanaian philosopher, said that "race is just as misunderstood as nationality—with disastrous consequences."[5] Kwame Gyekye, on the other hand, identified a common ethnic unity and label among Africans that makes the category of race real.[6] These two perspectives constitute two sides of the same coin. The real distinction between the two is a matter of emphasis. The category of race is real. The issue of racism is also real in the

---

[3]Jean-François Lyotard affirmed that the postmodern era is characterized by the collapse of all the grand, all-encompassing sacred stories through which human beings interpreted life in their respective cultures. See Lyotard, *The Postmodern Condition: A Report on Knowledge*, trans. Geoff Bennington and Brian Massumi (Minneapolis: The University of Minnesota Press, 1984).

[4]Lamin Sanneh, *Whose Religion Is Christianity? The Gospel Beyond the West* (Grand Rapids: Eerdmans, 2003), 56.

[5]Hannah Ellis-Petersen, "Racial Identity Is a Biological Nonsense, Says Reith Lecturer," *Guardian*, October, 18, 2016, www.theguardian.com/society/2016/oct/18/racial-identity-is-a-biological-nonsense-says-reith-lecturer.

[6]Kwame Gyekye, *An Essay on African Philosophical Thought*, 2nd ed. (Philadelphia: Temple University Press, 1995), ix-xxxii.

history of Christian missions in Africa. It cannot be swept under the carpet. In the American context, the passionate narratives of movements such as Black Lives Matter, white nationalism, and neo-Nazism compel us to avoid treating race matters as abstract and nonsensical. Discourses about race matters have the power to awaken individuals' and communities' deep-seated dreams, imaginations, and frustrations. Race is not simply about skin pigmentation; rather, it conveys attitudes, feelings, and worldviews.

The concomitant responses to these sensibilities are integral to African imaginations concerning mission and piety. These responses are also connected to the unexpected moments and movements in African Christianity. These surprises under the sacred canopy have provided the impetus for a post-Western Christianity. Andrew Walls and Kwame Bediako have asserted that Africa provides a litmus test for assessing the parameters and credentials of a post-Western Christianity.[7] Contextual theologies take the issues of race and identity seriously. These two categories must be properly recognized and analyzed in order to come to terms with the deep connections between the Gospels and redemptive transformation in different contexts. In this vein, the issues of race and identity go beyond mere rhetoric or abstract philosophical construct. They underscore an essential aspect of the nitty-gritty of human life. Contemporary global events from Charlottesville to Kigali compel us to challenge structures, injunctions, and ideologies that suppress human dignity and freedom. Christian mission must provide the platform for proclaiming the prophetic profile of the Christian gospel.

One of the tasks of prophetic missiology is to "take the crucified down from the cross," to quote Jon Sobrino, a Latin American liberation theologian.[8] From a South African perspective, Takatso Mofokeng has discussed the experience of the crucified among the crossbearers.[9] This chapter seeks to analyze the intersections between mission and race within African Christianity. It further seeks to tease out new avenues and approaches beyond the colonial

---

[7]Andrew F. Walls, *The Missionary Movement in Christian History: Studies in the Transmission of Faith* (Maryknoll, NY: Orbis, 1996), see chap. 7; Kwame Bediako, *Christianity in Africa: Renewal of a Non-Western Religion* (Maryknoll, NY: Orbis, 1995), see chap. 1.

[8]Quoted in James H. Cone, *The Cross and the Lynching Tree* (Maryknoll, NY: Orbis Books, 2011), 161.

[9]Takatso Afred Mofokeng, *The Crucified Among the Crossbearers* (Uitgeversmaatschappij: J. H. Kok, 1983).

paradigms navigating mission and race in Africa. The linkages between mission and race are deeply embedded in the litany of cultural shifts within colonizing forces, as well as events and responses at certain historical moments in African Christianity. I will use some of these narratives as heuristic categories to flesh out the implications of race matters for mission and vice versa.

Before I go on to identify the specific heuristic examples engaging mission and race in Africa, it is crucial for us to foreground significant cultural paradigm shifts that contorted and hindered the efficacy and validity of Christian mission in Africa. These cultural paradigm shifts, which took place at the height of the European Renaissance and Enlightenment, were so significant that they introduced race and racial identity as a theological issue. The epistemology of the Enlightenment was characterized by the escape from old paradigms of control into freedom and independence marked by reason and the rational mind, which precipitated breakthroughs in science, philosophy, and theology. These paradigm shifts in epistemology would have costly affects on Western mission on the African continent.

The first cultural shift took place as Europe emerged out of the so-called Dark Ages. Spurred on by the Renaissance, science emerged from the medieval category of mystery and magic into a legitimate field of inquiry. Thus, the Enlightenment was conceived. Beginning with Copernicus and the scientific revolution, science began to be studied throughout Europe under new conditions of scientific methods involving controlled experiments, observations, and measurements.[10] The nature and validity of truth shifted from the lofty ecclesiastical heights of Rome and Canterbury to Schleiermacher's "Cultured Despisers." It was during this time period that the invention of race as a distinctive human category of difference gave birth to "scientific racism." According to this understanding, humans were arranged into a hierarchy according to value. Under the guise of natural science, Europeans no longer classified races in terms of biblical genealogical descent, but according to biological observation of characteristics such as cranial size, facial angles, and phenotype.[11] Carolus Linnaeus, Johann Friedrich Blumenbach, Arthur

---

[10]Alfred Cobban, *In Search of Humanity: The Role of the Enlightenment in Modern History* (New York: G. Braziller, 1960), 40.

[11]Colin Kidd, *The Forging of Races: Race and Scripture in the Protestant Atlantic World, 1600–2000* (New York: Cambridge University Press, 2006), 81.

Gobineau, Carl Gustav Carus, and other European and American scientists used distorted scientific methods to classify human races.

Carolus Linnaeus, a Swedish botanist known for his *Systema Naturae*, created the original version of the species classification system still used today. In addition to categorizing plants, Linnaeus identified four species of human: *homo americanus*, *homo asiaticus*, *homo europaeus*, and *homo africanus*, which he specifically described as "black, phlegmatic, lazy, freaky."[12] These racial stereotypes were later used by missionaries in their correspondence as pejorative epithets to refer to the African people they encountered.[13] German physician Johann Friedrich Blumenbach furthered the field of scientific racism by coining the term *Caucasian* to represent the "most beautiful and perfect of humans," that is, White people.[14]

For Arthur Gobineau, race was not only a biological theory but above all a spiritual mindset. Gobineau claimed that in order to understand issues concerning nations, civilization, and humankind, we should start to "think in a racial way."[15] And by thinking in this way, one can explain and understand various social and cultural phenomena. Without Arthur Gobineau, race would have become a categorical constant, but instead it became a law of life and a master key to unlocking the enigma of humankind. Continuing in this vein, Samuel George Morton states:

> Characterized by a black complexion, and black, woolly hair; the eyes are large and prominent, the nose broad and flat, the lips thick, and the mouth wide; the head is long and narrow, the forehead low, the cheekbones prominent, the jaws protruding, and the chin small. In disposition the Negro is joyous, flexible, and indolent; while the many nations which compose this race present a singular diversity of intellectual character, of which the far extreme is the lowest grade of humanity. . . . The moral and intellectual character of the Africans is widely different in different nations. . . . The Negroes are proverbially fond of their amusements, in which they engage with great exuberance of spirit; and a day of toil is with them no bar to a night of revelry.

---

[12]William E. Burns, *Science in the Enlightenment: An Encyclopedia* (Santa Barbara, CA: ABC-CLIO, 2003), s.v. "Linnaeus, Carolus."

[13]See Willie Jennings, *The Christian Imagination* (New Haven, CT: Yale University Press, 2011), chap. 3.

[14]Kenneth Barber, "Johann Blumenbach and the Classification of Human Races," in *Science and Its Times*, ed. Neil Schlager and Josh Lauer (Detroit: Gale, 2000), 105-8.

[15]Burns, *Science in the Enlightenment*, s.v. "Blumenbach, Johann Friedrich."

Like most other barbarous nations their institutions are not infrequently characterized by superstition and cruelty. They appear to be fond of warlike enterprises, and are not deficient in personal courage; but, once overcome, they yield to their destiny, and accommodate themselves with amazing facility to every change of circumstance. The Negroes have little invention, but strong powers of imitation, so that they readily acquire mechanic arts. They have a great talent for music, and all their external senses are remarkably acute.[16]

As the lucrative slave trade built wealth and prosperity for slave owners, the theories of scientific racism justifying the inferiority of men and women clothed in blackness grew in popularity and were surprisingly supported by the noblest minds of the day. This racialized tutelage molded missionary minds and fueled colonialist resentment among those who anchored on African shores in a new age of discovery.

The second cultural shift was philosophical and was produced by some of Europe's most influential thinkers and writers. These were men who captured the *Zeitgeist* and created it at the same time. Inspired by the Renaissance and emboldened by the French Revolution, thinkers of the Enlightenment broke out of old classical ecclesiastical paradigms into freedom marked by reason and a spirit of epistemological independence. The scientific methods developing in the field of natural science were introduced into the world of philosophy. This move brought about such seismic shifts in thinking that Enlightenment philosophers boasted that their "age of reason" surpassed all preceding unenlightened generations of Europeans combined.[17]

Significant contributors to the Age of Reason include Thomas Hobbes, who believed that knowledge came from testing our ideas against experience; René Descartes, who coined the popular Latin phrase *cogito ergo sum* (I think; therefore I am) and the idea that the world is comprehensible if we construct our understanding on irrefutable and verifiable experiences; and the British philosopher John Locke, who insisted that reason must be the final mediator of what we believe regarding politics, ethics, and religion.[18]

---

[16]Samuel George Morton, *Crania Americana; or, A Comparative View of the Skulls of Various Aboriginal Nations of North and South America; To Which Is Prefixed an Essay on the Varieties of the Human Species* (Philadelphia: J. Dobson, 1839), 183.

[17]Kidd, *Forging of Races*, 79.

[18]Kidd, *Forging of Races*, 105; Peter Gay, *Age of Enlightenment* (New York: Time Life, 1966), 16; and Jonathan Hill, *Faith in the Age of Reason: The Enlightenment from Galileo to Kant* (Downers Grove, IL: InterVarsity Press, 2004), 26.

Whatever its presentation or description, it had to pass through the scrutiny of reason, which was the unifying and central power of European Enlightenment and its ultimate priority.[19] Reason gave birth to rationalism, which was the primary trophy of European Enlightenment.[20] Through rational thought, humankind *can* ascend to understanding the world and her place within it. Although other major developments occurred in the world of philosophy during European Enlightenment, the construction of rationalism and the belief in the power of reason formed a foundational epistemology and their crowning idea.

German philosopher Immanuel Kant must be singled out here. Kant, a brilliant philosopher—though blinded by his own ethnocentrism—capitalized on each of these racialized insights of the European Enlightenment with such precision that he was able to make race a scientific, philosophical, and theological reality, simultaneously making theology a racialized issue.[21] With this White, normative, colonialist perspective firmly in place, White settlers placed themselves at the top of the racial hierarchy by creating entirely new systems of language to determine who was White, or who was close to whiteness, which continues to disease our social imagination to this day. This led to the creation of what Willie James Jennings calls a "colonialist theological subjectivity" in which Christian doctrine was reimagined through a White colonial gaze.[22]

Since Enlightenment morality held that reason was the apex of its values, European missionaries coupled reason with Christianity as a sanctifying power. This is the third cultural shift, namely, the detachment of Jesus from his racial and ethnic particularity. Because Enlightenment morality valued whiteness as the noblest virtue to be emulated, Jesus' Jewishness and non-whiteness were problematic. This tendency to project Jesus into an abstract space, racially and culturally stripping his human identity, is what Willie Jennings describes in *The Christian Imagination* and J. Kameron Carter

[19]Paulos Gregorios, *A Light Too Bright: The Enlightenment Today; An Assessment of the Values of the European Enlightenment and a Search for New Foundations* (Albany: State University of New York Press, 1992), 42.
[20]Hill, *Faith in the Age of Reason*, 113.
[21]J. Kameron Carter, *Race: A Theological Account* (New York: Oxford University Press, 2008).
[22]Willie James Jennings, *The Christian Imagination: Theology and the Origins of Race* (New Haven, CT: Yale University Press, 2010), 80.

addresses in detail in *Race: A Theological Account* with his deconstruction of Immanuel Kant's projection of White normativity and supremacy. Divorcing Jesus from his Jewish roots as a hermeneutic for reading salvation history we may attribute to the mind of Immanuel Kant.[23]

This would later have a profound impact on the value of culture and cultural traditions as a means of "earthing" Christianity within the particularity of people, language, and land in an African context. White Europeans and American missionaries who went to Africa indoctrinated Indigenous people into this distorted theology of the Eurocentric viewpoint that deemed White people superior to all other races.[24] The binary "scale of existence" between Black and the whiteness of Jesus allowed Europeans to exploit the Indigenous people and extract their land while continuing to save their spiritual lives.[25] It was in the greed for land that Christology and epistemology became the distorted disease of rationalization, removing people from their land, language, people group, and identities, with only an unrooted Christology of whiteness for an uprooted people.[26] Howard Thurman laments,

> How different might have been the story . . . on this planet grown old from suffering if the link between Jesus and Israel had never been severed. For the Christian church has tended to overlook its Judaic origins . . . the fact that Jesus of Nazareth was a Jew of Palestine.[27]

This unmooring, or displacement, of Christian thought, pedagogy, philosophy, and theology from the soil of Africa created a vacuum in which Christian vision was given space to tie itself to the colonial project. The decoupling of Jesus from his Jewishness created a scenario in which mission work became primarily occupied with the forced assimilation of African people into a White theological vision. In this White theological vision Scripture is demoted and turned into a philosophical, historical, moral, and cultural set of documents detached from the possibility of Christian theology born from African land, language, and culture. Thus, the trifecta of

---

[23]Carter, *Race.*
[24]Jennings, *Christian Imagination*, 8, 32.
[25]Jennings, *Christian Imagination*, 23-27.
[26]Jennings, *Christian Imagination*, 39-63.
[27]Howard Thurman, *Jesus and the Disinherited* (1949; repr., Boston: Beacon Press, 1996), 42.

these three European Enlightenment projects—science, philosophy, and theology—constitute the backdrop of European mission to Africa. We have taken the time to briefly outline these wide-sweeping cultural shifts in Europe because of the way they racialized mission in Africa and distorted the Christian vision.

MISSION AND RACE IN CONTEXT: THE STORY OF AJAYI CROWTHER

The African terrain in the nineteenth century was saturated with conflicting claims about the purpose of mission. In this period, Victorian representations and narratives about race, wittingly or unwittingly reinforced by the hubris of White missionaries, elicited various responses from Africans. Colonial structures provided the institutional framework for several racist policies and programs. These attitudes gave the impetus to creative reappropriations and rediscovery of Christianity in Africa. They also contributed to what Lamin Sanneh has described as "acute indigenization."[28] Committed agents laid the foundations for the selfhood of the church in Africa, and when serendipity mingles with fate, the outcome is a mixture of stark bewilderment and sublime surprises. In a context characterized by what Richard Gray has described as "Black Christians and White missionaries,"[29] the interplay between piety and power was intense and intentional.

The nineteenth century was characterized by political uncertainties and social upheavals in many African societies. It was also a time when new political and theological parameters were introduced to many African communities. In this season of constant flux in political, social, and civic life, missionary initiatives flourished in many African societies. The Church Missionary Society (CMS), which represented what Paul Jenkins has called "the Protestant internationalism," was at the forefront of this spiritual revolution in Africa in the early nineteenth century.[30] However, the high handedness and hubris of some of the missionary agents cast a very dark shadow on an otherwise lofty enterprise in spiritual matters. Nonetheless, their racist attitudes were often tempered by local realities and resistance.

---

[28]Sanneh, *Whose Religion Is Christianity?*, 92.
[29]Richard Gray, *Black Christians and White Missionaries* (New Haven, CT: Yale University Press, 1959).
[30]Paul Jenkins, "The Church Missionary Society and the Basel Mission: An Early Experiment in Inter-European Cooperation," in *The Church Mission Society and World Christianity, 1799–1999*, ed. Kevin Ward and Brian Stanley (Grand Rapids: Eerdmans, 2000), 43-65.

Bold heuristic narratives that confronted whiteness as a theological ideal for Africans include Zulus Nxele (*unzaul*) and Ntsikana (*unsikana*) during the Zulu war with the British in 1811 and 1819. Along with (Cosha) Xhosa Christian prophets, Nxele (*unzaul*) and Ntsikana resisted the British colonizers and missionaries in their various ways with a liberating message that fused Xhosa traditional religion and Dutch Christian theology. This was indeed an early example of Indigenous Christian resistance against a colonizing and missionizing agency.

The heroic story of the African woman known as Kimpa Vita (a.k.a. Donna Beatrice) is an exciting example. At the beginning of the eighteenth century, Vita advocated for a more spirited and emotional expression of faith in the face of the cold, formal, and legalistic Roman Catholic Church in the Congo. Kimpa led a protest movement against the imposed Christianity that coupled the Christian faith with whiteness and white supremacy. She preached that Africans should do away with the White Jesus presented by Catholic missionaries in favor of a Black Christ who sided with Africans through his suffering.[31]

In addition to Kimpa—who exhibited one of the earliest expressions of Black theology—there were others such as Mantsope Makheta (b. 1793) in Lesotho; Hendrik Witbooi, a type of political messiah among the Herero in South West Africa (1905); Enoch (Gijima) Mgijima in South Africa (1921); and the Chilembe rebellion in Nyasaland (1915), which prepared the way for the nineteenth-century emergence and development of Ethiopianism in the broader context of Pan-Africanism. Let us not forget also the powerful stories surrounding African prophets such as William Wade Harris (a Kru from Liberia), Walter Matiffa (Lesotho), Simon Kimbangu (Belgian Congo), and Samson Oppong (Ghana, formerly Gold Coast). These and myriad other African Christians fought gallantly against racist ideologies that sought to impose whiteness as God's theological ideal for African converts.

The story and legacy of Bishop Ajayi Crowther is a powerful example and will constitute a more detailed case study. In spite of being afflicted with a mild stroke at the age of eighty-five, he continued to fret about the prospects

---

[31]See "Kimpa Vita (Donna Beatriz) 1684–1702," in *Dictionary of African Biography*, ed. Emmanuel K. Akyeampong and Henry Louis Gates Jr. (Oxford: Oxford University Press, 2012), 2:181-83.

of the church in Africa. The bishop was feeble, but he continued to contend with the storm within the church. The church was dealing with a crisis of legitimacy, but on the surface, it was business as usual. One of the crucial issues at this period was the role of the Native ministry, that is, the role of African church leaders in the churches established by missionary societies. The real bone of contention was the question of whether the experiment of consecrating Crowther as a bishop in charge of the Niger Mission was a monumental failure that should not be repeated. Crowther's story revealed the acute tension between the Church Missionary Society (CMS) and the so-called native question.[32]

Crowther was born in Nigeria in the year the slave trade was outlawed by the British Parliament. As a youngster, he was captured in his village, Osoogun, by Muslim slave raiders and sold into slavery in Lagos. In Lagos, he was put on a slave ship heading for Brazil. As fate would have it, he was rescued by the British Naval Squadron and relocated in Freetown, a settlement founded in 1787 for the primary purpose of settling freed slaves. From the time of resettlement, Crowther took on the role of an antislavery crusader. At Freetown, he enjoyed the mentorship of many missionaries. Within six months, he was able to read the New Testament, and he was recognized by his peers as an unusually gifted man. The hallmark of his ministry and episcopate was charity. He was surrounded by the turmoil and savagery of the slave trade; consequently, he became an avid proponent of freedom and justice. He invoked the words of Isaiah to assail the deeds of slave traders: "For Zion's sake will I not hold my peace, and for Jerusalem's sake I will not rest, until the righteousness thereof go forth as brightness, and the salvation thereof as a lamp that burneth" (Is 62:1 KJV). He championed the movement that sought to abolish the slave trade in Nigeria. He did this well into his eighties.

Crowther's pioneering work as an abolitionist set the tone for his other projects in West Africa in the nineteenth century. He embarked on translation projects that aided an Indigenous discovery of Christianity. At a time when Victorian practices were insensitive to other cultural norms, Crowther's vision of Christianity was colored by tolerance to certain aspects

---

[32]For a full story of Crother's life see *Samuel Crowther: The Slave Boy Who Became Bishop of the Niger* (London: Forgotten Books, 2012).

of Africa's indigenous worldview, Islam, and the Catholic faith. His Yoruba Bible of 1851 was the first one in an African language. Ade Ajayi described Crowther as a "patriot to the core." Crowther's favorite prayer up to his death was that "God who called me first from among my people to the important post of His service, may give me grace to set a good example for others to follow."[33]

Crowther led the Niger Mission that started in 1841. The main agents in the mission were Africans. Its overall purpose was to produce a self-supporting African pastorate, one that would foster cooperation between autonomous African churches and Canterbury. It carried on successful projects in the Niger Delta as well as at Lokoja and other areas in the Upper Niger. The active partners in the mission were Africans, including a large contingent of Sierra Leoneans with Nigerian connections.

The role of Henry Venn in Crowther's saga was very important. Venn was the honorary secretary of the Church Missionary Society (CMS) for thirty-one years (1841–1872).[34] He was very supportive of efforts to create "self-governing, self-supporting, self-propagating" churches in Africa. Just like the CMS, his work grew out of two different movements: the evangelical and the humanitarian. Venn supported the abolitionist strategy to regenerate Africa by "the Bible and the Plough." This was a tactic that depended on thousands of liberated Africans in Sierra Leone, West Indies, and Brazil. His proactive policy of development boded well for the church despite the fraught circumstances.

Venn thought that Crowther should spearhead the mission in the Niger, establish a coterie of devoted African church leaders, and, in so doing, contribute to the realization of a "euthanasia of mission." However, things did not turn out as he planned. According to Lamin Sanneh, "the adverse view the CMS came to take of the work of Bishop Crowther in the Niger Mission was a significant factor in generating an active reservoir of separatist sentiment from which Independency was to gush forth in bursts of quick

[33]Ade Ajayi, "Bishop Crowther: A Patriot to the Core," a paper delivered to commemorate the death of Crowther at the Emmanuel College of Theology, Ibadan, December 20, 1981, 2.
[34]On Venn, see E. A. Ayandele, *The Missionary Impact on Modern Nigeria 1842-1914: A Political and Social Analysis* (London: Longmans, 1966); and J. F. A. Ajayi, "Henry Venn and the Policy of Development," in *The History of Christianity in West Africa*, ed. Ogbu U. Kalu (London: Longman, 1980), 63-75.

succession."[35] Crowther was the sacrificial victim on the altar of racial purity and power. His episcopal rights were curtailed by the powers that be, and the poor man was reduced to a mere shadow of himself. A financial committee, chaired by the Rev. J. B. Wood, was constituted by the CMS to investigate the activities of the Niger Mission. This was the final coup de grâce in the effort to oust Bishop Crowther. Wood summarily dismissed the Niger Mission as a monumental failure without any concrete evidence and sources. He sent his report to the CMS in London, and that was the final nail in the coffin of Crowther's denigration and defeat. He was denied his right to read the report. Crowther and his African agents were rudely assailed by overzealous CMS agents. Their worth and decency were impugned in reports they were not allowed to challenge.

By discrediting the African agents, European missionaries were inexorably planting themselves at the helm of affairs for the Niger Mission. A group of young and ambitious European missionaries condemned the Niger Mission as spiritually stale and too extravagant. Their motive was too obvious: they wanted Crowther and his associates out of the picture so that they could show the whole world the best modus operandi for proclaiming the good news in Africa. This was the beginning of an aggressive Europeanization. These young church officials were gravely offended that Africans would consider themselves equals to Europeans rather than humbly confine themselves to the low order of nature. The prevailing colonial order and ideology in the nineteenth century supported this racist attitude. "Crowther and his Creole compatriots were vilified . . . as half-reclaimed barbarians clad in dishcloths, inferior specimens, savvy niggers, hybrid and uppity Africans, effete and degenerate."[36]

Imperial mandates about missions were often anchored on an unmitigated "teacher complex," to borrow a phrase from Kosuke Koyama.[37] This perspective operates in a one-dimensional mode: one party eternally knows the truth, and the other group should simply sit back to be perpetually taught and spoon-fed. Crowther "was spiked on the twin prongs of a sharpened European imperial drive into the African interior and the

---

[35]Lamin Sanneh, *West African Christianity: The Religious Impact* (Maryknoll, NY: Orbis Books, 1983), 169.

[36]Sanneh, *Whose Religion Is Christianity?*, 91.

[37]Kosuke Koyama, "Christianity Suffers from Teacher Complex," in *Mission Trends No. 2: Evangelization*, ed. Gerald H. Anderson and Thomas F. Stransky (Grand Rapids: Newman Press, 1975), 73.

exploited mixed fortunes of the Niger Mission."[38] Crowther's efforts to save his loyal assistants were met with resistance and rejection by the CMS. On this final face-off with the CMS, one observer wrote, "few scenes could have been more painful to watch than the grey-haired . . . Bishop of over 80 . . . , tormented and insulted by the young Europeans, trembling with rage as he never trembled before, as he got up to announce his resignation from the committee."[39] This was the final dénouement in the perplexing and jaw-dropping saga of Bishop Crowther. However, it would not be fair to say that his ministry was entirely afflicted with what Geoffrey Chaucer described as "a thoroughfare of woes." He was very effective in organizing local pastors and watering the seeds of an autonomous African church. He also engineered a robust mechanism for evangelism in the Niger Delta.

The humiliation of Bishop Crowther was a bitter pill to swallow by many loyalists and nationalists. In August 1891, a group of people seceded from Anglican and Methodist churches in Lagos and formed the United Native African Church in solidarity with Mojola Agbebi, who had formed the Native Baptist Church in 1888. Since once bitten twice shy, these new congregations were very intentional about maintaining their ecclesiastical autonomy and power. In the nineteenth century, the issues of race and autonomy compounded the ambiguities of the missionary venture in Africa. The story of Bishop Crowther was the tipping point in the complex relationship between foreign missionary agents and Indigenous church leaders. Missionary attitudes and sensibilities about race gave the impetus to the creative appropriation of Christianity in Africa. In the later part of the nineteenth century, African priests and prophets were empowered by the Holy Spirit and the ability to read the Bible in indigenous languages. This phenomenon has been described by Andrew Walls as the "cross-cultural process" in Christian history.[40] The top-down syndrome of Christendom with societal standards as the norm was eventually replaced with voices from the underside of history. This bottom-up movement started in the late nineteenth century and flourished in the twentieth century.

---

[38]Sanneh, *West African Christianity*, 172.

[39]Sanneh, *West African Christianity*, 173.

[40]Andrew F. Walls, *The Cross-Cultural Process in Christian History: Studies in the Transmission and Appropriation of Faith* (Maryknoll, NY: Orbis Books, 2002).

Crowther's death could be described as an end of an era for Western colonial missions in Africa. Eugene Stock, the CMS editorial secretary, remarked that Crowther "may not have possessed the highest spiritual gifts, but he was a plain, practical, patient, hard-working Christian man."[41] His death created a moment of respite for the CMS. The one person the organization did not know how to control in their effort to assert the hegemony of the European officials of the CMS over the churches in Lagos, Yorubaland, and Upper and Lower Niger missions was finally out of the picture. The CMS was tightly wedded to a conventional missionary template of the normative sender and receiver of the gospel. Crowther's legacy is about a radical deconstruction of this idea. His story revealed the promise and perils of the Indigenous church in Africa.[42] The saying that "when you turn over a rock, you can't put back all the critters that start crawling out" is a telling one indeed. The events after Crowther's disgrace confirmed that unmitigated missionary patrimony engendered dissenting voices and movements in African Christianity.

Bishop James Johnson, who took over the Niger Mission after Crowther, was also a tour de force in piety and orthodoxy. He advocated for an Anglican church with African leadership, African worldview, and African theology. According to him, "It is more helpful that a people should be called to take up their responsibilities . . . than be in the position of vessels taken in tow."[43] He vehemently opposed the heterodox views of a former associate, Garrick Braide, and excommunicated him from the church. Johnson became known as Holy Church for his personal piety and prayer life.

"Missionaries Go Home": Unmasking the Moratorium Debate

The debate on moratorium (1971–1975) generated pertinent issues related to mission and race in African Christianity. It started as a harmless conversation,

---

[41]Quoted in Ajayi, "Bishop Crowther: A Patriot to the Core," 2.

[42]Bolaji Idowu elaborated on some of these challenges in his *The Selfhood of the Church in Africa* (Lagos: Methodist Church Publications, n.d.).

[43]*Dictionary of African Christian Biography*, s.v. "James 'Holy' Johnson," https://dacb.org/stories /sierra-leone/johnson-james/. On Johnson, see E. A. Ayandele, *Holy Johnson: Pioneer of African Nationalism, 1836–1917* (London: Frank Cass, 1970); and Jehu J. Hanciles, "The Legacy of James Johnson," *International Bulletin of Missionary Research* 21, no. 4 (1997): 162-67.

but it soon developed into a full-blown debate about indigenization, autonomy, and reverse mission. In postcolonial Africa, the Zeitgeist of autonomy was raging high. It naturally had a concomitant effect on theological and spiritual matters. The clime and context were calling for serious conversations about the credentials of the Christian faith in Africa. While the story of Bishop Crowther evokes an accommodationist model in mission and race, the moratorium debate exhibited a rejectionist model in the history of missions in Africa. The fundamental issue underlying the moratorium question was one about the enduring connections between church and mission. It was a wake-up call related to the responsibility to be obedient to the Great Commission.

The debate was an integral part of the indigenization project in African Christianity. It vividly underscored African frustration and impatience with the lackluster mode of mission-initiated indigenization. It paved the way for a wave of reverse mission by Africans to North America and Europe in the twentieth century.[44] Paul Freston has, however, suggested that reverse mission is more than a geographical inversion; it also represents a movement from below.[45] This phenomenon opened the door for what we will call an adventurist paradigm in mission and African Christianity. An important contributing factor to the boldness that spurred on the moratorium was African Pentecostalism. Although African Pentecostalism is not often situated within discussions of race in Africa, African Pentecostalism is part of a broader movement of African independence and self-sufficiency.

In 1892, the *Sierra Leone Weekly News* published a fiery speech by Mojola Agbebi on the theme of autonomy and the African church. Although he was repeating the words of Edward Blyden, it was hard to dismiss his stern warning. According to Agbebi: "It does not seem that it is appointed to foreign teachers with their countless sects and myriad dogmas to clothe

---

[44]On reverse mission, see Richard Burgess, "Bringing Back the Gospel: Reverse Mission Among Nigerian Pentecostals in Britain," *Journal of Religion in Europe* 4 (2011): 429-49; Roswith Gerloff, "The Significance of the African Christian Diaspora in Europe," *International Review of Mission* 89, no. 354 (July 2000): 498-510; Matthews A. Ojo, "Reverse Mission," in *Encyclopedia of Missions and Missionaries*, ed. Jonathan Bonk (New York: Routledge, 2007); Afe Adogame, "Mapping Globalization with the Lens of Religion: African Migrant Churches in Germany," in *New Religions and Globalization*, ed. Armin W. Geertz and Margit Watburg (Germany: Aarhus University Press, 2008), 189-213; and Jehu J. Hanciles, *Beyond Christendom: Globalization, African Migration, and the Transformation of the West* (Maryknoll, NY: Orbis Books, 2008).

[45]Paul Freston, "Reverse Mission: A Discourse in Search of Reality?," *PentecoStudies* 9, no. 2 (2010): 153.

African personality with the toga of manhood. The sphinx must solve her own riddle. The genius of Africa must unravel its own enigma."[46]

Agbebi was setting the tone for the reconceptualization of mission in Africa. This agitation later crystallized into the moratorium debate in African Christianity. The call for moratorium was issued by John Gatu, the secretary-general of the Presbyterian Church in Kenya, during a visit to the United States in 1971. He shocked his hosts by boldly declaring that he had come not with a begging bowl to solicit for funding but to humbly request that missionary aid in money and personnel should cease for at least five years so that African churches could stand on their own. Burgess Carr, the secretary of the All Africa Council of Churches (AACC) in Nairobi, applauded his message. He invited African churches to Alexandria to draft an African confession of faith.

The essence of the moratorium debate lay in missiological partnerships and cooperation between the West and Africa. It was not based on a total repudiation of mission; rather, it was an utter rejection of the patrimony that characterized missionary work in Africa in the nineteenth century. The moratorium debate was not a brazen attempt to repeal and replace mission but a concrete effort to add mutuality and reciprocity into the lexicon of missiological ventures. Mission remains the raison d'être of the church. The challenge is how to develop the capacity to create an elastic space for its modalities and actualization. Rather than treating the debate as the angst of a toothless bulldog, it is more pragmatic to think of it as a response to an ingrained sense of hubris and lopsidedness in mission. It was a call for Africans to engage in mission on their own terms and to design theological templates that were suitable to the African context. An African proverb states that "as long as you sleep on a mat that belongs to someone else, you will never sleep easy." It was imperative to develop missiological and theological categories that emanated from the African worldview. The issue of moratorium is a perennial one in missiological circles. C. Peter Wagner called for a moratorium (he used the term *reform*) on four levels: Western chauvinism, paternalistic church aid, theological and ethical imperialism, and unproductive missionary work.[47]

---

[46]*The Sierra Leone Weekly News*, March 5, 1892; and E. W. Blyden, *The Return of the Exiles and the West African Church* (London, 1891).

[47]C. Peter Wagner, *The Future of the Missiological Enterprise: In Search of Mission* (New York, 1974), 63.

Toward an Ubuntu Kenosis Missiology

We conclude this chapter by presenting Ubuntu kenosis missiology as a way to navigate the issue of mission and race in an African context. The African social philosophy known as Ubuntu has been applied to everything from board games to corporate leadership mottos. In spite of the liberality of its usage and sometimes abuse, it is a concept that carries profound meaning that resonates around the world. *Ubuntu* is an African word for a universal concept. It is a Zulu word that captures the spirit of the philosophical foundation of African societies as a collective whole. It is a unifying vision or worldview enshrined in the Zulu maxim *umuntu ngumuntu ngabantu*, that is, "a person is a person through other persons." The essence of this African aphorism is the understanding that we are contingent beings. In our discussion of mission and race in Africa, we would like to posit the idea of an Ubuntu kenosis missiology as a response to the normative gaze engineered by the Enlightenment philosophy in its reification of White superiority as a universal norm. Given the brevity with which this must be done, we would like to use three broad delineating strokes that emerge from a possible Ubuntu missiology, grounded in the biblical concept of kenosis from the Christian tradition. We are anchoring our usage of *kenosis* on the biblical text taken from Philippians 2:5-8:

Let the same mind be in you that was in Christ Jesus,
who, though he was in the form of God,
did not regard equality with God
as something to be exploited,
but emptied himself,
taking the form of a slave,
being born in human likeness.
And being found in human form,
he humbled himself
and became obedient to the point of death—
even death on a cross.

I would like to posit the idea that Ubuntu (connectedness) and kenosis (self-emptying) are complementary ingredients that provide a corrective against colonial abuse of power and privilege as described in this chapter. The concept of kenosis disrupts scientific racism and the racialized philosophy of projected White normativity described above.

The kenosis theory is based on Philippians 2:6-7, which states that Christ, "though he was in the form of God, did not regard equality with God as something to be exploited, but emptied himself, taking the form of a slave, being born in human likeness." Focusing on the term *emptied* (translating the Greek verb *kenoō*; noun *kenosis*), it is understood that the preexistent Son of God voluntarily relinquished or "emptied" himself of all maximal divine attributes, power, prerogatives, and glory that were incompatible with his becoming truly human.[48]

Such an incarnational approach to mission stands in stark contrast to the approaches evident in colonial missiology adopted by Infante Henrique, José de Acosta Porres, or John William Colenso as graphically portrayed by Willie Jennings in *The Christian Imagination*, or in the treatment of Samuel Crowther at the hands of CMS missionaries as described above. Ubuntu invites us to consider in practical terms how this self-emptying might be realized in affirmation of our common humanness and connectedness. First, Ubuntu affirms a respect and acceptance of others. This notion of mutual respect is premised on the idea that all of us are God's offspring and part of the *imago Dei*. The basic notion of African people as human and a part of the human family is and has been under constant assault and questioning. Ubuntu affirms a respect for the other as a religious other. Dirk Louw argues that this attests to the spiritual foundation of African societies.[49]

The intrinsic concept of Ubuntu speaks to the value of the human spirit, precisely because it is created in the image of God and not valued according to pigmentation or phenotype. Louw suggests that the concept of Ubuntu defines individuals in terms of their several relationships with others and stresses the importance of Ubuntu as a religious concept. An Ubuntu kenosis missiology invites us to empty ourselves of prejudice, stereotype, and whiteness in exchange for a profound interconnectedness and shared human identity. For the Yoruba, the individual cannot be separated from the community, and societal reality is interlaced with the other: "I am not

---

[48]Richard Plantinga, Thomas Thompson, and Matthew Lindbery, *An Introduction to Christian Theology* (Cambridge, UK: Cambridge University Press, 2010), 249.

[49]Dirk Jacobus Louw, *Ubuntu and the Challenges of Multiculturalism in Post-Apartheid South Africa* (n.p.: Expertisecentrum Zuidelijk Afrika, 2002), 390.

because we are not" or "I am ill because we are ill."[50] For them, individualism has a limit; indeed, the purpose for individual existence is intricately connected with the purpose and health of communal and social existence, and hence individual existence cannot be reached without living within society.[51] A South African Venda saying, *muthu u bebelwa munwe* (a person is born for the other), captures the spirit of this approach of interdependence between self and community. Thus, Gyekye avers:

> For the Akan, religion is not seen as hindering the pursuit of one's interests in this world. . . . Akan humanism is the consequences not only of a belief in the existence of a supreme being and other supernatural entities but more importantly I think of the desire to utilize the munificence and powers of such entities for the promotion of human welfare and happiness.[52]

The tragedy of Western Christian mission as exemplified in the treatment of Samuel Crowther is in its denial and violation of this basic human principle in order to champion white privilege and normativity.

The second way Ubuntu invites us to kenosis pertains to the extremely important role of agreement, consensus, and mutuality. Wherever colonialists and Christian missionaries went, far too often the religion of the people they encountered was rendered pagan and thus illegitimate, and the culture was declared barbaric and the people savages. Hence they were considered fair game for colonization, land dispossession, and imperialism, and the history of the people was deliberately distorted in order to justify and rationalize acts of conquest and domination. Consensus is an important value within African societies in which decisions are traditionally made in consultation with community elders who represent the interest of the local constituents. Traditional African democracy operates in the form of lengthy discussions in the quest for consensus and agreement between parties.[53] An

[50]A key effect of communal life is the deep sense of hospitality, which permeates African social relationship; see Chima J. Korieh and Ugo G. Nwokeji, *Religion, History and Politics in Nigeria* (New York: University Press of America, 2005), 16.
[51]Olusegun Gbadegesin, "Destiny, Personality and the Ultimate Reality of Human Existence: A Yoruba Perspective," *Ultimate Reality and Meaning* 7, no. 3 (1984): 173-88.
[52]Kwame Gyekye, *An Essay on African Philosophical Thought: The Akan Conceptual Scheme* (Philadelphia: Temple University Press, 1995), 144-45.
[53]See Jesse Mugambi, *African Christian Theology: An Introduction* (Nairobi: Heinemann, 1989), 4.

Ubuntu kenosis missiology invites us to recognize the innate value in the culture and tradition of others.

This brings us to a third connection between the Ubuntu way of life and a decolonized invitation to kenosis living that we want to highlight. This third dimension pertains to dialogue, or what Louw calls "mutual exposure,"[54] which epitomizes the conduct prescribed by Ubuntu. In a similar manner Jabu Sidane asserts that "Ubuntu inspires us to expose ourselves to others, to encounter the difference of their humanness so as to inform and enrich our own."[55] Ubuntu entails respect for the particularities of the cultures, beliefs, and practices of others. Above, we mentioned the decoupling of Jesus from the particularity of his Jewishness. This decoupling paved the way for White normativity to silently fill the cultural vacuum created by the cultural neutrality of an Enlightenment hermeneutic. The kenosis that Ubuntu invites us to is especially emphasized by a striking, yet lesser-known translation of *umuntu ngumuntu ngabantu*, that is, "a human being is a human being through [*the otherness of*] other human beings."[56] An important part of this respect of particularity is respecting the historicity of others. Respecting the historicity of the other means respecting his or her history, culture, and value system. The flexibility of the other is well noted by Ubuntu, and the creation of "scientific racism" has done violence to this sacred truth.

CONCLUSION: MISSION, NOT MANIPULATION

In the grand scheme of things, God's grandiose plan for the world transcends all human tendencies to control and manipulate the good news. The beauty of mission lies in freedom, mutuality, and justice. Racism is one of the potentially divisive factors in human societies. It has been used in many contexts to contradict *missio Dei*. However, human manipulations are bound to falter and fail. Eventually, God's plans for the least of these are unleashed with remarkable power and gusto. In this new development, a divine fellowship emerges that transcends myopic and selfish manipulations. This is a divine rainbow that evokes diversity and richness.

---

[54]Louw, *Ubuntu and the Challenges of Multiculturalism*, 390.
[55]Jabu Sidane, *Ubuntu and Nation Building* (Pretoria: Ubuntu School, 1994), 45.
[56]Willie L. Van der Merwe, "Philosophy and the Multi-cultural Context of (Post) Apartheid South Africa," *Ethical Perspectives* 3, no. 2 (1996): 1-15.

In contemporary times, there is a need to reevaluate the meaning and purpose of mission. In light of personal and societal fractures, mission can become the balm in Gilead that heals all brokenness. Racism contributes to what sociologists have described as a "bias of categorization." This relates to the human tendency to separate and create oppressive hierarchical structures in society. This is the height of human manipulation. The good news of Jesus Christ, on the other hand, provides the power to embrace the other. Such a vision is crucial in our postcolonial world yearning for peace, redemption, and unity.

Racism is the veil that keeps humanity from experiencing God. It is a blatant contradiction of the powerful concept of *imago Dei*, which affirms that all human beings are created in the image of God. It is a resounding affirmation of the dignity of every sacred soul. Racism is also a potential mask that prevents people from encountering the true face of God. It blurs people's vision of the kingdom of God. It also constitutes a deep scar on God's beautiful creation. Mission provides auspicious spiritual strategies for removing this debilitating obstacle and blemish. Our human ego must be sublimated in order to let God be God and allow God's reign to prevail in the world. This is a missionary agenda that is centered on the crucified mind rather than being driven by a teacher complex. Mission is about welcoming the other in the same manner that God continues to embrace everyone. This dimension transcends the puerile paternalism that racism evokes and celebrates.

The crux of the issue in our contemporary world is how to construct missiological paradigms that contribute to human dignity and flourishing. Mission is about standing together to proclaim the good news. It is firmly based on building bridges, not walls. It is unequivocally anchored on the transformative power of the gospel. Mission promises a prophetic profile and template that can move communities beyond tragedy.

"Lord, I believe; help thou mine unbelief" (Mk 9:24 KJV).

PART III

Race and Mission to
Latin America

5

. . . .

Siempre Lo Mismo

Theology, Rhetoric, and Broken Praxis

Elizabeth Conde-Frazier

I am of Puerto Rican descent. On one side of my family we have been Protestant for three generations, and on the other side we are Catholic. An itinerant preacher came to the Yunque area traveling on horseback throughout the countryside evangelizing, sleeping in a hammock at night, and preaching to the homes he encountered. My great grandparents became Protestant because of his work. Later, when the family immigrated, they continued their Christian commitment in New York City at the Central Baptist Church of the American Baptist Churches USA. For three generations we drank deeply of the Scriptures and lived as a covenantal multicultural faith community.

As the work in the city of New York among Latinos/as continued to grow, the structure of the denomination included Latino/a leaders in the development of the new work. These leaders advocated for the funding of new congregations and for representation of Latin@s at different levels of the denominational structure. In the American Baptist Churches, Latin@ leaders were at first part time while pastoring a church and sometimes were bivocational.[1] They were the leaders who carried out the vision of the work. In the American Baptist Churches, it took about thirty years before Latin@s became leaders in the denominational structure.

---

[1]The history of these origins has not been formally published. Some of it may exist in denominational reports and meeting minutes of the mainline denominations but is yet to be brought to light by a historian. One book that summarizes some of this history among the Hispanic American Baptist Churches is a bilingual book by Santiago Soto Fontánez, *Misión a la Puerta/Mission at the Door* (República Dominicana: Editora Educativa Dominicana, 1982).

THE CHURCH AND ITS MISSION: *CHABIENDAS*
RECURRENTES—SIEMPRE LO MISMO

In 2003 I attended a meeting for Latin@ leaders to discuss the strengthening of Hispanic churches.[2] At that point I had been working with Latin@ church leadership for approximately twenty years as a pastor, as a director of a Hispanic program in a seminary, and as a professor at a theological school. The leaders at this meeting were asked to meet in groups in order to identify needs and strategies with the purpose of attending to those needs. We were an ecumenical group that included Latin@ Mainline, Catholic, and Pentecostal Christians.

As we returned from our groups I listened to the reports of each one. The pressing needs we identified at this summit of leaders were similar across groups:

> better opportunities for formal education, training for laity to assume leadership responsibilities. Increased cultivation of second and third generation Latino youth, initiatives that would help church leaders to advocate for the social needs of their communities, programs to provide lay leaders and clergy with practical administrative skills and a permanent national dialogue on Hispanic pastoral leadership.[3]

While my brothers and sisters who come from Latin@ concilios may be able to avoid dealing with White structures, we still read translated books, and today we take online courses from White evangelical schools who maybe know Justo González but do not expose us to the rich theological coffers of persons of Color. This further perpetuates the idea that we do not generate our own theology and that we must continue as a conduit for *la sana doctrina* (sound doctrine), the "real theology" as interpreted by the Anglo church. This teaches us that White evangelical voices have more authority. We listen to them on the airwaves and encounter them in other media. It is how many Latin@s were duped into thinking that Trump was chosen by God, and now they wonder why the chosen one is turning their

---

[2]The subhead describes the frustrations Latin@s have faced in seeking more responsibility in the church. A *chabienda* is a very bothersome incident or reality. In this case, it is a recurring (*recurrentes*) set of realities, which is precisely what *siempre lo mismo* means: perennially persisting without change.

[3]Edwin I. Hernández, Milagros Peña, Kenneth Davis, and Elizabeth Station, *Strengthening Hispanic Ministry Across Denominations: A Call to Action*, Pulpit & Pew Research Reports (Durham, NC: Duke Divinity School, 2005), 3.

lives upside down in such unjust ways. All that is to say that even if we have not come from Anglo-run church structures, the theological ideological structures have still proliferated throughout our lives.

At the meeting in 2003, we concluded that we needed to understand how to do community work. We were looking for pastoral skills for counseling, especially for family, marriage, and parenting, with an understanding of how these dimensions of our lives are affected by immigration. We needed to understand poverty and lacked tools for generating economic empowerment. We needed resources for our communities, especially lay-leadership development for our ministries if we were to accomplish effective ministry.

Some of the broader discussions around these issues exposed the absence of our theology or histories in theological education. This was compounded by the fact that our missionary heritage had not taught us a theology that would allow us to become involved in politics, and therefore community work was not something that every pastor saw as allowable to the fullest extent. Research indicates that the participation rates of Latin@s in political or social-action groups is similar to those of non-Latin@ Whites; it is significantly lower than that of African Americans.[4] This meant that most had not become vocal leaders in their communities around the very issues that most affected and disempowered their congregants and the communities they served.

Seminary courses that would teach us the aforementioned skills, and the spaces for doing our own theological reflection, were not accessible.[5] We did not have faculty who had been in our communities, who got it when we discussed the matters at hand. Instead, Latin@ pastors and leaders often found ourselves always having to explain, to educate those whom we expected by now to have educated themselves about the peoples they were supposed to be working with. The books we read did not represent our realities.

Hispanic leaders of the different church structures were supposed to act as our middle persons, our intercessors and interpreters of the mission of the Hispanic congregations. Most of the church bodies with an episcopal structure required four years of college and three years of study for a master

---

[4]See Edwin I. Hernández and Kenneth G. Davis, *Reconstructing the Sacred Tower: Challenge and Promises of Latino/a Theological Education* (Scranton, PA: University of Scranton Press, 2003).
[5]Hernández and Davis, *Reconstructing the Sacred Tower.*

of divinity degree before ordination.[6] This was financially prohibitive, and, given that the curriculum was not relevant, our leaders were reluctant to make the investment. Many times the ordaining bodies did not understand our theology and pastoral praxis but required that we give credence to the models used for the churches of the dominant groups. If we used alternative models of theological education, we would not gain the full rights of ordination. This could mean that, when we represented the interests of our congregations in the full body of the church, we did not have full vote in the assemblies. It was too similar to our status as second-class citizens or noncitizens in society. What was the difference between the mainline church and the rest of society as we engaged in these different arenas?

In my ministerial experience, resources were rarely allotted in accordance with needs. Latin@ pastors were at the margins, the afterthought of those creating budgets. I was hearing Hispanic pastors and denominational leaders referring to themselves as the dogs waiting for the crumbs to drop from the main table. When we received funds, the criteria for how long and how much we received had middle-class expectations assigned to them. Growth was defined in accordance with the assumptions of the dominant in society. Each of these (lack of ordination pathways, lack of theologically appropriate texts, lack of appropriate tools in ministry, and lack of budget) was a demonstration of my lack of understanding about racism in the structures and a colonized mentality. I had grown up with the fruits of this evil.

During this time, the denomination had afforded me opportunities that taught me so much about how to become a contributing citizen. I also knew that these opportunities had been advocated for by my preceding generation of Latin@ leaders and those who were allies, including other groups of Color. There were also those persons who had affirmed me in very powerful ways and executives who had stepped aside to allow leaders of Color to come into positions of power.

It took me a while to realize that understanding developed not because of an academic degree but because one had opened up the heart to the other,

---

[6]This chapter reflects my own experience with the varied episcopal and free-church structures of mainline denominations and some Pentecostal denominations. It is here acknowledged that some Latin@ church bodies represented at the meeting do not require education of their ministers at all. These were usually run by Latin@ leaders themselves. Their theologies and ordaining requirements were contextualized.

and now the desire to know was authentic. This was a knowledge that only compassion could generate. Until I learned this, I was sorely disappointed or frustrated with those who required explanations for matters that seemed to me common sense and therefore general knowledge. I had failed to see that general knowledge of issues of power and privilege, or of who we are as Latin@s, was absent even after so many years of coexisting with us in the church. We had not come to the *compenetración* or the perichoresis of "communion" or of fellowship. What history and theology have informed this?[7]

In this essay I hope to be able to show how this personal experience has its roots in racism embedded in colonialist practices by which Anglophone missions were established. I will describe the historical context in which colonialist mission takes place and show examples of the church and the missionary endeavors from the mid-1800s to the 1920s, when much of the missional theology and spirit of the United States began to take form. Efforts that the church may have made toward eradicating racism will be noted as well as times when the church has betrayed her witness of Christ for other gains. Along the way, definitions and some analysis of what racism is and how it expresses itself today as an agenda of white supremacy will also be made. I will end with a theological framework of *misión integral* to inform how the mission of the church might move in new directions of faithfulness to recognize Jesus' teachings of the *basileia*.[8]

Racism as Sin: An Evangelical Theological Perspective

The history of racism implicates all of us whether we play the role of oppressed or oppressor in it. Racism is a dance, a relational pattern, and it takes both sides to keep it going. I borrow from the words of Paul in his epistle to the Romans: "all have sinned and fall short of the glory of God" (Rom 3:23). Sin requires repentance. Repentance is more than guilt. Guilt

---

[7]While much of this is a personal testimony, one can see from the references that the issues have been documented as well. The diversity of Latin@ churches is great and includes a vast variety and range of dependence and independence. Nonetheless, the Pulpit & Pew report referenced earlier (Hernández et al., *Strengthening Hispanic Ministry Across Denominations*) speaks to Hispanic ministry across denominations in the United States, including Catholics. Structural independence from Anglos does not exempt the Latin@ church from the racism of the larger evangelical church context.

[8]*Basileia* will be used to refer to the "kingdom of God" as it is a more neutral term that does not bring to us images of hierarchy or patriarchy or any other earthly models of governance.

makes us culpably blameworthy, responsible for the wrong perpetrated, but doesn't create change. Guilt is like a stagnant body of water overgrown with algae—a cesspool. It can therefore paralyze our lives at times. But this is only looking at the psychological dimensions.

Shame is similar. It is chagrin, embarrassment, discomfort, humiliation, or distress caused by the consciousness of wrong behavior. The difference is that guilt can be a private or simply legal matter while shame speaks more to the dishonor, disgrace, ignominy we face as we confront community or the public when we do something wrong.

Sin is deeper, for it points to a breach in relationship and to the indebtedness that results from our actions. It's interesting that Leviticus 5:14–6:7 and Numbers 5:5-10 speak of the restitution owed to the one wronged as well as the guilt offering owed to God. Full restitution is owed the neighbor plus an extra one-fifth; then a guilt offering must be made to the Lord since we have violated the order of relationship God prescribes.[9] In guilt we do not find the power or the process for change. Though we may admit culpability and experience feelings of remorse and distress, we may not initiate change. What then would bring about change, a new direction, a *shuv*?

Repentance in the New Testament is the verb *metanoeō*, the turning from evil and returning to God to embrace the good or righteousness, right relationships. To turn away from God is apostasy. When in a state of apostasy, we are practicing idolatry. In returning to God we recognize the wrong and commit to change, examining both our motives and our deeds. The practice for repentance is reflected in the prophetic words of Isaiah:

> Wash yourselves; make yourselves clean;
>> remove the evil of your doings
>> from before my eyes;
> cease to do evil,
>> learn to do good;
> seek justice,
>> rescue the oppressed,
> defend the orphan,
>> plead for the widow. (Is 1:16-17)

---

[9]See Stephen Motyer, "Guilt," in *Baker's Evangelical Dictionary of Biblical Theology*, ed. Walter A. Elwell (Grand Rapids: Baker Books, 1996).

To turn to God is a practice that begins with confession. We are reminded in 1 John 1:9 that confession is a part of repentance and necessary when we ask God's forgiveness. Repentance was accompanied in the Old Testament by public ceremonies, fasting, displays of sorrow such as ashes and sackcloth, liturgies, and songs, most probably songs of lament. But at times, the prophets chided the people for carrying out these rituals with no true desire to change. They would urge the people to convert or to obey God. Change in relationship with God was necessary to bring the people to repentance. Obedience is dependent on trust in God, which engenders faithfulness to the actions that God requires.

All good evangelicals know this already. Why rehearse it in this space? As highly intelligent people, we are able to rationalize our sins well. So, over the years, we have set policies that have fit the realities of those we know, and the missional and institutional goals and structures have arisen from those policies. We have continued to give privilege to the peoples we are most familiar with. Our structures have relegated the others to marginal spaces and diminished budgets. If and when they command our attention, they become objects for charitable, not missional, actions.

Mission should come from a deep conviction of the lordship of Christ and radical discipleship. Pity creates distance between the ones suffering and the one helping. The helper is seen as the strong one and the suffering as weaker. However, in mission, there is empathy, an identification that leads to mutuality in weakness. Empathy also leads to cooperation of the two parties in creating structures of justice together. It builds the fellowship needed for perseverance in doing the works of justice. These matters are about not only the personal realm of our lives but also the institutional arenas in which we move. While on a personal level we may all be sinners, at the institutional level, not all have the power to channel their sin of prejudice into a system that affects all realms of society.

The particular sin I am addressing here is the sin of racism. As I am using the word *racism*, it excludes internal reflections and considerations about the other; racism is about power at an institutional level. Institutions perpetuate ideologies and practices that give expression to this exclusionary power. Roots of the sin of racism become the white supremacy of today. White supremacy is defined by Robin Harvey Gorsline as "the operation of

social practices by individuals and institutions, including political and economic mechanisms, to achieve and maintain the political, social and economic dominance of white people and the subjugation of peoples of color."[10]
From a sociological perspective, racism is a socially constructed term. It is
the use of a social continuum for categorizing persons of Color, a continuum
that marginalizes them and assigns characteristics to them in order to
portray them as inferior to those of the majority group so that the majority
can rationalize why they should have more power and privilege over the
groups of Color and perpetuate that power.[11] This power is over the bodies,
the property, the destinies, and the movements of persons. Philosophy, theology, economics, science, culture, the media, and the arts are all used to
rationalize the perpetuation of power based on race.

Racism comprises "attitude, action, institutional structure or social policies that subordinate persons or groups because of their color."[12] It can be
expressed in covert as well as overt ways. Mark Hearn speaks of colorblind
racism and theology and how these relate to the practices of the church. He
describes colorblindness as a method of racism today, involving "the false
assumption that all people begin from the same starting point, when in reality they do not." He posits that "refusing to acknowledge the effects of color
in society contributes to the meritocracy argument and thus an attitude of
superiority over those who have not achieved the same," adding to the negative perceptions of persons of Color and placing them in subordinate and
marginalized places.[13] It is racism that "otherizes softly ('these people are
human too')."[14] Colorblindness denies the existence of public racism and
charges persons of Color with seeking to bring disunity and racial tension
where there is none. Hearn states that it is this type of colorblind racism that
exists in the evangelical church today.

---

[10]Robin Hawley Gorsline, "Shaking the Foundations: White Supremacy in the Theological Academy," in *Disrupting White Supremacy from Within: White People on What We Need to Do*, ed. Jennifer Harvey, Karin A. Case, and Robin Hawley Gorsline (Cleveland: Pilgrim Press, 2004), 34.

[11]In this statement, I am not including Whites who are able to see themselves as persons, and not
always as having color.

[12]Derald Wing Sue, *Overcoming Our Racism: The Journey to Liberation* (San Francisco: Jossey-Bass,
2003), 31.

[13]Mark Hearn, "Color-Blind Racism, Color-Blind Theology, and Church Practices," *Religious
Education* 104, no. 3 (May-June 2009): 276.

[14]Eduardo Bonilla-Silva, *Racism Without Racists: Color-Blind Racism and the Persistence of Racial
Inequality in the United States*, 2nd ed. (Lanham, MD: Rowman & Littlefield, 2006), 3.

In the work of James H. Cone "Theology's Great Sin: Silence in the Face of White Supremacy"[15] Cone points to Reinhold Niebuhr's work *The Nature and Destiny of Man*, where Niebuhr speaks about the sinfulness of man and points to the sinfulness of racism of both the oppressed and the oppressor: "the sinfulness of man makes it inevitable that a dominant class, group, and sex should seek to define a relationship which guarantees its dominance, as permanently normative. It is a fact that those who hold great economic and political power are more guilty of pride against God and of injustice against the weak than those who lack power and prestige."[16]

RACISM, COLONIALISM, AND MISSION

While we could speak of racism beginning with the era of colonialism, Fredrickson explains that its roots go back further, to the Middle Ages when Christians promoted the belief that Jews were responsible for the crucifixion of Christ, thus demonizing Jews and placing them outside the realm of humanity. Fredrickson places some of the history of racism in fifteenth- to sixteenth-century Spain when *conversos* (Jewish converts) were seen as incapable of true conversion because they were of impure blood.[17]

Colonialism and its need to dominate others and prevent their self-determination in order to appropriate the land fueled the social construction of race. Peruvian sociologist Anibal Quijano posits that racism was the better organizer of colonialism in the Americas.[18] It depended on biblical interpretation and theological tenets to rationalize the political dominance of the colonial powers. It conquered by creating an opposing worldview to that of the colonized by creating confusion and disrupting the way of life of the conquered people.

Religion provides the ultimate roots of a group's identity. Theologian Virgilio Elizondo reminds us that "they [religious symbols of the colonized people] are the ultimate justification of the worldview of a group and the

---

[15]James H. Cone, "Theology's Great Sin: Silence in the Face of White Supremacy," *Black Theology: An International Journal* 2, no. 2 (2004): 139-52.

[16]Reinhold Niebuhr, *The Nature and Destiny of Man: A Christian Interpretation* (New York: Charles Scribner's Sons, 1941), 1:282.

[17]See George M. Fredrickson, *Racism: A Short History* (Princeton, NJ: Princeton University Press, 2002).

[18]See Anibal Quijano, "Coloniality of Power, Eurocentrism, and Latin America," *Nepantla: Views from South* 1, no. 3 (2000): 533-80.

force that cements all the elements of the life of a group. . . . When such symbols are discredited or destroyed . . . the worldview moves from order to chaos."[19] This is the ultimate conquest of the dominant group.

Persons of Latin American and Caribbean descent inherited the gospel from the people of the Americas who were conquered militarily. The symbols and sacred text of Christianity, whether in its Catholic or Protestant expression, were used to bring peoples into submission by powers that raped, robbed, and killed. At the same time, the missionary work provided education and positive social change. The missionary leaders showed deep commitment to the work and to the peoples while unconsciously continuing to relate from a position of superiority. It is difficult to describe how this felt within Latin@ culture, which respects those more educated and those who show compassion. How do we come to terms with the prejudices, discrimination, and structural racism of white supremacy implicit in the structures of the church and the missiological endeavors of people who were not bad people?

Immigration of peoples from Latin America and the Caribbean to the United States further complicates matters of missions and race, particularly at the border between the United States and Mexico during the time of US expansion. Let us look at how racism becomes essential to the expansion of the United States and the role of religion in the formation of the ideology of manifest destiny. During the nineteenth century, manifest destiny was a philosophy with a theological underpinning that was used to rationalize the expansion of the United States into Mexican territory and that included the removal of Native Americans from their lands.[20] This belief justified the Anglo-Saxon mission to civilize and expand into these territories in order to establish what was thought to be a superior society because it brought forth the full potential of the land and the people by way of developing political and economic institutions to further liberty and progress.

Manifest destiny was undergirded by social theory, science, and theological/biblical understandings. Americans in the United States were God's

---

[19]Virgilio P. Elizondo, "*Mestizaje* as a Locus of Theological Reflection," in *Frontiers of Hispanic Theology in the United States*, ed. Allan Figueroa Deck (Maryknoll, NY: Orbis Books, 1992), 107.
[20]The phrase was first employed by John L. O'Sullivan regarding the annexation of Texas in an article in the July-August 1845 edition of the *United States Magazine and Democratic Review*, which he edited; see Matthew Pinsker, "Manifest Destiny," *History*, A&E Networks, www.history .com/topics/manifest-destiny.

chosen people, and as such they were destined to take the land. God's creation, natural and human, existed for the benefit of the chosen nation. Expansion and slavery fed on each other. The philosophy of manifest destiny was founded on an understanding of the god of Protestantism—the chooser was this god. Once we have established God's unique favor and choosing, it becomes a very powerful concept. Its implications are capable of creating much inequality, hatred, and violence. Forrest Wood made the claim that Americanism and Protestantism were synonymous at the time.[21]

Divine chosenness and capitalist economic interests went hand in hand. As theology and the endeavors of Christianity were coopted by the colonists, theology generated knowledge of white supremacy, not of the *basileia* of Christ—practices of oppression, not salvation or liberation. Economics and race were about control of the land. The idea of inferior races was necessary for rationalizing the control of the land and human resources. By 1840 race had become a topic of general intellectual and popular interest. Phrenology, a popular science, concluded that Caucasians were capable of infinite improvement while other races were irredeemably limited by the deficiencies of their original cerebral organization.[22]

In the Americas the colonial powers enslaved the Indigenous peoples on their lands. Later, Africans were brought to the Americas to be enslaved as well, especially after the Indigenous populations died of illnesses brought by the Europeans and from the effects of slavery. These enslaved peoples, Indigenous and African, in Latin America and the Caribbean, were defined as an inferior species created to serve Europeans. They were a species that had mental and spiritual deficiencies requiring them to live under Christian tutelage as a way of correcting their deficiencies. The slave trade, *encomienda*, therefore, was legitimate within the parameters of human and divine laws.[23] Slaves were mandated by God to serve masters. Their freedom was only from personal sin. The Bible was used as justification for policies that gave

---

[21]See Forrest G. Wood, *The Arrogance of Faith: Christianity and Race in America from the Colonial Era to the Twentieth Century* (New York: Knopf, 1990).

[22]Reginald Horsman, *Race and Manifest Destiny: The Origins of American Racial Anglo-Saxonism* (Cambridge, MA: Harvard University Press, 1981), chap. 8.

[23]The Spanish crown would grant to soldiers an estate of land that included the inhabiting American Indians. This system was instituted in 1503. The inhabitants were said to be under the protection of the Spanish crown, paying for this protection with their servitude. The soldiers were required to evangelize the inhabitants.

Europeans control over every aspect of the lives of the enslaved and of peoples in their own lands. The physical traits that marked the differences of these persons—pigmentation, lips, hair, and so on—were considered the biological evidence of their inferiority. These biological traits were then used as ways of categorizing and targeting persons for discrimination.

Christianity and its missiological endeavors therefore have been strongly criticized in the twentieth century for being the religious arm of the European colonial powers and later of the United States.[24] However, this was not as clean cut as one may think; oftentimes the missionaries defended the rights of the peoples they served. This demonstrates the motive and intention of love beyond the structural purposes of colonization. It is this intention that bears fruit to the work of true mission.

This convoluted legacy of the gospel understanding, and self-understanding, of subjugation because of racial difference has been embedded in the religion and culture. It continues to shape the ways we relate to one another. Racism has built the epistemologies, worldviews, laws, and educational institutions of our times. There isn't a perspective or institution that has not been marked by this legacy of hatred and its accompanying violence. Colonialism has colored the very lenses with which we read Scriptures and understand ourselves as the colonized and the colonizers.

Racism has depended on the categories of racialization. These have taken a variety of different forms. As documented by Steve Martinot, after slavery was abolished in the United States, racial segregation took the form of Jim Crow and debt servitude, but after civil rights were legally restored, police profiling, the prison-industrial complex, and felonized disenfranchisement were employed to effectively maintain segregation.[25] The anti-immigrant movements in the United States and across Europe are also a part of the new racialization. In the United States, detention centers have become an extension of the prison-industrial complex.

---

[24]See Luis N. Rivera, *A Violent Evangelism: The Political and Religious Conquest of the Americas* (Louisville, KY: Westminster John Knox, 1992). Also see Steven Maughan, "An Archbishop for Greater Britain: Bishop Montgomery, Missionary Imperialism and the SPG, 1897–1915," in *Three Centuries of Mission: The United Society for Propagation of the Gospel, 1701–2000*, ed. Daniel O'Connor et al. (New York: Continuum, 2000), 358-70.

[25]See the discussion by Steve Martinot, "The Coloniality of Power: Notes Toward De-Colonization," www.ocf.berkeley.edu/~marto/coloniality.htm.

Immigration is interrelated with the global economy. Industrialization in the late nineteenth century was accompanied by colonization, which required a mass of workers with no rights.[26] Deindustrialization in the late twentieth century commodified the bodies of persons needed for the large service economy it had created. Immigrants have come from former colonies, and some have been brought for forced labor and sexual slavery by human traffickers. When people of Color have migrated to the lands of their colonial powers, the deep roots of racism have come to the surface. Slippery arguments today have masked racism, depicting it as an issue of citizenship rights.

Aviva Chomsky, in her book *They Take Our Jobs!" and 20 Other Myths About Immigration,* asks: "What makes a person eligible for rights? Do we all have rights by virtue of being human? If rights are restricted to a select group of people-citizens, then who decides who is a citizen?"[27] How do the political views compare to the biblical views?

The *imago Dei* is the biblical grounding for the rights of all persons based on their equality at creation. However, those who have substituted racialization categories for the biblical narrative categorize the immigrant as an illegal alien. Some churches have gone as far as refusing to baptize those who are alternately documented because they are "in sin" since they are living outside of the law. No attempt has been made to determine if the law is aligned with the values of the gospel. Still others have exiled congregation members who have voted for the rights of the immigrant, labeling them traitors to the United States and to God because God has chosen the United States; thus a vote for the undocumented immigrant defies the will of God to bless this nation. I have also seen flyers recruiting persons to be minutemen at the door of a church in Nogales, Arizona. The church has chosen loyalty to the law without critical theological reflection that would define loyalty to Christ in light of the law and the situation. Let us examine the rights of persons according to the law.

In 1948, after World War II, when the world experienced the horrors of Nazism, the United Nations General Assembly passed the Universal Declaration of Human Rights, which asserts that everyone has all rights and

---

[26]See Aviva Chomsky, *"They Take Our Jobs!" and 20 Other Myths About Immigration* (Boston: Beacon Press, 2007).

[27]Chomsky, *"They Take Our Jobs!,"* xvii.

freedoms without distinction of race, color, sex, language, religion, political or other opinion, national or social origin, property, birth, or other status. It also guarantees social and economic rights, like rights to work, to equal pay, and to education, food, housing, and medical care.[28]

In the United States, however, the Supreme Court in Sosa v. Álvarez-Machain (2004) concluded that the United Nations General Assembly's passage of the Universal Declaration of Human Rights "does not of its own force impose obligations as a matter of international law."[29] This makes the constitution more ambiguous so that the rights that belong to "the people" are not the same as the rights that belong to all people. This ambiguity has been used to exclude some persons from rights and to benefit employers who can then exploit by excluding. It has been argued by Loida Martell-Otero, and I agree, that exclusion by citizenship is based on racism and used for the same reasons that the construct of racism was invented—to create a mass of rightless workers. Illegality is a new codification of inferiority used to maintain coloniality, a social construct with the financial goals of the wealthy in mind.[30] Does it remotely remind us of the codifications and goals of slavery?

As a final point, in 1868 the Fourteenth Amendment was passed extending to all persons citizenship, except Native Americans. It states that "no person can be denied equal protection under the law."[31] However, the amendment leaves it to the courts to decide who fits into the "no person" category. Supreme Court cases have given contradictory rulings over the

---

[28]Chomsky, "*They Take Our Jobs!*," xviii.

[29]Sosa v. Álvarez-Machain, 542 U.S. 692 (2004); see summary of Sosa v. Álvarez-Machain 542 U.S. 692 (2004) at Justia: US Supreme Court, https://supreme.justia.com/cases/federal /us/542/692/. See also David Weissbrodt, Joan Fitzpatrick, and Frank C. Newman, *International Human Rights: Law, Policy, and Process*, 4th ed. (New Providence, NJ: LexisNexis Group, 2009).

[30]For a fuller discussion of the comparison of mass incarceration with immigrant detention and a theology of the *basileia* as sacrament see Loida I. Martell-Otero, "*La Nueva Encomienda*: The Church's Response to Undocumented Migrants as Mass Incarcerated," in *Thinking Theologically About Mass Incarceration: Biblical Foundations and Justice Imperatives*, ed. Antonios Kireopoulos, Mitzi J. Budde, and Matthew D. Lundberg (Mahwah, NJ: Paulist Press, 2017), 161-93.

[31]The United States Naturalization Law of March 26, 1790, only granted citizenship to free White persons of good character. The Chinese Exclusion Act of 1882 excluded Chinese from US citizenship, and each Black counted as half a citizen and had no citizenship rights. See "History of Laws Concerning Immigration and Naturalization in the United States," Wikipedia, https:// en.wikipedia.org/wiki/History_of_laws_concerning_immigration_and_naturalization_in_the_ United_States.

years. For example, in 1971 the court ruled against discrimination due to legal status when it comes to welfare benefits to noncitizens, and the 1996 welfare reform included discrimination against legal immigrants. The Fourteenth Amendment is violated daily when noncitizens are denied any protection under the law. These laws and their interpretations show some glimpses of how legal status and race are used to discriminate against persons of Color in the United States. The expansion and reform periods of US history have been marked by definitions of exclusion and how these definitions have been used to maintain a pool of workers for a secondary labor market. The interpretations of such definitions have also changed in accordance with the economic and sociopolitical climate.

Here are just a few quick examples: in 1942 the Bracero program in the Southwest and later Operation Bootstrap in the Northeast were both used to bring in workers from Mexico and Puerto Rico to work in agriculture. Notice that *bracero* means "arms." The term designated Mexicans not as persons but as arms. Later, in light of consciences awakened to civil rights, the popular discussion deemed that the treatment of persons under the Bracero program could not be reconciled with the values of a democratic society. In 1965 as women worked full time in the areas of private care—areas such as fast food, elder care, and cleaning—such work became a public industry. Immigrant groups from Asia filled this care deficit. Because they were the workers without social and economic rights, they were recruited to provide this low-wage labor force. The changing economy at this time also allowed for a secondary sector of jobs that were subcontracted, and these jobs moved from regulated to unregulated sector jobs while other jobs were being outsourced. Many rights that laborers had won over the years slipped away as a result.

The economic hopelessness that this created for poor populations, the "war on drugs," and today the "war on terrorism" have increased the prison population and detention centers, creating a new industry of prisons and security.[32] Prison corporations had doubled their revenues from the immigration detention business in the years between 2005 and 2012.[33] They

---

[32]Geiza Vargas-Vargas, "The Investment Opportunity in Mass Incarceration: A Black (Corrections) or Brown (Immigration) Play?," *California Western Law Review* 48, no. 2 (Spring 2012): 355-56.
[33]Aviva Chomsky, *Undocumented: How Immigration Became Illegal* (Boston: Beacon Press, 2014), 111.

now have a powerful lobby base and have lobbied for harsher sentences. It behooves us to wonder whether the incarcerated under such a system are not really political prisoners. We have seen how prisons have provided income for small towns, making prison and security a prime economic strategy for these towns. Growth in the prison population has become a return on investment for stockholders. Detention is a part of mass incarceration and a new source of income for investors.

This historical continuum of racism and its variety of expressions in the different institutions of our society have confronted the church with a challenge. How has her mission addressed or failed to address these challenges? Below we will see how the church's self-understanding, which informs her mission, is mixed with the worldview of her times, causing her to side with other gods.

THE DISCIPLES OF CHRIST IN TEXAS

Church historian Daisy L. Machado writes of the Disciples of Christ in Texas from 1888 to 1945, the years that the manifest destiny ideology and its race economy and ideals of chosenness were prevalent.[34] The Disciples were expanding toward the frontier, as were other Christian groups such as the Methodists and Presbyterians, and were doing mission work in Mexico as a part of their foreign mission. However, the work with Mexican Texans was considered homeland mission, and because the Mexican Revolution (1910–1920) took place during that time, the work was complicated. Many migrants crossed the border, but the border ethos saw Mexicans in Texas as inferior to others. Machado quotes Boren's statement about the work of the Disciples with Mexican Texans:

> Indifference and racial prejudice largely characterized the relationship of the Texas Disciples toward opportunities for service among both Negroes and Mexicans. The size of these racial elements in the state, especially in regard to Mexicans and their limited economic and social status, have offered unusual opportunities for an extensive program of service that has been neglected.[35]

---

[34]Daisy L. Machado, *Of Borders and Margins: Hispanic Disciples in Texas, 1888–1945* (New York: Oxford University Press, 2003).

[35]Carter E. Boren, *Religion on the Texas Frontier* (San Antonio: Naylor, 1968), 340, quoted in Machado, *Of Borders and Margins*, 111.

Resources were not invested for the development of Indigenous leaders or materials in Spanish to facilitate a Latin@ church in the margins. Latin@ pastors were poorly paid, yet they continued to work faithfully and with a vision that came from love for the people as part of the mission of Christ. If the work advanced, it was due to their faithful perseverance. Some churches found it difficult to continue and had to close during this time.

The view that leaders of the Disciples church had toward Mexican Texans echoed that of the culture of the time.[36] Mexicans were seen as low-status persons without education who would hamper the advancement of the work. The Mexican leaders were seen as helpers and were not given equal status with their Anglo counterparts. Leaders from the Mexico missions and churches were brought to pastor the churches in Texas rather than equip the Mexican Texans living in the area. When the work did prosper, God was praised, but when it didn't, there was no analysis. Blame was placed on the Mexican Texans, which made the work that much more difficult because they were seen as "ignorant, irresponsible, roving and superstitious."[37] This population was considered other not only because they were not White but because they were also Catholic. Mexican Texans were also seen as the people who lived in the undeveloped territory that now became the responsibility of the Anglos under manifest destiny. The agenda of this ideology eventually displaced the Tejanos from their land.[38]

Part of the history of displacement, including lynching of people of Mexican origin or descent between 1848 and 1928, is documented by Carrigan and Webb.[39] During this period the lynching rate was 27.4 per 100,000 of the population. During the same time period, the highest rate of lynching for African Americans was in Mississippi with 52.8 victims per 100,000 of the population.[40]

---

[36]The term *Mexican Texan* is used to describe the fluid reality of the frontier between Mexico and Texas that created a mixing of races and cultures with their foods, music, and unique traditions. It was, in 1821, the Hispanic frontier of North America. For a fuller discussion see Machado, *Of Borders and Margins*, chap. 1. Also see Phyllis McKenzie, *The Mexican Texans* (College Station: Texas A&M University Press, 2004).

[37]Machado, *Of Borders and Margins*, 111.

[38]*Tejanos* is the Spanish term that refers to the Mexicans living in Texas.

[39] Only in the last ten to fifteen years have scholars begun to unearth this history. See the groundbreaking work of William D. Carrigan and Clive Webb, "The Lynching of Persons of Mexican Origin or Descent in the United States, 1848 to 1928," *Journal of Social History* 7, no. 2 (Winter 2003): 411-38. From a legal perspective see Richard Delgado, "The Law of the Noose: A History of Latino Lynching," *Harvard Civil Rights–Civil Liberties Law Review* 44 (2009): 297-312.

[40]Carrigan and Webb, "Lynching of Persons," 414.

Lynchings of persons of Mexican origin and descent were rarely investigated except under federal pressure after some years of diplomatic pressure by the Mexican government. President Porfirio Diaz's efforts to facilitate trade links between the two countries finally led to the documentation of injustices and abuse along the Texan border. The US government would not respond to the reports until 1890, when the lynching of four men in a courthouse square took place before the men were brought to trial. At the same time, after the massacre of Chinese miners in Wyoming and attacks on Sicilian immigrants in Louisiana, the United States attempted to show the international community that foreign nationals would be safe. President McKinley then responded to the demands of the Mexican government for accountability by recommending to Congress a one-time payment of a $2,000 indemnity. This established a precedent.[41]

Land interests and resentment toward the Tejano owners surely discouraged empathetic mission among the Tejanos. Machado posits that the issue of land ownership, its use and development, had an influence on the missions theology of Protestant denominations.[42] The history of expansion in the Southwestern border states sheds light on the issues of immigration today. Negative attitudes toward people of Mexican descent and other immigrants are new acts of racism masked by the rhetoric of citizenship.

This is an example of how the power and influence of an ideology shaped not only the political and socioeconomic agenda of the Southwest border but the mission of the Protestant church as well.[43] Had the Disciples been able to employ the Scriptures to reflect critically and regulate external forces, they could have become an influential witness at the border, shaping its ethos differently. Instead, their theological paradigms mirrored their sociopolitical worldview, and their missional practices and patterns were shaped by the Southwestern ideology of conquest, which created racial paradigms of inferiority and otherness.[44]

Today, the White evangelical church is divided about the issue of immigration. There are those who have protested President Trump's orders, which

---

[41]Carrigan and Webb, "Lynching of Persons," 428.
[42]Machado, *Of Borders and Margins*, 110.
[43]Carrigan and Webb, "Lynching of Persons," 109.
[44]Carrigan and Webb, "Lynching of Persons," 108.

place a ban on particular groups of peoples coming to the United States. Others judge immigrants by a law that criminalizes immigrants. They respond by quoting Scripture about respecting the law of the land without asking if that law is just or if it reflects biblical directives regarding how the foreigner is to be treated in one's land. Still others remain publicly silent so as not to stir division among their ranks. This silence has condoned the unjust treatment of immigrants in much the same way that the Disciples church condoned the treatment of Mexican Texans. These same churches will conduct missions in Mexico or other Latin American countries. They feel good about these missions without seriously reflecting on why it's okay to love your neighbor on the other side of the border while criminalizing the same neighbor who moves to this side of the border.

THE ORIGIN OF CHRISTIAN MISSIONS IN LATIN AMERICA

Perhaps a wee bit of history of American Protestant missions in Latin American will shed some light on the issue. Protestant missions took place at different times in different parts of Latin America as each country responded to varying circumstances that made it feasible to enter and evangelize. Missiologist Samuel Escobar tells us that as early as 1556 Reformer John Calvin sent two Protestant missionaries to Brazil, but their efforts failed almost immediately due to the Catholic Church's strong control.[45] It was not until the 1800s, when the countries began to break free of Spain, that the religious climate became more hospitable to missions. Pioneers like James Thomson, who was sponsored by the British Foreign Bible Society, came from England to Buenos Aires in 1816 and went from there to Uruguay, Chile, Peru, and Mexico. These were independent movements. Colporteurs peddled the Bible and other devotional materials. The Methodist Episcopal Church was the first to send American Protestant missionaries to Argentina and Brazil in 1836. In 1870, the American Baptist Home Mission Society started a mission in Mexico, and the Presbyterian Church in the United States sent missionaries to Colombia in 1856.[46]

---

[45]Samuel Escobar, "Protestantism Explodes: Why Is a Traditionally Catholic Region Turning Protestant?," *Christian History* 35 (1992), https://christianhistoryinstitute.org/magazine/article /protestantism-explodes.

[46]Svenja Blanke, "Civic Foreign Policy: U.S. Religious Interest Groups and Central America, 1973–1990" (PhD diss., Freie University, Berlin, 2001), 20, www.diss.fu-berlin.de/diss/receive

By the time that La Conferencia Protestante Panamericana or Congreso Misionero took place on February 10-20, 1916, in Panama, there were sixty missionary societies in Latin America. There were 235 delegates, of which only 27 were Latin Americans, and the official language of the congress was English.[47]

Christian education, one of the main topics discussed at La Conferencia, played a primary role in the evangelization of the peoples. The purpose of education was the formation of character and of the whole personality. In the course of time, the purpose was to enlighten with Christian thinking and guide in daily life with Christian ideals so that the evangelized could become the new society. Christian education was to Christianize, to inspire the people to dedicate their lives to a noble purpose. This is an important step toward the attainment of all that the Lord's day on earth is destined to achieve for humankind. Christian schools were designed to develop the new leaders of a society.[48] These sentiments and strategies reflect the understanding that to Christianize a group or a nation was to completely change the ideologies and concepts of a people on the way to a Christian worldview.

Education shapes society. The instruments of society such as the family, the church, the community, the economy and its agencies (banks, assets, and roots), the legal system (courts), health care infrastructure (hospitals, clinics), and mass media (newspapers, TV, the internet) serve as the axes of education. Throughout its history, the church has developed agencies and instruments by which it has fulfilled its teaching task using the other axes or institutions of society. Associating closely with US institutions meant that evangelization and Americanization became closely intertwined with the economic and political systems.

Two theological lines of thought existed in the formation of the different educational agencies: (1) the fundamentalists, who did not see the importance of establishing social institutions to educate, heal the body,

---

/FUDISS_thesis_000000000975. See also David Shavit, *The United States in Latin America: A Historical Dictionary* (New York: Greenwood, 1992).

[47]See Juan Francisco Martínez Guerra, "Panamá 1916: Sus raíces y sus frutos en el mundo evangélico latinoamericano," unpublished paper presented at the Confraternidad Latinoamericana, Wheaton College, summer 2016.

[48]See Report of Commission III, chaired by Charles Gore, *Missionary Conference, 1910: Report of Commission III; Education in Relation to the Christianisation of National Life* (New York: Revell, 2910), vol. 3, chap. 9, 444.

and regenerate the society, and (2) the liberal sectors, who understood that changes occur only in the individual. A variation within the fundamentalist camp understood that Christ would not come until every creature was preached to. In order to perfect society, it would be necessary to use the scientific method to solve poverty. The political regime was seen as part of the regeneration of the world. From this theological perspective, the missionary project was helping to create a civilization in which educational, medical, theological, and journalistic institutions were established, which gave form and strength to a Protestant foundation within society, creating a North American concept of the world. The more theologically conservative groups saw mission as effecting change in daily living based on the principles of faith, creating a rupture with the past and a construction of new social and cultural practices. Together, the fundamentalist and the more liberal theological understandings of the purpose of mission created a new colonial and Americanizing concept.

US Christian missionaries played an important role in promoting foreign aid in Latin America as they turned to wealthy individuals for funding. Indirectly, they became agents of US interests. One example of a wealthy supporter is John D. Rockefeller, who saw his cooperation with the evangelical Summer Institute of Linguistics as a way "to secure resources and 'pacify' indigenous peoples in the name of democracy, corporate profit and religion."[49] Scholars writing about missionaries dispersing American policies abroad agree that while it may have been done unconsciously, missionaries were the carriers of the American dream.[50] Scholarship shows how evangelization carried a colonizing attitude from the perspective of Anglo-Saxon superiority.

THEOLOGY, SPIRITUALITY, AND PERSPECTIVE TRANSFORMATION

White supremacy lives within a matrix of structures, attitudes, and behaviors that maintain the dominance of those at the top despite challenges from people of Color and those in alliance with us. "Maintaining the practice of

---

[49]See Gerard Colby with Charlotte Dennett, *Thy Will Be Done: The Conquest of the Amazon; Nelson Rockefeller and Evangelism in the Age of Oil* (New York: HarperCollins, 1995).
[50]See Emily S. Rosenberg, *Spreading the American Dream: American Economic and Cultural Expansion 1890–1945* (New York: Hill & Wang, 1982).

racism in place does not require the help of anyone for it is self-perpetuating and not self-correcting."[51] Elsewhere I have written about this matter, pointing out that

> the practices and mechanisms of this form of dominance are invisible to those that carry them out. It is a social construct whereby knowledge of the world is filtered through the lens of whiteness. These are the judicial systems, the structure of government and the educational and legislative systems. They are promoted by way of the media, the arts, religion and education. As such, it makes up the world of white persons and becomes the norm. As the norm, it makes up the world of others as well. One inherits the construct as a process of socialization that teaches one to adapt and fit into it as one makes meaning of life situations.[52]

I always heard my mother say, "Las estructuras crean hábitos." Structures create habits. Structures and habits hold together the basic facilities, services, and installations needed for the functioning of an organization, community, or society. They regulate life, the texture of our social existence. Therefore, our spiritual living is impacted by a complex web of structures. Structures incarnate the ideologies or philosophies that define the values of our institutions. As such, they can be an expression of righteousness or of injustice. Structures create a consciousness out of which people live their lives. This consciousness, whatever it has become, causes our brains to act like echo chambers in which beliefs and processes endure and become a part of who we are. These beliefs and processes influence us because they persist as thoughts and patterns of behavior.

To transform an ideology and hence its power, one needs to generate a new consciousness with the purpose of developing critical movements or mobilization that requires group action and practices for engaging one's energy in ways that reinforce a different ideology and that have the goal of changing an unjust system. Generating a new consciousness involves coming to an awareness of one's cultural blinders and ideological filters through which we interpret the world.[53] This may sound like an unending

[51]Gorsline, "Shaking the Foundations," 34.
[52]Elizabeth Conde-Frazier, "Thoughts on Curriculum as Formational Praxis for Faculty, Students, and Their Communities," in Teaching for a Culturally Diverse and Racially Just World, ed. Eleazar S. Fernandez (Eugene, OR: Cascade Books, 2014), 141.
[53]Adapted from Elizabeth Conde-Frazier, "Theological Illiteracy Through World Religions," Spotlight on Theological Education 3, no. 1 (May 2009): viii; available at http://rsnonline.org/images/pdfs/2009MaySpotlightonTheologicalEducation.pdf.

academic exercise of critique. However, the strongest critique takes place not in a classroom but in seeking to identify with the oppressed—through solidarity. It is this lived-out exercise of discipleship that transforms perspective. In this relational dynamic our worldview collides with the lives of others, and we come to consider new viewpoints. Convictional experiences are needed to disrupt our previous assumptive world and puncture our previous ways of making meaning so that we can reground and realign our ways of seeing and being.[54]

Christian spirituality is meant to sustain our new life of discipleship through attentiveness to the Holy Spirit and participation in his initiatives. The *basileia*, the kingdom, is a communal initiative of the Spirit that emphasizes the corporate nature of our lives of faith. Covenant, the knitting together of those lives, is needed for forming and equipping a community whose character makes visible the gospel. If we are to learn and live in continued change, we need communities of support and accountability that allow us to reread the Scriptures with an eye for a new identity. This may commence as personal understanding but must move to a critical social consciousness that engenders a theology that inspires us to live the gospel through our actions in our local communities as we seek to transform injustice and alienation. Only the incorporation of commitment into concrete action will sustain transformational learning that becomes incarnational.

MISIÓN INTEGRAL: A THEOLOGY FOR RENEWED RELATIONSHIP

As they have articulated a theology of *misión integral*, Latin American theologians present a Christology of mission that offers an avenue for shifting our loyalties. It is based on the confession of Jesus as Lord or *Kyrios*.[55] The confession of Jesus as *Kyrios* is the recognition of his sovereignty over all of human life and all that works against that life and all of creation. To confess Jesus as Lord affirms that the reign of God is a present reality in our history, through the person and work of Jesus via the Holy Spirit. This theology provides a powerful critique of society that can move us to radical

---

[54]For further reading see James E. Loder, *The Transforming Moment: Understanding Convictional Experiences* (San Francisco: Harper & Row, 1981).
[55]See Tetsunao Yamamori and C. René Padilla, eds., *The Local Church, Agent of Transformation: An Ecclesiology for Integral Mission* (Buenos Aires: Ediciones Kairós, 2004).

discipleship as it calls for rejection of all ideologies/gods that do not represent the values of the *basileia* of Jesus, the *Kyrios*. Jesus invites disciples to participation in the world in order to proclaim the values of the gospel in their midst. It is what our young people are thirsting for and social entrepreneurs are attempting by funding endeavors that restore to the economy services and life-enhancing activities that offer equal access to all. This requires unraveling the images and values of other gods that oppose the values of the *basileia*.

Love, service, and the cross are the triad of this diaconal and prophetic communal living. These values demand the practice of mutual help, the confession of our sins, hospitality, and financial partnership with those who are in need. This is a picture of mission under a theology of *basileia* with Jesus as the *Kyrios* who is reconciling all things to himself (Col 1:19-20).

Mission as trinitarian redirects us. God is a triune God, Creator, Son, and Holy Spirit, a God in community and therefore a God of diversity within Godself. This relationship is called *perichoresis*. The term literally means "to dance around" and in Christian tradition became synonymous with interpenetration and interdependence. Jesus is in the Father as the Father is in him. Jesus, through the Holy Spirit, invites us to be in this community, this intimacy, this dance with the Father, and to invite others into community as well. We are invited to embody this understanding of community.

This is a profoundly incarnational epistemology because God is profoundly incarnational. God is present in human history, not only through the person of Christ but also through the Spirit who is present in the lives of people, particularly those who are invisible to us. "This understanding of God's presence, embodiment and diversity as imago Dei does not allow for anyone to be treated like a stranger, a foreign body in any space."[56] It does not allow for anyone to be treated as an inconvenience or an other to our policies or structures. It opens our eyes to the reality that institutions are to be sacred spaces for attention to the presence of God in others, a space where we may welcome a diversity of people to learn new things in new ways.

In this perichoretic dance, we internalize each other so that you are always present to me even when physically we are apart. You have changed

---

[56]Loida I. Martell-Otero, "From Foreign Bodies in Teacher Space," in *Teaching for a Culturally Diverse and Racially Just World*, ed. Eleazar S. Fernandez (Eugene, OR: Cascade Books, 2014), 64.

my world, and now I see it differently because I see it with you in it. Thus, when I am using my power, my privilege, I am compelled to make decisions about policies and take actions that advance the *basileia*. This understanding of your presence in me, *presencia*, means that "we are attuned to the value of people in the *communitas* because they are holy and are conduits of divine blessing for us all, even as we are conduits of blessings for the community."[57]

A significant element in mission is the preaching of the gospel. Missional preaching entails the proclamation of *dabar*, "word," the Hebrew notion of a word becoming reality as it is being pronounced. This concept is a part of the understanding of oral cultures. Literary cultures only see words as black-and-white symbols on a page. John, in his Gospel, describes God's great love, healing, and salvation for us by saying that the Word of God, the grace of God, became real in the person of Jesus: "the Word became flesh" (Jn 1:14). Preaching is not for stimulating minds so that the hearers can talk about it, process it, or comfort themselves with it. Preaching is intended to activate the love and grace of God to the poor in whatever condition they find themselves. If this love is to confront white supremacy, it must persevere in the practices of social critique, the study of the Word, prayer, and mission as justice—an incarnational Word.

Orlando Costas discusses proclamation as a sign of the kingdom of God:

> The kingdom is a symbol of God's transforming power of his determination to make "all things new" (Rev 21:5). The Kingdom of God stands for a new order of life. . . . This new order includes reconciliation with God, neighbor, and nature and therefore participation in a new world. It involves freedom from the power of sin and death. . . . It encompasses the hope of a more just and peaceful moral order. . . . It is a call to a vital engagement in the historical struggles for justice and peace.[58]

This signifies that the *kerygma* is more fully expressed when there is both a knowing dimension and a doing dimension. It is a witness through both words and deeds. No faithful proclamation can take place without an action that points toward the salvific activity of Jesus' death and resurrection.

[57]Martell-Otero, "From Foreign Bodies," 65.
[58]Orlando E. Costas, *The Integrity of Mission: The Inner Life and Outreach of the Church* (San Francisco: Harper & Row, 1979), 6.

Obedience to the ideal of the *basileia*, the lordship of Jesus, forced those who followed it into a profound identification with the interests of the poor and oppressed of society, those suffering from the ills of slavery. The strongest critique and missional gate toward the transformation of white supremacy is solidarity. Such missional proclamation motivates people to become involved in sharing the benefits they are receiving with others as subjects and not objects.

Biblically based mission is in harmony with the good news. Full understanding of the good news does not come to us except as we walk in the way, as we turn into action the words we have heard. When we are hearers as well as doers. We have full access to that word, and it activates the love and grace of God for those oppressed by white supremacy, both oppressors and oppressed. Biblically based mission is an enfleshed word, the place where we see the social performances of the Christian life as a countercultural stance, as witness to the *Kyrios* in all structures: government, the arts, media, education, the courts, and medicine, to name a few. Such a word becomes a movement, a force, the power of love as God is love, the *dynamis* that transforms.

This is not a lofty ideal. It has been carried out before. In the 1830s, Theodore Weld held the position of immediate abolition while others believed in gradual abolition and colonization. Weld entered Lane Theological Seminary in Cincinnati, Ohio, intending to introduce antislavery sentiments by having the whole subject thoroughly discussed. In the spring of 1834 he convinced fellow students to challenge others to an eighteen-day debate on the two positions. At the conclusion the students voted almost unanimously in favor of immediate abolitionism, and they organized an abolition society whose officers were all Southerners. The students worked with the Black residents of the city by conducting literacy classes, lectures on academic subjects, research regarding their financial and social problems, and Bible classes. Their most radical activity was treating the Black residents as their social equals.[59]

The students also started churches across the South and preached abolition. For this, some of them were lynched. They also rescued runaway

---

[59]For a full discussion see Donald W. Dayton with Douglas M. Strong, *Rediscovering an Evangelical Heritage: A Tradition and Trajectory of Integrating Piety and Justice*, 2nd ed. (Grand Rapids: Baker Academic, 2014), chap. 4.

enslaved persons from their captors by kidnapping the runaways and sending them off to freedom through the Underground Railroad. For this, the students went to jail. Eventually the students had to leave the seminary because they were banned from carrying doctrine into practical effect. A new institution was started that became known as a seedbed of radicalism. It was Oberlin College, which perpetuated the revivalism and social positions of Charles Finney, who refused to serve Communion to anyone who owned a slave because slave ownership was sin.

Where are the radical Christians today? Today we cannot simply express a concern for the topic of racism; we need a commitment. We can't just have a theology; we need motivation. We need to move from conversation to concrete witness and manifestations of the Spirit of God's love. From this point forward let us ask ourselves in the presence of God in prayer, What would God have us to do as we read this book so that the next conference that leads to new reading will be about the stories of the abolition of racism— our Christian witness to the glory of God?

6

Constructing Race in Puerto Rico

The Colonial Legacy of Christianity and Empires, 1510–1910

Angel D. Santiago-Vendrell

Puerto Rico has a long and contested history of race and racialization. As in missiology, where context shapes interpretations of reality based on understandings of God, Scripture, and human beings, issues of race are also contextually propagated and implemented.[1] This essay presents the concept of race as a process of exclusion based on biological, physical, cultural, and socioeconomic realities in Puerto Rico. First, it describes the history of the purity-of-blood statutes in Spain, which serves as the first step to understanding the concept of race in Puerto Rico. Second, I offer a description of how the concept of purity of blood was transformed in Puerto Rico to preserve social dominance based on the place of birth and traces of African or Amerindian blood. Third, I point out that when the United States took possession of Puerto Rico in 1898, the first Protestant missionaries encountered a different environment with regard to racial issues than the one they had back home. They were amazed at the mixing between the races, and, without understanding the deeper notions of race and class in the island, they praised Puerto Rico as a place where racism did not exist. Fourth, this essay offers a critique of the perpetuation of racism based on notions of sameness

---

[1]Clara E. Rodríguez and Hector Cordero-Guzmán, "Placing Race in Context," in *Rethinking the Color Line: Readings in Race and Ethnicity*, ed. Charles A. Gallagher, 3rd ed. (Boston: McGraw-Hill, 2007), 85-91.

constructed around terms such as *Mestizaje* and *Mulatez,* which operate as central images in US Hispanic/Latinx theology. Finally, it offers missiological reflection based on a theology of evangelism represented by the inbreaking power of the Holy Spirit that denounces racism as the original sin of the United States.

PURITY-OF-BLOOD LAWS IN SPAIN

We have to go back in history to understand the racialization of Puerto Rican society. Scholars have argued, for good or bad, that the mixing of races is the foundation of Puerto Rican identity, which starts at the nexus of Spanish colonial power, the church, and the Taino population.[2] The annexation of the kingdom of Granada with Castilla, accomplished by the marriage of Ferdinand and Isabella in 1469, played a crucial political role in the formation of what is known today as Spain. The *Reconquista* (War of Reconquest) was spiritualized with an aspiration to the universal kingship of Christ. The chroniclers of the king's court interpreted the events as providential signs of the grace of God to the kings, and the events represented the political war as a battle to implement the Christian faith. Thus, the War of Reconquest had both a secular and a religious dimension: on the one hand, it was an armed movement of expansion in search of wealth, and on the other hand, it was a religious holy crusade against the ideological-religious enemy of Islam.

Despite the importance of these events, recent scholarship on the social and economic history of Spain has debunked this traditional approach. Instead of recognizing the political importance of 1492, which symbolized the union of the kingdom, the expulsion of the Jews and later of the Moors, and the discovery of the New World by Christopher Columbus, historians are proposing an approach that reveals the creative tension and continuity

---

[2]For more on Puerto Rican identity, see Maritza Quiñones Rivera, "From *Trigeñita* to Afro-Puerto Rican: Intersections of the Racialized, Gendered, and Sexualized Body in Puerto Rico and the U.S. Mainland," *Meridians: Feminism, Race, Transnationalism* 7, no. 1 (2006): 162-82; Eric Williams, "Race Relations in Puerto Rico and the Virgin Islands," in *Portrait of a Society: Readings in Puerto Rican Sociology,* ed. Eugenio Fernández Méndez (Río Piedras: University of Puerto Rico Press, 1972), 39-47; Maxine W. Gordon, "Race Patterns and Prejudice in Puerto Rico," *American Sociological Review* 14, no. 2 (April 1945): 294-301; and Alan West-Durán, "Puerto Rico: The Pleasures and Traumas of Race," *Centro Journal* 17, no. 1 (Spring 2005): 47-69.

between the Middle Ages and the modern period.[3] In this transition between the Middle Ages and modernity, one aspect that guided Spain was the concept of purity of blood. Spain adhered to statutes about purity of blood, which originally served as a mechanism to exclude converted Jews from participating in important positions in government and in ecclesiastical positions. In other words, color was not the main element in racial identity but religious difference; Spaniards were more intent on excluding people on the basis of their Jewish heritage. In actuality, the purity statutes were directed mostly toward *conversos* (Jewish converts to Christianity).[4]

The zeal of the Roman Catholic Church on the Iberian Peninsula against the Jews dates back to the fourth century when, in the Council of Elvira, Spanish ecclesiastics tried to protect Christians from Jewish contamination. The Roman Catholic Church referred primarily to the Bible and the church fathers in constructing the statutes about purity of blood. After more than ten centuries of sporadically returning to the topic of anti-Judaism, by the fourteen century it was firmly established in Iberian society.[5]

The Bible narrates many events based on the genealogical linage of its protagonists. For example, Genesis 4 conveys the story of Adam and Eve and their sons; Genesis 5 traces the genealogy of Adam through Noah and his sons; Genesis 9 expands on the story of Noah and his sons; and Genesis 10 presents the table of nations listing the Japhethites, the Hamites, and the Semites and culminates in Genesis 11 with the genealogies from Shem to Abram. In the New Testament the ancestors of Jesus of Nazareth are presented in the Gospels of Matthew and Luke in two different genealogies. The Catholic Church in Spain used the Bible's admonitions regarding transmission of sins from the parents to their children to the third and fourth generation (Ex 20:5; 34:7; Num 14:18; Deut 5:9) to construct the statutes about purity of blood in an attempt to tag Jews for exclusion and

[3]Marcel Bataillon, *Erasmo y España: estudios sobre la historia espiritual del siglo XVI* (México: Fondo de Cultura Económica, 1950); William A. Christian Jr., *Local Religion in Sixteenth-Century Spain* (Princeton, NJ: Princeton University Press, 1981); Helen Rawlings, *Church, Religion and Society in Early Modern Spain* (New York: Palgrave, 2002); and Teofilo F. Ruiz, *Spanish Society, 1400–1600* (Harlow, UK: Pearson Education, 2001).
[4]Albert A. Sicroff, *Los estatutos de limpieza de sangre: controversias entre los siglos XV y XVII* (Madrid: Taurus, 1979), 43. Jewish converts to Christianity were also called *Cristiano nuevo, converso,* and many other derogatory names such as *marrano, confeso,* and *maculado.*
[5]Sicroff, *Los estatutos,* 45.

persecution. Finally, they used Matthew 27:25, "Then the people as a whole answered, 'His blood is on us and on our children!'" to show the presumed eternal guilt of Jews for killing Jesus.[6] The Bible, when using genealogical materials, presents a narrative that mingles biological and moral issues.

The church fathers also had conflicting views on human sexuality, sin, and morality. An example of this presumed correlation between sexuality, sin, and morality can be seen best in Augustine of Hippo. According to Justo González, for Augustine "the result of original sin is that it involves all humanity as a mass of perdition subjugated to death, ignorance, and concupiscence."[7] Concupiscence, as argued by Augustine, is mostly expressed in sexual intercourse because as fallen beings humans are incapable of having sex without objectifying the other person. For Augustine, even marriage was no more than a device to control lust, and concupiscence was transmitted to every child born in the world. With this biblical and theological rationale, Spaniards saw Jewish people as disciples of an irrational doctrine, without an exit from sin and condemned for eternity for killing Jesus of Nazareth, the savior of the world.[8]

Zeal for the Christian religion was not the only factor in persecuting Jews; political and economic capital also played a role. In a hierarchical society in which honor was derived from lineage, occupation, and property of land, honor operated as symbolic and actual power. Therefore, it should be guarded and protected, especially against Jews, Muslims, and heretics. According to Hering Torres, in the fourteenth century there were many anti-Jewish decrees in the Courts of Zamora (1301), Valladolid (1322), Madrid (1329), and the Council of Salamanca (1335); all took away the control of the financial system that was run by Jews.[9] This animosity against the Jews for their financial and political capital culminated in a great persecution in Sevilla in June 1391, in which thousands were killed and their properties confiscated. The persecution spread like wild fire to Cordoba and to the north, and by August the majority of the provinces in Iberia were

---

[6]John Edwards, "Race and Religion in 15th and 16th Century Spain: The Purity of Blood Laws Revisited," *Proceedings of the World Congress of Jewish Studies* 1, no. 2 (1989): 159-66.

[7]Justo L. González, *Historia del pensamiento cristiano* (Miami: Editorial Caribe, 1992), 2:46.

[8]Max S. Hering Torres, "La limpieza de sangre: Problemas de interpretación: acercamientos históricos y metodológicos," *Historia Crítica* 45 (September-December 2011): 32-55.

[9]Torres, "La limpieza de sangre," 36.

complicit in persecuting Jews by killing them and taking their possessions. After the persecution of 1391, Jews converted to Christianity en masse. It is estimated that just in Valencia one hundred thousand Jews converted to Christianity in order to escape the slaughter and pillage of their properties.[10]

Conversion to Christianity to survive the persecution and preserve their possessions initiated an assimilation process that allowed new converts to take part again in all aspects of social, cultural, economic, and religious life as new Christians.[11] The otherness of the Jews that was visible through their clothing, religious celebrations, customs, dietary rules, and housing disappeared from sight. However, such invisibility meant that many of the religious practices, dietary rules, and customs continued to exist in secret. María Elena Martínez points out, "The issue of identifying 'authentic' versus 'false' Christians produced a great deal of commotion within several institutions, especially some of the religious orders, and by the mid-fifteenth century it was feeding suspicions that the new converts were threatening to undermine the faith."[12] As *conversos* were gaining positions of power, rumors of crypto-Jews (*conversos* who continued to practice Judaism in secret) multiplied, prompting the Catholic rulers Ferdinand and Isabel to implement the Inquisition in Castile.[13] Therefore, a new legal definition to identify the new converts (*conversos*) emerged, giving prominence to their past or origin, which was traceable through bloodlines.

The first law passed in Toledo in 1449 when the constable of the town stated "that all the aforesaid converts descendants of the perverse lineage of the Jews, in whatever guise this may be should be held, as the law has and holds them, as infamous, unable, incapable, and unworthy to have any public and private benefice and office in the city of Toledo."[14] The main argument of the statutes of blood was that in the blood of the new converts, despite their conversion to Christianity, remained the seed of indecency, immorality, and heresy. Thus they could not be trusted in their claims of

---

[10]Sicroff, *Los estatutos de limpieza de sangre*, 45-47.

[11]María Elena Martínez, "Interrogating Blood Lines: Purity of Blood, the Inquisition, and *Casta* Categories in Early Colonial Mexico," in *Religion in New Spain*, ed. Susan Schroeder and Stafford Poole (Albuquerque: University of New Mexico Press, 2007), 196-217.

[12]Martínez, "Interrogating Blood Lines," 197.

[13]Martínez, "Interrogating Blood Lines," 198.

[14]Quoted in Edwards, "Race and Religion in 15th and 16th Century Spain," 159.

conversion to Christianity. On this foundation the statutes about purity of blood were solidified from the fifteenth to the eighteenth century.[15]

THE TRANSFORMATION OF THE PURITY-OF-BLOOD STATUTES IN EARLY COLONIAL PUERTO RICO

There is a growing consensus among historians that Black slaves and freed Blacks were introduced to the New World very early in the explorations of the conquistadors.[16] The first Blacks to arrive in the New World came not from Africa but from Seville. Black, Moorish, and Morisco slaves and freedmen in Seville were part of those first expeditions to the New World.[17] The life of slaves in Seville was difficult as they were exploited for profit. Many times slave owners depended completely on the work of slaves for their daily living. To complicate matters, slaves were not allowed to work in many occupations, adding to the city's unskilled working force.[18] On the other hand, the lot of Black freedmen was not better. Pike states, "Enfranchisement was not a step toward economic and social betterment for Negroes, and mulattoes remained on the lower rungs of the social ladder, whether slaves or freedmen."[19] Facing many difficulties in Seville, some Black freedmen saw the opportunity for a new beginning in the New World.[20]

Christopher Columbus "discovered" Boriquen and named it San Juan Bautista in his second voyage to the New World but paid little attention to the island. It was not until August 12, 1508, that Juan Ponce de León began the

---

[15]Martínez, "Interrogating Blood Lines," 197-202; Hering Torres, "La limpieza de sangre," 37-48; and Sicroff, *Los estatutos de limpieza de sangre,* 51-347. For the argument about *limpieza de sangre* at the end of the nineteenth century and the beginning of the twentieth century, see Joshua Goode, *Impurity of Blood: Defining Race in Spain, 1870–1930* (Baton Rouge: Louisiana State University Press, 2009).

[16]R. R. Wright, "Negro Companions of the Spanish Explorers," *American Anthropologist* 4, no. 2 (1902): 217-28; Peter Gerhard, "A Black Conquistador in Mexico," *Hispanic American Historical Review* 58, no. 3 (August 1978): 451-59; Matthew Restall, "Black Conquistadors: Armed Africans in Early Spanish America," *Americas* 57, no. 2 (October 2000): 171-205; and Jalil Sued Badillo and Ángel López Cantos, *Puerto Rico Negro* (Río Piedras, PR: Editorial Cultural, 1986).

[17]Ruth Pike, "Sevillian Society in the Sixteenth Century: Slaves and Freedmen," *Hispanic American Historical Review* 47, no. 3 (1967): 344-59. Pike argues, "People usually referred to Moorish and Morisco slaves as *esclavos blancos* [white slaves]. The Moors were most often North African prisoners of war; the Moriscos came from Granada" (344).

[18]Pike, "Sevillian Society," 353.

[19]Pike, "Sevillian Society," 356.

[20]Sued Badillo and López Cantos, *Puerto Rico Negro,* 17-18; Pike, "Sevillian Society in the Sixteenth Century," 358.

colonial enterprise in San Juan Bautista. Born in 1460 into a noble family in
Santervás, Valladolid, Spain, Ponce de León served as an assistant in the royal
court of Aragon. He later became a soldier, fighting in the Spanish campaign
against the Moors in Granada and distinguished himself in the wars against
the natives of Hispaniola. Because of his skills as a soldier, Ponce de León was
appointed by Governor Nicolás de Ovando to be a lieutenant of Juan Esquivel,
who was engaged in pacifying the province of Higuey in Hispaniola. It was at
Higuey that Ponce de León learned about the natives of San Juan who came
to trade with the Spaniards.[21] In that first voyage to San Juan Bautista, Ponce
de León was accompanied by fifty conquistadors, among them a freed Black
man named Juan Garrido and a Mulatto named Francisco Mexia.

According to Matthew Restal, "wherever Spaniards set foot in the
Americas as members of conquest companies they were accompanied by
black conquistadors."[22] Most of the historiography of Blacks in the New
World can be found in concentrated form in the story of Juan Garrido.[23]
There is an account of Garrido's *probanza* (proof of merit) to the king dated
September 27, 1538, that claimed:

> I, Juan Garrido, black in color of this city, says he of his own free will, became
> a Christian in Lisbon, was in Castile for seven years, and crossed to Santo
> Domingo where he remained an equal length of time. From there he visited
> other islands, and then went to San Juan de Puerto Rico, where he spent much
> time, after which he came to New Spain, appeared before Your Majesty and
> stated that I am in need of making a *probanza* to the perpetuity of the king, a
> report on how I served Your Majesty in the conquest and pacification of New
> Spain, from the time that the Marqués del Valle entered it; and in his company
> I was present at all the invasions and conquests and pacifications which were
> carried out, always with the said Marqués, all that I did at my own expense
> without being given either a salary or allotment of natives or anything else.[24]

Another of Ponce de León's companions, the free Mulatto Francisco
Mexia, was born free after his parents obtained their freedom by buying it

[21]R. A. Van Middeldyk, *The History of Puerto Rico* (New York: Arno Press, 1975), 18.
[22]Restall, "Black Conquistadors," 175.
[23]Ricardo E. Alegría, *Juan Garrido: el conquistador negro en las Antillas, Florida, México y California
c. 1503–1540* (San Juan, PR: Centro de Estudios Avanzados de Puerto Rico y el Caribe, 1990);
Restall, "Black Conquistadors"; and Gerhard, "Black Conquistador in Mexico."
[24]Alegría, *Juan Garrido*, 6. Author's translation.

or working toward it with their previous master. Nicolás de Ovando recruited both Francisco and his freed father Anton Mexia in Seville. Anton was married to a woman named Violante Gómez. There are no references to Violante's life, but it could be assumed that she was a *Morisca* (White slave) or a White Spaniard since Anton was Black and Francisco Mulatto. According to Ruth Pike, Black and White slaves had friendly relations in Seville where "miscegenation and common-law unions were frequent" and even "members of the clergy maintained illicit relations with female households slaves, and in some instances recognized their illegitimate children."[25] It would appear that Anton and Violante acquired their freedom in 1485. In that year they looked for the services of a lawyer, which was the custom of newly freedmen and freedwomen, to take care of their paperwork and defend their freedom in any case against them. It seems that Anton was the assistant of a crossbowman in Hispaniola named Juan Mexia and was paid thirty-five maradevies per year. Sued Badillo and López Cantos argue that probably Juan Mexia was Anton's master back in Seville and freed him from servitude. It was not uncommon that after slaves were freed they continued to serve the interest of their previous master, and "many accompanied their former masters to the new world as servants."[26]

For his part, Francisco decided to accompany Ponce de León in the colonization of San Juan Bautista in 1508. He worked for Ponce de León as a supervisor of his *encomienda* of natives working in the mines, and in the gold smelting of 1511 he registered for Ponce de León seven hundred thirty pieces of gold. He also worked for the crown, picking Natives to work in the mines for a regular salary of fifty pesos of gold a year.[27] Alegría points out, "Men, woman, and children were forced to work long hours digging gold from the mines and washing it in the rivers."[28] In 1513 the ill treatment of the natives precipitated a great rebellion against the Spaniards but also against the *caciques* that were helping the Spaniards by offering natives to work in the mines. When Francisco was picking natives from the tribe of *cacica*

[25]Pike, "Sevillian Society," 357.
[26]Pike, "Sevillian Society," 358.
[27]Sued Badillo and López Cantos, *Puerto Rico Negro*, 20.
[28]Ricardo E. Alegría, *Discovery, Conquest and Colonization of Puerto Rico, 1493–1599*, 2nd ed. (Río Piedras, PR: Colección de Estudios Puertorriqueños, 1983), 49.

Luisa, the native liberators burned the village, killing her and Francisco.[29] The lives of Anton and Francisco Mexia and Juan Garrido are important for several reasons because, notwithstanding some discrimination, they were able to enjoy some privileges like bearing arms and owning investments. However, this racial accommodation changed in the second half of the sixteenth century with the mass introduction of African slaves.

During the second half of the sixteenth century, White colonizers reacted against freed Blacks by limiting their opportunities and privileges in society. As in Spain, freedmen were excluded from practicing certain jobs such as gilders, hatters, silk spinners, chandlers, or painters.[30] Another sector in which Black freedmen were excluded was in the military. Stories like those of Francisco Anton and Juan Garrido ceased to exist, and by 1573 there were no Black freedmen enlisted in the military or allowed to carry weapons.[31] Now the same restrictions that were enforced in Spain against *judeo-conversos*, as well as practicing Jews, were also taking shape according to racial indicatives—free Blacks were not distinguished from Black slaves.

During the first decade of the conquest of Puerto Rico, Black slaves were mostly introduced as domestic servers to the conquistadors, who probably brought them from Spain. At this early stage of colonization, Natives were populous; nonetheless, as the Native population began to shrink due to fatalities from the intense work, and laborers were needed to work in the mines, Black slaves took their place.[32] According to Stark, based on Governor Francisco Manuel de Lando's census, "by 1530, Africans comprised 2284 or 69% of the island's enslaved laborers, while Amerindians accounted for the remaining 1043 or 31%."[33] Luis Rivera-Pagán states, "when the conquistadors came to the Indies, there were approximately 100,000 Amerindians; by 1570, the population was barely 500."[34]

---

[29]Sued Badillo and López Cantos, *Puerto Rico Negro*, 21. A *cacique* or *cacica* was the chief of a particular tribe. In Puerto Rico there were female *cacicas*, as the case of Luisa indicates.

[30]Sued Badillo and López Cantos, *Puerto Rico Negro*, 47.

[31]Sued Badillo and López Cantos, *Puerto Rico Negro*, 39.

[32]David M. Stark, "A New Look at the African Slave Trade in Puerto Rico Through the Use of Parish Registers: 1660–1815," *Slavery and Abolition* 30, no. 4 (December 2009): 491-520.

[33]Stark, "New Look," 493.

[34]Luis Rivera-Pagán, *Evangelización y violencia: la conquista de América* (San Juan, PR: Editorial CEMI, 1990), 289.

Not only did the Amerindian population decline drastically at the end of the sixteenth century, but also African slaves declined from approximately fifteen thousand to a low of five thousand to six thousand slaves by 1594. There are several reasons for the decline of the African slave population: in some cases slave owners moved to more lucrative endeavors in Mexico and Peru and took their African slaves with them; in other cases African slaves were sent to Cuba to work on military fortifications; and third, runaway slaves escaped to the interior of the island accompanied by Amerindians.[35]

Two major players in the mass introduction of African slaves into Puerto Rico were the Roman Catholic Church and the Spanish monarchy, who were both deeply complicit in organizing the social infrastructure of Puerto Rico by introducing African slaves. According to Rivera-Pagán,

> To affirm . . . that the discovery-encounter quickly became domination and conquest does not solve the fundamental question of the goals and objectives of its Spanish protagonists. It is not sufficient, either, to point out the obvious *colonization* process that transferred to the New World Spanish settlers who exploited its natural riches to benefit the metropolis. Certainly, material interests were there from the beginning. . . .
>
> But the principal participants in the debate about the conquest pointed to another objective that was of a religious and transcendental nature: the Christianization of the new lands and towns.[36]

The principal objective presented was the conversion of the natives. Evangelization was the theoretical banner that the Spanish state waved during the conquest, and Christian religion became the official ideology for imperial expansion. The epistemological role of Catholic religious ideas in the colonization of the Americas is well illustrated by the *bula* of Pope Alexander VI, *Inter caetera* (1493). This *bula* established the donation from the pope to the Spanish crown in perpetuity of the lands already discovered and those discovered in the future. According to Rivera-Pagán, "the evangelization of the natives has an important political consequence. The missionary task implies political hegemony. The effective Christianization of

---

[35]Ángel G. Quintero Rivera, "Cultura en el Caribe: la cimarronería como herencia y utopía," *Estudios Sociales Centroamericanos* 54 (September-December 1990): 85-99.

[36]Luis N. Rivera-Pagán, *A Violent Evangelism: The Political and Religious Conquest of America* (Louisville, KY: Westminster John Knox, 1992), 24.

the discovered lands becomes the juridical-theological foundation for the donation in perpetuity of political authority."[37] The same rationalization to evangelize the Native peoples as a way to compensate for their miserable condition as slaves and bring them from darkness to the light of the Roman Catholic Church was used with Black slaves. Hence, as the slave trade developed, the church had no option but to defend slavery in the New World as a divine prerogative to save the souls of those they enslaved.

In the first two centuries of the conquest of Puerto Rico, many cases of miscegenation took place among various ethnoracial groups. Spaniards took Indigenous, *Morisca*, and Black women as concubines, and African freedmen and runaway slaves also took Indigenous women as wives and concubines. Ileana Rodríguez-Silva points out, "Although Spanish origins and whiteness were prized commodities to secure a place in the upper strata of society, people frequently transgressed racial boundaries."[38] However, the amalgamation of the races did not create a better society, which was always ruled by White elites because for them racial impurity disqualified individuals from citizenship and responsibilities.[39] As in the case of the purity-of-blood statutes used to exclude *judeo-conversos*, now the litmus test for exclusion would be based on the taint of an individual's Black or Indigenous blood.

Whitening was the most effective route to acquire the honor and privileges of the White ruling elites. *Hay que mejorar la raza* (we have to improve the race) was a common statement that still persists today in Puerto Rican society. Whitening was accomplished through marriage or illicit relationships, as White came to represent honor, prestige, and social standing. The fruits of this process would not be available to the first generation, but with time the process of whitening would provide future generations with a new identity rooted in becoming White. However, already in 1765, the prelate of San Juan Mariano Martí affirmed "it was difficult to discern in that city because of the mixing between the races who was white and who was mulatto, as they share the same women."[40] For this reason, Mulattos were despised even more than Blacks by the White elites since they represented

---

[37]Rivera-Pagán, *Evangelización y violencia*, 48-49.
[38]Ileana M. Rodríguez-Silva, *Silencing Race: Disentangling Blackness, Colonialism, and National Identities in Puerto Rico* (New York: Palgrave Macmillan, 2012), 22.
[39]Rodríguez-Silva, *Silencing Race*, 22.
[40]Quoted in Sued Badillo and López Cantos, *Puerto Rico Negro*, 259.

the closest threat to the White hegemony of the elites of Puerto Rican society. One of the major players to police or prevent mixed marriages was
the Roman Catholic Church. In 1739, Bishop Pérez Lozano promulgated an
edict arguing:

> That no marriages should be dispatched to unequal persons as white with
> mulattoes as I have observed since being appointed to this bishopric, moti-
> vated to this prohibition by the families that are in this city that can obtain
> the offices in the government and military and between clerics and Friars, as
> had happened by marriages between mulattoes with the whites elites, and
> even blacks with white women, that the republic would be left without persons
> of distinction to occupy such jobs.[41]

Even though Sued Badillo and López Cantos present a picture in which
racial mixing or *Mestizaje* was a harmonious occurrence among distinct
racial conglomerates, miscegenation was something that White elites despised and guarded against at all costs through governmental policies,
church edicts, and the plantation economic regime. These processes were
clearly articulated by White elites in the late eighteenth century through
the nineteenth century and even after emancipation (1873), when the
boom of the sugar industry demanded a new work force constituted by
African slaves and the absorption of freedmen.[42] According to Rodríguez-
Silva, "slavery in Puerto Rico had such an appeal that even some committed abolitionist liberals found ways to reconcile slavery with liberal
modernity."[43] For the abolitionists, the slave population could gain their
right to be productive citizens and free individuals if they treasured their
new status after emancipation and became not just producers of wealth
but also consumers.

The abolitionist paradigm gave space to personal reform and moral uplift
in spite of the color of their skin but never as equals in class or race. In a
postslavery society, abolitionists thought that former slaves would be
grateful to their colonial masters for granting their freedom. For example,
abolitionist Segundo Ruiz Belvis pointed out,

---

[41]Quoted in Sued Badillo and López Cantos, *Puerto Rico Negro*, 281.
[42]Rodríguez-Silva, *Silencing Race*, 22-25.
[43]Rodríguez-Silva, *Silencing Race*, 23.

Once a slave is freed, no matter how perverted and lowly we believe they are, once a slave recognizes that they are indebted to us because of the great gift of freedom—because for him freedom is a bequest not the realization of their right, once he realizes that he is free to be with his family and has ownership over his labor and property, he surely will forget the indignities he had suffered. What is the ultimate goal of emancipating a slave? To give them back their personhood and their inalienable rights, it is to rescue him from arbitrary domination and transform him into a dignified man and citizen.[44]

The discourse of gratitude by liberal abolitionists was flavored with an inherent paternalism for the masses demonstrated through their perceptions of the other as childish and in need of tutelage. Some of this paternalism was directed at the racial composition of freedmen after emancipation, depicting them in terms of their blackness, immorality, and poor health while liberal elites emphasized their whiteness, good health, and sexual restraint.[45] Rodríguez-Silva points out, "At a moment in which most imperial politicians equated blackness with instability and destruction, particularly in the Caribbean, Puerto Rican liberals sought to represent themselves and the island population as white and hence harmonious and stable."[46]

A New Empire, a New Religion, and a New Understanding of Race

When General Nelson Miles arrived on the coast of Guanica, Puerto Rico, in 1898, he said, "We have not come to make war upon the people of a country that for centuries has been oppressed, but on the contrary, to bring you protection, to promote your prosperity, and to bestow upon you the immunities and blessings of the liberal institutions of our government."[47] In a surprise to Puerto Ricans, on August 12, 1898, the Treaty of Paris officially ceded Puerto Rico and Guam to the United States while Cuba gained its independence.[48] Within eighteen months, the US Congress passed the

---

[44]Segundo Ruiz Belvis, *Projecto para la abolición de la esclavitud en Puerto Rico* (1867), quoted in Rodríguez-Silva, *Silencing Race*, 37.

[45]Ruiz Belvis, *Projecto para la abolición*, 61-64.

[46]Ruiz Belvis, *Projecto para la abolición*, 65.

[47]General Nelson Miles, quoted in Mario Murillo, *Islands of Resistance: Puerto Rico, Vieques, and U.S. Policy* (New York: Seven Stories Press, 2001), 9.

[48]Murillo, *Islands of Resistance*, 25

Foraker Act, making Puerto Rico the first unincorporated territory of the United States.[49] According to Manuel Maldonado-Denis, the United States envisioned Puerto Rico as one of its new territories, part of its attempt to expand its markets and control the Caribbean militarily.[50] Puerto Rico thus became the first colony of the United States, initiating a process by which the island became an object of the political, economic, cultural, and ideological apparatus of the United States.

Together with the new imperial power came Protestant missionaries from all denominations, who saw the new mission fields as ready to harvest using the Protestant version of the gospel. William Hutchison argued that in the period from 1880 to 1910, North American missionary efforts were directed by a postmillennial theology that saw civilization as a primary element in mission practice.[51] A contemporary editorial of the *Missionary Review of the World* read, "The momentous war with Spain seems destined to cause changes in the policy of the United States, and to greatly influence our future. It also already gives evidence of being the means of furthering the progress of the Kingdom of God on earth."[52] Another editorial read, "The present war with Spain has an important religious and missionary bearing. The government of Spain has denied to her colonies religious as well as civil liberty, and has kept them in moral darkness, as well as in material depression."[53] In this regard, the Methodist Episcopal Church compared "the nation's success with the will of God, and Manifest Destiny was equated to the providence of God."[54]

One of the most vocal theological proponents of US expansionism and Protestantism as civilization was Josiah Strong. Strong was the General Secretary of the Mission Society of the Congregational Church. In 1885 he

[49]Murillo, *Islands of Resistance*, 30.

[50]Manuel Maldonado-Denis, *Puerto Rico: una interpretación histórico-social*, 8th ed. (Coyoacán, Mex.: Siglo Veintiuno Editores, 1988), 65.

[51]William R. Hutchison, "A Moral Equivalent for Imperialism: Americans and the Promotion of Christian Civilization," in *Missionary Ideologies in the Imperialistic Era: 1880–1920*, ed. Torben Christensen and William R. Hutchison (Aarhus, Denmark: Aros Press, 1982), 167-77.

[52]J. T. Gracey, D. L. Leonard, and F. B. Meyer, "Editorial Department," *Missionary Review of the World* 11, no. 9 (September 1898): 698.

[53]Missionary Digest Department, "Spanish Rule in the Philippine Islands," *Missionary Review of the World* 11, no. 6 (July 1898): 520.

[54]Kenneth M. McKenzie, *The Robe and the Sword: The Methodist Church and the Rise of American Imperialism* (Washington, DC: Public Affairs Press, 1961), 31.

published what was to become a famous book, titled *Our Country, Its Possible Future and Its Present Crisis*. Strong interpreted the conditions in the United States as playing a major role in world history, and he understood the providence of God to be guiding the United States to establish the kingdom of God on earth.[55] Strong believed that men of that generation in the United States (1890s) would determine the course of the future of humanity.[56] He proposed that the progress of Christ's kingdom in the world for centuries to come depended on the actions of American Christians in that decade.

Strong's perception of the Anglo-Saxon race as superior and as having a divine command to Americanize or civilize the world played a crucial role in the imperialist discourse of American expansionism. The theme of white supremacy was present in all his theology, which represented the Darwinian position of "the survival of the fittest."[57] He wrote: "Some of the strongest races, doubtless, may be able to preserve their integrity; but, in order to compete with the Anglo-Saxon, they will probably be forced to adopt his methods and instruments, his civilization and religion."[58]

Strong's attitude of superiority dominated the encounter between Anglo-American missionaries and Puerto Ricans and was corroborated by many missionaries. Among them was Howard B. Grose, who pointed out,

> The Anglo-Saxon is superior in initiative and resourcefulness. The Latin knows the Anglo-Saxon methods as different from his, and also superior. Whatever his air of courtesy, however graciously he may seem to accept the inevitable, deep down there is a race barrier, that had yet never been overcome. Many students of the races think it never can be; all that he can hope for is a peaceable and friendly and mutually serviceable *modus vivendi*.[59]

---

[55]Josiah Strong, *Our Country, Its Possible Future and Its Present Crisis* (New York: American Home Missionary Society, 1885).

[56]Even though the missionary movement was characterized by many single women missionaries, Strong's language pointed to the masculinity of colonization and the exclusion of female missionaries. For a history of single female missionaries, see Dana L. Robert, *American Women in Mission: A Social History of Their Thought and Practice; The Modern Missionary Era, 1792–1992* (Macon, GA: Mercer University Press, 1997). For single female missionaries to Korea, see Misoon Im, "The Role of Single Women Missionaries of the Methodist Episcopal Church, South, in Korea, 1897–1940" (ThD diss., Boston University School of Theology, 2008).

[57]Richard Hofstadter, *Social Darwinism in American Thought* (Boston: Beacon Press, 1955), 170-200.

[58]Strong, *Our Country*, 176.

[59]Howard B. Grose, *Adventures in the Antilles* (New York: Presbyterian Home Missions, 1910), 211.

It is interesting to notice that Protestant missionaries also employed the same descriptive discourse against Blacks and Mulattos that White Creole elites used against that group. For example, in 1765, the prelate of San Juan Mariano Martí affirmed how difficult it was to differentiate who was White or Black because of the population's amalgamation. In comparison, Grose stated that "Porto Ricans are more homogeneous than Cubans and . . . there is no distinct color line, nor can be one drawn."[60]

One thing that both White Creole elites and Protestant missionaries shared was the exclusion of Blacks from those they designated Puerto Rican. Creole White elites wanted to present the island as harmonious, stable, and industrious by affirming their whiteness and excluding any Black element in their discourses.[61] Protestant missionaries were also affirming their whiteness by excluding blackness and denying the whiteness of the Creole elites. Grose pointed out, "You may find much to attract in the cities, but you will remember longest the country scenery and the welcomes you received from those who are classed as *jíbaros*. There is no better blood in the island that flows in the veins of many of these descendants of the Indians and Spanish."[62] For Grose and many missionaries, the African element was erased in their evaluation of the interior of the island. In defining Puerto Rican identity, Protestant missionaries saw only two streams of blood coming from the Indians and Spaniards while ignoring the vast majority of the population that was Black and Mulatto, just as Creole elites had in the nineteenth century.[63]

However, even the Spaniards were not recognized as of pure blood. Protestant missionaries noted that even among the "best families" in San Juan

[60]Grose, *Adventures in the Antilles*, 177.

[61]Rodríguez-Silva, *Silencing Race*, 59-90.

[62]Grose, *Adventures in the Antilles*, 189.

[63]Grose, *Adventures in the Antilles*, 177; George Milton Fowles, *Down in Porto Rico* (New York: Young People's Missionary Movement of the United States and Canada, 1910), 22; and S. S. Hough, "Porto Rico," in *Our Foreign Missionary Enterprise: United Brethren Mission Study Course* (Dayton, OH: United Brethren Publishing House, 1908), 171-215. J. Merle Davis, *The Church in Puerto Rico's Dilemma* (New York: International Missionary Council, 1942), 8, pointed out, "The typical family was white and consisted of five to seven members." R. A. Van Middeldyk, *The History of Puerto Rico, from the Spanish Discovery to the American Occupation* (New York: Young People's Missionary Movement of the United States and Canada, 1910), 215, wrote: "It has been impossible to ascertain in what degree they became amalgamated by intermarriage with the conquerors; yet, that it has been to a larger degree than generally supposed, is proved by the fact that many of the inhabitants, classed as white, have, both in their features and manners, definite traces of the Indian race."

the majority of them were of mixed blood. George Milton Fowles, a missionary with the Methodist Episcopal Church, wrote a book for the Young People's Missionary Movement of the United States and Canada, in which he affirmed: "The whites of Porto Rico must be considered in an entirely different sense from European and North American whites. They represent a genus of their own, the Porto Rican whites."[64]

American Protestant missionaries to Puerto Rico, by distancing themselves as a superior White race, were using the same social Darwinism that the Creole elites used to distance themselves from the Black and Mulatto population. In the same manner, by such distancing and denying the whiteness of Creole elites, Protestant missionaries established themselves as superior beings. As superior beings, White Protestant missionaries erased any claim of European whiteness for White Creole elites and treated them and all Puerto Ricans as children in need of tutelage. For example, for Fowles the verbal and nonverbal expressions of Puerto Ricans were disturbing. He pointed out, "In the plazas where they gather in groups of two or more, instead of a quiet and friendly conversation, you soon hear every group talking in high and loud tones, so that the plaza sounds like a school yard for children."[65] This habit of speaking loudly was learned from the Spaniards, who trained Puerto Ricans to be "as light-hearted and irresponsible as a set of children."[66] Fowles's position on what constituted a Puerto Rican went further than Grose's by not even including the Amerindian in his assessment. Fowles pointed out, "The Porto Ricans being chiefly of Spanish descent or having being closely associated with Spaniards, have many of the general characteristics of the Latin race."[67]

Such characterization of Puerto Ricans gave Protestant missionaries and the US government incentive to deny them true citizenship. This was clearly seen in the Insular Cases. The Insular Cases were a series of Supreme Court opinions in 1901 about the status of the newly acquired territories after the Spanish-American War. In the opinions of the Supreme Court, Puerto Ricans were considered an alien race incapable of understanding

---

[64]Fowles, *Down in Porto Rico*, 22.
[65]Fowles, *Down in Porto Rico*, 47.
[66]Fowles, *Down in Porto Rico*, 48.
[67]Fowles, *Down in Porto Rico*, 46.

Anglo-Saxon law, thus not able to be citizens because they were mongrels.[68] Protestant missionaries and the governmental establishment seized on this characterization on the political grounds that Puerto Ricans needed supervision, nurturing, and guidance and embraced the characterization of Puerto Ricans as children. Charles S. Detweiler, a Baptist missionary, pointed out, "They look up to us as little children to a big older brother, proud to have been freed from Spanish autocracy and to be under the protection of the most liberal of democracies, and cherishing the hope of ultimate independence by our aid."[69]

Taking Roman Catholicism as a failed religion and Spain as a weak and declining nation, North American missionaries worked to elevate the moral tone of Puerto Ricans through evangelism, education, and Christian institutions such as churches, hospitals, and orphanages. The impressive sanctuaries of the Presbyterian Church in Aguadilla and that of the United Brethren in Ponce were built within a decade of each other and resemble the same architectural structure of the sanctuaries built in the United States. The church structures illustrated that Protestant missionaries were transplanting their religion in all forms to Puerto Rico without considering the local customs or what Puerto Ricans wanted. José Irizarry pointed out,

> Since in this line of theological reflection the democratic state is on its ethical side identical with the ideal of the kingdom of God, the United States would embody this ideal by compelling people to work out a new peculiar destiny as Americans; therefore every citizen or inhabitant of the democratic state needed to be Americanized.[70]

Carlos Cardoza-Orlandi argued similarly:

> Seeking to define its mission, the North American missionary movement proposed a new model of life alien to what it had discovered, ignoring the

---

[68]Doug Mack, "The Strange Case of Puerto Rico: How a Series of Racist Supreme Court Decisions Cemented the Island's Second-Class Status," *Slate*, October 9, 2017, www.slate.com/articles /news_and_politics/politics/2017/10/the_insular_cases_the_racist_supreme_court_decisions_ that_cemented_puerto.html.

[69]Charles S. Detweiler, *The Waiting Isles: Baptist Missions in the Caribbean* (Philadelphia: Judson Press, 1930), 21.

[70]José R. Irizarry, "The Politics of Tradition in the Protestant Education Endeavor for Colonial Puerto Rico," in *Futuring Our Past: Explorations in the Theology of Tradition*, ed. Orlando O. Espín and Gary Macy (Maryknoll, NY: Orbis Books, 2006), 233.

Puerto Rican people, maintaining an exogenous character to the cultural Puerto Rican reality and proposing an accusatory, divisive, and violent attitude to everything that represented being Puerto Rican.[71]

For Cardoza-Orlandi, the first wave of Protestant missionaries was unaware of its own biases against the Puerto Rican people and treated them with great paternalism by defining Puerto Ricans counterculturally and in opposition to their cultural, social, economic, racial, and religious past.[72] Thus, the process of making Puerto Ricans Protestant was equated with making them loyal to the United States. This was clearly expressed by George Milton Fowles, who after criticizing Spanish literature as useless "for there is not much of a complimentary nature to be found there, while there is much hostility against America and American ideals," argued for what he thought to be the best way to Americanize Puerto Ricans: "If the people learn to read American literature and come to know our ideals of national life, if they are able to converse in an intelligent manner with American officials and citizens who reside in Porto Rico, it will not be long until this people shall be thoroughly American."[73] As Charles Detweiler stated, "Ought not the Porto Ricans to embrace the religion of their liberators as well as the other elements of their civilization?"[74]

MESTIZAJE AND MULATEZ IN LATINX THEOLOGY

Racial relations and tensions in Puerto Rico have been part of the island since its early history when Spaniards conquered Amerindians and introduced African slaves and freedmen. Before the conquest, Spain had developed its own rules to exclude Jews from public office in government, business, and clerical activities. The purity-of-blood statutes were renegotiated and implemented in the New World with new meanings and pedigrees that worked against people with Amerindian or African blood. My study has shown that in the beginning of the conquest in the sixteenth century, racial mixing was a historical fact. Since then, many scholars had

---

[71]My translation of a section from Carlos Cardoza-Orlandi, "Nos llamaron: mulatos, fiesteros, pero redimibles: Antropología misionera del protestantismo en Puerto Rico," *Apuntes* 14, no. 4 (Winter 1994): 109.

[72]Cardoza-Orlandi, "Nos llamaron mulatos," 110.

[73]Fowles, *Down in Porto Rico*, 87-88.

[74]Detweiler, *Waiting Isles*, 25.

argued for a colorblind society based on the myth of *Mestizaje* or race mixing and rooted in a national identity.[75] However, such racial mixing never changed the power dynamics of Spaniards and Amerindian or African concubines and their descendants. The story of the development of *Mestizaje* in Puerto Rico is much more complicated and conflictive than the rosy picture some scholars had portrayed.[76] White elites have always asserted their power based on their race, and "miscegenation was ultimately seen as a whitening of the black and brown, and not the opposite."[77]

Many Protestant missionaries of the first decades after the US invasion in 1898 appropriated the language of *Mestizaje* to praise Puerto Rico as a place where racial tensions did not exist. Baptist missionary Howard Grose wrote in 1910 that "in comparison Porto Ricans are more homogeneous than Cubans and . . . there is no distinct color line, nor can be one drawn."[78] Also in 1910, George Milton Fowles, missionary with the Methodist Episcopal Church, pointed out, "We believe that the present population is very largely an amalgamation of white, black and Indian blood."[79] Baptist missionary Charles Detweiler said in 1930, "There is comparatively little race prejudice, and on this account the colored people carry themselves with a certain dignity and poise and with an absence of race consciousness that is pleasant to see."[80] Earl Carvey and Ernest Fincher, missionaries with the Brethren Church stated in 1945,

> In a country that the color lines are not sharply drawn it is difficult to determine the number of Negroes, but it is estimated that approximately 30% of the population is colored. Many "white" Puerto Ricans have Negro blood. Thus racial discrimination becomes virtually impossible since a majority of the people are of mixed Indian, white, and Negro blood.[81]

[75]Salvador Brau, *La Colonización de Puerto Rico, desde el descubrimiento de la isla hasta la reverción a la corona Española de los privilegios de Cólon*, tercera ed., anotada por Isabel Gutiérrez del Arroyo (San Juan, Puerto Rico: Instituto de Cultura Puertoriqueña, 1966); Tomás Blanco, *El prejuicio racial en Puerto Rico* (Río Piedras, PR: Ediciones Huracán, 1942); and Sued Badillo and López Cantos, *Puerto Rico Negro*.

[76]Sued Badillo and López Cantos, *Puerto Rico Negro*.

[77]West-Durán, "Puerto Rico," 54.

[78]Grose, *Adventures in the Antilles*, 177.

[79]Fowles, *Down in Porto Rico*, 22.

[80]Detweiler, *Waiting Isles*, 6.

[81]Earl S. Garver and Ernest B. Fincher, *Puerto Rico: Unsolved Problem* (Elgin, IL: Elgin Press, 1945), 21.

The perpetuation of the picture of Puerto Rico as a place where there are no racial tensions, as a harmonious paradise, continues to be propagated until today based on a national identity that erases any trace of African Blackness.[82] "We are all Puerto Ricans" is an expression used mostly to deter any conversations about race and racial tensions.[83]

Curiously, the idea that Spanish Caribbean and Latin American racial tensions are nonexistent is rhetoric that has found a new home with Latinx theologians in the United States.[84] Hispanic Roman Catholic theologians, more than Protestants, have adopted *Mestizaje* as the predominant category to theologize Latinx race relations in the United States.

The first Catholic Latinx theologian who made reference to *Mestizaje* as a theological category was Virgilio Elizondo. For Elizondo, "Mestizaje is simply the mixture of human groups of different makeup determining the color and shape of the eyes, skin pigmentation, and makeup of the bone structure. It is the most common phenomenon in the evolution of the human species. . . . Biologically speaking, mestizaje appears to be quite easy and natural, but culturally it is usually feared and threatening."[85] Interestingly

---

[82]Quiñones Rivera, "From *Trigeñita* to Afro-Puerto Rican," 162-64. Quiñones Rivera points out, "On the island, the politics of difference are subdued, silenced, and embedded within imaginary nationalist discourse. One of these discourses involves the idea of *mestizaje,* or race mixing" (163).

[83]Rodríguez-Silva, *Silencing Race,* 1-3.

[84]Virgilio Elizondo, "*Mestizaje* as a Locus of Theological Reflection," in *The Future of Liberation Theology: Essays in Honor of Gustavo Gutiérrez,* ed. Marc H. Ellis and Otto Maduro (Maryknoll, NY: Orbis Books 1989), 358-74; Elizondo, *The Future Is Mestizo: Life Where Cultures Meet* (Oak Park, IL: Meyer-Stone Books, 1988); Elizondo, *Galilean Journey: The Mexican-American Promise* (Maryknoll, NY: Orbis Books, 1983); Arturo J. Bañuelas, ed., *Mestizo Christianity: Theology from the Latino Perspective* (Maryknoll, NY: Orbis Books, 1995); Allan Figueroa Deck, ed., *Frontiers of Hispanic Theology in the United States* (Maryknoll, NY: Orbis Books, 1992); Ada María Isasi-Díaz, *Mujerista Theology: A Theology for the Twenty-First Century* (Maryknoll, NY: Orbis Books, 1996); Roberto S. Goizueta, *Caminemos con Jesús: Toward a Hispanic/Latino Theology of Accompaniment* (Maryknoll, NY: Orbis Books, 1995). The term *Mestizaje* is also used among some Latino/a Protestant theologians: Mayra Rivera, *The Touch of Transcendence: A Postcolonial Theology of God* (Louisville, KY: Westminster John Knox, 2007); Justo L. González, *Santa Biblia: The Bible Through Hispanic Eyes* (Nashville: Abingdon, 1996); González, *Mañana: Christian Theology from a Hispanic Perspective* (Nashville: Abingdon, 1990); Rubén Rosario Rodríguez, "No Longer Jew or Greek but *Mestizo?* The Challenge of Ethnocentrism for Theological Reconstruction" (PhD diss., Princeton Theological Seminary, 2004); and Rodríguez, *Racism and God-Talk: A Latino/a Perspective* (New York: New York University Press, 2008). For a critique of *Mestizaje/ Mulatez,* see Néstor Medina, *Mestizaje: (Re)Mapping Race, Culture, and Faith in Latino/a Catholicism* (Maryknoll, NY: Orbis Books, 2009); and Michelle A. Gonzalez, *Afro-Cuban Theology: Religion, Race, Culture, and Identity* (Gainesville: University Press of Florida, 2006).

[85]Elizondo, "*Mestizaje* as a Locus of Theological Reflection," in Bañuelas, *Mestizo Christianity,* 27.

enough, the concept of race in Elizondo's *Mestizaje* is replaced with the concept of culture. In this sense, *Mestizos/as* would form a new humanity based on their cultural patrimony as *Mestizo/a* beings.[86] Perhaps because Elizondo is Mexican American, his construction of *Mestizaje* ignores and erases Africa and Blackness while privileging the Amerindian. When the language of *Mestizaje* is void of racial tensions it becomes a mythical discourse separated from reality. This is clearly seen in the definition provided by Espín and Díaz, which states that *Mestizaje* is

> the process of cultural (and often racial) mixing of the Spanish and the Amerindian in the Western hemisphere. The "product" of this process is the mestizo/a. The term is often used, in Latino/a theology, to refer to a much broader and deeper mixing of cultures, religious traditions, and so on, including the contributions of the European-American to contemporary U.S. Latino/a communities.[87]

According to Roberto Goizueta, *Mestizaje* transcends Western dichotomies of race as white and black because they contradict Latinx lived experience. In this sense, racism in the Latinx community is a betrayal of their own identity and history.[88]

Latinx Protestants also have adopted *Mestizaje* as a theological category to describe their plight in theological discourse. Mayra Rivera points out that "taking as a point of departure a concept that highlights impurity and fluidity, Latino/a theologies could contribute to a profound subversion of social values of purity and sameness, rereading a founding meta-narrative of Western theology (and philosophy) to reinscribe in it 'denied knowledge' and foreclosed otherness."[89] Teresa Chavez Sauceda sees *Mestizaje* as embodying a new social space in which the *Mestizo/a* is no longer tied to one specific reality using a "dual cultural citizenship."[90] However, once race is

---

[86]See Elizondo, *Future Is Mestizo.*

[87]Orlando O. Espín and Miguel H. Díaz, *From the Heart of Our People: Latino/a Explorations in Catholic Systematic Theology* (Maryknoll, NY: Orbis, 1999), 262.

[88]Goizueta, *Caminemos con Jesús,* 120.

[89]Mayra Rivera, "God and Difference," in *Building Bridges, Doing Justice: Constructing a Latin/a Ecumenical Theology,* ed. Orlando O. Espín (Maryknoll, NY: Orbis Books, 2009), 34.

[90]Teresa Chavez Sauceda, "Love in the Crossroads: Stepping-Stones to a Doctrine of God in Hispanic/Latino Theology," in *Teología en Conjunto: A Collaborative Hispanic Protestant Theology,* ed. José David Rodríguez and Loida I. Martell-Otero (Louisville, KY: Westminster John Knox Press, 1997), 22-32.

eliminated from the discourse and culture is adopted, Latinx theologians ignore the internal struggles of racism in Latinx cultures. "Even though these scholars want us to embrace *Mestizaje/Mulatez* as a harmonious pluralism devoid of conflict, struggle, and disharmony, reality is not that simple. Not only does *Mestizaje/Mulatez* essentialize the experience of US Latino/a Christians, but now the concept would swallow everybody who comes into contact with it as it symbolizes a new historical erasure of real difference."[91]

There are several scholars who are critical of the use of *Mestizaje* by Latinx theologians. For Néstor Médina, *Mestizaje* as used by Latino/a theologians covers up more than it reveals. It covers up the history of racism, classism, and sexism among Latinos/as, thus becoming a tool of empire and weapon of tyranny. It is impossible to have a unifying element that holds a race or a culture together and allows for an actual common experience.[92] As De La Torre and Aponte argue, "Unfortunately, the desire of Latino/a theologians to evoke a pan-ethnic unity diminishes the reality of how sexism, racism, and classism are alive and well within the social space occupied by Hispanics."[93]

CONCLUSION: KEY MISSIOLOGICAL IMPLICATIONS

There is something extremely bizarre in the irony that throughout the history of empires religion has played a central role in justifying colonization. As the now-famous quote from Lord Rosebury says: "What is Empire but the predominance of Race?"[94] From the biblical verses used to exclude Jews in Spain via the purity-of-blood statutes to its metamorphosis in the New World among enslaved Amerindians and Africans and its modern use to suppress marginal voices, religion has been at the forefront of creating an imperial vision of the world that has legitimized racial discrimination to perpetuate power structures that benefit the ones holding power in society. With this history, how could missionaries circumvent previous mistakes regarding issues of race made by Christians living in an empire?

---

[91]This critique of the term *Mestizaje* as a theological category for Latinx theology appeared earlier in Angel Santiago-Vendrell, "The Gospel in a New Tune! The Appropriation of María Isasi-Díaz's 'Historical Project' by Latina Pentecostals in the Formulation of a Theology of Evangelism," *Feminist Theology* 19, no. 1 (2010): 1-13.

[92]Medina, *Mestizaje*, 116.

[93]Miguel De La Torre and Edwin Aponte, *Introducing Latino/a Theologies* (Maryknoll, NY: Orbis Books, 2001), 147.

[94]Kenan Malik, *The Meaning of Race: Race, History, and Culture in Western Society* (New York: New York University Press, 1996), 115.

The first thing that Christians should consider is constructing evangelism as denunciation. The denunciation of a form of theology that legitimizes domination based on racialization and perpetuates power hierarchies should be of utmost importance in a process of evangelism. James Cone argues, "Unfortunately, American theologians from Cotton Mather and Jonathan Edwards to Reinhold Niebuhr and Schubert Ogden, including radicals and conservatives, have interpreted the gospel according to the cultural and political interest of white people."[95] Missiologist Orlando Costas thought that the United States should be considered a mission field in the 1980s because "the witness of American Christians is intrinsically related to their life and thought as a church and as an indissoluble part of their culture and society."[96] In this sense, Christianity in the United States is void of a prophetic utterance against the machinations of empire. In contemporary US Christianity, some segments of evangelicalism have surrendered their voice and integrity to pursue political power.

In the contemporary context of the United States, missiology and its evangelistic enterprise should involve the act of denunciation. Evangelistic denunciation would present the message of Christ as confronting systemic racism in a way that calls the oppressor to a radical transformation through repentance. It is only after denouncing racism that reconciliation can be accomplished. As Mortimer Arias says, "It is in the context of the in-breaking kingdom, of the mounting opposition it provokes, and with the confrontations with the powers that Jesus makes, that we understand better his call to radical discipleship."[97] Missiology and its evangelistic enterprise should take the form of denouncing all forms of oppression in society, and nothing is more destructive than the original sin of the European colonial enterprise along with US expansionism and its main ideological engine, racism. The history of the conquest of Puerto Rico cries out for a new missiology regarding race, one that sees human races as equal and not through racialized lenses of exploitation.

---

[95]James H. Cone, *The God of the Oppressed* (Maryknoll, NY: Orbis Books, 1997), 43.
[96]Orlando E. Costas, *Christ Outside the Gate: Mission Beyond Christendom* (Maryknoll, NY: Orbis Books, 1982), 72.
[97]Costas, *Christ Outside the Gate*, 52.

PART IV

Race in North America
Between and Beyond
Black-and-White

7

The End of "Mission"

Christian Witness and the
Decentering of White Identity

Andrew T. Draper

INTRODUCTION

There is a tradition in Hebrew poetry that those who worship idols will become like them.[1] The psalmist echoes this tradition in Psalm 135:15-18 when he reminds the house of Israel that the gods of the nations (the *ethnos*: the Gentiles) are of their own making and have no power to communicate of their own accord. The psalmist points to a mutually reinforcing circularity in the constitution of both the idols and their worshipers. Since these "no-gods" are fashioned by those who worship them, they bear the image of the idolater while the idolater, through continual veneration of the idol, in turn bears its image.[2] Throughout this paper, I will make the claim that whiteness is best understood as a religious system of pagan idol worship that thrives on a mutually reinforcing circularity between the image (the ideal or the form) and the social constitution of those who worship it.[3] As idolatry, whiteness must be dealt with like any such cultic system: its high places must

---

[1]See Ps 115:8; 135:18; cf. Is 44:9-20; also Rom 8:29, where Paul speaks of being "conformed to the image of [God's] Son."

[2]While the psalmist's notion of idolatry has been used as a tool of the powerful against indigenous peoples (see Willie James Jennings, *The Christian Imagination* [New Haven, CT: Yale University Press, 2010], chap. 2), this misreading of the social location of divine revelation means that whiteness can effectively be read as idolatry.

[3]Christopher M. Driscoll, *White Lies: Race and Uncertainty in the Twilight of American Religion* (New York: Routledge, 2016), makes a similar argument, although not from a Christian theological viewpoint.

be torn down and its altars laid low.[4] The purpose of this paper is to offer a few concrete practices in which White folks must engage to begin casting down our White idols.

Toward this end, I will use language of decentering to describe the posture needed for White people as we engage in these spiritual disciplines. For whiteness as idolatry to be cast down, White identity (traditionally European particularities) must be decentered and not held as normative.[5] Because White worshipers have centered ourselves in the economy of God's saving activity in the world, specific practices aimed at decentering White identity as universally normative constitute the best path toward tearing down the altars of whiteness. Because white supremacy is arguably the original sin of the West, the United States, and the church, we must speak of whiteness as an effective idolatry. While whiteness has historically been fashioned by White worshipers, its cultic power is such that all flesh may be tempted to render it homage.

How does one worship whiteness? By seeking to become like it, by assimilating to its form, by being enamored with its power, and by internalizing its standards of beauty and rationality. To become like whiteness is to disremember the manner in which whiteness competes with the rule and reign of Jesus as a site of identity constitution. In this state of affairs, reconciliation often entails learning to leverage the sociopolitical power of whiteness for one's own ends and thereby losing oneself—what Karl Barth would stress as one's creaturely particularity—in the process.[6] In this essay, I will retain language of reconciliation because of the rich biblical notion of the preeminence of divine agency that it invokes (see 2 Cor 5:16-21). While it is a contested term that has been used to encourage assimilation to whiteness and to remove the pursuit of justice as a precondition for the beloved community, it is central to my argument that the movement of diverse peoples to one another must be centered on the particularity of divine

---

[4]See Hezekiah's reforms in 2 Kings 18:1-6.
[5]This distinction arose out of Erin Dufault-Hunter's response to this paper when I delivered it at Fuller Seminary's 2017 Missiology Lectures. She correctly noted that if whiteness is idolatry, then simply *decentering* it is insufficient. Language of decentering runs the risk of granting whiteness a kind of finality. My claim is that the decentering of White particularities (what I have called White identity) works against whiteness as idolatry.
[6]Karl Barth, *Church Dogmatics III.4* (Peabody, MA: Hendrickson, 2010), 291-94.

revelation and not the universalizing tendencies of whiteness. Reconciliation is not reconciliation if the normativity of whiteness is left uncontested. As bell hooks has noted, White people must actively work against white supremacy and for racial justice rather than simply lament a lack of meaningful relationships with people of Color. She maintains that this integrity of praxis and this longing for the other will compel White people to be part of "the beloved community where diversity is a given."[7]

This chapter and the practices I am proposing have been birthed out of my experiences and relationships in the ethnically diverse and socioeconomically disadvantaged community in which my family and I have lived and ministered for fourteen years. Although we moved into "the hood" in order to be missional and to engage in incarnational ministry, this journey has pushed against these ways of imagining the movement of the gospel. It has consistently called me to be decentered; to realize that I am not the central actor in God's saving work in the world; to admit that common White assumptions about what is needed, what is right, what is healthy, and what is beautiful are constructed according to an implicit cultural hierarchy; and to recognize that I am very much in need of redemption and conversion.

I moved into my neighborhood with progressive anti-racist convictions, a passion for social justice, and a learned exposition of the struggle for racial equality in our country. However, being joined in relationships of love, intimacy, and mutuality with people different from me complicated these presuppositions; it messed me up. Not only were my passions and my resources not enough, but they allowed me subtly to picture myself as savior, the lived embodiment of Jesus in my community. Even though I would have been ideologically appalled at talk about myself as a "great White hope," evangelical theologies of mission had subtly inculcated in me a resistance to thinking of myself in any other way. My theological imagination was deficient.

I do not present my story in order to justify or condemn myself or others. Rather, I will reference my experiences—the good, the bad, and the ugly—to demonstrate that being joined in relationships of love and desire with people different from me has been the door through which God has participated in my continued conversion or, better yet, is the life of continued conversion

---

[7] bell hooks, *Teaching Community: A Pedagogy of Hope* (New York: Routledge, 2003), 65.

into the radical love of God. I will share ways in which I have been corrected and am still being challenged to be drawn into the way of Jesus in a manner that decenters White identity. I cannot claim that this process is easy. Being reminded of the idolatrous fascinations that still tug on one's heart is difficult and can tempt one toward defensiveness. However, if Christians are those who are being joined to the God made vulnerable, the Incarnate One, then we too must be marked by vulnerability: the discipline of standing open-handed with nothing of our own to offer. Being joined in relationships marked by difference decenters White self-fascination as we become enamored with the other.

In a lesser-known essay titled "The Souls of White Folk," W. E. B. Du Bois offers a sociological analysis of whiteness that sounds notes that would later be echoed and further developed through the discipline of critical race theory. In this essay, Du Bois draws a distinction between *White* as a skin color and *whiteness* as a way of being in the world that had to be discovered through modernity. In tantalizingly theological terms, Du Bois describes the conversion of White folks to whiteness, a system that is "the ownership of the earth forever and ever, Amen!"[8]

To develop my claim that whiteness is idolatry, I am reading Du Bois's prescient analysis in a theological register. If whiteness as a sociopolitical order entails a conversion and a sense of earth-ownership, then it makes claims in regard to soteriology and creation theology that are at odds with the salvation history of Scripture. To that end, I will be proposing several practices consonant with a deconversion from whiteness. If Christian theology is imagined as White theology and Christian mission is thought of as a White practice, it is necessary to proclaim the end of mission. If, however, Christian witness can be reimagined through the decentering of White identity, then the practices I am proposing may be a promising path forward.

Now, before several White listeners protest that being pigmently challenged is not inherently sinful, or before several non-White listeners register suspicion at a White theologian talking about race, may I offer the caveat that I am not attempting to essentialize race by talking about color. Additionally, it should be obvious that liking White things (skinny jeans, indie

---

[8]W. E. B. Du Bois, *Darkwater: Voices from Within the Veil* (Mineola, NY: Dover, 1999), 17-18.

rock, green bean casserole, and John Milbank, for instance) is not in itself the problem. The problem is that said particularities have been elevated as universally normative and theologically central, all the while being cloaked in conceptions of neutrality. I am attempting to demonstrate, as a White scholar-pastor being remade through joining, what it means for White people to work against whiteness. Theologically speaking, whiteness will not be overcome through uncritical reassertions of tradition but in learning to accept, by grace, a marginal seat at Christ's table. It is only in the decentering of White identity that White particularities will be included in the body of Christ in a redemptive manner.

Toward this end, I propose five practices in which White folks must engage to resist the sociopolitical order of whiteness: first, repentance for complicity in systemic sin; second, learning from theological and cultural resources not our own; third, choosing to locate our lives in places and structures in which we are necessarily guests; fourth, tangible submission to non-White ecclesial leadership; and fifth, hearing and speaking the glory of God in unfamiliar cadences. If, as Brian Bantum has compellingly claimed, whiteness is a way of life into which its novitiates are discipled,[9] then a Christian discipleship that entails a deconversion from whiteness is necessary if any true experience of reconciliation with God, others, the creation, and ourselves is to take place. When White people actively work against white supremacy in all its explicit and implicit forms, we allow ourselves to enter into the trajectory of divine desire that draws all people, even us, to a divine Center of which we are not mediator and in which we are not privileged.

REPENTANCE FOR COMPLICITY IN SYSTEMIC SIN

First, White people in general and White Christians in particular must repent for complicity in systemic sin. This includes a continual recognition of the legacies of colonization, destruction of Native peoples, imperialist seizures of land, the transatlantic slave trade, lynching, Jim Crow segregation, and the modern racialized criminal justice system,[10] which have

---

[9]Brian Bantum, *Redeeming Mulatto: A Theology of Race and Christian Hybridity* (Waco, TX: Baylor University Press, 2010), 19.

[10]See Michelle Alexander, *The New Jim Crow: Mass Incarceration in the Age of Colorblindness* (New York: The New Press, 2012).

created social structures that still benefit White people and marginalize others. For instance, it is worth noting that the median household income for Black households is still roughly 60 percent that of White households, a figure that aligns with the three-fifths compromise of 1787, which valued Black bodies at 60 percent of White bodies.[11] In my own community, I have recognized this disparity in the fact that I, as a White relocator, have access to familial inheritance, economic connections, and educational resources that have been denied historically to many communities of Color. Our confession entails recognizing that none of these injustices and disparities would have been possible without our assumptions about the universality of our traditions and the manner in which those assumptions effectively center whiteness as constitutive of the Christian body and the body politic.

When I utilize language of repentance, I am not referring to what is commonly understood as white guilt, the paralyzing sense of shame that would keep us from working against the effects of white power and privilege. While conservative claims about white innocence—the refusal to take seriously systemic white sin and white privilege—are historically illiterate, progressive white guilt also often functions as an exercise in self-justification. White innocence reads whiteness as sinless and pure while white guilt reads whiteness as the willing sacrifice for the sake of the world. Both ideological stances subtly read White folks into a christological trope, thereby reaffirming the centrality of the White Jesus whom J. Kameron Carter calls the "cultural reflex" Christ.[12] Both picture White folks as White saviors; both evince similarly self-obsessed postures. There are far too many papers, sermons, blogs, and books by "guilty White guys" resulting in little more than tearful confessions of our own ignorance while doing very little to tear down the altars of whiteness. As a scholar-practitioner, I know that my tears and my enlightenment alone are not meaningful for people of Color. Rather, we must identify the ways in which the structures in which we participate retain power for White folks, and then we must work toward the redistribution of power, even at our own expense. As a friend recently commented, "Some of these 'woke' folk need to take a nap."

---

[11] Carmen DeNavas-Walt, Bernadette D. Proctor, and Jessica C. Smith, "Income, Poverty, and Health Insurance Coverage in the United States: 2011," U.S. Census Bureau, September 2012, https://www.census.gov/prod/2012pubs/p60-243.pdf.
[12] J. Kameron Carter, Race: A Theological Account (Oxford: Oxford University Press, 2008), 80.

Moving away from White self-obsession also moves the conversation away from focusing solely on personal racial animus (as a matter of the will) to focusing instead on what Willie Jennings identifies as the collective racialized imagination characteristic of whiteness.[13] This is a way of avoiding the gridlock of trying to ascertain the supposed purity or impurity of one's intentions, instead beginning to speak about what is. Not only is purity of will an illusion, searching after it tends to function as a practice of works-righteousness antithetical to the gospel. Dietrich Bonhoeffer compellingly maintains that humanity's desire for the "knowledge of good and evil" is rooted in the idolatrous temptation to be "like God."[14] If this is the case, then focusing on will or intentions tends to be an exercise in white navel-gazing that further ensconces White folks in self-deification. We would do better to recall the Pauline exhortation that not being "aware of anything against [ourselves]" does not mean that we are "thereby acquitted." Rather, according to the apostle, it is the Lord who is the judge (1 Cor 4:4). By admitting that the Lord judges us, our systems, and our traditions, we are freed from the compulsion to obsess about our own perceived innocence or guilt and instead receive the gospel of grace as a gift. It is this invitation, extended even to Gentiles like us, that allows us to be freed from defensiveness, to be decentered from cultural self-obsession, and to repent of our self-imposed claims to power and control.

White folks need not protest that our hearts are in the right place but instead must focus on how the white economies of privilege we have constructed marginalize others. Imagine the transformation in relationships marked by difference if even a fraction of the grace that White folks extend to one another in regard to intentions were extended to all people. For instance, we as White people are often defensive when confronted with something offensive we have said and protest that "we didn't mean it that way." But, if our ignorance has hurt others, it doesn't matter how we meant it.

At the invitation of pastors with whom I am in relationship, I often preach in historically African American churches. Early on in this journey, I once

---

[13]Willie James Jennings, *The Christian Imagination: Theology and the Origins of Race* (New Haven, CT: Yale University Press, 2010).

[14]Dietrich Bonhoeffer, *Creation and Fall: A Theological Exposition of Genesis 1–3* (Minneapolis: Fortress, 2007), 111-14.

attempted to use the plural *you* by addressing a congregation as "you folks." A mother in the church took me aside after the service and explained to me that, although she knew I didn't intend to racially categorize the worshiping body, it would be interpreted that way if I continued to talk in this manner. Another time, an African American woman who sits on a board of which I am a member publicly confronted me with the way a popular community development book I was recommending pictured poverty as a black, urban phenomenon.[15] In these and countless other times, I have had the choice to apologize and change rather than dig in my heels and protest that "I meant well." It is common that some White people who are regularly defensive about being corrected are the first to become gravely offended when people of Color make statements that could be interpreted as unfair, even when those statements are made out of places of deep hurt. What if we as White people saw correction and anger as gifts given to us by people of Color, gifts that signal a desire to relate in a healthier manner?[16] And what if we reciprocated that grace by giving others the benefit of the doubt when what is said makes us feel prickly and vulnerable?

The repentance of which I am speaking is not a punctiliar confession of the sort that is had during events planned to encourage racial reconciliation nor even during the presentation of papers at missiology lectures. Think of the Promise Keepers events to which evangelicals flocked in the 1990s or more recent events planned by White mainline denominations to publicly confess the sinful racial history of the United States.[17] Although perhaps good starts, the inherent danger in focusing primarily on getting race questions "right" is that White folks can subtly define ourselves as good White people (i.e., the sort of people on the in crowd of race relations), be pleased with ourselves, and then be done. This posture risks treating the non-White body as an object upon which to unburden ourselves of the psychological guilt of personal prejudice or generational sin.

---

[15]Steven Corbett and Brian Fikkert, *When Helping Hurts* (Chicago: Moody Publishers, 2009), esp. chap. 4.

[16]This point was made at the Missiology Lectures by Elizabeth Conde-Frazier, who noted that when people of Color express anger to White folks, it demonstrates a commitment to pushing into relationship instead of simply walking away.

[17]See Jeremy M. Bergen, *Ecclesial Repentance: The Churches Confront Their Sinful Pasts* (London: Continuum, 2011), esp. chap. 7.

People of Color have borne the burden of White folks' sins long enough; they have suffered and still suffer violence, subjugation, criminalization, and marginalization. It is not their responsibility to doubly bear this burden by continually serving as confessors to a long line of White people plagued with knowing that the systems in which we live were created for, and are maintained to support, White privilege. Privilege is being able to do what you want to do, or to do nothing, regardless of how it affects others. This includes the assumption that people of Color should be glad to receive our overtures of sorrow. Better yet, we should do something to change power dynamics! We can voluntarily give up positions of power to open space for more people of Color to lead. These are complicated and difficult processes because they require White people in power to consider regularly how we are working ourselves out of certain roles and recommending people of Color for opportunities that come our way. While we may not always get this dynamic right, as we move in this direction, reconciliation will follow. Simply confessing personal or structural prejudice and ignorance can be an easy substitute for tearing down the altars of idolatry to which we are tempted to return (see Ex 16:2-3; Prov 26:11; Mt 12:43-45; Lk 11:24-26). It is to be remembered that the New Testament concept of repentance entails not just rational assent or recognition of sin but a continuous renewal of the mind embodied in a change of direction.[18]

For example, messianic Jewish theologian Mark Kinzer maintains that what are needed more than Gentile Christians' apologies for their anti-Semitic relationship to Jews are concerted efforts that dismantle the supersessionism that has marginalized non-European flesh for centuries.[19] The same can be said in regard to the need for White people to move beyond self-centered introspection toward working in solidarity with people of Color to dismantle whiteness. For White folks to disengage because we think such involvement is unnecessary suggests that we view white as raceless or neutral. Alternatively, for White folks to be discouraged from involvement in such work can lead us to adopt an even greater self-obsessed introspection that further reproduces

---

[18]Etymologically, the word *metanoia* means "to change one's mind" and carries with it the sense of turning.

[19]Mark S. Kinzer, *Post-missionary Messianic Judaism: Redefining Christian Engagement with the Jewish People* (Ada, MI: Brazos Press, 2005), 37. Supersessionism is the belief that the Gentile church has replaced Israel in the narrative of divine salvation.

the circuitous idolatry of whiteness. When I have made the choice to join organizations led by people of Color in their work to systematically address root causes of inequality, in social protest and in worship, I have consistently been welcomed to the table and treated with love too wonderful to be expressed. White people need to learn anew that we are nothing more than creatures and certainly not creators. Again, in Du Bois's poignant words about how African Americans observe the White body: "We whose shame, humiliation, and deep insult his aggrandizement so often involved were never deceived. We looked at him clearly, with world-old eyes, and saw simply a human thing, weak and pitiable and cruel, even as we are and were."[20]

If the message of the gospel is that humans are simply creatures awaiting the justification and judgment of God, then the universalizing tendencies of White folks' often optimistic theological anthropologies must be chastened. Western tradition has tended to see the human being as constituted by inherent capacities rather than by divine fiat. When we White folks think Western civilization is the apex of what it means to be human, we necessarily engage others from a self-imposed position of condescension. This indicates we believe that our theologies, our preaching, our art forms, and our worship practices are the standards while the practices of people of Color are specialist interests, ethnic experiences, missions initiatives, or expressions of diversity. In the words of Paul's chastisement of Gentile soteriological hubris: "So do not become proud, but fear" (Rom 11:20 ESV).

Many will note that I am implicitly drawing on Willie Jennings's contention that the theological deformity of supersessionism contributes to the formation of the racialized imagination, yet it is not the purpose of this chapter to retrace this genealogical account in detail but rather to offer a treatment of the posture necessary for White Christians as we work to resist whiteness. Suffice it to say that I find compelling Jennings's treatment of the genesis of the racialized imagination in the age of colonial conquest and J. Kameron Carter's extension of this thesis into his treatment of the maturation of the racialized optic in modernity.[21]

To buttress my claim that White people must repent for our complicity in systemic sin, I will briefly present a reading of the earlier

---

[20]Du Bois, *Darkwater*, 20.
[21]Jennings, *Christian Imagination*; Carter, *Race*.

Christian tradition that is sympathetic to the contention that supersessionism is a theological development animating modern racism. My
contention is that the tradition (or traditions) of Western Christian orthodoxy, while not monolithic in a reductionist sense, is nonetheless best
understood as one particular enculturation (or cluster of Hellenized ap-
propriations) of faith in the Jewish Messiah and should not be read un-
critically in a universalizing manner.[22] I find compelling Justo González's
claim that the Nicene Christian tradition more sufficiently reflected on
the doctrinal implications of the claim that the Jewish Jesus of Nazareth
is the Savior of the world than the comparatively overly systematized
heresies of the first few centuries of Gentile Christian faith.[23] At the
same time, González notes the psychological, sociological, and racial
implications of the Nicene tradition's use of language and formulations
foreign to the biblical witness.[24]

Similarly, Kinzer compellingly demonstrates that both the patristic luminaries and the conciliar formulations went to great lengths to define *Christianity* as a religious system distinct from, and even opposed to, Judaism and
continued Jewish adherence to Torah.[25] Whereas, in Acts 10–15 the discussion had focused on the extent to which Gentiles must adhere to Jewish
practice in order to be joined to Jesus, in early church history the discussion
shifted to focus on how much Jews must become like Gentiles in order to
worship their own Messiah. The burden of proof transferred from Gentiles
to Jews, privileging Hellenistic praxis in the process. In contrast to this trajectory, by reading the Christian tradition as a particular enculturation of

---

[22]Whether through theologies expressed in terms of early Platonic idealism, medieval scholastic
realism, modern Kantian rationalism, or postmodern Hegelian dialecticism, it should go without saying that schools of thought from other Gentile traditions (e.g., sub-Saharan African,
Asian, Native American) have been underemphasized, if present at all, in the tradition. A good
step for White folks would be to recognize this reality, even if the development of Christianity
as Hellenized was in some sense necessarily so. This Hellenization is apparent in the focus on
essence rather than *being* in the great creedal affirmations. At Nicaea, for instance, much ink was
spilt in deciding between *homoousios* and *homoiousios* as the proper term to describe the relationship between the eternal nature of Christ and the nature of the eternal Father, while relatively little discussion was had about the particular Jewish humanity of Jesus.

[23]Justo L. González, *A History of Christian Thought*, Vol. 1, *From the Beginnings to the Council of
Chalcedon* (Nashville: Abingdon, 1979), 394-95.

[24]Justo L. González, *Mañana: Christian Theology from a Hispanic Perspective* (Nashville: Abingdon
Press, 2010), 102.

[25]Kinzer, *Post-missionary Messianic Judaism*, chap. 5.

faith in the Jewish Messiah that is both helpful and problematic, we are free to read with the "communion of saints" in both generous and critical ways.

Especially from the time of Constantine, Christian orthodoxy effectively forgot that it was itself syncretistic in nature and thereby began to see itself as the ideal that would then be translated into non-Western cultural forms.[26] It is not too far a leap from this way of conceiving the relationship of the particularity of the divine and the universality of humanity to viewing European peoples as the "hope of the nations." It is this self-centering impulse in Western Christian faith that animates whiteness and from which White Christians must repent. If Christian orthodoxy is a specific Gentile appropriation of the claim that God was in Christ, then it need neither be enthroned in a universal sense nor discounted out of hand through a hermeneutic of suspicion.

Theological projects that derive their energy primarily from reclamations of the tradition often underestimate the extent to which their doctrinal systems and ecclesial practices reenact the memory of White pagan gods of race and religion.[27] This theological hubris has far-reaching implications for how we think about mission, race, wealth, and criminality and is the core of the systemic sin of which White Christians must repent. This means that common Western missiological questions related to protecting against syncretism in the proclamation of the gospel are fundamentally flawed because they tend to position Western Gentile Christians as capable of judging the relative cultural merits of others while forgetting our own cultural situatedness.

---

[26]This contention can be demonstrated through reflection on the development of the Christian calendar. Most holidays are Christianized versions of pagan festivals celebrating connections between place (seasons and harvests) and pagan religious conceptualities (spiritism and animism, for instance). My point is not that such enculturations of the gospel are without merit but rather that we should acknowledge their social location. Our understanding of the gospel is necessarily connected to particular places, peoples, and pre-Christian understandings of the world, the remembrance of which should mitigate against viewing the Western tradition as an immutable religious ideal.

[27]For an example of accounts that reclaim tradition in ways that center White identity, see Alasdair MacIntyre, *After Virtue* (Notre Dame, IN: Notre Dame University Press, 2007), and John Milbank, *Theology and Social Theory: Beyond Secular Reason* (Oxford: Blackwell, 2006). While their critiques of modernity and liberalism are not unwarranted, I contend that they drastically underemphasize the manner in which many of the problems of secularism are legacies of the supersessionist theological tradition reenacted in their accounts. For an extended treatment of my critique, see Andrew T. Draper, *A Theology of Race and Place: Liberation and Reconciliation in the Works of Jennings and Carter* (Eugene, OR: Pickwick, 2016).

Repenting of whiteness entails recognizing that the tortured history of race in the West is animated by a theological history of White centrality that made it possible for "Christian" nations to order their political practices so as to marginalize and subjugate non-White bodies. If White Christians are serious about pursuing reconciliation, we must recognize that our theological traditions of appropriating the Christ event, while perhaps confessionally faithful, are nonetheless culturally particular. Christian missiologies and theologies of race must therefore read the tradition in both a confessional and a subversive sense. Now that I have treated the practice of repentance in some detail, the remaining four practices can be treated in a more concise fashion.

Learning from Non-White Theological and Cultural Resources

As a second practice, White Christians must learn from theological and cultural resources not our own. The centering of whiteness is concomitant with situating the White male heterosexual abled body as constitutive of the Christian body (both individual bodies and the body politic). By making this claim, I am not suggesting that race, gender, and disability are interchangeable sites of identity, even less that they should be reified, but rather that whiteness tends to orbit around maleness and ableism as an ideal form of the human. Therefore, my claim that whiteness is idolatry is not a suggestion that all White folks experience white privilege in the same manner[28] but rather that the benefits and burdens of whiteness are leveraged and borne by many different groups of people in various ways and for various projects, an insight that is pursued in recent scholarship related to intersectionality.[29] It is through learning from theological and cultural

---

[28]A full third of residents of my city live below the federal poverty line. In my neighborhood, there are many White folks whose ancestors migrated north from Appalachia for factory jobs that no longer exist. The grinding poverty they experience points to a different appropriation of white privilege than my own. Economically disadvantaged White folks have been fed the lie that the only thing they have going for them is that they are not Black, which helps to explain the overt racism so common in impoverished White communities. For a popular account of these dynamics and how they contributed to the discontent expressed through the election of Donald Trump, see J. D. Vance, *Hillbilly Elegy: A Memoir of a Family and Culture in Crisis* (New York: HarperCollins, 2016).
[29]Kimberle Crenshaw, *On Intersectionality: Essential Writings* (New York: The New Press, 2017). Intersectionality describes the manner in which multiple sites of identity overlap, or intersect, to create a whole identity not reducible to its various parts. Likewise, various forms of oppression or bigotry intersect so that various marginalized people experience oppression in compounded ways.

resources that are not White (read: that are not traditioned accounts by only White males) that White folks can begin a process of decentering our own theological and philosophical presuppositions as universally normative while seeing whiteness for what it is: a weak and pitiable longing to be divine. In my own university teaching, I have had to recognize the extent to which my syllabi position the luminaries of the Western tradition as the systemic core while relegating female theologians and theologians of Color to specialist concerns or peripheral issues. I have worked and am still working to rectify this problem by ensuring that my students are learning from female and non-White theologians as they think about the doctrines of God and Christology, not in sections related to ecclesiology or missiology only. Allow me to demonstrate how non-White theological resources decenter whiteness while centering on the particularity of the Word made flesh.

Learning from liberation theology can help White folks resist our purely individualized or "spiritualized" interpretations of salvation while being attuned to the manner in which wealth, power, and whiteness have been aligned through the mechanisms of modernity.[30] In so doing, the universalizing nature of whiteness can be unmasked, and more diffuse and communal conceptions of both soteriology and economics can be appreciated. Theologies of liberation shine a light on the manner in which much of the Western Christian tradition has imbibed a Greek body-spirit dualism and has often operated in modernity as functionally neo-Gnostic. This spirit-matter dichotomy has influenced the split in Western theology between the spiritual conceptions of salvation common to white evangelicalism and the material conceptions of social justice common to white liberalism.[31] While liberation theology's "preferential option for the poor" may not be a full-orbed telos for Christian community, it can be a propitious step toward resisting the primacy of whiteness.[32] In general, Latin American and African American

---

[30]Gustavo Gutierrez, *A Theology of Liberation: History, Politics, and Salvation* (Maryknoll, NY: Orbis, 1988); James H. Cone, *God of the Oppressed* (Maryknoll, NY: Orbis, 1997); Nancy L. Eiesland, *The Disabled God: Toward a Liberatory Theology of Disability* (Nashville: Abingdon, 1994).

[31]See the classic introduction to the social gospel: Walter Rauschenbusch, *Christianity and the Social Crisis in the 21st Century: The Classic That Woke Up the Church* (New York: HarperCollins, 2007).

[32]While this strand in Catholic social teaching is preferable to religion being used as a tool to maintain oppressive systems of social control, it tends to essentialize who the poor are and does not necessarily mitigate against paternalistic ways of relating to the other. Additionally, inasmuch as liberation theology has at times been a tool for leftist regimes, it suggests that no system is exempt from being affected by humanity's propensity toward sin, power, and control.

theologies of liberation do not evince a sharp distinction between spirit and matter. For instance, in encouraging White evangelicals to a more holistic gospel, I have often cited my own church's focus on the spiritual and physical aspects of redemption. At the same time, I have not always adequately recognized that historically Black churches in my community have been faithfully focused on both for years, avoiding the dualism so common to much white Christianity. When we first began implementing justice initiatives in our community, I quickly learned that leaders of Color were already doing much of what seemed so revolutionary to me. Missiologically speaking, I was deconverted from thinking that I was starting a new work or a reclamation of a gospel that had been dormant until I arrived.

Similarly, resources from African American theological traditions give the lie to tacit assumptions of white cultural superiority. Rather than seeing African American religious traditions as specialist interests or intercultural concerns, we as White folks must recognize the liberative and cruciform nature of Black theology conceived on New World soil.[33] If the Christ event is salvation from sin (both individual and communal), liberation from oppression (both spiritual and material), and justification by grace (both particular and universal), then resources from Black church traditions are arguably more Christian than most White theologies, split as they are between conservative defenses of traditional morality and liberal accounts of social justice. African American Christian traditions tend to address more readily both spiritual and material concerns, thereby bypassing the Western philosophical dualism undergirding the white conservative-progressive impasse.

Feminist theology illustrates the manner in which traditional Western Christian anthropologies and narratives of history have often been centered on the male body,[34] even to the extent of at times understanding the female body as a deformation of the original male ideal.[35] While feminist theology illustrates that maleness has often been the assumed anthropological ideal,

---

[33]James H. Cone, *The Cross and the Lynching Tree* (Maryknoll, NY: Orbis, 2011); Albert J. Raboteau, *A Fire in the Bones: Reflections on African-American Religious History* (Boston: Beacon, 1995).

[34]Elisabeth Schüssler Fiorenza, *In Memory of Her: A Feminist Theological Reconstruction of Christian Origins* (New York: Crossroad, 1994).

[35]Brian Brock, "Augustine's Hierarchies of Human Wholeness and Their Healing," in *Disability in the Christian Tradition: A Reader*, ed. Brian Brock and John Swinton (Grand Rapids: Eerdmans, 2012), 69-70. Although not exempt from formulations that we would today recognize as sexist, Augustine's theological anthropology pushes against these demeaning conceptions in fruitful ways.

womanist theology helps us see how maleness and whiteness are interconnected.[36] A womanist critique emphasizes the manner in which women of
Color experience the weight of whiteness and misogyny in multifaceted
ways and helps us see how traditional white feminism has often underemphasized the manner in which it benefits from White identity, therefore
tacitly reinforcing androcentricity. In *White Women, Race Matters*, Ruth
Frankenberg investigates the manner in which systems of power render
bodies raced and gendered in ways that both bestow privilege and contribute to marginalization.[37]

For example, in our local church, while I want to pat myself on the back
for the ways in which I have worked to empower women in leadership, I
regularly need to be reminded of the ways in which empowerment still
orbits around conceptions of male centrality. Several women in pastoral and
lay leadership at our church recently explained to me that, while listening
to what women have to say, I often repackage their insights in my own words
in a way that renders their voices silent. I did not recognize that I had in
effect been translating their speech into a male register and, in so doing,
claiming their contributions as my own. It hurts to recognize the ways in
which I deploy male privilege. However, the tragedy is women being hurt
by men as we move ourselves to the spotlight at their expense. Thankfully,
they corrected me in love and are helping me restructure my discourse and
the way I carry myself in meetings.

While learning from each of these trajectories is indispensable, one word
of caution must be noted in regard to contemporary humanist proclivities
toward collapsing theology into identity politics. While the particularity of
the incarnation should mitigate docetic tendencies in our thinking about the
divine, if talk about God is finally primarily talk about humanity, we have
ceased to do theology. This caution is not directed specifically at any of the
aforementioned texts (Gutiérrez, Cone, or Schüssler Fiorenza) but rather at
the manner in which some discourses within religious studies tend to characterize any sort of confessional Christian posture as necessarily oppressive,

---

[36]Delores S. Williams, *Sisters in the Wilderness: The Challenge of Womanist God-Talk* (Maryknoll,
   NY: Orbis, 2013).
[37]Ruth Frankenberg, *White Women, Race Matters: The Social Construction of Whiteness*, 5th ed.
   (Minneapolis: University of Minnesota Press, 1993).

thereby rendering divine revelation a subspecies of human experience.[38] The ability to make oneself is the temptation for human autonomy that humans have experienced since Babel and that Whites have tried to perfect. The danger in any reification of identity is that it creates new loci of power that trade against whiteness, which may be the latest—but certainly not the last—system that encourages us to put our hope in humanity rather than in God. The continuous parceling up of identity into subcategories may tend to be consonant with a capitalist "economy of desire" more than a gospel-centered economy of grace.[39] Such modern power brokering can be understood as the parceling out of the privileges of whiteness, often intensifying its idolatrous fascination.[40] While I am in no way criticizing the need for self-determination in freedom over against oppressive structures that objectify, it must be noted that self-deification is a temptation common to humanity.

To that end, I propose disability theology as a fruitful and underemphasized theological trajectory for resisting whiteness. Robust theologies of disability show that traditional theological anthropologies have often implied that there are real humans at the center against which marginal humans are compared. In other words, prejudicial theological assumptions about race often rest on a disability description of people of Color. In this center-periphery game, there are normal White people and then there are ethnic Black and Brown people. In resisting anthropologies centered on human capacity (what Brian Brock calls "best-case anthropologies"[41]), disability theology calls into question the existence of an ideal form of the human.

Christian theology has often struggled to overcome the prejudicial implications of its own "analogies of being" in relation to the question of the

---

[38]For example, I am thinking of the way in which Charles H. Long, *Significations: Signs, Symbols, and Images in the Interpretation of Religion* (Minneapolis: Fortress, 1986), 197, lauds the "new god" of the "religious primordium" and the "human spirit" that has replaced the "older theological languages." I address this dynamic in the first chapter of my book *A Theology of Race and Place*. For an example of a theologian who successfully combines identity issues with a robust theological anthropology, see Eugene F. Rogers Jr., *Sexuality and the Christian Body: Their Way into the Triune God* (Oxford: Blackwell, 1999).

[39]Daniel M. Bell Jr., *The Economy of Desire: Christianity and Capitalism in a Postmodern World* (Grand Rapids: Baker, 2012).

[40]This can be seen in the way in which more stereotypically masculine traits (power, control, violence, sexual prowess) are often leveraged in power brokerings in corporate America, for example.

[41]Brian Brock, introduction to Brock and Swinton, *Disability in the Christian Tradition*, 1.

imago Dei.[42] In recognizing the dehumanizing implications of focusing on capacities such as rationality as constitutive of the human, Christian tradition has often been awkwardly forced into clarifying that people with disabilities are, in fact, human. By stressing the constitution of the human as reliant upon the free command of God alone and as imaging the relationality of the Trinity, robust disability theologies resist the problematic anthropological implications of whiteness.[43] In denying productivity as a suitable modality in which to consider human value, disability theology rejects works-righteousness for the doctrine of justification. In more satisfactorily reflecting on what it means to be human, disability theology reveals the prejudicial ways in which White theology has pictured the non-White body as less rational, less productive, or less human.

When our church moved into a historic church building on the dividing line of segregation in our town, I was attracted to the ramifications this location had for racial unity, all the while assuming that the building would be welcoming to people with disabilities because it had an elevator. I did not first consult the members of our church with physical disabilities. A woman with cerebral palsy led me through the building and showed me how our lift did not work well for people with disabilities, how the pews forced people with disabilities into a segregated disability section, how the doorways were too narrow for independent movement, and how all of this combined to form an exclusionary environment. While I had asked her to lead accessibility issues at our church, it took a tearful and angry interchange to help me recognize the extent to which disability, like race, is a site of identity that incurs marginalization in many church communities. As a result of her leadership, our church began learning from disability communities and shifting the priorities of our budget to reflect the need for increased accessibility. She invited me to spend a day with her, riding around our town in a motorized wheelchair, learning how even ADA (Americans with Disabilities Act)

---

[42]See Brock's work on Augustine in "Augustine's Hierarchies of Human Wholeness and Their Healing." For a classic formulation of human capacity, in this case rationality, as constituting the *imago Dei*, see Thomas Aquinas, *Summa Theologica* (London: Burns, Oates & Washbourne, 1920–1922), II-II, Q. 66, Art. 1.

[43]Amos Yong, *The Bible, Disability, and the Church: A New Vision of the People of God* (Grand Rapids: Eerdmans, 2011), 11. See also Bonhoeffer's description of the *imago Dei* as an *analogia relationis* (analogy of relationship) in Bonhoeffer, *Creation and Fall*, 60-65.

accessibility does not guarantee a welcoming environment. Disability calls into question ableism as human normativity and shines a light on how racial segregation has often operated according to a logic of disability.

Finally, in reclaiming the potential of Christian theology to subvert cults of race, gender, ability, and nation, the Christian tradition itself can be reread in generous ways. While the usual suspects of patristic, medieval, and Reformation thought may not often speak in language attuned to our modern sensibilities, it does not mean that their projects cannot be helpful in resisting dehumanizing ways of thinking about humanity. In fact, a convincing case can be made that, limitations notwithstanding, Christian tradition has been more affirming of the created dignity of humanity than both ancient Greco-Roman society and modern secular humanism.[44] While justly criticizing the tradition for the manner in which it has tended to universalize its own particularities and forget its own peripheral place in the divine drama of salvation, a process of learning from non-White theological resources likewise encourages us to act charitably in refusing to anachronistically stereotype patristic thought or render it monolithic.

The insights about Christology and theological anthropology raised in these diverse treatments of Christian identity highlight a crucial question: Whose Jesus are Christians worshiping? Is he the White Jesus of the West, the aesthetically idealized ur-human into whose flesh pagans may be grafted? Is he the triumphant Christ of colonization, political empires, military campaigns, targeted policing, and mass incarceration? Or is he the Jesus whom Ted Smith proclaims as beaten, chained, enslaved, lynched, and raped at gunpoint, whom James Cone calls "the Jesus of . . . the Spirituals" and Fanny Lou Hamer, the Moltmannian "crucified God"?[45] If White Christians are to meet this latter Jesus, we must learn from theological and cultural resources not our own. If Christians are called to live or minister in communities not our own, it is especially important that we learn from people in those communities. Specifically, White, male, able-bodied

---

[44]See Milbank, *Theology and Social Theory*, chap. 10, and Stanley Hauerwas and Charles Pinches, *Christians Among the Virtues: Theological Conversations with Ancient and Modern Ethics* (Notre Dame, IN: Notre Dame University Press, 1997), chap. 4.

[45]Ted A. Smith, *Weird John Brown: Divine Violence and the Limits of Ethics* (Stanford: Stanford University Press, 2015), 153-54; Cone, *God of the Oppressed*, xiii; Jürgen Moltmann, *The Crucified God* (Minneapolis: Fortress, 2015).

Christians cannot claim to be missional without experiencing how God's
mission to us is embodied in theologies of liberation from people of Color,
women, and people with disabilities.

LOCATING OUR LIVES IN PLACES AND STRUCTURES NOT OUR OWN

As a third practice, White folks must choose to locate our lives in places and
structures not our own. Place matters; it is identity constituting. In Barthian
terms, it is through participation in the particularities of the created order
that a human recognizes that she is a creature and that she is this particular
creature and not another.[46] Of all people, Christians must recognize that we
are "strangers and aliens" (see Eph 2:19; 1 Pet 2:11) who necessarily enter new
physical and social spaces as guests.[47] However, Christian tradition has
often seen its vocation as one of hospitality, conceived in a way that positions Christians as hosts to the world—as arbiters more than recipients of
divine hospitality.[48] While this may sound innocuous, and while it may not
be completely without merit, by reading ourselves into the center rather
than the periphery of the salvation narrative, White Christians have tended
(and still tend) to enter places not our own as divinely appointed owners
who think we know better what is needed in those spaces than the people
who already live there.[49] Such a conception cannot but encourage paternalistic assessments that orbit around a racialized hierarchy.

Consider how Christian mission has often functioned as a methodology
of evaluation and social control: non-Christians and people of Color who
are already Christians are often treated as objects of White mission or
become forced recipients of White welcome. While the positive legacies of
Western mission include a more global recognition of the story of salvation
in Israel's Messiah and, at times, even resistance to empire in solidarity with

---

[46]Barth, *Church Dogmatics: Volume III.4*, 291-94.

[47]If this was the case for Jewish exiles in the Dispersion, how much more so for Gentiles who are
joining to them?

[48]Luke Bretherton, *Hospitality as Holiness: Christian Witness amid Moral Diversity* (Surrey, UK:
Ashgate, 2006).

[49]Christians thinking of ourselves as host to the world may be appropriate inasmuch as, through
the Messiah, we are joined with the people of Israel as ambassadors of reconciliation (2 Cor
5:18-20). However, this hosting is a secondary action only. We as Gentiles must remember that
God first makes his appeal through the Jewish apostles that we might be reconciled to God
(2 Cor 5:20). Therefore, Gentile Christians must think of ourselves as guests who are being
drawn into a story not our own and must enter particular places accordingly.

Indigenous peoples, its worst legacies include colonization, genocide, and slavery. Modern mission trips, crosscultural experiences, community development work, and urban ministries (of the sort of which I am a part) are not automatically exempt from similarly dangerous paternalistic tendencies. Only by entering as guests (i.e., learning as much as we can about a place and its cultural traditions, learning from our hosts what is appropriate) can Christians in general, and White people in particular, practice a witness consonant with the One who was a stranger on earth (see Jn 1:9-11). White hospitality often forecloses Christian reciprocity.

A few years after moving into our neighborhood, the church that I pastor was still not a very diverse body. I knew this was not the reality to which God had called us, and I would pray in tears and agony for this to change. However, the Lord convicted me that I was praying for reconciliation on my terms rather than asking for our city to be reconciled to one another whether or not I was at the center of that work. I was asking and acting according to the missional imagination bequeathed to me by my faith. In effect, I was lamenting that I had not been successful in leading the joining across ethnic and socioeconomic lines, which revealed the extent to which I thought of myself as host. It was soon thereafter that God allowed me to meet leaders of Color in our community who were willing to take me under their wings. I had to learn to be a guest.

A mark of whiteness is the ability to think of created place in terms of a mandate for earth ownership.[50] Western Christians have often thought of ourselves as the primary actors in Jesus' call to "make disciples" (Mt 28:19) in a way that reads our own locales (i.e., our Jerusalems) as central and imagines the lands of non-White peoples as "the ends of the earth" (Acts 13:47) positioned in concentric circles radiating outward from us.[51] Whiteness entails thinking that all the world should be open to us while simultaneously forgetting that many places are not open to (or safe for) people of Color. Fear of immigrants, the repeal of DACA (Deferred Action for Childhood Arrivals), anti-Muslim rhetoric, and America First doctrines, embodied in the

---

[50]Contra Ps 24:1. One can see such a doctrine of use value and ownership clearly articulated in John Locke, *Two Treatises of Government* (Cambridge: Cambridge University Press, 1988), 294-96.

[51]While Gentiles certainly bear a responsibility to witness to the good news of the Messiah, the Great Commission was foremost given to Jewish disciples who, as they were dispersing from Jerusalem, were to make disciples of those of us at "the ends of the earth."

"Whitelash" of the Trump election, are manifestations of believing that the land belongs to us. One need only think of Trayvon Martin's fatal transgression of gated space in Sanford, Florida, to recognize the manner in which racialized policing of place has become ubiquitous in modernity. Throughout the world, space has often been divided up and parceled out by the dictates of capitalist markets, which have historically been oriented toward segregationist practices and the alignment of relative socioeconomic status with racialized hierarchies.[52] If capitalism is constituted by economies of desire and if whiteness is best understood as a self-constituting cult of worship, they are, in effect, made for each other.

In this state of affairs, we plan the locations of our homes, our work, our faith communities, and our children's schools according to perceived values of market potential, safety, or desirability without recognizing how those factors have become inherently racialized. White folks often engage in this constellation of choices as if it is an unassailable good and then maintain that we should not be implicated when our ecclesial communities are segregated and homogenous. For instance, White folks have historically moved farther and farther away from communities of Color while citing colorblind reasons like home resale value, high-performing schools, and proximity to recreational activities and consumerist centers. We have ignored the fact that pulling economic resources out of communities contributes to an inequitable distribution of resources. I have experienced this way of imagining space when suburban or rural White folks who visit our urban neighborhood feel uneasy or fearful because of society's perceptions about race, place, violent crime, and criminality. While our family has experienced fights and shootings on our street (including a bullet through our window), the majority of violence in our community is not random; it is related to drug abuse and trafficking, which are statistically no less prevalent in suburban or rural neighborhoods.[53] The main differences are the varying ways

---

[52]I am thinking here of the complicated historical mix of segregation, industrialization, urbanization, red-lining, suburbanization, gentrification, and the war on drugs, and how these economic processes are best understood as race policies. For a theological account see Scott Prather, *Christ, Power, and Mammon: Karl Barth and John Howard Yoder in Dialogue* (London: T&T Clark, 2014).

[53]Jonathan Rothwell, "How the War on Drugs Damages Black Social Mobility," *Social Mobility Memos* (blog), The Brookings Institution, September, 30, 2014, www.brookings.edu/blog/social-mobility-memos/2014/09/30/how-the-war-on-drugs-damages-black-social-mobility.

in which policing, education, employment, and economic distribution function in our respective communities. Militarized police forces treat my neighborhood as a war zone!

All the while, many White conservatives and progressives alike imply that the difficulties marginalized communities face are related to internal cultural or familial dynamics, effectively exculpating themselves for historical participation in, and contemporary promulgation of, segregation and injustice. Once the world has been fashioned according to our liking, it costs White folks very little (and means very little) to claim that we are welcoming or desiring of diversity. We have ordered space so that the requisite assimilation to whiteness carries with it both desirable socioeconomic benefits and the lamentable experience of cultural disintegration.[54] Rather than a Christian hospitality concomitant to whiteness, Christian guesting is a more promising practice for joining in relationships marked by difference.

Christian guesting requires that White Christians intentionally live our lives in places in which we must be offered hospitality, in which we must learn how to be led. While I am not ignorant of the structural economic inequities maintained by segregationist divisions of space, I am not speaking here of gentrification or downward mobility, which both tend to assume an essentialized link between poverty and nonwhiteness. I am also not speaking of relocation in a unilateral incarnational motif, which tends to read those doing the relocating into the position of Jesus.[55] Rather, I am describing a complicated and messy process of choosing to live, work, and worship as guests in places that are not our own, of taking concrete steps forward out of a desire to be joined with others who are different from us.[56] For example, when Christians in our neighborhood and church eat together, it means White folks learning how to eat greens with ham hocks and hot sauce and Black folks wondering what in the world green bean casserole is all about. When hospitality is extended from the hand of another, we can join in and

---

[54]Jennings, *Christian Imagination*, 247.

[55]I am borrowing this language from the Christian Community Development Association, which in recent years has worked to mitigate against this unilateral understanding of the incarnation. See Wayne Gordon and John M. Perkins, *Making Neighborhoods Whole: A Handbook for Christian Community Development* (Downers Grove, IL: InterVarsity Press, 2013).

[56]Jennings refers to this process as "transgressing the boundaries of real estate" so that bodies may join together as they touch the body of God. *Christian Imagination*, 287-88.

confess that we don't know what we are doing rather than doubling down on being comfortable and in control. Living in connection to land, place, food, and people offers White people a way to remember that we are merely human.

In regard to Christian mission, Amos Yong has maintained that being guests of the other must be the central frame in which Christians imagine missional engagement with people of other faiths.[57] Whether in regard to relationships across ethnic lines or relationships with neighboring faiths, little more can be said theoretically about the process of guesting without universalizing what it entails and so collapsing diverse peoples and places into the sort of ethnic comparisons common to whiteness. The contours of this movement cannot be predetermined but must be experienced in specific spaces. Such is the vulnerability necessary for the decentering of white identity.

TANGIBLE SUBMISSION TO NON-WHITE ECCLESIAL LEADERSHIP

A fourth practice is intrinsically connected to the third and helps to further clarify the nature of Christian guesting. White folks must practice tangible submission to Black and Brown ecclesial leadership. In both church and society, White folks often retain positions of power and control for themselves and then lament the noninclusion of people of Color in their activities. In this schema, racial reconciliation usually means submitting to white cultural ways of doing things. For reconciliation to be more than assimilation, White Christians cannot unilaterally start churches, plan worship services, move into neighborhoods, organize community activities, plan events, and then invite others to join them. Rather, a necessary spiritual discipline for White folks is joining churches or ministry associations in which they are a minority and which are led by people of Color.

In the church I pastor, the shift from a fairly homogenous worshiping body to a community diverse at every level of leadership began after I joined African American ministry associations. I asked the bishop of a historically African American church in our community that was engaged in justice initiatives to mentor me and then joined him in his community development work. He met with me weekly, guiding me as a younger pastor with the wealth of his thirty-five years of ministry experience. For instance, rather

---

[57]Amos Yong, *Hospitality and the Other: Pentecost, Christian Practices, and the Neighbor* (Maryknoll, NY: Orbis, 2008).

than our church starting our own addiction recovery/transitional housing program, we partnered with his. When we travel to conferences, we still often travel together. Our families visit and stay in each other's homes. While we have preached in each other's churches, this has not been a pulpit-sharing initiative. We have encouraged congregants to move their attendance to each other's churches (with varying levels of success). He invited me to join an activist ministerial association led by Black pastors. As I joined work that was already happening and submitted to the leadership of people of Color, our church grew into a community better reflective of the diversity of the kingdom. To this day, I serve under and join with initiatives led by people of Color. This joining has led me to take stances that often place me at odds with the White church culture of my upbringing and tradition. Joining requires White folks to submit, which requires a shifting of allegiances.

The regrettable fact is that White people will often not join an organization or a mission unless Whites are leading it. To counter this proclivity, White folks must join diverse ecclesial communities not to lead them but to be mentored and to be led. While I am not suggesting that Christ does not call people with white skin into positions of ecclesial leadership, I am claiming that the default setting for relationships marked by difference has been one in which White people (especially males) automatically assume that we are gifted to lead before being called to follow. Because the body politic in the West has been ordered around the white body, people of Color regularly experience many settings where they are expected to defer to White leadership (in education, business, politics, religion, and law). Because of this tortured history, working against whiteness will necessitate White people intentionally deferring to non-White leaders both publicly and privately.

I am not speaking of the sort of enforced submission historically demanded of Black, Brown, or female bodies by White males. For instance, the language of submission must be differentiated carefully with regard to female and male bodies.[58] Rather, I am speaking of voluntary submission to

---

[58]For women, submission has often meant sacrificing the sanctity of their own bodies for the desires and dictates of men—whether through work, sexuality, marriage, or worship. Scriptural accounts of the *haustafeln* can be read as culturally situated subversions of such a trajectory. See Rachel Held Evans, "Submission in Context: Christ and the Greco-Roman Household Codes," personal blog, June 5, 2012, https://rachelheldevans.com/blog/mutuality-household-codes.

one another with only Christ as head.[59] Instead of abandoning language of submission, I propose reclaiming this biblical notion in a way that subverts objectification and points to mutuality. In much the same way that I am trying to reclaim language of reconciliation in a nonassimilationist manner and attempting to read the tradition in both subversive and redemptive ways, I am suggesting that submission be reconsidered in ways that encourage mutual vulnerability. If we do not do this, we risk being left with little more than individualist moral autonomy and the warring of identity factions.[60]

Mutuality does not mean that women and people of Color must be vulnerable to White males unilaterally but that vulnerability on the part of White males can help to open up more spaces where marginalized people are safe to be themselves and diverse peoples are free to open up to one another. For instance, as I have opened myself to criticism, women, people of Color, and people with disabilities have welcomed me, led me, and even followed me, in ways that could have been risky for them. Because whiteness and maleness have claimed dominance for so long, these rich biblical conceptions of mutuality must be rediscovered in ways that decenter and dethrone whiteness. For White males, whose bodies usually take up space without fear of marginalization or objectification, submission means rediscovering the body of Christ by following the members of the body whose bodies have been encroached upon by whiteness and maleness.

A Pauline notion of submission recognizes that the body politic is present only when there is a diversity of body parts functioning together in somatic unity (1 Cor 12:14-20). When leadership has been historically denied to certain members of the body, the body parts that have been overexercised must be rested and the marginalized body parts must assume greater prominence so that the body can begin to function in a holistic unity. Whiteness causes and feeds on the atrophy of all other body parts. While each individual is ultimately accountable to the authority of Jesus Christ, a sign of the kingdom is the voluntary laying down of power so as not to lord over others, a propensity Jesus identified in we who are Gentiles (Mt 20:25-28).

---

[59]See Eph 5:21, in which the idea of mutual submission should be joined with the following pericope about marriage, the church, Christ, and the body.

[60]See 1 Cor 3, in which the church identifies herself according to dueling allegiances, even to the point of claiming Jesus for one's own group (which is what whiteness has done).

In regard to theological education and missions, this is an especially complicated dynamic. Many majority world leaders come to Western institutions for theological education and are therefore socialized into Western modalities. While Western institutions hiring more non-White leaders is a good and necessary step, the centering of Western education usually entails the centering of historically white theological norms, pedagogical practices, and conceptions of truth and beauty. We as White folks must recognize that practicing submission to non-White leadership means that we must be open to new conceptions of theological rationality and Christian education. For instance, I have come to realize my lingering desires to remain central and in power when words I have spoken about self-determination or lessons I have taught about historical struggles against injustice come back to decenter me as I am called to take a back seat to someone else's dreams, desires, and goals.

HEARING AND SPEAKING THE GLORY OF
GOD IN UNFAMILIAR CADENCES

Fifth and finally, White Christians must practice hearing and speaking the glory of God in unfamiliar cadences. The gift of the Spirit on the day of Pentecost enabled people "from every nation under heaven . . . in our own languages [to] hear them speaking about God's deeds of power" (Acts 2:5, 11). To be addressed by the Word of God means first to hear rather than to speak. For White Gentiles to listen first reminds us that we are first recipients, rather than arbiters, of divine grace. This does not preclude God calling us to speak—and speak we must, when called—but is a reminder that we must think of ourselves first as hearers and thereby become accustomed to listening to others. When the church imagines the call to proclamation as her primary calling, rather than the call to joining, the call to reception is easily precluded. Speech acts are performative. The meaning of words cannot be removed from the interplay of speaker and hearer in particular cultural locations.[61] Our speech and our way of being in the world are mutually articulating. Especially in regard to the work of reconciliation and joining, it may be helpful to think of language as "a form of life."[62]

---

[61]J. L. Austin, *How to Do Things with Words* (Oxford: Oxford University Press, 1975), 1-11, 94-108.
[62]Ludwig Wittgenstein, *Philosophical Investigations* (West Sussex: Blackwell, 2009), 11.

The process of which I am speaking takes time. It means being hosted in a community such that one begins to recognize, appreciate, and participate in the worship of the God of Abraham in linguistic cadences not one's own. It means more than occasionally attending a crosscultural worship experience because it is fun or interesting. For example, as Dianna Watkins-Dickerson has observed, when White folks attend worship services in historically Black religious communities, we are often engaged in "surveillance" more than "participation."[63] While experiencing dislocation is unavoidable when initially pursuing reconciliation, the temptation to assuage these feelings of unfamiliarity by quickly moving to evaluation of the other precludes the greater experience of shared mutuality. When encountering previously unfamiliar modes of discourse and expressions of embodiment, White folks must learn to practice sustained involvement rather than exercising the ethnographic gaze.[64]

As I am a guest in a community not my own, as I submit to others different from myself, I begin to recognize what love and desire sound like when spoken to me in ways with which I was not previously familiar. As my ears are attuned to the glory of God being shouted and sung and preached and whispered, I imagine the God of Jesus differently. I fumblingly attempt to reciprocate the voices of love and desire I hear speaking over me. I begin to theologize differently, to preach differently, to pray differently, and to love differently. I am not speaking here of repackaging an immutable message, as if a sharp distinction can be drawn between form and content, a distinction prevalent in many projects related to mission, enculturation, and translation.[65] Likewise, I am speaking not of trying to learn another language to relate better to people different from me but of entering a new thought world through joining with others, a process that has to be mutually navigated. As I recognize Jesus in ways I had not known him, my white idols begin to be

---

[63]Dianna Watkins-Dickerson, "'You Are Somebody': A Study of the Prophetic Rhetoric of Rev. Henry Logan Starks, D.Min." (paper presented at the Sacred Rhetoric Conference, Winebrenner Theological Seminary, June 2, 2017).

[64]The gaze is the tendency of White folks to classify and categorize the cultural practices of people of Color according to an implicit racialized hierarchy.

[65]For examples of a form-content dichotomy in missions and translation, see Andrew F. Walls, *The Missionary Movement in Christian History: Studies in the Transmission of Faith* (Maryknoll, NY: Orbis, 1996), xvi-xix, 7-8; and Lamin F. Sanneh, *Translating the Message: The Missionary Impact on Culture* (Maryknoll, NY: Orbis, 1989), 1-6.

cast down. As I am immersed in a mutually participatory proclamation, the way I preach changes; I may even have found a little "hoop" in me! But it is because of love and conversion, not because of religious marketing or diversity packaging.

As I have been immersed in the art of preaching in many African American church traditions, I have experienced a mutuality of proclamation akin to the psalmist's invocation of responsorial praise in the Jewish assembly but foreign to many white European church traditions. Much like the manner in which jazz musicians improvise on a common progression while circling back to an original theme, proclamation is a shared enterprise. This call and response is inherent to the life of Christian faith. In the words of the apostle: "What should be done then, my friends? When you come together, each one has a hymn, a lesson, a revelation, a tongue, or an interpretation. Let all things be done for building up" (1 Cor 14:26).

It is easier and more comfortable to be affirmed in one's own identity by living life with people from similar ideological and cultural backgrounds. However, for White people to continue to do so entails continuing to worship our own White images instead of Jesus. Life together with a diverse variety of people means that our own prejudices and paternalisms will be regularly checked and confronted. While having the deficiencies, blind spots, and bigotry of one's whiteness or maleness on full display is not always comfortable, it is the only path forward if we are serious about casting down the idolatry of whiteness. If we faithfully work through this messiness, we will experience an unparalleled and unexpected community of difference and beauty.

Only when our lives are intertwined with others in relationships marked by difference can we learn to recognize the Word of God meeting us in the other. As our ears are opened through this miraculous move of the Spirit, we begin to repeat back to each other the glory of God in the new way we have come to receive it. Together, we proclaim the end of mission as we tear down the altars of whiteness and lay low its idolatrous high places. As together we worship the living Word, whiteness is cast down as a site of identity constitution and White people are grafted back in as simply human. This then is mission: decentering white identity so as to be joined to others who are also making the journey to a Center not of our own making.

Community, Mission, and Race

A Missiological Meaning of Martin Luther King Jr.'s
Beloved Community for Racial Relationships
and Identity Politics

Hak Joon Lee

Martin Luther King Jr. is one of the most influential spiritual moral
leaders of the twentieth century. He is known to the world as a leader of the
civil rights movement, a preacher, a prophet, a theologian, and a martyr.
Amazingly, all these titles are accurate descriptors of King, and he performed
such multiple roles with excellence. The inspiration of his life and ministry
for humanity is strong and enduring, and many who study them are deeply
touched by the scope of his achievement and its ongoing legacy.

During his movement, King traveled a hundred thousand miles per year
to mobilize people of every walk for the cause. He met countless people.
He led marches and demonstrations; he was harassed and beaten by mobs
numerous times, and frequently imprisoned. In his short life of thirty-nine
years, he accomplished for the public more than any other ordinary citizen
was able to accomplish. His achievement is symbolized today by his memorial in the entrance to the national mall in Washington, DC. How was
this magnificent achievement possible? King was a mission-driven person.
Although he was not a missionary in the typical sense, King lived an intense, mission-oriented life. The unwavering sense of dedication and
passion rooted in his faith guided his life and ministry. Facing false accusations and threats to his life, he stood firm on his core identity: a Black
Baptist pastor.

This paper studies King's missiology with a focus on a constructive role that his vision of the beloved community played for his public ministry, in particular the dismantling of segregation in the United States. In a popular Christian understanding, mission usually means crossing cultural or language barriers in sharing the gospel with unchurched people and non-Christians. Associated with the work of evangelism, church planting, and Christianizing civilization, Christian mission has to do with the exposure, propagation, and expansion of Christianity in the world.

Going beyond a traditional ecclesiocentric view, King's life and ministry offer a wonderful example of the holistic nature of Christian mission. King's view of mission was thoroughly theocentric: Christian mission flows from God, and it exists to achieve God's will and desire, which King articulated as the beloved community. In God's mission, God invites humanity to be companions in achieving that goal. I claim that King's idea of the beloved community and his missional life offer a communal moral purpose and a sociopolitical contour to Christian mission. To identify the beloved community as the historical goal of *missio Dei* has huge implications in understanding Christian mission. It not only makes the communal-political engagement and social witness an integral—not optional—part of Christian mission but also delineates how Christians missiologically approach public issues. That is, it answers the questions: What do we want to achieve with evangelism and church planting? How would the redeemed world really look when God's mission is fulfilled? What means do we use and what steps do we take to achieve the goal, and why?

In studying King's missiology, this paper focuses on race relations as the primary topic of its analysis. Although King's campaign was never confined to racism but always included two other interlinked evils of classism and militarism, racial issues were what sparked his public campaign and marked his major achievements. The study of race will reveal how his vision of the beloved community concretely guided King's public campaigns to achieve racial reconciliation.[1] After the missiological analysis of King's approach to

---

[1] Informed by his Christian faith (especially Jesus' Sermon on the Mount), King's idea of racial reconciliation is predicated on a just, equal, interdependent relationship among different races through the confession of sins, implementation of justice, forgiveness, and love. King's idea of the beloved community envisions a fully reconciled community that overcomes all sorts of conflicts, alienations, and enmities, including race.

racial reconciliation, the paper seeks the implications of his missiology for identity politics in our time, exploring how King's insights and experiences guide us in our journey toward the beloved community.

THE BELOVED COMMUNITY

Scholars identified King's idea of the beloved community as the organizing principle and capstone of King's theology and ethics because it was a vision that consistently inspired and pulled his movement.[2] King's vision of the beloved community, later rephrased as "the great world house," offers an encompassing vision of Christian mission for King and his followers.[3]

King's vision of the beloved community was derived from a long-standing communal spiritual tradition of African and African American communities.[4] The idea of community has been at the heart of a traditional African understanding of humanity and spirituality. For African peoples, a community has paramount moral significance.

Unlike the Western liberal idea of a society as the voluntary contract among rational individuals, a community in the African cosmology is created by the supreme deity as the sacred moral entity.[5] The African view of community is based on unique anthropological assumptions that a person is incomplete apart from a community; a person becomes a true person in interaction with others in a community. A person owes his or her existence, growth, and fulfillment to a community; thus he or she is required to fully participate in the life of that community.

African American Christians inherited this spiritual tradition.[6] In their fight against racism in the United States, they theologically adapted and

---

[2]See Kenneth L. Smith and Ira G. Zepp Jr., *Search for the Beloved Community: The Thinking of Martin Luther King Jr.* (Valley Forge, PA: Judson Press, 1998), 129; and Walter E. Fluker, *They Looked for a City: A Comparative Analysis of the Ideal of Community in the Thought of Howard Thurman and Martin Luther King, Jr.* (Lanham, MD: University Press of America, 1989), 82. The notion itself originated with Josiah Royce and R. H. Lotze. See Josiah Royce, *The Problem of Christianity* (Washington, DC: Catholic University of America Press, 2001).
[3]Martin Luther King Jr., *Where Do We Go from Here: Chaos or Community?* (Boston: Beacon Press, 1967), 167.
[4]Hak Joon Lee, *We Will Get to the Promised Land: Martin Luther King, Jr.'s Communal-Political Spirituality* (Cleveland: Pilgrim Press, 2006), 26-31, 91.
[5]Peter J. Paris, *The Spirituality of African People* (Minneapolis: Fortress, 1994), 51.
[6]The African moral goal of preserving and promoting community was expressed in many ways in the community life, songs, and folklores of African Americans (Paris, *Spirituality of African People*, 51-61). The cohesive, extensive family, naming rituals, and the leadership of elders disclose this deep African spiritual communitarian root.

expanded further into their distinctive church tradition: "the parenthood of God and the kinship of humanity."[7] Identified as the spiritual essence of the gospel, the principles of "the parenthood of God and the kinship of humanity" envision a society free from any form of racism, a society in which all humanity is in a loving harmony in God. For African American Christians, these principles provided a theological justification for their political struggle for freedom, equality, and solidarity. It is not difficult to see that King's idea of the beloved community was the outgrowth and articulation of the Black church tradition, centered on these principles. Building upon the Black church tradition, King understood the whole of humanity as a single family—with God as their parent and all others as their brothers and sisters.

Like his African ancestors, King understood a community as the creative purpose of the universe intended by God.[8] In particular, King regarded the building of the beloved community as the specific content of *missio Dei*, hence the goal of Christian mission. King believed that all Christian mission and ministry flow from God's heart and strive toward the beloved community; hence, community constitutes the final goal of all human spiritual and moral efforts. In this spirit, King declared, "He who works against community is working against the whole of creation."[9] The following statement, framed in trinitarian theology, concisely sums up God's goal and determination in building the community:

> The cross is the eternal expression of the length to which God will go in order to restore broken community. The resurrection is a symbol of God's triumph over all the forces that seek to block community. The Holy Spirit is the continuing community creating reality that moves through history.[10]

The idea of the beloved community as God's purpose reflects God's person and character. For King, God is personal and relational, not remote and impersonal as a deist claims. King noted, "So in the truest sense of the word, God is a living God. In him there is feeling and will, responsive to the deepest yearnings of the human heart; this God both evokes and answers

---

[7]Peter J. Paris, *The Social Teaching of the Black Churches* (Minneapolis: Augsburg Fortress, 1998).
[8]Lee, *We Will Get to the Promised Land*, 91.
[9]Martin Luther King Jr., *Stride Toward Freedom* (New York: Harper & Row, 1958), 106.
[10]King, *Stride Toward Freedom*, 105-6.

prayer."[11] Created in the image of God, human beings are endowed with spiritual and moral capacity to communicate with one another and with God. God and human beings, as persons, work together to build the beloved community through their eternal companionship. God intends fellowship (community) with humanity. The idea of God's personhood is important in King's theology because only a person can enter fellowship and form a community.

Then what is the distinctive moral nature and characteristics of the beloved community? How is it different from other kinds of communities, such as racial, ethnic, or neighborly ones? The beloved community is an inclusive, interdependent, and egalitarian community that transcends race, ethnicity, sex, and class. As a rephrasing of the Christian idea of the kingdom of God, the beloved community refers to an inclusive, interracial democratic society characterized by freedom, justice, and friendship of all. King's idea of the beloved community envisioned a fully reconciled society—racially, socially, and economically—where enmity, bias, and alienation are removed but love and justice prevail, and where the dignity of every person is respected and his or her potential is actualized.

Many Americans confuse King's idea of the beloved community with a liberal view of an inclusive (tolerant) society. However, King's vision was different from the latter because of its strong communal nature. Beyond freedom, tolerance, and inclusiveness, mutuality and cooperation characterize the beloved community. The beloved community cannot be legislated; it is based on the voluntary participation and cooperation of all members.[12] It is a community in which each person is responsible for others as brothers and sisters and each member arduously seeks friendship with others. The beloved community denotes a universal family of God in which all humans live as free and equal intimate brothers and sisters. However, it is not naturally given; it is eschatological—something that is possible by God's power alone. Nevertheless, all humanity is called to work together to accomplish this community.

---

[11]Martin Luther King Jr., *Strength to Love* (New York: Harper & Row, 1963), 141-42.

[12]In a biblical sense, his social vision of the beloved community embodies a fully actualized covenant relationship that is characterized by love, justice, mutual respect, and care in God. Covenant is a mechanism to build the right, mutually committed relationship among different individuals and groups.

For King, the vision of the beloved community is not only normative but also empirical. It was not only a rephrase of the kingdom of God for the public but also reflected human creativity in addressing common challenges. It becomes even more so in the context of the undeniable rising reality of interdependence and exchange that globalization and technology create today.

King's idea of the beloved community was not a fancy utopian moral ideal but a concrete goal of Christian mission for the nation and all humanity. King applied this vision to his movement. Going beyond dismantling segregation, the civil rights movement aimed at building the beloved community. King's speeches, sermons, writings, and actions were constant, relentless striving toward the goal of inviting US citizens to this noble vision. This vision helped participants in the movement go beyond their narrow political interests, parochial loyalties, and tribal allegiances to work together for the common good of the nation and humanity.

The Communal-Political Nature of Christian Mission

With the beloved community as the purpose of the *missio Dei*, the Christian mission inevitably takes a political and social nature because the beloved community is not an otherworldly reality nor a utopian dream but a moral community based on justice and righteousness and love. Social injustice, such as racism, classism, and militarism, inevitably undermines and frustrates its actualization. One of the first steps toward building the beloved community is to arrange social relationships that respect human dignity, freedom, and equality.[13] In this context, King's notion of the organic relationship among love, justice, and power is useful in understanding the sociopolitical nature of Christian mission in striving toward the beloved community.[14]

Many Christians consider power and love in mutually exclusive terms. For them, love, defined as *agape*, is considered the complete resignation of power; they quickly point out that the cross is the prime example. This notion implies that power is intrinsically negative—something that good Christians should not pursue.

---

[13]The task of politics is to coordinate/adjudicate the conflicting claims and interests among different groups and promote the common good.

[14]Lee, *We Will Get to the Promised Land*, 100-101. The idea was originally Paul Tillich's, but King creatively adapted it to his own situations in addressing racial, economic, and international relationships.

King had a different understanding of power.[15] He believed that power is not intrinsically evil; it is indispensable for the survival and flourishing of every life.[16] It is an essential aspect of human life, a gift from God from the moment of creation. At the same time, King was very conscious of the precarious nature of power—its destructive potential, especially since the fall. He claimed power in itself could never be the end; it should be guided always by justice and love.

> One of the greatest problems of history is that the concepts of love and power are usually contrasted as polar opposites. Love is identified with a resignation of power and power with a denial of love. What is needed is a realization that power without love is reckless and abusive and that love without power is sentimental and anemic. Power at its best is love implementing the demands of justice. Justice at its best is love correcting everything that stands against love.[17]

This statement of King's implies that power is presupposed in love. He said, "Love is the most durable power" in the universe.[18] It is a creative force that sets people free from fear, selfishness, and isolation toward the liberating relationship in a community.[19] Without power, love becomes sentimental or emotional, even masochistic, and it cannot but helplessly surrender to the harsh reality of injustice. King understands *agape* not as a sheer resignation of power but rather as a sublimated exercise of power in the form of voluntary self-sacrifice for others. Such an act of self-sacrifice presupposes the free exercise of power (not helpless capitulation) since it requires the ability to transcend oneself. Conversely, without the guidance of love and justice, power inevitably becomes abusive and even demonic.

In a triadic relationship, justice mediates the reality of power by adjudicating conflicting claims, self-assertions, and the accumulation and imbalance of power, to progress toward the goal of love. Justice demands that a person, in the exercise of power, at least does not harm others and respects

---

[15]For King, power describes the ability of a moral agent to achieve his or her intention despite obstacles and resistance.

[16]In fact, Scripture acknowledges and praises God's power as "the Maker of heaven and earth" (e.g., Ps 115:15), refuge and liberator of the oppressed (Ps 9:9; Lk 4:18-19), and conqueror of death (2 Tim 1:10), which is implausible without power.

[17]King, *Where Do We Go from Here?*, 37.

[18]Martin Luther King Jr., "The Most Durable Power," in *A Testament of Hope: The Essential Writings of Martin Luther King, Jr.*, ed. James M. Washington (New York: HarperOne, 2003), 11.

[19]King, "An Experiment in Love," in *Testament of Hope*, 20.

the rights of each person. Justice receives from love a moral vision, horizon, and motivating energy for moral actions, just as love is concretized through justice in every relationship. Without the guidance of love, the norms of justice are abstract and fragmented. Because of its intrinsic relationship to justice, God's love is a righteous love, affirming and celebrating the rights and uniqueness of each person. Because of love and justice, God's power is correcting, redeeming, upbuilding, enabling, and reconciling power. Because of its relation to love, God's justice is a restorative, reconciling justice. In short, justice indicates the minimum condition and fulfillment of love while love is the maximum actualization (the purpose) of justice.

Theologically, for King the triad elaborates the sociopolitical nature of God's kingdom. By definition, God's reign is political and therefore includes the exercise of power and implementation of justice in attempting to actualize the beloved community. Thus the political and social nature of God's kingdom inevitably makes Christian mission political and communal because Christian mission flows from and proceeds under God's reign. King believed that a delicate and dialectical balance among love, justice, and power should be always maintained in pursuit of mission. That is, Christians should address the reality of power, the demand of justice, and the eschatological vision of love simultaneously and dialectically. In light of this triadic analysis, King frequently preached "social salvation."[20]

RACISM

The vision of the beloved community (articulated by the triad of love, justice, and power) provided a missional reference point—the positive moral vision toward which all moral energies and strivings should focus, the criterion by which public policies and laws are assessed, and the standard by which the actions and strategies (words and deeds) of his movement were measured. This section takes racism as an example and briefly studies how the vision of the beloved community invigorated the dismantling of segregation and racial discrimination.

Taken to this foreign land against their will, African Americans were defined by racial oppression. Slavery and segregation represented a coercive

---

[20]Martin Luther King Jr., "Suffering and Pain," in *Testament of Hope*, 42.

and legally institutionalized form of racism/evil. The goal of these evils was the exploitation and subjugation of African Americans through intimidation, coercion, and violence. The evil of racism touched every aspect of their lives, exercising a negative constraining power on the life of every African American.[21] African American Christian ministry developed primarily in response to the evil of racism—in an endeavor to dismantle racism and to secure the conditions of survival and common flourishing as promised by God. In the process, African American churches developed a unique missiological perspective that combined their communal spiritual heritage with political activism.

Thus, the African American understanding of Christian mission is communal and political in nature. In addition to the ordinary religious activities of the church, they organized their limited resources in many different creative ways to empower their community by starting their own schools, colleges, and civic organizations. They did not make the work of justice optional or for the purpose of individual salvation, just as they did not romanticize the communal vision into a utopian ideal. Their communal tradition served as an indispensable asset for their survival as they provided the resource of community self-development and unity in fighting against racism, just as political activism offered the opportunity to publicly exercise their communal faith.

In opposition to white-supremacist Christianity, which justified slavery and racism, African American Christians relied on the liberating message of the Scripture, most notably the exodus story and the gospel stories of Jesus. Refusing to allegorize the stories to personal spirituality, they applied the stories to racial relations. African Americans also used the constitutional ideals of inalienable rights, freedom, and equality of every human being in supporting their cause. These spiritual, moral, and constitutional sources empowered African Americans to confront racism and endure hostile social realities without losing a sense of hope and self-dignity.

King inherited this African American communal-political missiological tradition and applied it to his criticism of racism. Racism is based on the belief that one race is congenitally superior to others and thus deserves

---

[21]The existential emotional predicament of African Americans under racial oppression is well articulated by Howard Thurman's book, *Jesus and the Disinherited* (1949; repr., Boston: Beacon Press, 1996).

special, privileged treatment. Racism explicitly promulgates the view that other races do not deserve equal treatment and respect and necessarily excludes others from one's moral community, reducing them to less than human and depriving them of legal protection. When its logic is followed to the extreme, racism unavoidably engenders violence and leads to exploitation (slavery), violence (lynching), and even genocide, as we saw in Nazi Germany. From King's perspective, racism is not a minor, tangential issue for Christian mission; it goes directly against the core moral convictions of the Scripture and God's goal for creation.

In particular, racism negates the core moral teachings of the Bible: the *imago Dei* (the source of human dignity) and the freedom, equality, and kinship of humanity. It violates the transcendental worth, equality, and interdependence of humanity intended by God. Created by the same God in the same image, all human beings, regardless of their skin color, are free and equal before God. Their dignity and worth are sacred and eternal. Racism is wrong because treating people of Color as intrinsically inferior to Whites goes directly against the sacredness (freedom and equality) of human life represented by the idea of *imago Dei*. It deprives people of Color of the opportunities to develop and flourish, which is God's intention for all creatures from the very moment of creation.

According to King, racism violates the interdependence of humanity in God. It is anticommunity. All human beings are interdependent as they share their common origin in God as creatures made in God's image. Racism inevitably creates distrust, hatred, and enmity among different races. It is the antithesis to the beloved community because it divides people on the basis of skin color. King saw how the well-being of African Americans was threatened by the systemic evil of racism and felt a strong need to address this issue politically and spiritually. His decision to be a minister was motivated by these deep social concerns that he experienced as an African American. Throughout his seminary years, King wrestled to overcome racism in a Christian way—that is, without contradicting Jesus' love ethics.

DESEGREGATION AND INTEGRATION

King applied his vision of the beloved community and the triad of love, justice, and power to his campaign to dismantle segregation. King's dialectical idea of desegregation and integration concretely displays the depth of his communal-political missiology in overcoming racism and building the beloved community in the United States. King believed that dismantling segregation required both desegregation and integration, judicial change as well as spiritual-moral transformation. Desegregation may break down the physical segregation of public schools, lunch counters, waiting rooms, and other facilities, but it cannot break down the walls of the heart, such as fear, pride, and prejudice.[22] If integration is the goal of the struggle, desegregation is a necessary step toward it.[23] The legal change was important because it regulated the evil, violent actions of people against people of Color. Segregation was a political and legal entity, not just a racially prejudiced act of a few individuals. It represented an institutionalized form of racism supported by laws and social customs. It could not be changed by moral persuasion or spiritual conversion alone.

Yet, King knew that a legal change must be yoked with spiritual and moral change—addressing how we respect and befriend people of different races. Integration requires mutual acceptance that begins with repentance and forgiveness. Unless these spiritual problems were addressed, there could be no meaningful and enduring social change. King said these inner attitudes were "unenforceable"[24]—beyond the reach of legal enforcement; they could be changed only by love. Hence, the solution to the race problem in the United States depended on how much members of a society were willing to follow the unenforceable obligations of love.

NONVIOLENCE

In undertaking desegregation as an immediate objective of Christian mission for African Americans, King never lost sight of the ultimate goal of God's mission: the beloved community. He chose the means to achieve this objective in coherence to this ultimate goal: nonviolence.

During his student years, King struggled to reconcile the tension between immoral power and powerless morality, the ideal of *agape* love and the

---

[22]King, *Where Do We Go from Here?*, 101.
[23]For King, integration did not mean the assimilation of African Americans into White culture and values; rather, it meant the formation of a new society on the basis of genuine freedom, equality, reciprocity, and respect for one another.
[24]King, *Where Do We Go from Here?*, 100.

reality of oppression. After a long intellectual search, he discovered in nonviolence a practice that respected theological integrity as well as political effectiveness in bringing about the social change he desired to see. For King, nonviolence met the communal (love) and political (justice) dimensions of Christian mission. Nonviolence served two objectives: to overcome racism and to build the beloved community. Nonviolence is a collective moral exertion of power to achieve the goal of love by confronting the injustice that stands in the way of love.

Theologically, nonviolence is deeply rooted in the notion of the sanctity and intrinsic interdependence of humanity in God. Passively, it refuses to harm other human beings, even one's enemies, but, actively, it aims to build the beloved community. The heart of nonviolence is to respect others as brothers and sisters in God. Politically, nonviolence is the exercise of power to dismantle injustices. King recognized that moral persuasion alone couldn't change the reality of injustices. Oppressors never voluntarily give up their power and privileges.[25] Collective political activism is indispensable to achieve justice. Power must be checked by another power; yet that power must be a nonviolent, moral one and consistent with love because the goal of the struggle is the beloved community. Love cannot be achieved by an immoral means, such as violence. Unlike a secular approach, King approached nonviolence as more than a political tactic. He rejected the utilitarian idea that the end justifies the means. A moral means must be consistent with the moral end it pursues; the end is preexistent in the means.

King's idea of nonviolence presupposes that humans have the moral capacity both to love and to come to recognize this love and the good it represents. Such love includes the possibility of suffering for the sake of the well-being of others through the exercise of a redeeming good will toward one's opponents. King believed that redemptive suffering and sacrifice were necessary for social change and considered such suffering a virtue of his life and that of his followers.[26] He said,

> Now I pray that, recognizing the necessity of suffering, the Negro will make of it a virtue. To suffer in a righteous cause is to grow to our humanity's full

---

[25]Martin Luther King Jr., "Letter from Birmingham City Jail," in *Testament of Hope*, 292.
[26]Martin Luther King Jr., "Suffering and Faith," in *Testament of Hope*, 41.

stature. If only to save ourselves from bitterness, we need the vision to see the
ordeals of this generation as an opportunity to transfigure ourselves and
American society.[27]

Nonviolence is not only a political action but also a virtue that requires
constant practice and training within a community for its formation.
Through workshops and regular mass meetings, King consistently taught
and trained the participants of his movement with theological and moral
values embedded in the beloved community. He did not allow those who
refused to publicly pledge their absolute commitment to nonviolence to
participate in demonstrations he organized. Participation in the training
programs and nonviolent struggles transformed them from onlookers to
actors, from victims to change agents.

Like racism, the evils of classism and militarism created major structural
obstacles standing in the way of the beloved community. King applied the
same vision of the beloved community and the political practice of nonviolence to these evils. By doing so, he inspired numerous people, both
Christian and non-Christian, toward justice work.

THE CIVIL RIGHTS MOVEMENT

King's communal vision and nonviolent method shaped his movement.
Throughout his entire movement, the vision of the beloved community offered guidance in exercising and asserting power by setting the tone and
stipulating the choice of political means in achieving the goal. He used persuasion, nonviolence, and coalition building to carry out the mission. Such
deep theological commitment and practices shaped the spiritual character
and moral nature of the movement.

Guided by King's deep theological understanding of God and Christian
responsibility and mission, the civil rights movement was not merely a
political movement but a spiritual-moral renewal movement of the nation.
This collective, social aspect of mission was most explicitly evidenced in
the motto of the Southern Christian Leadership Conference—"to redeem
the soul of America"—which was inspired by the vision of the beloved

---

[27]Martin Luther King Jr., "Creative Protest," an address delivered in Durham, North Carolina, during the lunch counter sit-down by black students (King Center Archives, February 16, 1960).

community. Similarly, the movement's creative and sustaining power largely came from the churches. African American churches were not only instrumental in initiating the movement but also provided the constant spiritual, moral, and financial resources, and various local churches served as organizing centers throughout the movement.

One can see that the campaigns were almost like the spiritual enactment of the Christ event (the cross) in the public realm. As Jesus willingly suffered by taking the cross to confront the power of evil without compromising with evil, King and his followers took the blunt power of water cannons, dogs, batons, and mob violence to confront the evil of racism without returning evil with evil.

Thanks to King's leadership in providing a clear social-moral vision and setting the moral tone and the dedication of his followers, the civil rights movement is regarded as one of the most transformative and inspiring movements in US history. Throughout the entire history of Christianity, there was no such social movement organized by minority Christians under oppression that was so thoroughly saturated by an inclusive spiritual purpose and moral passion. It was the perfect amalgam of the religious and the civic, the heavenly and the earthly, the spiritual and the political.

IMPLICATIONS

United States society has considerably changed since King's death. It is culturally and religiously more diverse because of the influx of immigrants and demographic changes, and it is politically more contentious because of widening economic inequality. Our race relationships have become far more complex and volatile with the ascendance of identity politics that take a more secular, tribal, often violent form in their ideology and social expression. So, what is the church's mission for racial reconciliation in a secular, pluralistic age? What do King's ideas of the beloved community and his communal-political missiology teach us today when Christianity is losing its moral power and social influence? In this final section, I want to briefly explore King's legacy by engaging with race-based identity politics.

Theological engagement with identity politics is important because the latter increasingly defines the ideology and methodology of race relationships in the post–civil rights era, shaping attitudes toward other races and the nature of political engagements. In general, *identity politics* refers to political agendas and activities that are based on aspects of a person's identity such as sex, gender, race, ethnicity, age, religion, disability, nationality, and so on. Not all members of a concerned identity group are involved in identity politics, though identity-based politics gain influence in a pluralistic society.

On the one hand, many forms of identity politics result from a long-standing, ongoing resistance to the political and social hegemony of Whites since the era of the European colonialism. Many of these new assertive voices of identity are necessary to protect their basic human rights, and many of them are even historically belated.[28] For example, Asian American political voices are long overdue given rampant bullying, social stereotypes ("model minority," "forever foreigner," "yellow fever"), and marginalization (e.g., the internment of Japanese Americans during World War II; the 1992 Los Angeles Upheaval). On the other hand, the rise of identity politics has to do with the structural and demographic changes taking place in our society. Among various factors, the structural forces of globalization, migration, and postmodern ideology of self-construction contribute to a social condition that is conducive to the rise of identity politics. In a highly mobile, fragmented, radically pluralistic society, there is growing psychological need and social pressure to discover or affirm one's existential anchor in a community with the most tangible identity markers that provide a clear boundary: race/ethnicity, sex, gender, age, and so on. That is to say, structural forces push people to cluster around the markers of a clear boundary. Each group creates its own feeders, networks (e.g., Facebook and news media that selectively feed information), and cultural enclaves, and politicians manipulate this insularity for their political interests.

Identity politics relies on a secular liberationist or poststructuralist social philosophy, notably related to Marxism or Michel Foucault's social analysis of power relationships and the social construction of identity. It frames politics in terms of oppressor/oppressed relationships while aiming to undo or deconstruct the oppression or social control of a particular social group through social stigma, ostracism, and bias to reclaim one's sense of identity, agency, and a community free from a negative social script on its identity.

---

[28]For example, the Black Lives Matter movement is necessary to publicize and confront police brutality against African Americans and other people of Color.

In the following, I want to critically engage with the secular ideology and practice of current identity politics in light of King's vision and prophetic ministry. Contemporary identity politics has a lot to learn from King who, a staunch advocate of justice, is often regarded as a forerunner of liberation theology. Liberationist and poststructuralist philosophical assumptions (e.g., hermeneutical privilege of the oppressed, the hermeneutics of suspicion, deconstructionism), *when essentialized*, have unintended adverse effects and interfere and impede the community-building process. Rather than create an opportunity for dialogue, essentialism could build barriers and result in alienation between groups because each group operates within virtual intellectual and cultural enclaves.

Increasingly confined to the echo chamber of like-minded people, a reified form of identity politics may create blind spots. Racism, as King perceptively noted, is always interlocked with economic interest, colonial history, and ecological degradation. Other important issues of our polis, such as jobs and health care, cannot be ignored or treated as secondary; this only further fragments our society. Ignoring complexity, intersectionality, and other crucial social issues, identity politics could slide into sociological reductionism.

In this global, interdependent society, such an essentialist approach, together with the dichotomous logic of identity politics, is not a realistic way to address the threats that humanity faces. It is ultimately detrimental to the political goal and moral cause of identity politics in the long run. For example, to frame racism in terms of the Black-White dichotomy alone is no longer relevant to our complex multiracial relationships. In a pluralistic society, we need a common vision to coordinate our conflicting interests and struggles so that we may more effectively achieve our goal.

A deconstructionist logic that denies the existence of universal moral truths (though their historical interpretations may vary) and any possible public adjudication of truth claims, leads to moral relativism. This indirectly offers a pretext for the rise of white nationalism in the West. Borrowing from other identity politics, white nationalists identify themselves as the victims of current government policy and liberal media; they claim that Whites experience reverse discrimination, and thus they need to protect the rights of White citizens. Other white nationalists are more blatant in their assertion that modern civilization is the work of Whites; they are the ones who provide the benefits and convenience of modern medicine, science, and technology for other races. In short, white privilege is the result of their merits, not a historical fabrication or oppressive tool used to control people of Color. Is the assertion of white nationalism another legitimate form of identity politics? By what moral criteria do we adjudicate its claims?

I personally welcome a search for a healthy, critical, contextualized White ethnic identity, but we need to make a careful distinction between white nationalism and other legitimate White racial identity claims.[29] However, the assertion of White victimhood is preposterous because Whites in the United States are still in control of the power and resources of the nation in almost all major institutions; the United States is still the strongest economy, and its corporations are thriving under neoliberal arrangements. Some white nationalists claim that their assertion of identity is a necessary response to the assertions of other racial groups. Yet white identity has a long history in the United States. White identity in the form of white supremacy was in fact the origin of all identity politics. Whites invented the modern idea of race with pseudoscience and theology, perpetuated the racialization of humanity, and justified the systematic exploitation and subjugation of people of Color.[30]

In addressing white nationalism, a simple binary liberationist logic is not helpful because it does not allow us to see a full picture of complex social reality and intersectionality of various forms of oppression and injustice. For example, the recent surge of white nationalism in the United States has to do with the deep, widespread discontent of White blue-collar workers and poor White people who have lost their jobs and livelihood because of outsourcing and the advance of technology. Out of anger toward the callousness of professional politicians of both parties, toward their loss of jobs, and toward the breaking down of families and neighborhoods, they overwhelmingly voted for Donald J. Trump for president, and some of them joined the

---

[29]See Beverly Daniel Tatum, "*Why Are All The Black Kids Sitting Together in the Cafeteria?" And Other Conversations About Race* (New York Basic Books, 2003), chap. 6.

[30]For a more detailed discussion on the origin of racialization in the United States, see Hak Joon Lee, "Redeeming Covenant: A Critical Reflection on Puritan Covenant Theology, Democracy, and Racism in the U.S.," *Theological Conversations*, www.presbyterianmission.org/wp-content/uploads/TheologicalConversation_RedeemingCovenant.pdf.

misguided cause of white nationalism. In an ordinary situation, the claims of white nationalists should be regarded as absurd, but a postmodern epistemology of self-construction and relativism provides the intellectual justification for them, especially in the current social milieu in which many poor Whites feel their legitimate concerns are not properly addressed by the political system.

On a practical side, growing White identity politics among White blue-collar workers is not beneficial to people of Color. As economic issues are racialized, these two groups are pitted against each other in a divide-and-conquer tactic by ruling plutocrats. It is unwise to antagonize the entire race without giving a space for conscientious moral individuals. Rigid race or identity politics may unnecessarily undermine its otherwise legitimate cause by alienating people outside its own identity group or isolating itself from potential supporters. For example, in the area of racial politics, achieving racial equality requires a change of power imbalance between Whites and people of Color, which is not possible without the substantial support and collaboration of many Whites who have financial resources and institutional positions. However, the growth of white nationalism may make many average Whites look relatively moderate or acceptable and further delay the transformation of institutional and cultural racism in a mainstream society. The energy and resources to fight institutional and cultural racism are now diverted to resisting white nationalism, and average Whites may assume they are not complicit in racism in any manner.

More importantly, the binary logic of liberationist ethics framed by the oppressor versus the oppressed is morally and politically limited because it is not completely free from the hegemonic framework that created racial oppression. Under this logic, the identity of the racial victims is defined in reaction to the perpetrators. That is, the category of the oppressed depends on that of the oppressor; there are no oppressed without the oppressors.[31]

---

[31]Eboni Marshall Turman's book, *Toward a Womanist Ethic of Incarnation: Black Bodies, the Black Church, and the Council of Chalcedon* (New York: Palgrave Macmillan, 2013), makes an important contribution on this subject. Analyzing the two logics of incarnation in the Chalcedonian Formula, namely *kata sarka* ("according to the flesh") and *en sarki dei* (God's active presence in the flesh), she claims that the current ethical paradigm of black churches for their liberation is predominantly based on the *kata sarka* model, which contributes to the perpetuation of a binary hierarchal structure between men and women and falls into the trap of the "white gaze" in the final analysis. Instead, Turman claims that liberating ethics for black women must secure the

Furthermore, a rigid binary logic (oppressor-oppressed) could operate by the sheer logic of power—the dead end that Foucault's and Nietzsche's philosophies lead to—and inadvertently result in another form of marginalization. "Just as dominant groups in the culture at large insist that the marginalized integrate by assimilating to dominant norms, so within some practices of identity politics dominant sub-groups may, in theory and practice, impose their vision of the group's identity onto all its members."[32] In other words, fighting against oppression, the oppressed may imitate their enemies.

Instead of a binary logic (hermeneutical privilege of the oppressed), we need to take an inductive, critical realist approach, examining each situation carefully in light of historical facts, evidence, and warrants. We need to give a moral and emotional space (empathy) for each group of people to express and share their pain and suffering, and have a sense that they are being heard.

In this context, King's vision of beloved community and the triad of love, justice, and power have something valuable to offer us. Among many possible areas of his contributions, I want to focus on his understanding of the relationship between liberation and community, justice and love: how to conceive the relationship between liberation and community is critical for the long-term consequence and direction of the movement. The beloved community presents the idea of the common good that coordinates diverse interests without suppressing the necessity of liberation and particularity of its participants. King said: "A true alliance is based upon some self-interest of each component group and a common interest into which they merge."[33]

In the beloved community, as aforementioned, each group celebrates a distinctive cultural and historical and religious tradition, but in collaboration with others under the principles of justice. It is covenantal in nature as it is built upon a clear interpersonal, intergroup egalitarian principle; each

---

priority of *en sarki dei* over *kata sarka* because only the presence of God in humanity (*en sarki dei*) "makes room for a vindicated tomorrow by propelling humanity toward another way of being in the world" (48).

[32]*Stanford Encyclopedia of Philosophy*, s.v. "Identity Politics," rev. March 23, 2016, https://plato.stanford.edu/entries/identity-politics/.

[33]Cited in Donald T. Phillips, *Martin Luther King, Jr. on Leadership: Inspiration & Wisdom for Challenging Times* (New York: Business Plus, 1998), 153. In a similar vein, King was critical of the separatist philosophy of the Black Power movement. He said, "There is no salvation for the Negro through isolation" (*Where Do We Go from Here?*, 48).

group finds its own space, voice, and claim to a seat at the table. The vision of the beloved community offers the antidote to overzealous, sometimes divisive identity politics. A true community should be based on just and righteous relationships and protection of equal rights among the members. Each needs to think of its own identity and politics in light of the common good, asking: what kind of society do we want to create together, and what should our contribution be?

From a Kingian perspective, liberation is necessary but not sufficient; it is the first step but not the final step, just as the exodus was the first step, not the final goal. Metaphorically, the covenant at Sinai and the time in the wilderness were as important as the exodus for the Israelites to enter the Promised Land. Although it is not possible without liberation, the beloved community does not automatically emerge after liberation, either. "In a multiracial society no group can make it alone. . . . To succeed in a pluralistic society, and an often hostile one at that, the Negro obviously needs organized strength, but that strength will only be effective when it is consolidated through constructive alliances with the majority group."[34] Liberation and the beloved community need each other as the process and the goal. We need *ante-* (love) as much as we need *anti-* (liberation).

Without this emphasis on love, the boundary between violence and nonviolence becomes morally blurred, which is already found in many demonstrations. The means we choose (violent or nonviolent) and the tone of our claims and criticism inevitably matter for the kind of society we inhabit and build and the kind of neighbor with whom we want to live. The vision of the beloved community and the idea of love affect how we proceed and engage with our political struggles in relationship with others. King's vision stipulated how love is expressed and practiced from the very beginning and in every step of a social struggle for justice. Otherwise, we may unconsciously imitate the binary worldview of Whites—that is, White versus the rest—and end up unknowingly pursuing the same desire of domination and control over others, weaker ones.

King's communal approach is not only theologically faithful and constructive but also politically more effective because realistically systematic

---

[34]King, *Where Do We Go from Here?*, 50.

racism cannot be dismantled by one racial group alone without the collaboration among others races, including Whites. Rigid identity politics may unnecessarily alienate the people of good will in other racial groups. Without a coalition among people of Color (the victims of racism), the struggle for racial justice could be susceptible to the divide-and-conquer tactic of the dominant group.

In a global, pluralistic society, creating a community has become a moral mandate because ongoing competition for depleting resources threatens the future well-being of the entire humanity and the planet. Global peace and justice cannot be achieved by any one race, one nation, or one religious group alone; the destiny of humanity is tied together. In our claim of legitimate rights, we also need to heed King's insight that the formation of a community indicated the most creative turn of human history: a true sense of human civilization arose when primitive persons put aside their stone axes and decided to cooperate with one another.[35]

CONCLUSION

King's idea of Christian mission was communal and political, which placed community building and prophetic witness at the center of Christian mission. King teaches us that Christian mission cannot be discussed abstractly at the exclusion of social justice, power relationships, and community building. This communal-political interpretation of the gospel is unique because many Christians fail to specify building the beloved community as the goal of their mission, awareness of and addressing power as the intrinsic aspect of human condition, and justice as the integral part of Christian proclamation and mission.

Here are some of King's lasting contributions:

King helps to rediscover the beloved community as the *telos* of Christian mission. If Martin Kähler's assertion that "mission is 'the mother of theology'" is true,[36] then for King, his search for the beloved community was the source and inspiration of his mission. I think King's claim is biblically faithful: the idea of community (associated with the people of God) is

---

[35]King, "The Ethical Demands for Integration," in *A Testament of Hope*, 122.
[36]Cited in Berhard Ott, *Understanding and Developing Theological Education* (Carlisle, UK: Langham Global Library, 2016), 166.

central to God's mission. God's reign is not individualistic but communal, ultimately encompassing the entire creation for the fulfillment of shalom. Whenever God's reign takes place (that is, whenever *missio Dei* happens), God gathers people and a new community arises. There is no kingdom of God without the gathering of people and building of the beloved community.

King demonstrated that social justice can be approached missionally without compromising theological convictions and identity. Justice is also integral to Christian mission, just as almsgiving and evangelism are. For King, the fight against segregation and racism expressed his sense of Christian mission. Christian mission is not purely a spiritual or religious matter in a narrow modernistic sense or as the premise of the two-kingdom theory defines.[37]

Through his successful movement, King showed that the church's mission is not just saving souls, comforting the wounded, planting more churches, and sending missionaries to foreign lands. It also involves transforming society through the prophetic witness of justice and of the nonviolent practice of redemptive suffering. Through his deep understanding of the communal nature and prophetic aspect of mission, King contributed to expanding the nature and content of Christian mission by restoring its intrinsic social and eschatological impetus. However, his advocacy for social justice relied not on a thin and abstract moralism as many liberals do but on a thick christological ground. Critical balance and integration of a thick theology and deep social transformation are his lasting missiological contribution.

King demonstrated that Christian love can be equally militant, justice can be inclusive, and power can be life affirming. In our unwavering pursuit of justice, King offers an inclusive, egalitarian communal vision with nonviolence as the only morally valid and politically practical method. His approach, far from being outdated, is more relevant in a racially pluralistic society when the nation still has a long way to go in achieving racial reconciliation. When we follow King's example, we may be more truthful to the painful history of the past, generous and hopeful for the future, and patient and firmly committed to the work of love and justice in the present.

---

[37]Advocated by Reformer Martin Luther, the two-kingdoms theory denotes distinctive roles for church and state in history under God's rule, the former assigned to spiritual matters (such as preaching of the gospel) and the latter to the maintenance of order and law in a society. For the integrity of each, the two realms (domains) should not be mixed or confused. The church should not exercise its power over the government; nor should the secular government rule the church.

King gave everything he had to fulfill his mission of living out the beloved community in concrete terms of racial justice, economic equality, and global peace. To the fullest extent, King lived a dedicated life as a Baptist pastor, consuming his intellect, energy, and spirit for his mission. King's relatively short life displays the beauty of the dedicated, missional life of a person in Christ. We desperately need a shared vision, such as the beloved community, and missional leadership for humanity in a technologically reliant and highly interdependent but ideologically and politically divided and culturally fragmented world. It is my hope that King's mission-driven Christian life helps to rekindle in us the same fire of justice, love, and peace and to chart a way to navigate our radically pluralistic and complex society with a sense of confidence and hope.

"The Spirit of God Was Hovering over the Waters"

Pressing Past Racialization in the Decolonial
Missionary Context; or, Why Asian American
Christians Should Give Up Their Spots at Harvard

Jonathan Tran

Postracialism is the idea, held by many people, that America is no longer determined by racism and its racializing effects. In a volume focused on what missional living requires and enables in the context of contemporary racialization, it is worthwhile to think about whether postracialism is a reality, or even something to be hoped for.

In the following I consider an instance of different racial minorities being wedged against each other, namely, Asian Americans against other minorities not Asian American, and apply three theories of postracialism in order to assess their respective abilities to describe the situation morally, if not quite provide answers to it.[1] I conclude by arguing that one combination of the three theories does hold promise but will only work if buttressed by concepts supplied by decolonizing missionary discourses that allow for both receiving the presence of the past and working toward vital futures.

The instance I have in mind is the recent affirmative-action controversy involving Asian and Asian American undergraduate applicants to Harvard

---

[1]For analysis of wedging, or what she calls "triangulation," see Claire Jean Kim's "The Racial Triangulation of Asian Americans," *Politics & Society* 27, no. 1 (March 1999): 105-38; and her *Bitter Fruit: The Politics of Black-Korean Conflict in New York City* (New Haven, CT: Yale University Press, 2000).

University. For the sake of simplicity, I will refer to all people of Asian descent as Asian Americans, though I recognize that whether Asians and Asian Americans should be taken as an aggregate whole or disaggregated from each other is a question that is itself part of the problem.[2] Since my concern is to consider the kind of problem for which postracialism is proposed as an answer, namely, racism and racialization, I will construct the problem in a particular way. Specifically, I will imagine a situation in which Harvard University admissions officials did exactly as charged, that is, rig a system in which qualified Asian American applicants were denied admission precisely for the sake of diversifying an otherwise homogenous freshman class. I concede that what I have imagined may not be the case, or at least not in such a straightforward manner. Since my goal is to test a theory rather than solve a complex case, I will control for one aspect of the complexity for the sake of its analysis. By granting for the sake of argument that Asian Americans are being racially discriminated against, I can test how postracialism helps us understand and think about what is happening at Harvard and America more broadly. The current controversy at Harvard, like many others besides, is a controversy about the viability of postracialism as an ethical idea.

My larger point will be to suggest that Christians think about affirmative action from the perspective of missional people, people who believe that the Spirit is ushering in a new future to which Christian lives bear witness. My belief is that if Asian American Christians can see themselves as missionaries to the context of racism and racialization, that vision will turn out to be a crucial intervention in how Asian American Christians live. I conclude my argument by suggesting that Asian American Christian students give up their Harvard acceptances to those whose lives under racism do

---

[2] Throughout I use the phrase *Asian Americans* as shorthand for both Asians and Asian Americans. On the important question of disaggregating Asians and Asian Americans, see Hansi Lo Wang, "'Racist Bill'? Chinese Immigrants Protest Effort to Collect More Asian-American Data," heard on "All Things Considered," *NPR*, August 5, 2017, www.npr.org/2017/08/05/541844705/protests-against-the-push-to-disaggragate-asian-american-data. I recognize the limits of using the category Asian Americans to capture the wide diversity of those the category is meant to represent; however, I do so here for ease of argument (and I do not, I think, believe my argument is undermined by the limitations of the category's use) and as placeholder for histories that more sophisticatedly represent that diversity. See for example, Erika Lee, *The Making of Asian America: A History* (New York: Simon & Schuster, 2016).

not afford the same kind of access. Such dispossession is one form missional living takes in the mission field called racialized America. To be sure, my suggestion will prove for most to be impossible and unimaginable, and impossible because unimaginable. But not for all. For those raised in the traditions of thought and practice of the church's divestments for the nations, in its Spirit-driven missionary enterprise, where dispossession is imagined as the very possibility of missions, more will be given, and more will be received.

Three Kinds of Postracialism

I should start by acknowledging that the very idea of postracialism strikes many, especially in progressive academic circles, as not only empirically absurd but also, and for that reason, morally dubious.[3] Insofar as paying heed to the idea looks like a denial of racial injustice and suffering, even considering the idea that racism and racialization no longer play determinative roles in society is offensive. Given this tenuous state of affairs, I wonder if there is a way to hitch our considerations onto something like the following: "I have a dream that my four little children will one day live in a nation where they will not be judged by the color of their skin but by the content of their character."[4] In hitching these considerations to Martin

---

[3]Scholarly literature on postracialism is vast. As representative of critical orientations, see Eduardo Bonilla-Silva, *Racism Without Racists: Color-Blind Racism and the Persistence of Racial Inequality in America*, 5th ed. (Lanham, MD: Rowman & Littlefield, 2017; Keeanga-Yamahtta Taylor, *From #BlackLivesMatter to Black Liberation* (Chicago: Haymarket Books, 2016); Kathryn T. Gines, "A Critique of Postracialism: Conserving Race and Complicating Blackness Beyond the Black-White Binary," *Du Bois Review* 11, no. 1 (2014): 75-86; and Joseph R. Winters, *Hope Draped in Black: Race, Melancholy, and the Agony of Progress* (Durham, NC: Duke University Press, 2016). Illuminating as well are recent debates in critical race theory about the ongoing viability of racial formation and systemic racism theory. See, for instance, Joe Feagin and Sean Elias, "Rethinking Racial Formation Theory: A Systemic Racism Critique," *Ethnic and Racial Studies* 36, no. 6 (2013): 931-60; and, in defense, Michael Omi and Howard Winant, "Resistance Is Futile? A Response to Feagin and Elias," *Ethnic and Racial Studies* 36, no. 6 (2013): 961-73.

[4]To pose the question of King's dream and its relation to postracialism is, as Gary Dorrien's recent histories have shown, to pose the question about the racial vision of the black social gospel. On this, see Gary Dorrien, "King & His Mentors: Rediscovering the Black Social Gospel," *Commonweal*, January 14, 2018, www.commonwealmagazine.org/king-his-mentors; and Dorrien, *Breaking White Supremacy: Martin Luther King Jr. and the Black Social Gospel* (New Haven, CT: Yale University Press, 2018). Also consider Richard Lischer's classic *The Preacher King: Martin Luther King, Jr. and the Word that Moved America*, rev. ed. (New York: Oxford University Press, 1997).

Luther King Jr.'s words, I am not trying to ascribe to him a notion of post-racialism. At minimum, that would beg the question. Rather, it is simply to say that if we have reason to think that there was something biblically prophetic about King's dream, then we should see if theories of postracialism hold up in the light of King's dream. In other words, we should all want to live in a world where race and racialism do not determine the course of our lives; the question is whether postracialism as a theory gets us closer to that world. It is what the philosopher of race Paul C. Taylor calls taking postracialism seriously.[5]

I have in mind three versions of postracialism. The first is largely a descriptive picture of the world that says that while race *once* played a controlling role in American society, it no longer does. This version begins, it thinks, by acknowledging racism's terrible past and concludes by observing that the past is now past, that racism is no longer. Subscribers to this view take the two-term election of Barack Obama to the US presidency as evidence that racism and racialization have ended, and tend to consider people who talk a lot about present-day racism as confused or unhelpful or both. When people of this view actually do witness actual racist incidents, they cast them as aberrations, at most death rattles of a bygone, or maybe mostly bygone, era. We will call this version *simple postracialism*. We could also call it naive postracialism.[6]

The second I will call *biological postracialism* because it believes that the meaning of race is tied to things we say about its biological, or physical,

---

[5]Paul C. Taylor, "Taking Postracialism Seriously: From Movement Mythology to Racial Formation," *Du Bois Review* 11, no. 1 (2014): 9-25. Also see Taylor's primer *Race: A Philosophical Introduction* (Cambridge, UK: Polity, 2013), along with J. Kameron Carter, *Race: A Theological Account* (New York: Oxford University Press, 2008).

[6]For examples of simple postracialism, see Daniel Schorr, "A New, 'Post-Racial' Political Era in America," heard on "All Things Considered," NPR, January 28, 2008, www.npr.org/templates /story/story.php?storyId=18489466; Shelby Steele, "Obama's Post-racial Promise," *Los Angeles Times*, November 5, 2008, www.latimes.com/opinion/opinion-la/la-oe-steele5-2008nov05- story.html; and MSNBC host Chris Matthews's comment that he "forgot [President Obama] was black," YouTube, published January 27, 2010, www.youtube.com/watch?v=TQUMBHPUmNI. As one example of analysis, see Ta-Nehisi Coates, "My President Was Black: A History of the First African American White House—and of What Came Next," *Atlantic*, January/February 2017, www.theatlantic.com/magazine/archive/2017/01/my-president-was-black/508793/, along with Peniel Josph, "Obama's Effort to Heal Racial Divisions and Uplift Black America," *Washington Post*, April 22, 2016, www.washingtonpost.com/graphics/national/obama-legacy /racism-during-presidency.html.

constitution; that is, we speak as if there are biologically White people and biologically Asian people and so on. Due to factors like immigration and interracial procreation, in the future the physical phenotypes signified in race talk will no longer be discernible, and hence race will lose its significance. When this happens, racialization will no longer be a factor, mainly because it no longer can be a factor. Even if the racist still wanted to be racist, his racism would be severely circumscribed because he would not be able to pick out the racial traits he hates so much.[7] While biological postracialists do not think postracialism is currently a reality, and hence acknowledge our current racial difficulties, they say, "Just give it some time." For them, simple postracialism is a fantasy because our society is too dependent on racialization to get past it; our only hope is that one day race will no longer matter because we will be literally unable to see race. If everyone looks like Tiger Woods, then no one will denigrate or favor anyone who looks like Tiger Woods.[8]

The third version is *aspirant postracialism*. Aspirant postracialism combines features of simple postracialism and biological postracialism. Like biological postracialism, it sees itself as not so foolish as to think that the description held by simple postracialism will now or any time soon be realized. But the aspirant postracialist values what motivates simple postracialism, a world in which race no longer determines our lives. Unlike biological postracialism, it refuses to wait around for glacially slow immigration and procreative processes. Or it doesn't want to *just* wait around. Aspirant postracialism encourages us to act now as we wish to be later. It aspires to some possible world because it takes that state of affairs as better than what we have now. Its big idea is that if we start acting as if racialization has

---

[7]One might also consider phenomena where whiteness is inscribed to darker skin tones, hence diminishing the stark contrast racism presumes. See D'Vera Cohn, "Millions of American Changed Their Racial or Ethnic Identity from One Census to the Next," Fact Tank, Pew Research Center, May 5, 2014, www.pewresearch.org/fact-tank/2014/05/05/millions-of-americans-changed-their-racial-or-ethnic-identity-from-one-census-to-the-next/.

[8]For accounts of biological postracialism, consult David A. Hollinger's work—for instance, Hollinger, "The Concept of Post-Racial: How Its Easy Dismissal Obscures Important Questions," *Daedalus* 140, no. 1 (Winter 2011): 174-82; "Obama, the Instability of Color Lines, and the Promise of a Postethnic Future," *Callaloo* 31, no. 4 (2008): 1033-37; and *Postethnic America: Beyond Multiculturalism*, 10th ed. (New York: Basic Books, 2006).

ended, then racialization will end, or at least it will begin to end.[9] Aspirant postracialism was given voice in US Supreme Court Chief Justice John Roberts's argument against affirmative action: "the way to stop discriminating on the basis of race is to stop discriminating on the basis of race."[10]

THE HARVARD CASE

With these three theories in mind, we can now have a look at the Harvard case and see what the theories do for us. The case revolves around, at least ostensibly, an antidiscrimination lawsuit against Harvard University based on Title VI of the Civil Rights Act of 1964. The suit alleges that the university systematically discriminates against otherwise qualified Asian American undergraduate applicants.[11] They have done so, the suit claims, in order to (1) keep down the total number of Asian American students in order to (2) diversify its admitted ranks, where the first proposition is seen as required for the second. The idea here is that if Harvard admitted every qualified Asian American, Harvard would become so Asian American that there would be little room for others, including Whites and non–Asian American ethnic minorities. The discrimination occurs, as conjectured, by requiring of Asian American applicants 140 more SAT points than rival non–Asian American applicants. These plaintiffs take as damning the fact that Asian Americans *never* comprise more than 20 percent of Harvard's freshman class while elite schools that do not use affirmative-action delimitations have

---

[9]For helpful correctives of aspirant postracialism, see Winters, *Hope Draped in Black*, and Brian Bantum, *The Death of Race: Building a New Christianity in a Racial World* (Minneapolis: Fortress, 2016).

[10]See opinion in Parents Involved in Community Schools v. Seattle School District No. 1, 551 U.S. 701 (2007); on the legal difficulties surrounding racial discrimination, see David A. Strauss, "Discriminatory Intent and the Taming of Brown," *University of Chicago Law Review* 56, no. 3 (Summer 1989): 935-1015; Strauss, "'Recognizing Race' and the Elusive Ideal of Racial Neutrality," *Columbia Law Review Sidebar* 113, no. 1 (2013): 1-8; and Larry Alexander, "What Makes Wrongful Discrimination Wrong? Biases, Preferences, Stereotypes, and Proxies," *University of Pennsylvania Law Review* 141, no. 1 (1992): 149-219.

[11]See Anemona Hartocollis and Stephanie Saul, "Affirmative Action Battle Has a New Focus: Asian-Americans," *New York Times*, August 2, 2017, www.nytimes.com/2017/08/02/us/affirmative-action-battle-has-a-new-focus-asian-americans.html?mcubz=0; see also Laura Jarrett, "Justice Dept. Investigating Harvard over Affirmative Action Policies," CNN Politics, updated November 21, 2017, www.cnn.com/2017/11/21/politics/harvard-affirmative-action-justice-department/index.html; and Jeannie Suk Gersen, "The Uncomfortable Truth About Affirmative Actions and Asian-Americans," *New Yorker*, August 10, 2017, www.newyorker.com/news/news-desk/the-uncomfortable-truth-about-affirmative-action-and-asian-americans.

tellingly different numbers: Berkeley is 32.4 percent Asian American, and Caltech is 42.5 percent, counterexamples suggesting what might be the case at a nondiscriminatory Harvard.[12]

For the sake of argument, we are assuming that the relatively low figure of 20 percent is the result of a highly calculated and effective plan to minimize Asian American numbers at Harvard. The plaintiffs suggest that without the discrimination, Harvard would be nearly 40 percent Asian American, over twice what it is now. The constitution of the rest of Harvard's admitted class could, if not for the discrimination against Asian Americans, go a few different ways, but let us imagine one scenario. With no affirmative-action limitations in place, not only might there be lots and lots of Asian Americans, there might also be, given how the benefits of privilege work, lots and lots of Caucasians and very little of anything else.

Now that we have an initial construction of the Harvard case, I will apply our three postracial theories and see what results, and see how we feel about the results. For simple postracialism, this would be a case of no harm, no foul. Indeed, for the simple postracialist, not only would the absence of affirmative action turn out this way; things *should* turn out this way. Remember that affirmative action was historically justified by two subsequent drivers, first the goal of diversification and second the goal of reparations.[13] Any program that puts race in the rear-view mirror precludes the need for reparations going forward. The same program could accommodate diversity affirmative action, yet its simple postracialist viewpoint could only commit to pursuing diversity of nonracial kinds, intellectual or economic or what have you. It is when we pair the reparations goal with the diversification goal that affirmative action gets racial and, hence, racially discriminating.

The biological postracialist thinks race-based affirmative action is still necessary, but not for much longer. Non–Asian Americans would be strategically pursued under the goal of socially engineering a postracial society. As society increasingly moves toward biological racial integration through mix-raced persons, only those persons who were not racially mixed would

---

[12]Harvard and other elite institutions have for decades now faced similar accusations and investigations. See Dana Y. Takagi, *The Retreat from Race: Asian-American Admissions and Racial Politics* (New Brunswick, NJ: Rutgers University Press, 1992).

[13]Hugh Davis Graham, *Collision Course: The Strange Convergence of Affirmative Action and Immigration Policy in America* (New York: Oxford University Press, 2002), 65-210.

count for the sake of diversification and reparations; they would be intentionally dropped into the Harvard mix. At its worst, biological postracialism tracks with the dark lights of the eugenics movements of the past, the hope that problems will be genetically worked out by natural selection.

This brings us to aspirant postracialism. One version is straightforward enough. Chief Justice Roberts says the way to stop racial discrimination is to stop racially discriminating. While it seems beneficial in the present to deploy diversifying and reparative interventions, doing so, on this view, unwittingly continues racism and racialization. If influential places like Harvard University act now how we all want to be later, then they will do everyone a big favor.

Having applied each postracial theory to the Harvard case, we can now assess what each gives us. We need not rehearse all the quantitative and qualitative data that constitute the founding premise of simple postracialism, that race and racialization no longer play a role in American life, untrue and hence its argument unsound. Perhaps we should observe that its very function, what people are seeking to do when making simple postracial claims, demonstrates its falsity. Part of what makes racialization so powerful is that it conceals its operations from its beneficiaries. This is what we mean by white privilege. If said beneficiaries recognized that they benefited at the cost of others, it would be less beneficial, not to mention less desirable. Much of the privilege of white privilege is this operational blindness to white privilege. Consequently, beneficiaries of our current racial reality had to create the idea of simple postracialism. Whiteness has always had as part of its repertoire something like simple postracialism, believing that the infrastructures that enable its privilege do not exist. It is out of this context, or maybe into this context, that the claim that race no longer plays a determinative role in society is made, and has to be made. This allows for the peculiar situation in which White people can go about their privileged world as long as its enabling structures remain invisible to them. Postracialism is a necessary constituent of the White world.

In the case of Harvard's affirmative-action strategy, the simple postracialist, happily ignorant of white privilege and delighted by notions of historical progress, sees race-based affirmative action as unnecessary and for that reason morally problematic. The clever simple postracialist might even posit prior affirmative action as precluding the need for future affirmative action. Affirmative action was a temporary measure that has efficiently worked itself out of a job. To further this case, the simple postracialist will tug on another part of the simple postracialist imprimatur, the myth of the model minority. The presence of successful Asian Americans both demonstrates that racism has ended and models how to be a postracial minority, serving up a convenient counterpoint to pro-affirmative-action arguments: "See what happens when you use race-based measures. The very people you previously helped, you now harm." As is becoming clear, simple postracialism is anything but simple. It requires sophisticated and sustained upkeep; self-deception usually does.[14]

Biological postracialists recognize all of this and do not expect things to improve anytime soon. Instead, they coach, we ought to keep the long view in mind. We should look for a time when there will be no racism because there will be no race, or no discernible race. Biological postracialism puts its hope in immigration and interracial progeny who will scuttle the fraught meaning of race.

The great political philosopher John Rawls suggested we imagine ourselves ordering the world as it should be rather than as it is, a thought experiment he called the "veil of ignorance."[15] In biological postracialism we find updated Rawls's thought experiment, a veil of physiological ignorance. Both are extensions of Kant's formalist approach to ethics, morality divorced from the world, for the sake of the world. I mean to say that biological postracialism asks of us absurdities, demanding either too much or too little. The aforementioned eugenics stratagem asks too much. Seeking to avoid that, another version of biological postracialism might go in the other direction, asking far less, settling for Kant's moral proceduralism. It does not take long to notice that this works by ignoring a whole lot—which is awkwardly the point. Hence, the veil of ignorance. By harkening to some distant future, biological postracialism, having separated itself from the present, hears nothing and says nothing. It stands nowhere and speaks in a vacuum. A politics of the echo, it can only hear its own voice.

---

[14]For an account of this see Wendell Berry, *The Hidden Wound*, 2nd ed. (New York: Counterpoint, 2010).

[15]See John Rawls, *A Theory of Justice* (1971; repr., Cambridge, MA: Belknap, 2005), 118-94; and Rawls, *Political Liberalism*, expanded ed. (New York: Columbia University Press, 2005), 289-371.

About biological postracialism, I want to say that it is right to think of the present in terms of the future, an aspect of practical reason I will later claim as constitutive of Christian missionary life. But biological postracialism does so by distorting the relationship between present and future, mainly by blocking the past. Applied to the Harvard case, the scheme is as ethically unfeasible as the too-much-eugenics approach is morally problematic: there may be too many Asians now and not very much diversity of other kinds, but one day diversity will be embodied in *every* applicant; wait and see.

Biological postracialism could be critically improved if combined with aspirant postracialism. But not enough to save it. Let me explain: if the problem with biological postracialism is that its picture of the future leaves adherents in an idle waiting game, then allying with an already-but-not-yet aspirant postracialism would infuse a deontological sense of duty toward some as-of-yet-unrealized future, something Kant himself envisioned as a postulated immortality.[16] We would begin to look for ways to live now that would enable and betoken this future state of affairs. Drawn by a hope that things won't always be this bad and beguiled by racially ambiguous children, this postracialist relates to society as it will be, so many generations into the future. The forward-looking hope becomes the lens through which to see the world. Ordinary activities situate themselves amid all these desires and processes, pushing away some things and pulling toward others. This adherent becomes the ultimate postracialist: driven by biological postracialist hope and enabled by an aspirant postracial spirit, he or she becomes a complex postracialist.

But it does not work, for it cannot, despite its gains, do what it most needs to do in order to succeed. It cannot outrun the past.[17] Postracialism rightly understands racialization as a product of history. What it wants is the obliteration of that history, for it sees that history as paralyzing the present by laying into the present with all the hard trauma of the past. Postracialism imagines futures free from history and its effects. In the case of simple postracialism, willful ignorance paves the way. With biological postracialism,

---

[16]See Immanuel Kant, *Critique of Practical Reason*, trans. Thomas Kingsmill Abbott (London: Longmans, Green, 1909; repr., Mineola, NY: Dover, 2004), first part, bk. 2, chap. 2, section 4, "The Immortality of the Soul as a Postulate of Pure Practical Reason."

[17]I develop this at greater length in Jonathan Tran, *The Vietnam War and Theologies of Memory: Time and Eternity in the Far Country* (Malden, MA: Wiley-Blackwell, 2010).

escapist projection is the route. In aspirant postracialism, fantastical idealism becomes our champion. We can never forget, and Kant never did. Without erasure, moral duty is not possible. Kant's categorical imperative, like the veil of ignorance proposed by neo-Kantians like Rawls, names the process by which historical determinants are eliminated. And this erasure of history, again as Kant saw, can only be done formally, by thought experiment.

Yet, in the real world, ghosts remain. Applied to our temporally complicated reality, as demonstrated by the Harvard case, postracialism recycles tortured memories from the past into the present and the future. Unless we are satisfied with what we get when we apply our three postracial theories to the Harvard case, we are going to have to come to terms, in some form or fashion, with the past. But dealing honestly with the presence of the past is exactly what those propounding postracialism try to avoid. It is no wonder that we are drawn to imaginative thought experiments.

An unfortunate example of this can be found in many Christian accounts of reconciliation, the upshot of which is that there is finally not much in need of reconciling, which is the reason why reconciliation can issue without reparative work. As Jennifer Harvey has persuasively argued, Christian accounts of reconciliation presume the past can be expunged and rejoice when that will be the case.[18] But the presumption is wrong, and so the expectation wrongheaded. This picture of reconciliation puts an enormous amount of weight on forgiveness as the mechanism that exorcizes the past.[19] But too often reconciliation goes forward without the ameliorating work of reparations, without addressing the past for the sake of the future, leaving reconciliation incomplete. Forgiveness tied to an incomplete picture of reconciliation is not strong enough to carry all the weight this picture of reconciliation puts on it. Without reparations there can be no forgiveness, and without forgiveness there can be no reconciliation. Because incomplete reconciliation looks so enticing, because we want it so badly precisely for the work it leaves undone, we miss this simple fact about reconciliation and keep piling our postracial hopes onto it. Its collapse is readily visible in Christian America, most recently in the disgraceful fact that White evangelicals, those most

---

[18]Jennifer Harvey, *Dear White Christians: For Those Still Longing for Racial Reconciliation* (Grand Rapids: Eerdmans, 2014).

[19]See L. Gregory Jones, *Embodying Forgiveness: A Theological Analysis* (Grand Rapids: Eerdmans, 1995).

prone to insufficient theology, installed an unapologetic racist into the White House. As Ta-Nehisi Coates recently wrote: "Certainly not every Trump voter is a white supremacist, just as not every white person in the Jim Crow South was a white supremacist. But every Trump voter felt it acceptable to hand the fate of the country over to one."[20] Witness the fate of Christian postracialism.

BETWEEN DECOLONIAL PASTS AND MISSIONARY FUTURES

If we are going to aspire rightly to a world where race and racialization no longer determine our lives, we will need to learn to live futurally into the thick presence of the past.[21] Needed will be concepts of moral agency that both acknowledge conditions so haunted by the past that the present feels unlivable and gesture toward possibilities within and beyond those determinations. What is needed is a future. Yet the future is as it has always been; the only future we can have is the future we can imagine from within the investitures of the past. If we cannot see it, we will not have it.[22] This is what makes our past and present so deadly, what makes the present yield to, among other things, abstract formulations. The presence of the past can incapacitate what can be seen or imagined, obscuring the future.

We might, perhaps counterintuitively, begin by looking at things the other way around, to see if the past and the death brought by the past might enrich soils of the present and grow something new, so long as we let it, so long as we let the past be more than past. The work of seeing and imagining—enabled, encouraged, and energized by natural conventions that arise with human adaptation to ecologies that both threaten and enliven—comes from the rich soil of previous life, life that has been good and cruel and rich and damaged.[23] What if we imagine the past as nutrient soil out of which comes

---

[20]See Ta-Nehisi Coates, "The First White President: The Foundation of Donald Trump's Presidency Is the Negation of Barack Obama's Legacy," *Atlantic*, October 2017, www.theatlantic.com /magazine/archive/2017/10/the-first-white-president-ta-nehisi-coates/537909/. See also Stanley Hauerwas and Jonathan Tran, "A Sanctuary Politics: Being the Church in the Time of Trump," ABC Religion & Ethics, updated March 31, 2017, www.abc.net.au/religion/articles/2017/03/30 /4645538.htm.

[21]Sheldon S. Wolin, *The Presence of the Past: Essays on the State and the Constitution* (Baltimore: Johns Hopkins University Press, 1990).

[22]Toni Morrison, *Beloved* (New York: Knopf, 2006), 104.

[23]See Enrique Dussel, *Twenty Theses on Politics*, trans. George Ciccariello-Maher (Durham, NC: Duke University Press, 2008), 114-21; and Dussel, "Beyond Eurocentrism: The World-System and the Limits of Modernity," in *The Cultures of Globalization*, ed. Fredric Jameson and Masao

new life, always determined, but as transacted with other life not only so. Decolonialist thought envisions life in the clearing of late modernity as "de-colonial options start[ing] from the principle that the *regeneration* of life shall prevail over primacy of the *production and reproduction* of goods at the cost of life (life in general and of *humanitas* and *anthropos* alike!)."[24] With Asian Americans specifically in mind, Lisa Lowe describes decolonization as "the social formation that encompasses a multileveled and multicentered assault on [capitalist and late capitalist] forms of colonial rule; that project of de-colonization is carried forth in the 'postcolonial' site but may equally be deployed by immigrant and diasporic populations."[25] The work of revolution, liberation, and emancipation cannot be separated from the conceptual work of "de-linking from the modern, political episteme articulated as right, center, and left; it is an opening towards another thing, on the march, searching for itself in the difference."[26] Armed with futures conceived by our words, insurgent life springs forward by living into the constraints and entailments of time, by making good on those wild words and engaging in the powerful work of living as if the new world were already the case. "The future must be a construction supported by [the human] in the present. This future edifice is linked to the present insofar as I consider the present something to be overtaken." That last bit comes from the inestimable Frantz Fanon.[27]

Miyoshi (Durham, NC: Duke University Press, 1998), 3-31; and more generally Michael Hardt and Antonio Negri, *Multitude: War and Democracy in the Age of Empire* (New York: Penguin, 2004). On "natural conventions," see Jonathan Tran, "Linguistic Theology: Completing Postliberalism's Linguistic Task," *Modern Theology* 33, no. 1 (2017): 47-68.

[24] Walter D. Mignolo, "Epistemic Disobedience, Independent Thought and De-Colonial Freedom," *Theory, Culture & Society* 26, nos. 7-8 (2009): 3. See also Mignolo, *Local Histories/Global Designs: Coloniality, Subaltern Knowledges, and Border Thinking* (Princeton, NJ: Princeton University Press, 2012); and Anibal Quijano, "Coloniality of Power, Eurocentrism, and Latin America," *Nepantla: Views from the South* 1, no. 3 (2000): 533-80.

[25] Lisa Lowe, *Immigrant Acts: On Asian American Cultural Politics* (Durham, NC: Duke University Press, 1996), 108. For analysis of Lowe, see Viet Thanh Nguyen, *Race and Resistance: Literature and Politics in Asian America* (New York: Oxford University Press, 2002).

[26] Walter D. Mignolo, "Epistemic Disobedience and the Decolonial Option: A Manifesto," *Transmodernity*, Fall 2011, 50. Also see Walter D. Mignolo, L. Elena Delgado, and Rolando J. Romero, "Local Histories and Global Designs: An Interview with Walter Mignolo," *Discourse* 22, no. 3 (2000): 7-33. It only makes sense to speculate whether theory comes before practice or vice versa if one has somehow missed the natural status of concepts, if one misses that the world comes to us in our life in words.

[27] Frantz Fanon, *Black Skin, White Masks*, trans. Richard Philcox, rev. ed. (New York: Grove Press, 2008), xvii, 201. In the poetic conclusion, Fanon resolves, "I am not a prisoner of History. I must not look for the meaning of my destiny in that direction. . . . The density of History determines none of my acts" (204-5).

For better or for worse, I envision Harvard admissions policies, set as those policies are against Asian Americans, as an attempt to overtake a present constellation of power, a constellation of power that required centuries to build up and now must be dismantled by the hard work of moral repair. Comprising that constellation are all the features that comprise most modern colonies of power: educational formations, municipal taxation, zoning codes, housing policies, health disparities, political gerrymandering, deep histories, food deserts, scarred bodies, straight-up prejudice, and so on and so forth. Affirmative action can be understood as a convention that came about naturally, which is not to say easily, within ecologies where inequality was allowed to run amok. At constellations like Harvard, the energy for the dismantling of power interestingly and ironically rises up out of and against those constellations. In other words, Harvard's affirmative action is Harvard trying to be better than itself; I see no reason why we should get in its way. In this I am like most Asian Americans, 75 percent of whom support affirmative-action measures of the kind taken by institutions like Harvard.[28]

I have been arguing that postracial theory does not work for the simple reason that it cannot do what it most wants to do, that is, outrun the past. Instead, I suggest we imagine present and future life growing out of the soil of past life. I have just delineated one necessary feature of that possibility, inspired by decolonial thought, where the past is given its proper place, but so is it also transcended by the very energies released as life expires and is received back into the earth. I now turn to the second conceptual feature, that is, the ability of future expectation to stimulate new life.

Fear arises out of the disasters of the past and will, if we let it, eat us alive. Thick conceptions of a completed future can rescue us from despair, enabling hope. But it will only endure if it arrives where we are from somewhere else. Christians call this future-present wind the Holy Spirit, and he enables, encourages, and enlivens everything he touches. He creates life

---

[28]See the data from the NAAS (National Asian American Survey), "Where Do Asian Americans Stand on Affirmative Action?," June 24, 2013, http://naasurvey.com/where-do-asian-americans -stand-on-affirmative-action/. Some Asian American applicants have joined the lawsuit, on the side of Harvard, in order to defend its affirmative-action policies; see "Breaking: Asian American Students File to Join Harvard Lawsuit and Defend Affirmative Action," *Reappropriate: Asian American Feminism, Politics, and Pop Culture!*, December 13, 2016, http://reappropriate .co/2016/12/breaking-asian-american-students-file-to-join-harvard-lawsuit-and-defend -affirmative-action/.

from the void, no matter whether that void is precreation or decreation, whether it is preflesh awaiting enlivening, enslaved flesh in exodus or entombed flesh resurrected. If the work of imagining life emerging from biopolitical determinations finds its bearings in decolonial thought, so reception of the Spirit comes through missionary residence in the strange new world of the Bible. Here we find hope amid temptations to despair.

This feature entails what the missiologist Amos Yong speaks of in describing "a postcolonial Trinitarian apocalyptic." Along with Christian T. Collins Winn, Yong writes,

> Whereas Christology and eschatology have been effectively severed from each other in [colonizing theologies], the alternative we propose begins with a reintegration of Christology and pneumatology with eschatology. The apocalyptic unveiling is thus not of a coming age of the Spirit but the revelation of the full depth and power of the messianic life, manifest in the Jewish carpenter from Nazareth, now working among those who have been filled with the Spirit of his resurrection. The Spirit-anointed Christ and his Spirit-anointed followers together embody a challenge to the status quo because the form of life raised from the dead in Jesus, and now shared by the Spirit of the resurrection, is radically different from the world as it is.[29]

We will need something like a *presently* embodied hope for the future among the incursions of the past. All parts of Collins and Yong's description of Christology, pneumatology, and eschatology do this type of work through the vestigial trinity of present, past, and future, which is why there has never been in Christian theology a serious eschatology that does not conceptually bank on God as revealed in Christ inhabiting time through the Spirit.

This, unlike postracialism's vaunted but fallow hope, chastens eschatological desire for the future by requiring of its adherents residence in the scary lands of the present. This eschatology looks to the future through the present/past, and its future orientation facilitates viewing those determinations in terms of their eventual redemption. The eschatological hope does not diminish the deadliness of past and present injustice. Indeed, from the

---

[29]Christian T. Collins Winn and Amos Yong, "The Apocalypse of Colonialism: Notes Toward a Postcolonial Eschatology," in *Evangelical Postcolonial Conversations: Global Awakenings in the Theology and Praxis*, ed. Kay Higuera Smith, Jayachitra Lalitha, and L. Daniel Hawk (Downers Grove, IL: InterVarsity Press, 2014), 150. See also Grace Ji-Sun Kim, *Embracing the Other: The Transformative Spirit of Love* (Grand Rapids: Eerdmans, 2015).

vantage point of their redeemed future and what that redemption costs—
nothing less than Christ's submission to the determinations of injustice,
what we might call reparations writ large—does one come to see just how
deadly is our current racial world, how much the relationship between past
and present produces a dynamic by which violent injustice reverberates
endlessly. Christ ushers in a revolution of the fullness of humanity. Against
the acedia of postracialism, we have the faithful re-membering of dis-
tended but testifying temporal existence. The arrival of Christ's redemption
does not involve a subordinationist god flitting above creaturely history in
order to offer an opaque image to which religious people might gesture.
The draw for someone like Arius was the idea that God could not suffer,
nor do anything new, just as those who followed such a god might not
suffer, or do new things.[30] In contrast, an eschatologically appropriate
trinitarian theology, which is just to say a post-Nicaean Christology, has
God entering into history, including its temporal torrents, determined like
any creaturely body by the currents of time, desirous of the future he
himself embodies, and waylaid by the catastrophic distending of time
Scripture names as sin, as he himself embodies. Rather than requiring no
work, and instead realizing in his person Arius's greatest fear, Christ be-
speaks redemption in ways that cannot help but collide with the expectations of those who believe that the future can be had only by reinstituting
a nostalgic past. Hence crucifixion, but also revolutionary new life.[31] Indeed,
crucifixion as revolution. Refusing to believe that such a present, like our
own racial moment, is the only future to be had, Christ heralds in the past-
present-future-past-present, a productive circularity that does not forget
or ignore that time as creature is given to witness and invites those who
follow to live into time-as-witness, just as Christ himself does. Something
similar is possible for all who claim humanity. Revolutionary mission is
what humanness looks like.

---

[30]See Rowan Williams, *Arius: Heresy & Tradition*, rev. ed. (Grand Rapids: Eerdmans, 2002), 233-
46. See also Justo L. González, *Mañana: Christian Theology from a Hispanic Perspective* (Nashville:
Abingdon, 1990).

[31]Revolution as a theological theme is central in Willie James Jennings, *Acts: A Theological Commentary on the Bible* (Louisville, KY: Westminster John Knox, 2017), 18; see also Jennings's
magisterial *The Christian Imagination: Theology and the Origins of Race* (New Haven, CT: Yale
University Press, 2011).

Note how the decolonizing liberationism and the eschatological missiology importantly work together. The decolonizing logic acknowledges and advances from colonized sites of discourse toward revolutionary possibility. The eschatological structure of revelation illumines and authorizes political action, rendering it confident while disciplining its patience. Decolonial forces, like the Spirit, surge forward, and Christology gives it shape and direction. Without the pneumatology, revolution goes it alone. And without the decolonizing commitments, American suburban pieties will domesticate the name of the Spirit. As the Spirit breathes life into the moribund colonized body, racial life is made to participate in God's triune economy.

Giving Up Harvard

The implications for Asian American Christians looking to live missionally follow. Asian Americans are tempted to live beyond history, as if white supremacy has not done what it has done, is doing, will continue to do. As if Asian Americans have not lived that history. As if they have not sometimes perpetrated it, often benefited from it, in every instance suffered it. Living beyond this reality entails living beyond the model-minority myth. Harvard, in the mythical version of the American Dream, is presented as that which both embodies and enables the dream's realization. Follow this route long enough and not only will Asian Americans make up 40 percent of schools like Harvard, but they should, for they unlike other ethnic minorities perform the script as it is written. They are accorded model-minority status exactly because they execute the fantasy so well. White supremacy loves this kind of racial life because it expedites the white privilege of simple postracialism. It especially likes its wedging effect that makes for minority-on-minority violence, Asian Americans pitted against other minorities, including recent Asian immigrants.

Something better would require Asian Americans to inhabit time more honestly. While they are neither Black nor White, Asian Americans can come to accept the truth that there will be no foreseeable time when Black-and-White does not touch everything about America, where the long and ongoing history of white supremacy does not kill, or at least seek to kill, in whatever way it can muster every aspect of Black life. Victims and victimizers, Asian Americans are conduits for this history's continuation. Like good Arians, they

can seek escape by living out their Harvard-enabled and -embodied fantastical dreams. Hence, the nearly 40 percent Asian American presence at
Harvard if not for that school's attempt to help them out of this fantasy.

Asian American Christians might look to participate in the Spirit's reparative missional work of God in Christ, the full and therefore vulnerable
inhabitation of history that inscribes them in lives that might, as imagined
through Philippians 2, recognize Asian American privilege where it obtains
(it certainly does not always) and where it is recognized (it certainly is not
always) and learn to, in good Philippian fashion, not consider privilege
something to be held on to. Asian Americans can find some solace in the
fact that the same privilege (again where it applies) that assisted their
Harvard acceptances will continue even if they do not attend Harvard. The
inverse may not be the case for other racial minorities. An Asian American
with an elite degree is usually just an Asian American, in the best sense,
whereas an African American with an elite degree is usually rendered just
an African American, in the worst sense. This solace can be turned to action
if the past is allowed to properly inform the future. The Harvard case would
be helped by one simple act: Asian American Christians admitted to
Harvard going elsewhere, leaving available spots for non–Asian Americans,
divesting themselves of the privileges and benefits that may have paved their
way to places like Harvard. Obviously, not many Christians will choose this,
not many will imagine its possibility or recognize its necessity or significance, but for those who do even more will be given. Through platforms
gained by such moral courage, these Christians might utter the following
missionary messages to America:

- "I studied very hard to get into Harvard, but I recognize I was reared in
  an environment where doing so was encouraged and often rewarded.
  That same rearing will serve me wherever I go, and while Harvard might
  help my career, so will many places. That may not be the case for these
  other students."

- "My grandparents immigrated under quite difficult circumstances from
  India to America. They would not have survived those circumstances if
  not for the warmth, encouragement, and charity of other immigrants. I'm
  simply paying it forward like those folks did for me."

- "In high school, my friends and I read Toni Morrison's *The Bluest Eye*, and it made me realize that I share with other minority women the burden of culturally endorsed self-hatred. To me this is an act of solidarity with my fellow sisters of Color."

- "I struggle as much as the next person with idolatry. I don't know what better way to smash my biggest idol than to give up this one career path in order to see what other things God has for me. My second-generation Chinese American church taught me to trust God."

- "Look, we're all members of the body of Christ. Why wouldn't I share the privilege of that body with others? The Bible says we share all things in common."

- "Growing up I always wanted to go to Harvard. But when my youth group went on a mission trip to Guatemala City last summer, the experience of coming face-to-face with great poverty kind of put that dream in perspective. I started worrying about how I might end up competing with applicants who grew up in that kind of need, and how much more they can do with a Harvard education. I still love the idea of going to Harvard, but I love this idea more, I guess."

- "I grew up as the only Asian kid in my neighborhood. A lot of these kids, even though they too were minorities, picked on me, calling me 'Chink' or 'Nip' or 'Gook.' Maybe giving up my Harvard spot is one way of loving my enemies?"

- "Why in the world would I want to go to a place that doesn't want me? If they want Latino kids more than me, fine. I'll go to Caltech or Cal. The weather is better there anyway."

- "Three kids from my Korean church got into Harvard this year. In previous years, it was the same kind of thing. Our parents came to America for this reason. But they also raised us Christian, and the three of us decided to do this together, to live the American dream in a way different from what everyone, including our parents, expects."[32]

---

[32]These ordinary, imagined utterances were inspired by Christina M. Qiu's op-ed in *The Harvard Crimson*: "Asian Americans Are Not Tools," updated August 4, 2017, www.thecrimson.com /article/2017/8/4/qiu-asian-americans/.

These are small enactments of Fanon's proclamation, "I am not a prisoner of History. I must not look for the meaning of my destiny in that direction. . . . The density of History determines none of my acts."[33] These enactments of Asian American Christianity presume a whole lot, not least of which is the truth that kids with the luxury of this decision tend to come from certain backgrounds. I'm not talking, mind you, about stable, financial, educated backgrounds. Remember that the model-minority myth isn't true, just like Harvard's admissions policies are not blind. These young Christians would have had to have been formed in the upheaval of thought that is life in the Spirit as described in Philippians 2.[34] It comes down to the question of whether our churches are capable of producing youth who see privilege as something *not* to be held on to. If we think not, if our children have not been raised to live missional lives, if the greatest ambition for them is Harvard, I'm not sure what we Christians are doing. But if Asian American churches can imagine their children's futures in terms of *moral* education, as developing children in the ways of making disciples of all nations, then the resourcing of occupational goods can take a backseat to vocational possibilities that can properly situate those goods.

Giving up Harvard could have the effect of rendering the Title VI lawsuit numerically moot.[35] But that is just the beginning of it. Substantively, it would mean that the zero-sum logic that affirmative action presumes would be broken open, creating space in which diversifying and reparative efforts can issue with less drama. It does more work still. Asian Americans are afforded if not White privilege, Yellow privilege, and often at the cost of other ethnic minorities.[36] Our dispossessive act, where and when it is possible, would reverse the lines of moral agency usually at play for ethnic minorities under strains of white supremacy, as evidenced by the lawsuit's wedging strategies. Instead, acting out of and toward mutuality, something always in

---

[33]Fanon, *Black Skin, White Masks*, 204-5.

[34]I borrow from Martha C. Nussbaum's wonderfully worded title, *Upheavals of Thought: The Intelligence of Emotions* (New York: Cambridge University Press, 2001).

[35]One would imagine it would be difficult to track down actual numbers of Asian American Christians at Harvard, but consider Rebecca Y. Kim, *God's New Whiz Kids? Korean American Evangelicals on Campus* (New York: New York University Press, 2006).

[36]See Jerry Z. Park, Brandon C. Martinez, Ryon Cobb, Julie J. Park, and Erica Ryu Wong, "Exceptional Outgroup Stereotypes and White Racial Inequality Attitudes Toward Asian Americans," *Social Psychology Quarterly* 78, no. 4 (2015): 399-411.

need of attentive maintenance, such acts would avail and empower moral agency, a performative moment that explodes the model-minority myth. The many prudential realities of race in America combined with Asian American Christians living missionally in America make acts of dispossessive empowerment—say, academically able students reparatively giving up spots at Harvard, Southern Californian families applying the same principle when enrolling or *not* enrolling their children in elite elementary and high schools, high-paid engineers gladly committing to graduated tithes, fantastically trained seminary professors risking their status by making public arguments for the cause of justice, male clergy vacating pastorates in order to make way for their equally gifted but patriarchically inhibited sisters—neither necessary as a manner of Christian discipleship under racism nor sufficient for it. But this does show what Yellow Christianity might look like.[37]

---

[37]Through conversation and research and editorial assistance, Tyler Davis substantially contributed to this essay. I am also grateful for comments from editors and from Daniel Lee.

PART V

Scriptural Reconsiderations
and Ethnoracial Hermeneutics

10

··

Intercultural Communication
Skills for a Missiology of
Interdependent Mutuality

Johnny Ramírez-Johnson

INTRODUCTION

This chapter deals with very sensitive matters of feelings and emotions about race and the reasoning behind them. You are invited to identify with all and or any one of the persons or examples presented throughout the chapter. This adventure in race relations from a personal emotional level promises to be a cumbersome trip. Only those seeking understanding of the other are advised to pursue the adventure.

We all experience the world via emotions even as it is widely agreed that any rigid distinction between emotions and other kinds of thinking is indefensible.[1] Our goal is to move from emotional-cognitive awareness to the development of skills for intercultural and interethnic relations. In this chapter, the word *skill* is used to refer to the cognitive-emotional approaches that are demanded of anyone seeking understanding of themselves and the other. The following outlines an intercultural missiology of everyday communications between peoples of different races, ethnicities, nationalities, and languages in our racialized Western English-speaking societies.[2]

---

[1]Marvin Minsky, *The Emotion Machine: Commonsense Thinking, Artificial Intelligence, and the Future of the Human Mind* (New York: Simon & Schuster, 2006).

[2]*Race*, a catchall term in Western English-speaking popular culture used as a synonym for nationality, ethnicity, skin-color-classifications (White, Black, etc.), identifies members of a unique cultural group. See Bill Ashcroft, Gareth Griffiths, and Helen Tiffin, *Post-Colonial Studies: The Key Concepts*, 2nd ed. (New York: Routledge, 2007), 20-21.

Herein I employ the epistemological perspective of practical theology where the biblical characters, experiences, and teachings are read as natural members of the Christian community without the need to make central the use of historical or textual criticism. This approach is what Swinton and Mowat call "ideographic truth," which allows for living in the Bible times as we live in our times without being enslaved by historical or textual critical methods as definers of truth. Here truth is relational and ideographic, not lineal and positivistic as demanded by the so-called correct reading.[3] Thus, I see a dialogue between Peter and the church today as authentic and truthful, and dealing with similar issues of inclusion and intercultural communications. The arguments are built on the platform of biblical insights that serve as models of intergroup conflict resolution in the missionary accounts in the book of Acts. Following a description of God's vision for diversity and Christian inclusiveness, the chapter argues for the need to engage across race groups as a Christian missiological mandate.

The chapter unfolds in six sections. I open with a story from my own life to illustrate how a White institution racializes the individuals in its context. Then, I explore the evolution of race as a social construct in the West through cultural anthropology. Third, I sketch a biblical definition of human anthropology and suggest a model for personhood as presented in the Genesis creation account. Fourth, I examine race relations based on reflection on Acts 10–11 and Acts 15, urging that the hermeneutics of intergroup relations in these passages can be applied to interracial relations in the church today. This leads, fifth, to discussion of how cognitive-emotion experiences become self-evident with the help of the Image-IQ inventory questions. Finally, the chapter ends with an unavoidable and sensate question about how we define our relationship with God and our racially other neighbors.

A RACIALIZED SOCIETY

Operationally, people experience a racialized society as an institution in which individuals consciously and unconsciously assign privileges to others by race in the context of relationships. The very first foundational step is understanding the category of race and how individuals, institutions,

---

[3]John Swinton and Harriet Mowat, *Practical Theology and Qualitative Research* (London: SCM Press, 2006), 43, 44.

and society manage such categories. Here I relate a story that shows how race categories operated in one episode from my life in a predominately White institution.

"You are not Black, and yet you signed with the Black faculty. This letter you signed cannot be truthful."[4] This was said to me in a private conversation inside his car, by the president of the institution. Because I was chair of the Human Relations Committee (HRC), I received many complaints. Consequently, when a Hispanic friend was fired, he informed me of his dismissal. When my president-friend denied remanding the adjudication of the case to my HRC, I called the faculty of Color to a meeting. The 1993 experience and its aftermath serve to exemplify how the unconscious views on race we all have learned guide our views of the other, just like Peter was guided in his views of the Gentiles (Acts 10–11; 15). The intercultural communication skills we were taught as we grew up shape how we view ourselves and how we categorize self and the other. These categorizations of self and other are culturally shared, though mostly unconsciously learned. By itself, categorizing people is an innocuous and normal practice that helps us navigate relationships. When dealing with intercultural exchanges, even if all involved have good intentions, the views we have about self and the other can cause us to stumble.

The Image-IQ intercultural and interracial theoretical framework that I am developing employs emotionally charged statements that help an individual identify his or her unconscious biases.[5] It should be obvious that no two people are the same and no two systems of racialization are the same. I propose that despite all political and cultural differences between Cornelius and Peter and my president-friend and me, both sets of relationships were shaped by two universal systems: (1) colonization and (2) racialization of the colonialized and colonizers. Both aspects of the Image-IQ are illustrated in this real-life vignette I experienced with my

---

[4]My president-friend, who is now retired, represents the best of his generation of the White leadership of the church. About this story I have alluded to, he responded as follows: "I do not remember the words spoken in my car that afternoon in 1993. Regarding the employment event, I did not use race as a criterion for any part of the logic for what happened. I do acknowledge that, in the opinion of the Black and Hispanic Faculty combined, meeting race was a factor."

[5]My forthcoming InterVarsity Press book (title still in progress) explains the four skills (Personal Awareness, Manifestation of Bias Vulnerability, Social Bonding Orientation, and Family Diversity Orientation) of the Image-IQ assessment (www.image-iq.org).

president-friend, and as we will see, they are also illustrated in the early church dramas depicted in Acts 10, 11, and 15.

The people of Color employed at the college unanimously challenged the firing as unjustified. The president responded with a protest. He was sure the issue had nothing to do with race while all minority faculty wondered how it could not be connected. His words were subdued in tone, seemingly characteristic of his European stereotypical demeanor. I felt, and the minority faculty felt, the firing was racially motivated. We all had witnessed how members of the same racial group as the president who were not stellar in their accomplishments had been treated with grace when they performed at lower than expected levels. We are trained to perceive our own group's mistakes as discrete incidents and the mistakes of the other are character traits applicable to the whole group.

In some ways, our Irish-descent president and we minorities have similar experiences. You need not be a person of Color to be a recipient of discrimination. As an Irish descendant, he belongs to a group that was historically discriminated against though they are not currently the object of discrimination in the Western world. Race is an elusive, ever-changing, always present, guiding category for Western cultural groups. The history of views on the Irish is indicative of the race-categorization argument and its sociopolitical purposes.

Race as a Construct in Cultural Anthropology

McClintock relates how the Irish nation was among the first conquered and classified peoples subjugated by the United Kingdom.[6] The Irish had been subject to the racial classifications applied to me—classifications based on what were thought to be obvious phenotypical characteristics. My president-friend was offended by my signing of a letter under the auspices of the Black Faculty Forum, for in his eyes I did not fit the classification.

Is race, as seemingly defined by my president-friend, a clear-cut, observable matter, a well-established set of categories? Looking at ourselves is paramount in seeing the other. Recognizing that we are each, everyone of us, a member of a cultural group that can be classified as a race is the first

---

[6]Anne McClintock, "The Lay of the Land, Genealogies of Imperialism," chap. 1 in *Imperial Leather: Race, Gender and Sexuality in the Colonial Contest* (London: Routledge, 1995).

step in building our intercultural communication skills. Race classifications started in Great Britain, at the birth of the scientific revolution, while the British were building their empire. As Prentiss argues, race as a social construct is constantly being reshaped and remade and includes the realization that each cultural, ethnic, and racial group constitutes a separate construction of race.[7]

In 1896 A. H. Keane argued that scientific taxonomical determinants for race were considered sufficient. These "materials have already been accumulated to justify de Lapparent's declaration that *l'heure des grandes synthèses a déjà sonné* [the hour of the great syntheses has already arrived]."[8] I am taking Keane's declaration as a sign of his and his scientific peers' views and the milieu in which they existed. Keane and his scientific peers, along with his society and cultural milieu, believed that race was a clear-cut and scientifically measurable human construct.[9] Seemingly this is true for many in the Western world even today.

For European culture of the nineteenth century a measurement of the protuberance of the jaw, also known as the "true or sub-nasal prognathism," was the primary scientific method for classifying races. Keane's hierarchically ordered list of races of prescribed intrinsic value included all those that he and his peers had measured. The list included White races, Yellow, Black, Guanches, and others living where the empire had gone.[10]

Western White populations were also divided into multiple races. The "Index of Nigrescence," a "scientific" measurement based on "algorithmic certainty" developed by the Ethnological Society of London and published under John Beddoe's name in 1885, defined whiteness.[11] Beddoe's work was used to categorize and scientifically justify the ideas about cultural superiority that translated into inherent rights for the politico-military hegemony of English speakers. Based on his work, the Irish, for example,

---

[7]Craig R. Prentiss, introduction to *Religion and the Creation of Race and Ethnicity: An Introduction*, ed. Craig Prentiss (New York: New York University Press, 2003), 2.
[8]A. H. Keane, *Ethnology, in Two Parts: I. Fundamental Ethnical Problems; II. The Primary Ethnical Groups* (Cambridge: Cambridge University Press, 1896), vii-viii.
[9]Keane, *Ethnology*, viii.
[10]Keane, *Ethnology*, 182.
[11]John Beddoe, *The Races of Britain: A Contribution to the Anthropology of Western Europe* (Bristol, UK: Arrowsmith, 1885).

were culturally considered "the white negroes."[12] Based on a nineteenth-century ethnology of hair color and jaw angles, skeletal and birth physiognomies were understood as visible and physical manifestations of the natural order of social hierarchies.[13] Since my president-friend is of Irish descent, he could have signed the letter himself!

White superiority requires the inferiority of Blacks. Such was the justification for slavery. The Duke de La Rochefoucault-Liancourt presented in written form a poignant example of the seventeenth century's logic of White superiority over Blacks. The duke's accounts of his travel to North America documented in vivid fashion the "decided superiority to the white colour, even in the eyes of the blacks." His words are very clear: "the abolition of the slave trade is the dream of a mistaken philanthropy. . . . The great danger a slave has to encounter after his emancipation is, that of not being able to provide for his wants."[14] The duke could not imagine Black slaves as full humans with reason; in order to survive they had to be guided like incapable automatons. For being Black, for being African, for being from a politico-militarily conquered group, the slaves were seen and treated as pseudohumans.

Even though "race has dubious value as a scientific classification system, it has had real consequences for the life experiences and life opportunities of African" descendants in the Western world. Sellers and colleagues indicate that race "is a socially constructed concept"; yet, the "arbitrary categorization of individuals into this racial group [i.e., Blacks] has resulted in the psychological unification of many individuals."[15]

Ogbu and Simons's anthropological insights about voluntary migration describe how Whites in most of the Western world "are almost entirely immigrants," making up the "dominant groups in settler societies." These Whites share "certain beliefs and expectations in common, including the

---

[12]Ralph J. Crane and Radhika Mohanram, *Imperialism as Diaspora: Race, Sexuality, and History in Anglo-India* (London: Oxford University Press, 2013), 78.

[13]Keane, *Ethnology*, 200.

[14]François-Alexandre-Frédéric de La Rochefoucauld-Liancourt, *Travels Through the United States of North America: The Country of the Iroquois, Upper Canada, in the Years 1705, 1796, and 1797*, 2nd ed. (London: T. Gillet, Salitbury Square, 1880), 3:358.

[15]Robert M. Sellers, Mia A. Smith, J. Nicole Shelton, Stephanie A. J. Rowley, and Tabbye M. Chavous, "Multidimensional Model of Racial Identity: A Reconceptualization of African American Racial Identity," *Personality and Social Psychology Review* 2, no. 1 (1998): 18-19.

belief in opportunity in their appropriated territory for self-improvement." Settler societies share a "cultural-ecological" milieu that includes "at least two kinds of minorities: those who have come to settle for the same reasons as the dominant group and those who have been made a part of the society against their will."[16] As a Puerto Rican, English-accented White Latino, I belong to an involuntary immigrant minority group. Puerto Rico was incorporated into the United States as part of President William McKinley's 1898 invasion during the so-called Spanish-American War.[17]

I recall my response to my president-friend's assertion that I was not being truthful in signing because I was not Black. In the heat of racial conflict I retorted: "You have a full-time job defining yourself. Do not pretend to have authority to define me." In the crowded front seat, we gestured passionately as we talked. His way of defining race was one that, seemingly, had closed boundaries while my own concept of race has an open definition grounded on self-expression. Race for me is permeable; I inhabit multiple definitions of race, not a single one. I am White, Black, Latino, Puerto Rican, and a bilingual Mestizo. I am a twenty-first-century member of José Vasconcelos's "cosmic race" and a Southern California inhabitant.[18]

BIBLICAL ANTHROPOLOGY

Brueggemann maintains that the Old Testament "has no interest in articulating an autonomous or universal notion of humanness."[19] Brueggemann further argues that such an idea of an autonomous human is not even possible in the Hebrew Scriptures. He maintains that the Old Testament presents an "interactionist mode of reality, so that humanness is always Yahwistic humanness."[20] Such interactionism means humans do not exist on their own—there is no individualized autonomy.

---

[16]John U. Ogbu and Herbert D. Simons, "Voluntary and Involuntary Minorities: A Cultural-Ecological Theory of School Performance with Some Implications for Education," *Anthropology & Education Quarterly* 29, no. 2 (1998): 155.

[17]Johnny Ramírez-Johnson, *An Ethnography of Social Mobility: Immigrant Membership in a Seventh-Day Adventist Puerto Rican Ethnic Church* (Lewiston, NY: Mellen, 2008), 29.

[18]José Vasconcelos, *The Cosmic Race*, trans. Didier T. Jaén (Baltimore: Johns Hopkins University Press, 1997).

[19]Walter Brueggemann, *An Unsettling God: The Heart of the Hebrew Bible* (Minneapolis: Fortress, 2009), 57.

[20]Walter Brueggemann, *Theology of the Old Testament: Testimony, Dispute, Advocacy* (Minneapolis: Fortress, 1997), 451.

To Brueggemann's interactionist definition of humanity, Joel B. Green adds nondualist and communitarian undertones—"the human person is utterly dependent on Yahweh for life, experiences human vitality only in relation to God, is a 'living being' that precludes any notion of dualism, and is human only in relation to the human community."[21] Neurophilosophers and neurocognitive scientists define humanity solely as biologically based though some acknowledge that there may be "'something more' with an ontologically distinctive entity such as a 'soul' or 'spirit.'"[22]

Green's definition of humanity marrying science and "biblical anthropology is not a speculative exercise, but grows out of interaction with perspectives on the human person in biology and philosophy."[23] Notions like this help us see race relations as embodied relations of and between individuals. Nancey Murphy's anthropology adds a spiritual dimension: "We are, at our best, complex physical organisms, imbued with the legacy of thousands of years of culture, and, most importantly, blown by the Breath of God's Spirit; we are *Spirited bodies*."[24] I follow Murphy, Green, and Brueggemann because in understanding race relations we need to see ourselves as spirited bodies in relationship. Such interdependence is crucial to this chapter.

Missiological skill sets for intercultural communication emerge from such a three-layered view of humanity: (1) All humans must define true existence in dependence on God. (2) No part of what constitutes the human is independent from God or the other. (3) Our very existence is tied to our interactionist reality, interactionist both with other humans in community and with God in community. In such a definition, humanity only truly exists in community. We are community when we communicate with our community members. Community before God is a created-in-his-image whole since excluding anyone from the whole community does not reconfigure it but causes that community to cease to exist.

According to Genesis 1, the actions of the Creator God were summarized six times with a positive statement that each part of creation "was good"

---

[21]Joel B. Green, *Body, Soul, and Human Life: The Nature of Humanity in the Bible*, Studies in Theological Interpretation (Grand Rapids: Baker, 2008), 9.
[22]Green, *Body, Soul, and Human Life*, 45-46.
[23]Green, *Body, Soul, and Human Life*, 16.
[24]Nancey Murphy, *Bodies and Souls, or Spirited Bodies?*, Current Issues in Theology (Cambridge: Cambridge University Press, 2006), ix (emphasis original).

(Gen 1:4, 10, 12, 18, 21, 25). In Genesis 1:31, the whole creation enterprise is judged "very good." This was not the case in the retelling of creation in Genesis 2. After God created the male *Adam*, he was not declared "good" but was judged in need of a companion ("not good that the man should be alone"). Thus God declares: "I will make him a helper as his partner" (Gen 2:18). "The details of this decision are told in two acts: the creation of the animals does not really meet the lack, but the creation of the woman does."[25] The narrative states that the man and, seemingly, God as he created each animal were searching together among the created beings for someone to be brought to Adam to be named his equal (Gen 2:20).

How do humans justify ceasing to see one another as community members, whether of the same or of different groups? Michel Foucault explains social exclusionary mechanisms as warranted by Western culture's bias in favor of scientific knowledge: "The Normal is established as a principle of coercion in teaching."[26] This "standardization," or creation of a norm, for people groups is what Jennings calls the "organizing conceptual frame" for the construction of whiteness. The "normalization" of whiteness is established via "Black bodies," who are the detectable counterbalance for the "invisible white identity."[27]

What Wilson Jeremiah Moses called "messianism," the idea that White Europeans were called by God for a "manifest destiny" to fulfill a special role "to bring about the kingdom of God on earth," has been used to define whiteness and in turn to create the myth of a White race.[28] Prentiss documented the role of religion in creating the White race myth as an elaborate Western social construction.[29] The whiteness myth was central in implying that God gave a superior status to royalty and that nonroyalty were inferiors and naturally defined as subjects of the queen or king. Because of their increased economic output and as a result of the industrial and scientific revolutions, the royal status of the elite was expanded to include the upper and

---

[25]Claus Westermann, *Genesis 1–11: A Commentary* (Minneapolis: Augsburg, 1984), 225.

[26]Michel Foucault, *The Foucault Reader*, ed. Paul Rabinow (New York: Pantheon, 1984), 196-97.

[27]Willie James Jennings, *The Christian Imagination: Theology and the Origins of Race* (New Haven, CT: Yale University Press, 2010), 25.

[28]Wilson Jeremiah Moses, *Black Messiahs and Uncle Toms: Social and Literary Manipulations of a Religious Myth*, rev. ed. (University Park: Pennsylvania State University Press, 2010), 4.

[29]Craig R. Prentiss, introduction to *Religion and the Creation of Race and Ethnicity*, 2.

middle classes.[30] As outlined by Foucault, degrees of normality indicated membership in whiteness, where whiteness is defined as the culture of European colonization.[31] This same perception of whiteness defined the seventeenth-through twentieth-century missionary, kingdom-building outreach movements, all seemingly playing a role in White European colonization.

The Foucaultian description of the Western scientific presumption that "the power of normalization imposes homogeneity" describes a homogeneity that diminishes, erases, and minimizes individual differences.[32] This statistically driven scientific classification delegitimizes individual differences "by making it possible to measure gaps, to determine levels, to fix specialties, and to render the differences useful by fitting them one to another."[33] What could be wrong with such a standardization process?

By eliminating diversity (i.e., individual differences) as the norm and creating an artificial mean for "the Normal," scientific stratification of knowledge explains why we are different and what such differences tell us about the other, and especially the nonconforming other. "It is easy to understand how the power of the norm functions within a system of formal equality, since within a homogeneity that is the rule, the norm introduces, as a useful imperative and as a result of measurement, all the shading of individual differences."[34] Foucault's project describes contemporary governmental approaches to race; today throughout the Western English-speaking world politics are defined by race.

Such scientific positivism, very much apart from biblical views, proposed how "the power of the norm" is used to confer equality. The first man (*Ish*), the biblical story tells us, required the presence of the first woman (*ishshah*) in order to establish such a social norm, in order to be declared good.[35] From a Western scientific perspective, it seems that the norm established by God provided formal equality when creating our first parents, yet that equality was not to last for long.

[30]Philippe Aghion and Steven Durlauf, eds., *Handbook of Economic Growth* (North Holland, Netherlands: Elsevier, 2005), 1A:1113-80.

[31]Foucault, *Foucault Reader*, 196.

[32]Foucault, *Foucault Reader*.

[33]Foucault, *Foucault Reader*, 197.

[34]Foucault, *Foucault Reader*.

[35]Justo L. González, *Mañana: Christian Theology from a Hispanic Perspective* (Nashville: Abingdon, 1990), 133.

In interpreting the words of Genesis 2:18, Justo González explains the importance of equality between humans for our social order. González sees the ontological power of the words of Genesis 2:18 as establishing a message of equality and declaring that humankind was "to have dominion over the rest of creation" but "not to have dominion over its fellow human beings."[36] For the colonial enterprise that established the Western world, one group imagined itself called to rule the others, to bring God to the others. God was not seen as already present, everywhere on earth. This missiology carried God from White Europe to the multiethnic world. As stated by Westermann, the norm at the time of creation was diversity as a definition of humanity, diversity in terms of male and female.[37] Human society moved from a view that legitimized diversity as the norm toward a view by which scientific categories were used to divide human groups and thus facilitate the epistemological creation of the other.

González described his Fuenteovejuna theology as a model for human social community, a paradigm in which unity is a communal reality based on shared experiences, not on shared identical human traits. Fuenteovejuna theology is defined by González as the social cohesion that shaped the Fuenteovejuna townspeople in Spain as an interconnected, indivisible group that was not separable into individual units. The residents of Fuenteovejuna frustrated the king and his emissaries in their attempts to identify the guilty party in the homicide of a cruel magistrate. These townspeople acted in unison in the face of adversity and saw their actions as executed by all without respect to individual autonomy.[38] Each reader, each individual Christian, every singular household, each institutional church, and the communities they inhabit have two choices for categorizing one another and the world they inhabit. The first choice is derived from Foucault's account of Western ways and involves categorizing humans as the Norm (Whites) and the other (deviant minorities). The second categorization, and the one I prefer for classifying humans, I derived from a synthesis of Brueggemann, Green, Murphy, and González, one I call the creation model.

---

[36]González, *Mañana*, 133, 134. Being fully human is being-for-others. This being-for-others is intended to occur in our many human relationships, and not only in marriage.

[37]Westermann, *Genesis 1–11*, 227.

[38]González, *Mañana*, 29.

Our shared humanity needs our shared dependence on God and is tied
to our interactionist reality, interactionist both with other humans in community and with God in community. God meant all of us humans to live in
interdependence in order to be human and in order to survive (Fuenteovejuna theology). González presents these ideas within an apocalyptic
view by which our experience is in conflict with "cosmic powers" (Eph 6:12).
Such was the view of the early church, such that its missionary enterprise is
seen in the book of Acts via an intercultural missiology of race relations.

RACE RELATIONS AS A READING OF ACTS 10–11; 15

The divisions of the early apostolic church were between two main people
groups—Jews and Gentiles. Acts 10:28 suggests that Jews were contami-
nated by the mere presence of Gentiles. These ideas were not grounded in
misanthropy but in deep covenantal commitments to purity, cleanliness,
and holiness as established in the Levitical Holiness Code (Lev 17–26).
When invited by God to eat unclean animals and not declare unclean what
God had cleansed, Peter in anguish responded to God saying, "By no
means, Lord!" (Acts 10:9-16). Then God challenged Peter, first by in-
structing him to visit the house of Cornelius, and second, even more
shockingly, by giving the Holy Spirit to the whole of Cornelius's household
of Roman citizens and slaves (Acts 10:17-48).

The "gift of the Holy Spirit" has been "poured" by God on them as in us
(Acts 10:45). This became the apostolic church's hermeneutical principle to
solve a great cultural, doctrinal, and liturgical conflict. Many words were
argued, spoken, and written by the early church about this very question, as
witnessed in the writings of the New Testament. This witness of acceptance
by God was repeated in the first Christian council as registered in Acts 15.
In his concluding remarks Peter testified that "God, who knows the human
heart," affirmed the Gentile converts "by giving them the Holy Spirit, just as
he did to us," that is, Jews who accepted Jesus' offered peace (Acts 15:8). By
such an outpouring of the Spirit, God cleansed Gentiles' hearts by faith thus
making "no distinction between them and us" (Acts 15:9). The church need
not, should not, ought not expect the other to look, feel, believe, and worship
exactly as they do. But of course that is easier said than felt, practiced, or
even believed.

F. F. Bruce argues that the Lukan record of the Council of Jerusalem creates a paradigm.[39] The first hermeneutical principle establishes that the actions and teachings of the Holy Spirit are to be superimposed on the words, teaching, and actions of Jesus. After all, the Holy Spirit is also called "the Spirit of Christ."[40] Thus, the teachings of Jesus are present today for the church as if Jesus were present among us, via the "law of the Spirit of life in Christ Jesus" (Rom 8:2). In fact, Jesus explained the role of the Spirit in John 15:26-27: "When the Advocate comes, whom I will send to you from the Father, the Spirit of truth who comes from the Father, he will testify on my behalf. You also are to testify because you have been with me from the beginning." These words of Jesus place in parity the testimonies to follow from the Holy Spirit with the testimonies coming from the disciples of Jesus. The very hermeneutical ideas behind the Jerusalem Council were registered in the letter sent to the Gentiles: "For it has seemed good to the Holy Spirit and to us" (Acts 15:28).

Second, the church established the hermeneutical principle of inclusion in the church community without conversion to Judaism or circumcision. This apostolic church conclusion is particularly revolutionary since the words of Jesus clearly established continuity with Jewish teachings (Matt 5:17-19). The Council of Jerusalem's decision in Acts 15 to cancel some of the traditions and laws of Moses for the Gentiles is a remarkable one. "Jesus . . . emphatically denies (twice, and thus with the greatest emphasis) that he has come καταλῦσαι, 'to destroy,' the law or the prophets."[41] In the Sermon on the Mount, at the dawn of his kingdom, Jesus declared his commitment to Jewish laws, yet here the revolutionary postresurrection church abrogates some of these traditions under the guidance of the Holy Spirit.

Third, the actions of the Council of Jerusalem established hermeneutical ground on the end of times and the fulfillment of the reception of the power of the Holy Spirit. The acceptance of a church member, the new friend of my son, or my daughter's fiancé is to be based on the reception of the Holy Spirit

---

[39]F. F. Bruce, *Commentary on the Book of Acts: The English Text with Introduction, Exposition, and Notes* (Grand Rapids: Eerdmans, 1954), 298.

[40]Romans 8:9: "Anyone who does not have the Spirit of Christ does not belong to [God]"; 1 Peter 1:11: "the Spirit of Christ within them"; Galatians 4:6: "the Spirit of his Son into our hearts"; and Romans 8:2: "the law of the Spirit of life in Christ Jesus."

[41]Donald A. Hagner, *Matthew 1–13*, Word Biblical Commentary 33A (Dallas: Word, 1998), 104-5.

and not their racial origins. We can relate these three hermeneutical principles to race relations for individual Christians, contemporary Christian
homes, and evangelical institutions for Christians in the world today.

These three apostolic hermeneutical principles are directly related to the
ways the Western heritage, White-majority church relates with people of
Color today. Led by the Holy Spirit, Peter, the apostolic church leaders, and
the early church as a whole concluded that they should accept the Gentiles
as equals and not force them to become Jews. God was found to inhabit the
land of all cultural groups and the spaces of all races of people. The gospel
message was and is about salvation and its ways via the person of Jesus, not
about bringing God to them (Acts 17:23-24; Rom 2:14-16). How did such a
process work itself out? Acts 15:19-31; 21:25 explain how the three hermeneutical principles outlined above were worked out operationally by the disciples (all from Jerusalem and all Jewish believers in Jesus).[42]

I propose that the stories of Acts involved a dialogue between gospel-
driven and Torah-driven values as seen by the Jewish religious leaders who
were in continual opposition to Jesus and Paul.[43] Drawing from cultural
traditions, eternal principles derived from the Ten Commandments, and
moral axioms, the apostolic church agreed to a prioritized list of requirements that the Gentiles needed to honor. Some of these elements were more
closely tied than others to essential mores defined by God, like the proscrip-
tions on consumption of blood based on old taboos regarding life (see Gen
9:4-6; Lev 17:10-14). The major matter concerned providing "a practical
modus vivendi for two groups of people [with] such different ways of life" to
live together.[44] The same skills of self-reflection and redefinition demanded
of Peter are required for us today: first, Peter saw himself and all Jews as the
people of God.

Second, as a result of the intense learning forced on Peter and the early
church by God, Gentiles and Jews were accepted equally as the people of God,
without requiring conversion of the Gentiles to Judaism. These self-reflection
skills that were forced by God on Peter are available to us today. You cannot

---

[42]"Operationally" here means the feelings involved in the decision-making process, seeing humans as emotional machines or as always behaving following emotional directions; thus "operationally" here means following feelings.

[43]Hagner, *Matthew 1–13*, 104.

[44]Hagner, *Matthew 1–13*, 104.

develop what you cannot see, and until Peter saw his biases clashing with God's ways, he could not welcome Gentiles as equals. This was not easy for him, and it is not easy for us today. The first step is the most difficult. The next section parses out in today's psychological language how these intercultural communication skills can be acknowledged and developed.

THE IMAGE-IQ INVENTORY: DEVELOPING INTERCULTURAL COMMUNICATION SKILLS

Recognizing that the integrity of our human spirit is directly connected to the existence of the mind, we must acknowledge that a mystery surrounds the social dimensions of intercultural communications. Most of the reasons for the preferences in our daily decision-making process at home, work, and church (simply anywhere and everywhere) remain unknown to us. The role race is playing in the decision-making process remains hidden to our conscious thinking even though race influences these social interactions on a daily basis. Westerners, mostly unconsciously, see people, particularly those that are the other, as racialized entities.

Research on "implicit attitudes" seeks to capture and define the etiology, thinking, consequences, and influences that guide and inform our dealings with people of other races. The race Implicit Association Test (IAT) is designed to capture the human social decision making triggered when in communication (directly or indirectly) with and about people from other racial and ethnic groups. The IAT attempts to measure human engagements or adjudications that are subject to the automatic control and evaluations that occur beneath human consciousness without the individual's awareness of that causality. In fact Greenwald, McGhee, and Schwartz document how useful the IAT is in measuring implicit attitudes; at the same time their findings indicate the pervasiveness of unconscious forms of prejudice.[45] How do implicit biases come to be? Even more importantly, how can we identify, name, and understand ways to fight them?

The Image-IQ, an emotion-cognitive intercultural-skills model that we will now examine, can assist in exploring and transforming implicit bias. The Image-IQ survey begins by describing two skills that help you look

---

[45]A. G. Greenwald and M. R. Banaji, "Implicit Social Cognition: Attitudes, Self-Esteem, and Stereotypes," *Psychological Review* 102 (1995): 6-8.

inwardly in order to consider the source of your preferences: "Personal Awareness" and "Manifestation of Bias Vulnerability." The survey continues by describing two additional skills that invite you to look outwardly and engage with the other in ever more intimate fashion: "Social Bonding Orientation" and "Family Diversity Orientation." The four emotion-cognitive communication skills in the Image-IQ survey help us conceive a way to walk in the steps that God forced on the apostolic church as it experienced intercultural clashes as reflected in the book of Acts. I will examine the emotions involved in the intercultural decision making in Acts 15 and describe the cognitive-emotional communication implied in the story.

As already indicated above, our emotions are involved in our social formation and decision making. A scripturally conceived missiology for change informed by social science therefore will help us in becoming conscious of these emotional aspects of our biases. This information will help us determine how our hidden logic, taught from infancy and learned as active agents of our lives, controls our minds and how our feelings shape our actions.

Before turning to a description of these four cognitive-emotional skills in the rest of this chapter, I offer a final word on the introspection involved in developing these skills. Advancing in interracial and intercultural communication requires deep personal awareness of feelings toward the other. Progress in communication depends on the degree to which a person embraces personal mindfulness. First, Peter saw Gentiles as unclean, just like he saw pork and reptiles as unclean, even though the Holiness Code in the Hebrew Scriptures does not explicitly define a Gentile as unclean in conjunction with food regulations. Still, this was the way Peter defined Cornelius and all Romans. For Peter, contact with the inhabitants of Cornelius's household would render him unclean. In other words, Peter was creating race categories, just like my president-friend and I do, and just like all members of the Western world do. Sechrest beautifully clarifies these ideas when she parses how New Testament Christianity, particularly via Paul, recognizes a discontinuity between notions of race in the past and in the present while Paul's theology of Christian character embraces a new racial identity.[46] Second, Peter saw Gentiles as a group to be differentiated. To identify and deal with similar feelings we must be willing to be introspective.

---

[46]Love L. Sechrest, *A Former Jew: Paul and the Dialectics of Race* (London: T&T Clark, 2009).

1. Personal awareness. The first skill involves becoming conscious of our own feelings about our cultural values, which initially are mostly hidden to us. This cognitive-emotional skill requires introspection and causes some discomfort when naming our likes and dislikes about self and others. However, this introspection helps us to see the contours of our own views. An acknowledgment of his own learned views about diversity came to Peter when he was asked to eat reptiles and God equated those reptiles with Gentiles (Acts 10:9-15, 28). God sees no favorites between Gentiles and Jews, and Peter is forced to acknowledge that alternative views on this question do exist (Acts 10:28-29). God resides with Gentiles. Our creator God, who owns the whole world, has never lost or given up ownership of the earth and all its inhabitants (e.g., Ps 24:1; 1 Cor 10:26).

Personal awareness also involves acquiring mindfulness of one's personal racial, ethnic, and cultural preferences. Do people see their preferences as the norm and even perhaps equivalent to the ways of God? Peter was first confronted with a clash of views about whom God accepts (Acts 10) and had to differentiate between the ways of his Jewish cultural-ethnic group and God's views. God was establishing via Peter's experience a new universal way to reach God based on total submission to God and inclusion of all who accept Jesus and receive the Holy Spirit.[47] Accepting God's magnanimous inclusion of all people was traumatic for Peter, and that is still true for us today. It requires total submission to God.

Answering the questions of the Image-IQ Survey will likely cause discomfort, perhaps similar to Peter's discomfort, discomfort that comes from answering, considering, or legitimizing the statements proposed in it. Often it will seem that no answer fits. All my views of diversity and all my personal feelings, values, and beliefs about my own and others' racial, ethnic, and cultural ideas were learned from childhood or as part of my life experiences. We are all, like Peter, told not to consider "profane" what "God has made clean."

My family and social experiences have formed the values of culture, race, and ethnicity that shape my customs, ideals, and ways of doing things. We

---

[47]The idea of submission is presented by James in his epistle, particularly Jas 4:7. See John Calvin, *Commentaries on the Catholic Epistles* (1855), Christian Classics Ethereal Library, 301, www.ccel .org/c/calvin/calcom45/cache/calcom45.pdf; and John Wesley, *The Works of the Rev. John Wesley*, 10 vols. (New York: J. & J. Harper, 1827), 17, www.archive.org/details/worksofrevjohnwe01wesl.

identify behaviors in others—like ways of dressing, musical tastes, smells, and other aspects of human diversity—that seemingly reflect values we consider less than ideal. We are unable to see our own ways as culturally grounded and to acknowledge that these ways are equally culturally derived.

2. Manifestation of bias vulnerability. The Holy Spirit facilitated Peter's acquisition of this skill set, but it took three times of seeing the same vision (Acts 10:16). Peter was "greatly puzzled," and the emotions aroused by the vision and its interpretation were apparently overwhelming (Acts 10:17). The second skill examined in the survey requires a posture of vulnerability about our biases and the ability to self-examine. Allowing such vulnerability leads to accepting other racial, ethnic, and cultural perspectives as valid. For Peter it took a vision and divine intervention for him to see how God made no distinction between people groups (Acts 10:34-36). According to N. T. Wright, Cornelius could have received the gospel message directly from the Holy Spirit via visions without requiring Peter to travel from Joppa to Caesarea.[48] It seems obvious that the meeting of the two groups was intended to build a new body for the church, an intercultural body that welcomed a Jew to the household of a Roman centurion. Such is the intercultural missiology here proposed. Only because God gave two clear-cut items of evidence of his acceptance of Gentiles did the Jews accept the Gentiles as equal. First, God gave a vision to Peter calling Gentiles clean. Second, through God's gift of the outpouring of the Holy Spirit on Cornelius's household, Peter and the apostolic church were invited to accept Gentiles as peers in the community of believers.

Bias vulnerability means that we must recognize our life preferences, insight that in turn forces us to see our dislikes and name them. You cannot have a preference without having something you like less. Peter was comfortable among Jews, but he was uncomfortable among Gentiles. In Joppa he was among his own, but on the way to Caesarea Peter became vulnerable and named his preferences. Peter declared that it was unlawful for him to be there in the house of Cornelius. Making decisions about truthfulness based on an individual's race is what I experienced with my president-friend. I am certain he did not see it, and still does not see it that way.

---

[48]N. T. Wright, Dale Larsen, and Sandy Larsen, *Acts: N. T. Wright for Everyone Bible Study Guides* (Downers Grove, IL: InterVarsity Press, 2010), 55.

We must also acknowledge that alternative preferences exist in the world. Recognition of his own preferences and acknowledgment that there are alternative ways to see the world were the result of Peter's coup d'état—Gentiles receiving the Holy Spirit (Acts 10:44-48). The outpouring of the Holy Spirit should be the final evidence of God's intentions for a multicultural church. It was the final argument for accepting Gentiles in the early church, and it should be the same for inviting the reader to embrace diversity. But such embrace only happens after we recognize that our ways are the ways of our cultural group.

The next set of skills invites us to recognize that other cultural, ethnic, and racial groups have lovable values and preferences, allowing us to see that alternative preferences exist. This was difficult for Peter, who was able to embrace this new value only because he remembered the command received in the vision. "What God has made clean, you must not call profane" (Acts 10:15) was a call to submit to God and embrace the other. Not everyone has the capacity to focus outside themselves. In fact, for White children who grow up among their own group, it is less likely that they can look outwardly and see equals. They are not able to see themselves as anything other than the norm.[49]

3. Social bonding orientation. The third skill set addresses our social bonding orientation, which is defined as the desire for pursuing interracial or interethnic cultural bonding. Only after Peter entered the household that he was forbidden to enter, according to his reading of the Torah, was he able to engage as the Holy Spirit engaged (Acts 10:47). As "it was, God had plainly accepted them, and Peter had no option but to accept what God had done."[50]

Unfortunately, plenty of churches, church members, families, and institutions of the church have rejected as different and inferior people of a different color of skin, ethnicity, language, or cultural beliefs. They are unable to seek, accept, and engage in diverse interracial relationships. In fact our

---

[49]Mary Jane Rotheram-Borus and Jean S. Phinney, "Introduction: Definitions and Perspectives in the Study of Children's Ethnic Socialization," in *Children's Ethnic Socialization: Pluralism and Development*, ed. Jean S. Phinney and Mary Jane Rotheram-Borus (Newbury Park, CA: Sage, 1987), 17. The differences in behavioral norms, expectations, values, and behavior patterns that distinguish groups are less frequently recognized by Whites because most live in contexts in which White norms prevail. Thus, many majority-group children are not even aware that they belong to an ethnic group.

[50]Bruce, *Commentary on the Book of Acts*, 230-31.

Christian day of worship, our Sabbath rest, is still today the most divided day by race. The only way to bridge this gap is to seek out relationships and thus be able to witness the Holy Spirit's embrace of those we see as the other. Such reaching out will afford us the opportunity that Peter was given.

Seeking diversity is not a natural human desire. Developing a desire to learn more about other groups' ethnic, racial, and cultural values and preferences results from the workings of God. Jesus informed us of his dream for a church that breaks all boundaries (John 17:11). Had Peter not been provoked with a divine fait accompli in the manifestation of the Spirit on Cornelius and his whole household, Peter would not have baptized them as he did.[51] Baptizing them meant accepting them as equal. An intercultural missiology was born from the Holy Ghost's inclusive ways when Peter accepted the call to submission. The same is true today: one individual can be an intercultural missiological agent for home, church, and the world—as long as we follow the Holy Spirit's prodding in submission.

Another aspect of a healthy social-bonding capacity involves the ability to critique diversity, which means getting emotionally involved. This skill is integral for learning to engage with the other. It is never about relativizing and minimizing differences. Differences need to be discussed openly and in an atmosphere of mutuality and respect. Peter did not behave as if nothing had happened. According to Bill Pannell, one's "personal hang-ups" for living together interracially are directly associated with one's Christian feelings about church and the doctrine of God.[52] Pannell's words are distressing, particularly in the context of the title of his book, *My Friend, the Enemy*, written back in 1968 in Pasadena, California, when he was the first full-time Black professor at Fuller Theological Seminary: "I am still puzzled by the level of animosity that I have received. This work of betterment of race relations is exhausting."[53] Pannell invites you and me to search for and identify our Cornelius, to express your feelings, ask your questions, and engage in dialogue as the only way forward. I believe that if you ask the Holy Spirit and request of God to take us to Cornelius, God will do so. In fact I believe the vision and dreams are available to us, so be sure to follow the instructions when received!

---

[51]Bruce, *Commentary on the Book of Acts*, 230.
[52]William E. Pannell, *My Friend, the Enemy* (Waco, TX: Word Books, 1968), 6.
[53]Based on personal dialogue with William "Bill" Pannell, June 2017.

4. Family diversity orientation. The fourth and last set of skills requires embracing a welcoming orientation toward diversity at the family level. This refers to the arduous process of learning to welcome racial, ethnic, and cultural diversity at home. Pannell agrees "with many others who suggest that the root of our agitation over race relations is sex."[54] Pannell further emphasizes the point by declaring that the two issues of sex and race are interrelated, that the "ghost of Negro sex prowess" and the myth of "white female purity still mocks us in the closets of our minds."[55] The feelings associated with our families and the sacredness of protecting our daughters comes to the surface for all, Asian, Black, Hispanic, Native, and White—for all.

The skills involved in embracing diversity in family bonding are all about breaking those stereotypes by getting to know the other. This includes learning to celebrate and embrace a child's union with a member of a different racial, ethnic, or culture group, or sharing lives, meals, worship time, and leisure time with other ethnic, racial, or cultural language groups. Neither of these two ideas may feel natural to you. It must have been emotionally and cognitively dissonant for Peter, especially because becoming one church family with Gentiles was something unacceptable. Only the Holy Spirit's work can help us build bridges. The first bridges are built by asking questions, exploring ideas, visiting uncomfortable subjects.

By no means are issues with ethnicity and sexual prowess limited to how Blacks were viewed by White culture. European missionaries described Cherokee women "as highly sexual natural beings, fruitful, fertile like the mythologized American continent itself."[56] Be it the macho Latino, the sexually free Cherokee female, the Black male sexual predator, or the sexually passive Asian male, all groups suffer grotesque stereotypical classifications that are meant to categorize the other in order to control them, and to defend our families from them.

This last skill set deals with personal choice in family bonding and has to do with learning to embrace the idea that, as long as it is a mutual choice, any person can elect to marry a partner from whichever racial, ethnic, or

---

[54]Pannell, *My Friend, the Enemy*, 104.
[55]Pannell, *My Friend, the Enemy*, 113.
[56]Joel Martin, "Almost White: The Ambivalent Promise of Christian Missions Among the Cherokees," in Prentiss, *Religion and the Creation of Race and Ethnicity*, 47.

cultural group they desire. David Livermore learned from Chinese friends who taught him "about *guanxi*, the personal relationship between people that obligates them to one another's needs and desires. In their minds, a relationship without any strings attached is no relationship."[57] While for many Americans and others of European descent, intercultural and inter-racial relationships, in fact all relationships, even family of birth relation-ships, are free and unattached, for many others this idea of freedom from attachments in relationship feels unreal, false, and vacant of meaning.

According to Livermore, to be ourselves and to build relationships with others, even at the family level, does not mean obliterating or relativizing our own values and beliefs. In order to build our intercultural communi-cation skills, we are called to bring our values to the surface and present them and, in a spirit of vulnerability, to defend our views while making in-quiry as to the views of others.[58] Jews continued to be Jews while embracing Gentiles as equals. Sharing in tension and building on their diversity made the church a worldwide institution. This feat is a product of the workings of the Holy Ghost. The missiology of intercultural relations that defined the New Testament church was full of contention and conflict, but was always interdependent and vulnerable. That is my invitation to you.

Relationship with God

Since this book addresses followers of Jesus and aims to stand on Bible-based truths of Jesus, I would do well to establish the motivation of God's commandments. At the same time, commandments need to be embraced and celebrated in operational ways. That is the task of heads of household, elders, pastors, bishops, and all leaders of the church. You are invited to embrace love as your motivation: "[These] commandments, . . . and any other commandment, are summed up in this word, 'Love your neighbor as yourself.' Love does no wrong to a neighbor; therefore, love is the fulfilling of the law" (Rom 13:9-10).

For John, the apostle of love, the love of God above all else is manifested via our love of neighbor.

---

[57]David A. Livermore, *Cultural Intelligence: Improving Your CQ to Engage Our Multicultural World* (Grand Rapids: Baker, 2009), 75.
[58]Livermore, *Cultural Intelligence*, 109.

> Those who say, "I love God," and hate their brothers or sisters, are liars; for those who do not love a brother or sister whom they have seen, cannot love God whom they have not seen. The commandment we have from him is this: those who love God must love their brothers and sisters also. (1 John 4:20-21)

The highest biblical value is love, and love is defined as sharing with the other, with the stranger. Are you a liar, or are you seeking to love God by loving the other?

This is the church's missiological task: to develop intercultural communication skills that are deep and real, communication based on mutuality and interdependence. These are not superficial, cosmetic, token relationships in which we never dialogue about differences and never invite people to our home or visit theirs. This is not an easy task, but a task of love, love that submits to God the Most High and manifests in an interdependent mutuality of loving your neighbor as yourself. A missiology of intercultural relations under the auspices of the Holy Spirit awaits the church that is ready for the final outpouring of God's Spirit. Are you embracing the end-time missiological outlook in Acts as your definition of an intercultural church composed of Jews and all Gentiles?

Our very relationship with God is defined by our relationship with one another. In particular, in loving and developing a relationship of interdependent mutuality with the other we learn about ourselves and them, and conversely we learn about God. There is no access to God without the steps of self-analysis, interdependent mutuality of love with the other, and thus relating with the God whose image abides in the other.

The question John presents is as valid today as it was in the first century: Do you love God by loving the other, or after all are you a liar?

11

"Humbled Among the Nations"

Matthew 15:21-28 in Antiracist Womanist Missiological Engagement

Love L. Sechrest

*Jesus responded and said, "I was sent only to the devastated
and broken sheep of the house of Israel."*

MATTHEW 15:24
(AUTHOR'S TRANSLATION)

INTRODUCTION

As I first began to engage theological questions about racism and patriarchy
in the church, I remember becoming increasingly uncomfortable with defenses of so-called biblical manhood and womanhood, and especially when
the explanations resulted in uneven and inconsistent morality. In particular, I
was told that the Bible commands, as stated in 1 Timothy 2:12, that women
refrain from teaching and leading men but that exceptions to this rule were
permissible in times and in contexts in which there is a dearth of male leadership. Thus, if a woman believed that she had gifts of teaching or leading, she
should be encouraged to seek out ministry opportunities that involved
teaching women or children if she wanted to teach domestically. If she preferred engaging adults, she would need to direct her ministry efforts toward
the mission field.[1] Though I keenly felt the denigration of women's teaching

---

[1]For more on trends regarding women in missions, see Frances S. Adeney, *Women and Christian
Mission: Ways of Knowing and Doing Theology* (Eugene, OR: Pickwick, 2015); Dana L. Robert,

gifts being depicted as inadequate for educating adult men—1 Timothy 2:13-14 clearly indicates that the prohibition is tied to inferior feminine intellectual capacities—I suspected that my White interlocutors had no idea of the racist and sexist logic at work in their reasoning.

Limitations on female teaching coheres with first-century culturally bound assumptions about women's intellectual abilities, which are inadequate to instruct what was then seen as the superior male rational mind:

> And since the elements of which our soul consists are two in number, the rational and the irrational part, the rational part belongs to the male sex, being the inheritance of intellect and reason; but the irrational part belongs to the sex of woman. . . . And the mind is in every respect superior to the outward sense, as the man is to the woman. (Philo, *On the Sacrifices of Abel and Cain* 1.103)[2]

> Theano, in putting her cloak about her, exposed her arm. Somebody exclaimed, "A lovely arm." "But not for the public," said she. Not only the arm of the virtuous woman, but her speech as well, ought to be not for the public, and she ought to be modest and guarded about saying anything in the hearing of outsiders, since it is an exposure of herself; for in her talk can be seen her feelings, character, and disposition. . . . For a woman ought to do her talking either to her husband or through her husband, and she should not feel aggrieved if, like the flute-player, she makes a more impressive sound through a tongue not her own. (Plutarch, *Advice to Brides and Grooms* 31-32)[3]

Further, both of these texts as well as the household codes in Colossians 3:18–4:1; Ephesians 5:21–6:9; 1 Peter 2:18–3:7; and Titus 2:1-10 draw on a common cultural root from Aristotle's *Politics*:

> The male is by nature superior, and the female inferior; and the one rules, and the other is ruled. . . . Of household management we have seen that there are three parts—one is the rule of a master over slaves, . . . another of a father,

---

American Women in Mission: The Modern Mission Era 1792–1992 (Macon, GA: Mercer University Press, 1997); Adeney, ed., *Gospel Bearers, Gender Barriers: Missionary Women in the Twentieth Century* (Maryknoll, NY: Orbis Books, 2002); Ruth A. Tucker, *Guardians of the Great Commission: The Story of Women in Modern Missions* (Grand Rapids: Zondervan, 1994); and Susan E. Smith, *Women in Mission: From the New Testament to Today* (Maryknoll, NY: Orbis Books, 2007).

[2]*The Works of Philo: Complete and Unabridged*, trans. Charles Duke Yonge, new ed. (Peabody, MA: Hendrickson, 1993).

[3]*Plutarch's Moralia*, trans. Frank Cole Babbitt, Loeb Classical Library (London: W. Heinemann, 1927).

and the third of a husband. A husband and father rules over wife and children, both free, but the rule differs, the rule over his children being a royal, over his wife a constitutional rule. For although there may be exceptions to the order of nature, the male is by nature fitter for command than the female, just as the older and full-grown is superior to the younger and more immature. . . . The relation of the male to the female is of this kind . . . but . . . the inequality is permanent. The rule of a father over his children is royal, for he receives both love and the respect due to age, exercising a kind of royal power. . . . The freeman rules over the slave after another manner from that in which the male rules over the female, or the man over the child; although the parts of the soul are present in all of them, they are present in different degrees. For the slave has no deliberative faculty at all; the woman has, but it is without authority, and the child has, but it is immature. So it must necessarily be with the moral virtues also; all may be supposed to partake of them, but only in such manner and degree as is required by each for the fulfillment of his duty. . . . Clearly, then, moral virtue belongs to all of them; but the temperance of a man and a woman, are not, as Socrates maintained, the same; the courage of a man is shown in commanding, of a woman in obeying. (Aristotle, *Politics* 1.1259b)[4]

The idea that women possess abilities that are sufficient to teach the immature reasoning abilities of children as well as adult men on the mission field effectively presents (dark and) foreign adult men as equivalent to domestic children.

Michael Omi and Howard Winant define racism as the perpetuation of hierarchy among racial groups. With its focus on *hierarchy*, this statement is an improvement over other definitions of *racism* that focus on the combination of prejudice and power.[5] When privileged individuals deny racism because they do not manifest personal prejudice and have little access to the levers of power, Winant's definition of racism challenges

[4]Aristotle, *The Politics*, trans. H. Rackham, Loeb Classical Library (London: W. Heinemann, 1932).
[5]Michael Omi and Howard Winant, *Racial Formation in the United States: From the 1960s to the 1980s* (New York: Routledge & Kegan Paul, 1986), 59-60; *Racial Formation in the United States*, 3rd ed. (New York: Routledge, 2015), 105-36; *Racial Formation Theory in the United States: From the 1960s to the 1990s*, 2nd ed. (New York: Routledge, 1994), 84-88; cf. Omi and Winant, "The Theoretical Status of the Concept of Race," in *Race, Identity and Representation in Education*, ed. Cameron McCarthy, Warren Crichlow, Greg Dimitriadis, and Nadine Dolby, 2nd ed. (New York: Routledge, 2005), 3-12.

them to focus on the manifestations of hierarchy that they do enjoy. Conversely, the personal prejudices of individuals from disadvantaged communities are certainly sinful but may not be racist if these individuals lack access to the means of promoting or establishing a hierarchy. Thus, the definition differentiates *personal prejudice* from *racism* and facilitates a focus on whether an institution, sentiment, or policy perpetuates racist social-group hierarchies of privilege. With hierarchy at the core of a conception of racism, an antiracist womanist agenda is one that operates to undermine structural advantages and level relationships among men and women and between diverse subgroups. What is less well recognized is the fact that sexism and racism focus on interlocking hierarchies of privilege and require a mode of analysis at the intersection of race and gender, like that found in womanist interpretation. By attending to black women's experience and reading strategies, womanist interpretation engages the Bible while attending to wounds inflicted by racism and sexism and all other oppressive "isms."[6]

Interpretation of the Gospel of Matthew represents an interesting site on which to reflect about the interaction of intertwining racial and patriarchal hierarchies and the missionary enterprise. On the one hand, in the missionary mandate of the Great Commission (Mt 28:18-20), Jesus directs disciples to take the gospel to foreign lands and other peoples. Yet on the other hand, the text evidences a sometimes exclusive inward focus on the mission to Israel, as in Matthew 15:24 (cf. Mt 15:26; 10:6). Indeed, though others would prefer to focus on the inclusivity of pro-Gentile passages in the gospel, like the Great Commission, it is not difficult to find interpreters who will see in Jesus' encounter with the Canaanite woman in Matthew 15:21-28 a perfect illustration of racial and gendered hierarchy in the New Testament. The story of the Canaanite woman is at the epicenter of both feminist and minority cultural critique; the ethnic and gendered dynamics in this text trigger a firestorm of protest. Many interpreters recoil at the Evangelist's portrait of a woman who seems to participate in her own denigration, while some readers might also resent the subtle anti-Semitism that emerges when critics label Jesus' behavior racist and then suggest that it was somehow

---

[6]For more on womanist biblical interpretation, see Mitzi J. Smith, ed., *I Found God in Me: A Womanist Biblical Interpretation Reader* (Eugene, OR: Cascade, 2015).

typical of Jewish thought of the time.[7] Yet, even though the scene is certainly analogous to the dynamics of modern-day racism and sexism, we must still ask whether the episode goes beyond prejudice and crosses the line into racism as defined by Omi and Winant.

Much like the underlying racialized and gendered logic presented to me regarding women's leadership on the mission field, missions history shows that the movement of the gospel was accompanied by the export of racist and gendered hierarchies of difference.[8] With that in mind, we might ask if, as well as promoting patriarchal hierarchies, the Gospel of Matthew is imperialistically racist, anti-Gentile, or both.[9] Or, on the other hand, should we engage a more sympathetic reading of the narrative that notes that it emerged in a context of oppression and imperialistic hierarchies? Is it possible that the Gospel of Matthew offers strategies to resist corruption of its intent to bring liberation from oppression? If we find it impossible to read the text about the Canaanite woman today without thinking about racism and sexism in light of hierarchical relations between groups in modern society, it would be advisable to consider the historical context of the Gospel. I contend that when read in light of the historical forces pressuring early Christian communities like Matthew's, Matthew 15:21-28 can provide opportunities to dismantle hierarchy through a reading that takes seriously the oppression of first-century Jews as well as contemporary women and minorities.

This essay focuses on questions about how the Gospel of Matthew engages questions about racism and sexism rather than questions about Jesus' racism and sexism. In other words, I am not concerned with the

---

[7]E.g., Amy-Jill Levine, "Matthew's Advice to a Divided Readership," in *The Gospel of Matthew in Current Study: Studies in Memory of William G. Thompson, S.J.*, ed. David E. Aune (Grand Rapids: Eerdmans, 2001), 25.

[8]See especially the volume edited by Mitzi J. Smith and Jayachitra Lalitha, *Teaching All Nations: Interrogating the Matthean Great Commission* (Minneapolis: Fortress, 2014), which interrogates the use of the Matthean Great Commission in Christian mission, education, and biblical and constructive theology. In addition, Musa W. Dube explores this dynamic in the Gospel of Matthew in *Postcolonial Feminist Interpretation of the Bible* (St. Louis: Chalice Press, 2000). Indeed Daniel Jeyaraj's essay in this current volume hints that interaction between the missionaries and the Tamil people of India unfolded in a way that reveals the missionaries' own attitudes about racial and social hierarchies.

[9]Patriarchal, imperialistically racist: Dube, *Postcolonial Feminist Interpretation*, passim; or anti-Gentile: David C. Sim, "The Gospel of Matthew and the Gentiles," *Journal for the Study of the New Testament* 57 (1995): 19-48.

question of whether Matthew 15:21-28 is historical or whether the historical Jesus shared the attitudes of the Evangelist who wrote about the significance of Jesus' life and work. Here I am attending to the historical pressures that likely shaped Matthew as the author as he adapted the episode for this Gospel. In addition, I am interested in the way that modern readers engage the text from the perspectives of their own cultures. In other words, I am bringing a historical-critical reading into conversation with a womanist analysis of contemporary interpreters in order to imagine how this ancient story can help us resist racism and sexism in a new cultural and temporal moment.[10] We will begin by considering the nature of racism in the context of early Christianity before moving on to consider how a synthetic reading of this text resists patriarchy and engages antiracist goals.

PRO-GENTILE VERSUS ANTI-GENTILE RHETORIC, OR "IS THE GOSPEL OF MATTHEW RACIST?"

Critical race theorists tracking the evolution of racism found that the *active* forms of racism that were more common in the first half of the twentieth century had given way to the *passive racism* and *symbolic racism* that were more socially acceptable at the start of the twenty-first century.[11] *Active racism* is typically exhibited in the ugly racial epithets, violent attacks, and physical segregation of the Jim Crow era and is recurring in Trumpism in the United States. It is seen in the mass incarceration of Blacks, Latina/os, and undocumented immigrants and in contemporary expressions of hate

---

[10]See Smith, *I Found God in Me*, 1-9. For a brief introduction to issues in historical criticism, cultural hermeneutics, and reader-response interpretation see Jaime Clark-Soles, *Engaging the Word: The New Testament and the Christian Believer* (Louisville, KY: Westminster John Knox, 2010). While evangelical interpreters are not often enamored of reader-response interpretation, which includes womanist interpretation, I suggest that evangelicals, who of all readers are among those most interested in faithful performances of the text, should be vitally interested in understanding where diverse communities of Christian readers encounter difficulties when engaging the biblical text (e.g., via texts that affirm slavery, feminine subordination, genocide, etc.). It is only after hearing these voices that the church can construct a Christian orthodoxy and orthopraxy that can promote fidelity to the God of the Bible, for Christians of all nations.

[11]For more on active, passive, symbolic, and internalized racism, see James M. Jones, *Prejudice and Racism*, 2nd ed. (New York: McGraw-Hill, 1997), 11-15, 124-31; and Love L. Sechrest, "Racism," in *The Dictionary of Scripture and Ethics*, ed. Joel B. Green et al. (Grand Rapids: Baker Academic, 2011).

against religious, ethnoracial, and sexual minorities.[12] *Passive racism,* on the other hand, is the racism that manifests itself in avoidance of raced individuals and racially charged topics and situations. Passive racism coincides with privilege because the capacity to avoid contact with racialized groups or ignore their issues is a luxury enjoyed only by those at the top of the racial hierarchy. Similar to passive racism is *symbolic racism,* which achieves racist outcomes via the use of more socially acceptable proxies for racist discourse. Symbolic racism might blame minorities for their poverty because they lack traditional values like a Protestant work ethic or respect for the law, without attending to systemic imbalances in society like racially ordered differences in criminal sentencing, school funding, or housing and mortgage lending.[13] Yet racism only works to the degree that a supporting ideology that creates hierarchy and mediates access to resources is present. If the prejudice of ethnocentrism is found in people of all hues, shapes, and epochs, the privilege that blesses some with extraordinary access to resources while denying others of that access creates the hierarchy that is the hallmark of a racist social system.

So, does evidence of racism exist with reference to what we know about the ancient world? In previous work, I found evidence that some Jews and early Christians did understand themselves to belong to different ethnic and racial groups, though, to be sure, the social construction of these groups differed in several ways from their modern analogues. Interestingly, some features of group identification among ancient Greco-Roman authors do line up with elements of modern ideas, and particularly with respect to the idea of calculating ethnicity via homeland or geographical origin. Many

---

[12]Michelle Alexander, *The New Jim Crow: Mass Incarceration in the Age of Colorblindness* (New York: New Press, 2012). The online news magazine *Slate,* referring to over a thousand hate crimes documented by the Southern Policy Law Center in the aftermath of Donald Trump's election, began a running tally of "individual incidents of racism, misogyny, Islamophobia, homophobia, transphobia, anti-Semitism, and anti-immigrant sentiment." Slate Staff, "Hate in America: An Updating List," *Slate,* August 14, 2017, www.slate.com/articles/news_and_politics/politics/2016/12/hate_in_america_a_list_of_racism_bigotry_and_abuse_since_the_election.html.

[13]We might also add here a mention of institutional racism, a concept that ascribes the differences in wealth between different groups to the social barriers for advancement that impede the participation of minorities in the American dream. This kind of racism is observable in statistics that document racial disparities in wealth from home ownership that emerged as a result of decades of racist policies and practices in the home mortgage and real estate industries, beginning in the post–World War II era with the misapplication of Veterans Administration benefits and decades of redlining.

Jews, on the other hand, did not distinguish races based on involuntary characteristics like territory of origin or ancestry. Instead, for this group, the Jewish race was constituted around the voluntary worship of the God of Abraham as mediated by the Torah.[14]

Since many insist that racism requires both a concept of race and the presence of a supporting ideology, a question about racism in antiquity must not only detect and understand the social construction of race in that era; it also needs to confirm the existence of a comparable cooperating worldview. On this point, classicist Benjamin Isaac identifies "proto-racism" in the ancient world by using a definition of racism that facilitates this kind of diachronic crosscultural comparison.[15] Isaac concentrates on the element of determinism as the critical component in the construction of a racist ideology in Greco-Roman texts that links undesirable characteristics to involuntary ascribed traits. In the classical period, ancients often associated negative characteristics with a people group by deterministically linking the character of a people to the group's territory of origin, that is, by assigning characteristics like hostility and brutality to people from harsh and unforgiving climates. This is deeply analogous to the way moderns have defined races by making associations between character traits like temperament and intellect with involuntary physical characteristics like gender or skin color. Thus, as documented by Isaac, according to the ancients, hot arid climates produce barbaric, uncivilized brigands, and mild temperate climates yield morally elevated, intelligent civilizations. Our question then is whether this ideology or a similar ideology is reflected in the Gospel of Matthew.

Instead of the climatological determinism described by Isaac, the Gospel of Matthew follows other ancient Jews by dividing the world based on a malleable characteristic centering on worship of the God of Abraham. Rather than excluding others who were born outside of the Jewish homeland, Matthew maintains that the good news of Christ is a precious

---

[14]Love L. Sechrest, *A Former Jew: Paul and the Dialectics of Race* (New York: T&T Clark, 2009).

[15]Benjamin Isaac, *The Invention of Racism in Classical Antiquity* (Princeton, NJ: Princeton University Press, 2004). In later work and in response to affirming feedback, Isaac acknowledged that he had been too tentative in naming the phenomenon identified in *Invention of Racism* and dropped the *proto-* prefix from his discourse. See Benjamin Isaac, Joseph Ziegler, and Miriam Eliav-Feldon, introduction to *The Origins of Racism in the West*, ed. Miriam Eliav-Feldon, Benjamin Isaac, and Joseph Ziegler (New York: Cambridge University Press, 2013), 1-31.

gift to be shared with *benign and discerning* Gentile outsiders (Mt 7:6).[16] The narrative has a concern for Gentile inclusion that pervades the work, from the worship of the magi at the outset of the story (Mt 2:1-12) to the climactic Great Commission that sends the gospel to the nations (Mt 28:19; cf. Mt 24:14).[17] Jesus' genealogy in Matthew 1:1-18 captures Matthew's particular blend of universalism and particularism by interweaving stories about four Gentile women into a Jewish tribal history.[18] Along with our passage about the faith of the Canaanite woman, Jesus heals a Roman's servant (Mt 8:5-13; cf. Mt 15:21-28), points toward a global eschatological banquet (Mt 8:11), and liberates two foreigners from oppressive spirits (Mt 8:28-34). The theme of universalism from Isaiah 42:1 finds its way into Matthew's description of the Messiah ("He will proclaim justice to the Gentiles"; Mt 12:18), and the Gospel borrows universalistic language from Isaiah 9:1 in describing Jesus' home and ministry ("Galilee of the Gentiles"; Mt 4:15-16). The kingdom parables of Matthew 21:28–22:14 point toward a Gentile mission, and the reference in Matthew 21:43 to giving the vineyard, that is, the people of Israel, to an ethnos that produces fruits of the kingdom may also have other-affirming elements.[19] The declaration of the Roman soldiers in Matthew 27:54—"Truly this man was God's Son"—gains importance in its climactic position in the narrative, depicting the third exemplary instance of a Gentile's confession of Christ (cf. Mt 8:5-13; 15:21-28).

---

[16]Love L. Sechrest, "Enemies, Romans, Pigs, and Dogs: Loving the Other in the Gospel of Matthew," *Ex Auditu* 31 (2015): 89-90.

[17]Eugene A. LaVerdiere and William G. Thompson, "New Testament Communities in Transition: A Study of Matthew and Luke," *Theological Studies* 37, no. 4 (1976): 567-97; Warren Carter, "Matthew and the Gentiles: Individual Conversion and/or Systemic Transformation?," *Journal for the Study of the New Testament* 26, no. 3 (2004): 259-82; David C. Sim, "The Gospel of Matthew and the Gentiles," *Journal for the Study of the New Testament* 57 (1995): 19-21; Schuyler Brown, "The Matthean Community and the Gentile Mission," *Novum Testamentum* 22, no. 3 (1980): 193-221; Donald Senior, "Between Two Worlds: Gentiles and Jewish Christians in Matthew's Gospel," *Catholic Biblical Quarterly* 61 (1999): 1-23; and Craig S. Keener, "Matthew's Missiology: Making Disciples of the Nations (Matthew 28:19-20)," *Asian Journal of Pentecostal Studies* 12, no. 1 (2009): 3-20.

[18]See John Hutchison's discussion of the common approaches to understanding Matthew's inclusion of references to Tamar, Rahab, Ruth, and Bathsheba in Matthew 1:1-18. John C. Hutchison, "Women, Gentiles, and the Messianic Mission in Matthew's Genealogy," *Bibliotheca Sacra* 158 (April-June 2001): 152-64.

[19]The common imagery of vineyard as a metaphor in Jewish thought and in the larger context of Matthew favor an understanding that the vineyard itself is not being replaced in this parable, but only the vinegrowers who tend the vineyard. Thus, the parable anticipates not a new and differently constructed people of God but a new set of leaders for the people of God. See Philip L. Culbertson, "Reclaiming the Matthean Vineyard Parables," *Encounter* 49, no. 4 (1988): 257-83.

Matthew also contains the striking command to *love* one's enemies (Mt 5:44), remarkable especially since, based on the consensus dating of the Gospel, it was penned in the immediate aftermath of a profound and humiliating military defeat.[20]

Nevertheless, the Gospel does contain evidence of stereotypic portraits of Gentiles that may incorporate hints of determinism.[21] Gentiles are hostile to outsiders (Mt 5:47) and worship vain idols (Mt 6:7); they are characterized by empty materialism (Mt 6:32) and are known as brutal and arrogant tyrants (Mt 20:25). Though the saying at Matthew 7:6 about giving holy things to dogs and casting pearls to swine is debated relative to whether the dogs and swine mentioned there refer to Gentiles, I find the unambiguous reference to outsiders as dogs in Matthew 15:26-27 to be decisive on this question (cf. 2 Pet 2:22).[22] Thus when Jesus tells the disciples to "go nowhere among the Gentiles" in the missionary discourse and again in our text, it can be read as excluding those people from missionary activity who are inherently unsuited for inclusion into the kingdom inasmuch as they pose a danger to Matthew's own recently defeated community (Mt 10:5-6; cf. Mt 15:26).[23]

Must we conclude, then, that Matthew does comport with the contours of racism we have sketched relative to the ancient world? Admittedly, the episode of the Canaanite woman comes closest to exhibiting the territorial determinism of ancient protoracism through the combination of the negative epithet and the mention of the woman's origin from

---

[20]Most biblical scholars date the Gospel in the aftermath of the Jewish War with Rome in 70-100 CE. See Raymond E. Brown, *An Introduction to the New Testament*, Anchor Bible Reference Library (New York: Doubleday, 1997), 216-17.

[21]Sim, "Gospel of Matthew and the Gentiles," 29-30. Sim's work has not been persuasive to many because scholars do not think that the passages discussed in this paragraph reflect Matthew's pro-Gentile viewpoint, though Sim sees them as communicating the editor's viewpoint. While Sim's conclusions about the anti-Gentile nature of the Gospel of Matthew are largely rejected (cf. Joel Willitts, "The Friendship of Matthew and Paul: A Response to a Recent Trend in the Interpretation of Matthew's Gospel," *Theological Studies* 65, no. 1 [2009]: 1-8; and Brown, "Matthean Community and the Gentile Mission"), his observations do point to the ambiguity in the Gospel's portrait of Gentiles.

[22]For a discussion about evidence that "dog" was a polemical reference to Gentiles, see Vincent Taylor, *The Gospel According to St. Mark*, 2nd ed. (New York: St. Martin's Press, 1966), 350; contra Levine, "Matthew's Advice," 32.

[23]For a nuanced development of this idea that takes into account Matthew's own minoritized experience, see Sechrest, "Enemies, Romans, Pigs, and Dogs."

Canaan.[24] Yet if we recall Isaac's contention that determinism was the characteristic that makes ancient ideology analogous to modern racism, the very fact
that most Jews did not construct identity around an involuntary element like
territory of origin but allowed for the welcome of outsiders through conversion
demonstrates the general lack of the key element of determinism. Indeed, Jesus'
final blessing on the woman and her child testify to this dynamic. In fact, the
female converts in Jesus' genealogy form key evidence that Matthew participated in a construction of Jewish identity that resists determinism;[25] likewise,
mention of the Pharisees' proselytism in Matthew 23:15 may be evidence that
Matthew knew that other Jews in the period held to this view.[26] Thus, though
the Gospel of Matthew may exhibit some prejudice in its use of negative stereotypes and symbolic beliefs about how Gentiles violate traditional values, it
also exhibits an inclusivism that goes well above and beyond more precise,
trans-historical definitions of racism.[27] Indeed, from a feminist perspective that
focuses on the striking inclusion of women in a genealogy, one scholar argues
that Jesus' relationship to divinely vindicated women such as Tamar, Bathsheba,
and especially Mary helps to establish his messianic bona fides.[28]

---

[24]It is interesting that Matthew describes her as a Canaanite (Mt 15:21), modifying Mark's description of her as a Syro-Phoenician (Mk 7:26). Does *Canaanite* function as a description of her land
of origin, her religious preferences, or her ethnic history? Given that models of ethnoracial
identification in the period encompassed all these elements, none of these options excludes the
possibility that the term is functioning as a racial identifier given that all these elements are
connected with the language of race in the period. For more on ethnoracial identification among
Jews of the period, see Sechrest, *Former Jew*, 54-109.

[25]E.g., see Eduard Schweizer, *Das Evangelium nach Matthäus*, Das Neue Testament Deutsch 2
(Göttingen: Vandenhoeck & Ruprecht, 1986), 9; Craig S. Keener, *A Commentary on the Gospel
of Matthew* (Grand Rapids: Eerdmans, 1999), 78-81.

[26]For more information about the ethnicity of the women in the genealogy, see Hutchison,
"Women, Gentiles, and the Messianic Mission," 154, 158-59. For more information on Jewish
proselytism, see James Carleton Paget, "Jewish Proselytism at the Time of Christian Origins:
Chimera or Reality?," *Journal for the Study of the New Testament* 18, no. 62 (1996): 65-103; and
Scot McKnight, *A Light Among the Gentiles: Jewish Missionary Activity in the Second Temple Period*
(Minneapolis: Fortress, 1991).

[27]For more on the phenomenon of prejudice, see Jones, *Prejudice and Racism*, 140-49. Indeed,
even some of the material supporting the pro-Gentile mission perspective can be viewed more
critically. For instance, see Warren Carter's discussion of the magi, picturing them as a fulfillment of the Isaianic vision of prostrate, gift-giving Gentiles (cf. Is 60:6; Carter, "Matthew and
the Gentiles," 273). Also in this vein is David Sim's observation regarding the confession in
Matthew 27:54, maintaining that the soldiers are examples of the Gentiles judged in Matthew
25:31-46, also noting that the Gadarenes completely reject Jesus ("Gospel of Matthew and the
Gentiles," 23-24).

[28]Peter-Ben Smit, "Something About Mary? Remarks About the Five Women in the Matthean
Genealogy," *New Testament Studies* 56 (2010): 191-207.

MATTHEW 15:21-28 AS RESISTANCE LITERATURE

Notwithstanding the discussion about whether the Gospel of Matthew is racist, we still have some distance to traverse before we can appropriate the troubling story of the Canaanite woman as part of a womanist antiracist agenda. Such work requires that we first consider the kinds of pressures in Matthew's milieu that would give rise to the negative polemics and prejudice in the narrative, and four considerations help establish the historical context.[29] First, it is easy to imagine how interethnic tensions in the aftermath of the fall of Jerusalem in the Jewish War with Rome could give rise to negative depictions of outsiders—war is, after all, the ultimate expression of ethnic conflict. Second, Matthew participates in the ensuing debates within Judaism about the future of the people in terms of their worship, society, and leadership. Matthew's conflict with the emerging rabbinic movement in the aftermath of the war is clear in his critique of Pharisees, as they became the dominant force in the fragmented remnants of Jewish society (cf. Mt 5:20; 21:43-45; 23:1-36). Third, there is also evidence that Matthew's community faced persecution and rejection on another front.[30] The Gospel was likely written in Syrian Antioch, where the Gentiles initiated violent anti-Jewish mob action in the postwar period, which was followed by repeated petitions to Rome that Jews be stripped of all the civil rights that had been previously guaranteed by the Romans.[31]

Finally, settled in an area where the Jesus movement was already pursuing a Gentile mission, Matthew's community possibly also faced internal

---

[29]This description of the pressures in Matthew's social milieu appeared earlier in Sechrest, "Enemies, Romans, Pigs, and Dogs," 86-88.

[30]Though some are more cautious, there is wide agreement about Syrian Antioch as the location for Matthew's composition. See Keener, *Commentary on the Gospel of Matthew*, 41-42, and the scholars cited there; cf. Donald A. Hagner, *Matthew 1-13*, Word Biblical Commentary 33A (Dallas: Word Books, 1995), lxxv, who is a bit more cautious.

[31]For a more detailed construction of the situation in Syrian Antioch, see David Sim, *The Gospel of Matthew and Christian Judaism: The History and Social Setting of the Matthean Community* (Edinburgh: T&T Clark, 1998), 166-86; and Wayne A. Meeks and Robert L. Wilken, *Jews and Christians in Antioch in the First Four Centuries of the Common Era* (Missoula, MT: Scholars Press, 1978), 1-54, esp. 4-5, 18. In "Gospel of Matthew and Gentiles," 30-38, Sim sees evidence of this conflict with Gentiles in Matthew 10:17-22; 24:4-14, and especially Matthew 24:9 ("hated by *all* nations"). Sim maintains that all but two of the prophecies in Matthew 24:4-14 contain descriptions that pertain to the community's present. Also see Warren Carter's discussion of the complicity of the Jewish leaders with the Romans and the Gospel's anti-Roman polemic in "Matthew and the Gentiles," 259-82. Similarly, Warren Carter, "Resisting and Imitating the Empire: Imperial Paradigms in Two Matthean Parables," *Interpretation* 56, no. 3 (2002): 260-72.

pressure from dedicated missionaries who wanted the community to welcome these Gentile converts and others beside them. Such associations might have increased the likelihood of opposition from the Pharisees, who might ridicule the Matthean community for being less observant and thereby prompt Matthew's stress on meticulous law observance, especially if any missionaries in the region were promoting a mission similar to the apostle Paul's work in Syrian Antioch (cf. Acts 13:1-3; Mt 14:19-22). Thus, any Gentile mission in Matthew's community would only be able to proceed on strictly Jewish terms (Mt 5:17-20; 7:15, 22; perhaps 24:11). In short, Matthew's ambiguity toward Gentiles may emerge from the fact that his group faced pressure on several fronts: (1) lingering tensions with Rome; (2) active Gentile persecution in Antioch; (3) hostility from Pharisees in the aftermath of the Jewish War; and (4) internal Christian-movement pressure to accept local Jesus-believing Gentiles. In such a context it is no wonder that we see ambivalence in the posture toward outsiders in the Gospel, as it insists on both Jewish priority and higher righteousness on the one hand (Mt 10:5-6; 5:17-20) while at the same time embarking on a Gentile mission on the other—but only so long as that mission is commensurate with "everything that [Jesus has] commanded" with regard to piety and practice (Mt 28:19-20).[32]

The tension between the prohibition of the Gentile mission in Matthew 10:5-6 and Matthew 15:24 and the commandment for a post-resurrection Gentile mission in Matthew 28:19 may thus be a bit less difficult to reconcile. The avoidance strategies reflected in the prohibition commands in Matthew 10:5-6 and Matthew 15:24 make sense in light of the evidence about Gentile hostilities toward Jews in the aftermath of the war, and similar devices are typical of stressed communities under analogous pressures in modern history, as seen, for instance, in immigrant enclaves in US cities. Since Matthew's Gospel

---

[32]Similarly, see Senior ("Between Two Worlds," 21; cf. 18): "What I am suggesting here is that Matthew . . . was attempting to bridge more than one divide at once. First of all, he was fending off attacks about his community's essential Jewish character from other factions within the Jewish community, but with equal conviction he wanted to communicate that heritage to a new generation of Christians, Jewish and Gentile." Somewhat similar is Schuyler Brown's conclusion ("Matthean Community and the Gentile Mission," 193): "The difficulty in finding a satisfactory theological explanation for the contradiction between Jesus' restriction of the mission to 'the lost sheep of the house of Israel' (Mt x 6) and his extension of the mission to 'all nations' (Mt xxviii 19) suggests that the gentile mission may have been an object of current controversy within the evangelist's community."

was written within years or decades of the fall of Jerusalem, the Great Commission is actually remarkable in view of what would be a more natural desire to avoid and reject anything associated with Gentiles. The Gospel represents a careful balance between prudent avoidance of known and past enemies (Mt 7:6; 10:5-6; 15:24, 26) and a remarkably idealistic ethical challenge that members would try to see a potential brother in such enemies (Mt 28:19; cf. Mt 5:44).

Nevertheless, there are few passages that are more scandalous for modern readers than Jesus' encounter with the unnamed Canaanite woman in Matthew 15:21-28. Indeed, the scandal is deepened by comparison with the source episode in Mark 7:24-30, whereby we see that Matthew removes several features from the earlier, milder version of the episode in Mark that communicates a greater welcome to Gentiles.[33] Matthew eliminates Mark's mention that Jesus actually enters a Gentile home and possibly eats there (cf. Mk 7:24; Mt 15:17-20); notably, in deleting the statement from Mark 7:27, "Let the children be fed *first*," Matthew also removes the implication from the Markan account of the encounter with the woman that Gentiles will *eventually* receive the benefits of Jesus' mission. Matthew changes Mark's identification of this woman from Syro-Phoenician to Canaanite in a move that frames this woman more clearly as an outsider and archenemy of the ancient Israelites.[34] In addition, the woman's response in Matthew is more submissive with her references to the "master's table" (Mt 15:27; cf. Mk 7:28) and her explicit confession that Jesus is Lord (Mt 15:22; cf. Mk 7:26). In Matthew,

---

[33]Regarding the differences between Mark 7:24-30 and Matthew 15:21-28, I do not conflate the details of the narrative as is common among lay readers of the Gospels, a method that was rejected by the church's embrace of four separate Gospels instead of a single harmonized account like the second-century Diatessaron. Instead, I am among the majority of biblical scholars who hold each of the Gospel narratives as a particular expression of the theological agenda of each respective Evangelist. For an introduction to the relationships among the Synoptic Gospels, see Clark-Soles, *Engaging the Word*, 35-76.

[34]Sharon Ringe, "A Gentile Woman's Story," in *Feminist Interpretation of the Bible*, ed. Letty M. Russell (Philadephia: Westminster, 1985), 155n8. Roy Harrisville thinks that use of the word *Canaanite* heightens the intensity of the religious conflict between Jesus and the woman (Roy A. Harrisville, "The Woman of Canaan: A Chapter in the History of Exegesis," *Interpretation* 20, no. 3 [1966]: 281), while Levine thinks that the word reminds readers of the Canaanite women of the genealogy ("Matthew's Advice," 26). Warren Carter (*Matthew and the Margins: A Socio-Political and Religious Reading* [Sheffield: Sheffield Academic, 2000], 222) thinks the word evokes the conflict over the land from the exodus and conquest; similarly, Donald A. Hagner, *Matthew 14–28*, Word Biblical Commentary 33B (Dallas: Word Books, 1995), 441.

Jesus initially refuses to acknowledge her request and possibly even her presence. When finally consenting to respond to her in Matthew 15:26, Jesus implies that the woman and all such Gentiles are dogs who should not receive the blessings reserved for the house of Israel. Accepting it as her due, her submissive acquiescence to that characterization in Matthew 15:27 is, to my female Gentile eyes, the most scandalous feature of the story.[35]

This dynamic—that is, the woman's embrace of a dehumanizing epithet—is akin to what today would be called *internalized racism*. We can see this by recognizing that responses to prejudice and racism can take many forms in the aftermath of any forced and painful disruption to a controlling narrative such as the one Matthew's community experienced after the Jewish War. *Internalized racism* is an unfortunate response to racism that further damages people oppressed by racism, as the marginalized begin to accept widely shared and durable negative stereotypes that take their toll on the community's self-esteem. Postcolonial discourse about Christian missiology documents numerous examples of the ways that the missionary endeavor wreaked violence on the internal self-conceptions of target populations.[36] Nor are these effects confined to missionary work—such damage is also a product of the internal race dynamics within the United States, which show that minorities sometimes internalize the same biases about themselves that majority groups hold, with the result that minorities have pro-White or anti-minority biases even with respect to their own groups. Thus the woman's ownership of the thinly veiled insult in Jesus' words is analogous to a phenomenon encountered in modern life; her complicit response showcases one of the soul-shredding effects of sustained prejudice against one's group.

Many interpreters suggest that Jesus' harshness serves to test the woman's capacity for faith,[37] while others insinuate that there is some use of humor

---

[35]Dube, *Postcolonial Feminist Interpretation*, 150.

[36]The classic exploration of this theme can be found in the Frantz Fanon's haunting and magisterial work *Black Skin, White Masks*, trans. Richard Philcox, rev. ed. (New York: Grove Press, 2008), but essays by Angel Santiago-Vendrell and Andrea Smith in the current volume also bear witness to this dynamic.

[37]J. Duncan M. Derrett, "Law in the New Testament: The Syro-Phoenician Woman and the Centurion of Capernaum," *Novum Testamentum* 15, no. 3 (1973): 162.

or teasing in the account.[38] Others soften the epithet "dog" to "puppy," framing it—unsuccessfully—as the use of an endearing, family term.[39] Another rescue attempt tries to empty the metaphor of its insulting associations, proposing that "dog" is conventional polemic about people who do not distinguish between clean and unclean foods.[40] More fruitful interpretations are clearly resistance stories that highlight the woman's agency in using Jesus' reply to her own advantage,[41] rereading her dialogue as a confrontation with an imperial, colonial oppressor that includes a demand for restitution.[42] Acknowledging the value of such feminist and culturally sensitive critiques of the passage, another scholar is intent on combating the caricature of Jews in these and other interpretations as misogynistic and racist.[43] Thus, this passage is a site of competing narratives. Some develop explanations that leave their worldview involving "benign hierarchy" intact while others resist the hierarchicalism in the passage that is analogous to modern modes of racist and sexist discourse.

One important and redemptive response to racism involves *antiracist activism*, defined as the development of a critical consciousness, alliances, practices, and advocacy work that seek to dismantle racism in material ways. Antiracism can be understood as an agenda that seeks to liberate both oppressors and victims from racism's warping effects so that the former seek alliances with the latter, and the latter seek their own liberation.[44] With reference to this passage, an antiracist reading would acknowledge

---

[38]E.g., William Barclay, *The Gospel of Matthew*, rev. ed. (Louisville, KY: Westminster John Knox, 1975), 2:122; Robert H. Mounce, *Matthew*, New International Biblical Commentary (Carlisle, UK: Paternoster, 1995), 153; Alan Hugh McNeile, *The Gospel According to St. Matthew* (London: Macmillan, 1915), 31; and R. T. France, *Matthew*, Tyndale New Testament Commentaries (Leicester: Inter-Varsity Press, 1989), 247; critiqued by M. Eugene Boring, *The Gospel of Matthew*, New Interpreter's Bible 8 (Nashville: Abingdon, 1995), 336n343.

[39]Derrett, "Law in the New Testament," 163; and Levine, "Matthew's Advice, 32: "As feminists frequently remark, being called 'little bitch' is no improvement to being called 'bitch.'" Compare with Harrisville ("Woman of Canaan," 283), who finds no justification for reading *dog* as a house pet since rabbinic materials see dogs as despised wild beasts.

[40]Hagner, *Matthew 14–28*, 442; Mounce, *Matthew*, 154; contra Levine, "Matthew's Advice," 32.

[41]E.g., Leticia Guardiola-Sáenz, "Borderless Women and Borderless Texts: A Cultural Reading of Matthew 15:21-28," *Semeia* 78 (1997): 69-81; and Mitzi J. Smith, "'Knowing More Than Is Good for One': A Womanist Interrogation of the Matthean Great Commission," in Smith and Lalitha, *Teaching All Nations*, 150.

[42]Guardiola-Sáenz, "Borderless Women," 76.

[43]Levine, "Matthew's Advice."

[44]Tammerie Day, "Constructing Solidarity," unpublished manuscript.

the oppressive dynamics in the text and the way that these dynamics reverberate in modern society and shape expectations about encounters with the other. Instead of seeking to remove the offense of this story, a womanist might try to use this passage as an entry point in the cultivation of a critical consciousness that is able to identify and resist processes of marginalization. Instead of deploying a counternarrative that attempts to domesticate or ignore the harsh realities of this text where it reminds us of situations in modern society, readers can choose to activate the responses generated by this text as a part of an antiracist program that seeks empathy with those on the margins.

Our womanist reading begins by acknowledging the power of the analogy that feminist and other interpreters have already located in this text, which highlights the dynamics of privilege and the ways that the text deploys power differentials that mimic those in modern society. Matthew's earlier similar story of an encounter with a centurion also narrated an outsider's request for Jesus' intervention on behalf of a dependent (Mt 8:5-13).[45] Instead of the dialogue there between Jesus and a more powerful male outsider, Matthew 15:21-28 puts Jesus firmly at the top of the implied social hierarchy vis-à-vis gender. Here his interlocutor is female, apparently unattached and thus vulnerable, rather than the powerful male representative of the recent Roman conquerors in the centurion of Matthew 8:5-13. By identifying the woman as a Canaanite, the narrator evokes the memory of hostilities between the Israelites and Canaanites so that Matthew's Jesus stands as a representative of a people who displaced her ancestors. When she calls him "Son of David," she is acknowledging Jesus as the legitimate king of the people who conquered her own (Mt 15:22). Instead of the comparison by which the centurion calls attention to the ways in which he and Jesus both command power, this woman desperately begs Jesus for an intervention, so importuning Jesus that Matthew records the awkward embarrassment of the disciples in the vicinity. The story reminds us of the invisibility that accompanies modern racism and sexism as the disciples dismiss and reject her as a person who can approach the Jewish king, and Jesus renders her invisible by refusing to engage her initial request. Adding

---

[45]Hagner, *Matthew 14–28*, 440.

to the work of these interpreters, we have already intimated that the story reminds us of internalized racism in the woman's tragic embrace of a racial epithet, a point that furthers the work of exposing privilege by highlighting its utter absence in her debased demeanor.

An antiracist program would also point out that the passage contains a strange mix of internalized racism and danger avoidance. Fear of the powerful, oppressive other also emerges subtly in Jesus' healing of the centurion's servant in Matthew 8:5-13. In light of the history of conflict between Romans and Jews in the aftermath of the Jewish War, it is possible that the episode represents Jewish servile deference to an oppressive colonizing power. This episode may reflect Matthew's own internalized racism, evident in his inability to engage with the representatives of the hostile party except through the indirect response of a hesitant, approval-seeking question in Matthew 8:7.[46] But the harshness of the racially loaded language of "swine" and "dogs" in Matthew 7:6 can also be heard differently. A reluctance to cast pearls before swine is essentially a partial restatement of the prohibition of the Gentile mission, as seen in the parallel phrase about giving holy things to dogs. These prohibitions may signal prudential danger avoidance rather than racism. As a character in Matthew's narrative, Jesus was a leader of a persecuted, oppressed, and defeated group in postwar Antioch, and the Jesus of that story has little in common with modern racist social hierarchies. When Jesus finally responds to the woman in Matthew 15:26, it could be that he implies that she and all such Gentiles are ravenous, ferocious, and irascible dogs who should not receive the blessings reserved for the postwar defeated, humiliated, and broken children of Israel.[47] Yet internalized racism may also be evident in that the encounter with this Gentile Canaanite recalls references to the other Gentile women mentioned at the outset of the Gospel. The hostility toward Canaanites implied in Matthew 15:21-28 can be understood as self-directed, inasmuch as the only other Canaanites mentioned in

---

[46]For more on the interpretation of Matthew 8:7 as a question, see Levine, "Matthew's Advice," 30-31. Mitzi Smith sees this collusion with imperialistic impulses as analogous to a "double consciousness," a survival mechanism developed by the oppressed. Smith thinks that this dynamic nonetheless coexists in the text alongside a more liberative generosity in which Jesus authorizes his disciples to continue his mission by coming alongside the marginalized and cast out (Smith, "'Knowing More Than Is Good for One,'" 142-55).

[47]Cf. Matthew 7:6, where dogs and pigs "trample . . . under foot and turn and maul you."

the story are those who appear in Jesus' own genealogy.[48] While it is unlikely that Jesus himself struggled with these issues, Matthew's portrait of the Canaanite woman episode may point to the Evangelist's struggle along these lines. In other words, it may be that only someone who gets internalized racism can paint a convincing portrait of it.

The healings of the centurion's servant and the Canaanite's daughter are traditionally reckoned as moments when Jesus recognizes unusual and unexpected models of faith. Yet if this episode and the Canaanite woman episode so like it function to identify Gentiles as models of faith, it is nonetheless a faith that demands that these Gentiles—and all Gentiles—recognize the particularity of the movement's Jewish character. It is a credit to Matthew that he is able to demonstrate generosity to the centurion, who represents the then-current powerful conquerors of Israel, even as it is additionally extended to a woman who represents a group historically and presently opposed to his community in Antioch. But it is nothing short of stunning that he does so by insisting that the conqueror assimilate to the conquered even while making requests of the vanquished.

Indeed, a major plank in our womanist reading of Matthew 15:21-28 as antiracist literature emerges from Matthew's insistence that a mission to Gentiles entails an explicit recognition by these Gentiles of the essentially Jewish character of the movement. Matthew's picture of the ideal Gentile emerges through the portraits of those encountered in the narrative. The magis' journey to the Holy City to do obeisance to the Jewish king of the empire of heaven performs the pilgrimage of the nations to Zion depicted in Isaiah 2:2-4 (Mt 2:1-12). The Canaanite woman, representing a history of hostility and strife, plainly subjugates herself to Jesus, explicitly acknowledging her inferior position vis-à-vis the Israelite people in an encounter with their king. The thoroughly Jewish character of the mission also appears in Matthew 25:31-46, where Jesus judges Gentiles who were unaware that their hostilities to Christian missionaries constitute hostility to the Messiah

---

[48]For more on the connection between the Canaanite women of the genealogy and the Canaanite woman of Matthew 15:21-28, see Hutchison "Women, Gentiles, and the Messianic Mission," 152-64. See especially Levine, "Matthew's Advice," 26, 36-37. Just like the findings of modern genetics that problematizes the idea of pure races, Matthew's genealogy suggests that the icon of Judaism, the Davidic Messiah-King Jesus, is mixed race.

himself.[49] For Matthew, one cannot enter the kingdom on anything other than very Jewish terms.[50] One must conform to the values and expectations of this thoroughly Jewish movement, as the fellow with the missing wedding garment found out to his distress (Mt 22:11-14).

In connection with the way that interpreters are fond of expounding on the theme of Matthew's universalism, I would be remiss if I did not comment on the deeply problematic nature of that theme when deployed carelessly in the modern context. Embedded in a great deal of Christian theology and practice, the idea of universalism is intertwined with the idea that Christianity is above or absent the particularism of a so-called inferior Judaism. When Western Christians assert universalism, this assertion often becomes in practice an affirmation of whiteness encountered as the universal norm of racelessness or colorblindness, as if difference and color are offensives that must be eradicated or ignored. Such an emphasis on the universalism of the Gospel ends up invalidating the particularism of Matthew's insistence on the Jewish character of the movement.[51] It may be the case that part of the scandal of Jesus' encounter with the Canaanite woman involves discomfort with this counterevidence of universalism. The tension between inclusivist tendencies and particularism in Matthew was ultimately resolved in favor of the former, given that the larger narrative ends with the Great Commission. But we cannot escape the fact that the essentially Jewish character of the movement is nonetheless embedded in the great invitation since Jesus commands that new disciples be taught to obey all that is taught in the Gospel. Further, we must not view the insistence on the Jewish character of the community as racist in view of our definition of racism since the Gospel neither withholds access to resources from outsiders nor perpetuates the existing hierarchies of the day. As an appeal from a minority movement, the Great Commission is an invitation to join a defeated ethnoreligious group that wholly lacks coercive power. This very particularistic Gospel may be

---

[49]Keener, *Commentary on the Gospel of Matthew*, 604-6; and Hagner, *Matthew 14–28*, 745-47. For a mediating position, see John Nolland, who thinks that fellow disciples are in view in Matthew 25:40 but that Jesus' concern expands to all the poor in Matthew 25:45. Nolland, *The Gospel of Matthew: A Commentary on the Greek Text* (Grand Rapids: Eerdmans, 2005), 1032-34.

[50]Andrew T. Draper, "The End of 'Mission,'" 196, esp. n49.

[51]Philip Culbertson, "Reclaiming the Matthean Vineyard Parables," *Encounter* 49, no. 4 (1988): 257-83.

offensive to the contemporary Christian metanarratives of universalism and inclusivism, but the power of the historically conditioned reading exposes the fact that Matthew's insistence on particularity is one that emerges in the context of a struggle for self-definition in the face of more numerous and powerful outside groups. On the contrary, this contextualized reading is deeply antiracist inasmuch as Matthew's particularism would resonate with any modern minority community that is attempting to resist the pressure to assimilate to dominate cultural norms in their struggle for self-definition.

Thus, in an antiracist program, this text would help expose and render visible the often soul-shredding pressures to assimilate that minorities face daily. It has the rhetorical effect of causing a predominantly white and Christian culture, with reference to religious, educational, and political structures, to confront the strangeness and difference of the particularistic Jewish movement at the heart of Christianity. By recalling Matthew's insistence that newcomers adopt the practices, norms, and teachings of this sect in contradistinction from every other socially ordered narrative in the majority culture, modern Christians—especially those enjoying the advantages of hierarchy—are able to see through this text dynamics that are normally invisible to them. They should not see themselves in the position of a Jesus who condescends to dispense healing to a marginalized person, nor see themselves as gatekeeper disciples, or even as the persistent woman who finally earns high praise.[52] Instead, those who normally profit from advantageous positions in the social hierarchy must learn to identify with the woman's humble posture. They must recognize that with reference to this very Jewish, very particularistic Jesus, they, like her, are humble outsiders with no birthright of entry or access—they must change their ways in order to participate in the new community.[53] Such persons can profit from

---

[52]Mark C. Thompson's interpretation of this passage imagines that readers will want to read themselves into the story as the woman because they will delight in hearing Jesus proclaim them people of great faith. Exposing his own privileged position in society, he notes that it is difficult to identify with her since "we . . . rarely find ourselves on our knees desperately crying out for help. Instead, we like to think of ourselves as being self-sufficient and independent, having the resources to take care of ourselves." Thompson, "Matthew 15:21-28," *Interpretation* 35, no. 3 (1981): 281-82.

[53]I still remember the startling metaphor that theologian Willie Jennings used when teaching seminary students to reckon with the Jewish particularity of this text: "It is as if God only speaks Hebrew!" He meant to impress upon us that it is only through Jesus that Gentiles gain access to the Jewish God of Abraham, Isaac, and Jacob. I am indebted to Jennings for initial insights about using this text in Christian antiracist activism.

a narrative that dislocates the ownership of the Christian tradition that prevails in Western theological discourse by reflecting on the fact that Matthew's Jesus demands assimilation to a very different type of community than that which survived into modernity. Rather than reading Matthew as a text that sanctions the political and cultural hegemony of modern Christian culture, it would do us some good to read it as a document that helps us non-Jewish Christians recognize how we gained acceptance to a group from which we were excluded by birth.

Conclusion

This reading of Matthew 15:21-28 and its attendant use in an antiracist missional agenda works by constructing analogies between the forces that marginalize today and the social pressures operating in Matthew's context. Armed with these similarities, we are able to conceive of an imaginative inversion of hierarchy that places modern Christian cultural hegemony into a humbled and marginalized subject position. To be sure, this particular use of the text to disrupt the complacency of those who normally define and occupy the center can have less sanguine implications for minorities if it is not used in combination with empowering reading strategies that emphasize the Canaanite's agency. Absent this important work, interpretations that stress the episode as modeling the proper attitudes of faith could tacitly and tragically encourage women and minorities to renew their identification with oppression when we are in reality seeking to give others a chance to have a taste of their normal experience. Indeed, the absence of humility is what ultimately helps pervert the missionary enterprise into an impulse that is complicit with empire.

Yet, a reading that fails to interrogate *all* the power dynamics at work in the larger narrative undercuts the liberative goals of womanists and other scholars on the margins. We can achieve a more liberative result by viewing all of the characters in this text through the prism of the oppressive historical forces that helped shape the text. While the narratives of interpreters on the margins are hugely important as resources to empower resistance to internalized racism, we must not forget that such readings run the risk of becoming damaging counternarratives in their own right. This reading attempts to place the Gospel of Matthew back in its historical milieu by interpreting it in light of our best historical reconstruction of the circumstances. A reading that ignores or denies that Matthew's community was beleaguered by the forces of oppression on as many as four hostile fronts risks participating in a narrative that creates a hierarchy of Jesus over Gentiles in a way that did not exist historically. It risks becoming complicit with narratives that rewrite history, like those that insist that slave owners were habitually kind and compassionate, that the Civil War was fought over states' rights, and that the Shoah[54] never took place.

Read as a narrative that resists oppressing women and minorities, Matthew's Gospel offers advice to marginalized groups who are forced into negotiating a hostile environment. Beyond a mere tolerance of difference and the renunciation of violence, Matthew begins by calling the community to embody an active love of enemies, proceeds to command the embrace of the other as brother and sister, and ends by enjoining care of all marginalized people for fear of overlooking fellow disciples (Mt 25:31-46). As if recognizing that a strategy of avoidance vis-à-vis powerful enemies might simply be impractical sometimes, Matthew also advises the cultivation of a reality-based, clear-sighted knowledge of the climate (Mt 7:1-6). Members of the community must not practice a naiveté that would leave them defenseless in the face of active hostility. Instead, in the sayings about offering holy things to ravening dogs in Matthew 7:6, they are called to practice discernment so as to avoid offering gifts to people who will despise, attack, or belittle their worth. At one level, Matthew counsels avoidance of hostile and possibly more powerful adversaries as seen in the advice in the missionary discourse (Mt 10:5-6). Yet on another level, Jesus' dignified mien in encounters with characters that represent the historical forces of conflict, persecution, and subjugation can be read as acts that deflect the power of stereotypes to marginalize. Altogether, the text counsels a posture that resists the corruption of internalized racism by encouraging discerned interaction with those who know your worth.

Matthew's insistence that a mission to the nations entails an explicit recognition by them of the particularly Jewish character of the movement is the main plank in our use of Matthew 15:21-28 as antiracist womanist

---

[54]*Shoah* is the preferred term for the Holocaust among many Jewish theorists.

missional literature. In context, the Great Commission is a humble, generous, and careful invitation to outsiders both powerful and weak; it is an offer that wholly lacks coercive power inasmuch as it first came from a humiliated and defeated people. Hence, our proclamation of the gospel must be an invitation to others by those who are themselves humbled among the nations, as we live out the gospel from one particularity to another. We do mission as those who have already traversed this territory, inasmuch as our own Gentile social location has already mimicked the Canaanite's embrace of a foreign king.

In the traditional translation of Matthew 15:24 Jesus rebuffs the Canaanite by saying, "I was sent only to the lost sheep of the house of Israel," but we must remember that in the historical situation of the Gospel of Matthew the first readers are better described not as just lost but as devastated, fractured, and oppressed as well. Matthew's record of Jesus' posture toward the Canaanite does not represent that of a privileged interlocutor who withholds mercy from the only marginalized person in sight. Rather, it is a portrait of one who is himself the leader of a defeated and humbled people; it is a portrait of a leader who recognizes that he has much work to do in serving among the marginalized close to home before turning and reaching out to remote others on the margins among the nations. This Jesus is the model for Christian missions today as we seek to do mission with a demeanor of humility and a heart of loving mercy, as those who have experienced oppression, exclusion, and marginalization firsthand.

Conclusion

Mission After Colonialism and
Whiteness: The Pentecost Witness
of the "Perpetual Foreigner" for
the Third Millennium

Amos Yong

In the final pages of this book, we will cursorily review what has gone on before in this book's triangulation of the themes of race, theology, and mission; conduct a frank assessment from this nexus of the current moment of particularly Christian theology of mission (or Christian missiology); and anticipate further what else it would take to reform Christian mission theology and practice so that good news can resound to the ends of the earth filled with many different peoples, ethnicities, cultures, and languages. Toward this end, I will suggest from my own Malaysian-born-American/US-naturalized location that the way forward involves at least in part what Asian Americans call a *perpetual foreigner* stance capable of empowering faithful Christian discipleship and witness amid and against the persisting forces of colonial imperialism and Euro-American whiteness regnant in the late modern world.[1]

---

[1] This essay both corrects and extends the theology of mission I have developed elsewhere—*The Missiological Spirit: Christian Mission Theology for the Third Millennium Global Context* (Eugene, OR: Cascade Books, 2014)—in the former case adding an analytical register informed by race and racialization perspectives and in the latter case promoting a specifically Asian American proposal and urging its normative Christian missiological implications.

MODERN CHRISTIAN MISSION: GOSPEL-HERESY-COLONIALISM

Christian mission as we know it at the beginning of the third millennium was formed out of and reshaped during the age of colonialism. From a certain set of conservative evangelical perspectives, there is much to celebrate in the way that the modern Christian mission brought the good news of Jesus Christ to the then (so-called) New World, into the heart of Africa, and across the vast Asian continent as well as Oceania. From other vantage points at sites attentive to the history of modernity, the Euro-American missionaries not only came with but also assisted the arrival of modern science, medicine, and technology; nurtured the curiosity, ingenuity, and inventiveness that propel such discoveries; and facilitated an embrace of the ideals of democracy, human rights, abolitionism, and the free market. In this telling, these various advances have combined over the last few centuries, within the overarching Christian religious frame, to elevate the quality of life around the world. Accordingly, for some, these results outweigh any collateral damage that might have accrued in the colonial mission endeavor.

But what if, as Willie Jennings's essay in this book eloquently articulates, the entirety of the modern project is based on a deformed vision of human perfection or maturation, one that heretically distorted the Christian theology of creation for the sake of a theology of private property and justified the colonial accumulation of land, land that had long been inhabited by other (non-White) peoples, ethnicities, and races?[2] What if the gospel, as Elizabeth Conde-Frazier and Angel Santiago-Vendrell both also explicate, was tweaked ever so slightly in this regard so that the biblical emphasis on the salvation of human souls was heretically disoriented toward an otherworldly destination (the attainment of everlasting heaven and the avoidance of eternal hell) for the sake of compartmentalizing Christian soteriology from colonial political ideology (thus separating church and state, and disjoining spirituality and materiality, etc.) and thereby unleashing the imperialist impulses of European expansionism and American manifest destiny? What if such a missionary gospel allowed Europeans and White Americans to bring the good news and the Bible to all other peoples in exchange for the "right" to lay claim to their land and to access and extract that land's natural

---

[2]See also Willie James Jennings, *The Christian Imagination: Theology and the Origins of Race* (New Haven, CT: Yale University Press, 2011).

resources for the colonial governments and peoples? As Andrea Smith's chapter intimates, the civilizing of the world went hand in hand with the humanizing of the barbarians, which not only made possible the salvation of these non-White creatures but also justified the means—genocidal in many contexts, exploitative otherwise along every economic register—toward such ends.[3] On these accounts, race and ethnicity are central rather than marginal to this history of modern Christian mission.[4]

To be sure, the European sense of ethnocentric superiority, seemingly grounded on Christian missionization, and the resulting racism enacted through establishment of hierarchies with Whites perched at the top, arguably is not sui generis in the human experience. Daniel Jeyaraj's essay unveils how the British came to South Asia and found a hierarchically structured civilization with layers of ethnic distinctions based on class and caste considerations. Further east, if we would have expanded the discussion of our book to include China and its Middle Kingdom—the literal translation of the Chinese self-designation *Zhonggou*—we would have seen that notions of Chinese ethnocentrism and especially Han ethnic superiority have persisted over millennia and that there is even a resurgent nationalism reacting to the perceived ascendency of the other minority ethnic groups that seeks to "make the Han great again."[5] And we also know that the transatlantic slave trade, as hinted at in Akinade Akintunde's chapter (with Clifton Clarke), built on intra-African ethnic, tribal, and related stratifications that have pitted sub-Saharan kinship groups and peoples against one another for

---

[3]For further details on these aspects of the Christian mission to native North America that Smith discusses, see the collection of essays in Barbara Brown Zikmund and Amos Yong, eds., *Remembering Jamestown: Hard Questions About Christian Mission* (Eugene, OR: Pickwick, 2010).

[4]E.g., Jane Samson, *Race and Redemption: British Missionaries Encounter Pacific Peoples, 1790–1920* (Grand Rapids: Eerdmans, 2017).

[5]Kevin Carrico, *The Great Han: Race, Nationalism, and Tradition in China Today* (Berkeley: University of California Press, 2017), 86-88; this is Carrico's description of the *Hanfu yindong* (China's Han Clothing Movement), which has sought to rejuvenate ancient—as opposed to those from the more recent Ming or Qing dynasties or even from the Maoist period—dress, ritual, images, aesthetics, and practices as central to contemporary Chinese political, economic, and social life. (Carrico does not reference the "Make American Great Again" slogan that has characterized the campaign and now presidency of Donald J. Trump in the United States, which is arguably also a response to the felt sense of threat that fifty years of ethnic minority civil rights gains and multiculturalism developments now pose to Whites across the Pacific.) See also Frank Dikötter, *The Discourse of Race in Modern China*, 2nd ed. (Oxford: Oxford University Press, 2015), for more on Middle Kingdom ethnocentrism.

the past millennia.[6] The point is that ethnocentrism (at best) and racism (at worst), with their accompanying systems of human slavery,[7] are not copyrighted by White European and North American colonizers. Rather, these reflect the most horrific vices of the human condition, albeit ones that now prevail in the neoliberal world order built off the backs, lands, and resources of those who found themselves on the underside of the modern colonial project.

But we have to be clear: many of us, including and especially myself as a contributor to this volume, are implicated in the imperial legacies of modern colonialism. As Jennings clearly explains, whiteness is less about the color of human skins than it is about the task of disciplining human creatures to live according to the telos—the ideal vision of human maturity—constructed by colonial modernity.[8] If White people are in the best position to access and harvest the advantages of such a teleological regimen, people of Color can also reap available benefits by participating and acting in alignment with European and white North American norms and standards. The following confession is in order: I earned my scholarly stripes and promotions by learning how to speak the language of the modern academy and then, during the first few years after completing my PhD, by devoting my analytical and constructive energies to waxing eloquent on topics that did not directly trouble either the (white) political establishment or its cultural protectors. In the last decade plus, however, I have embarked on a journey to (re)think about my work much more explicitly from the perspective of my own Asian American history and experience and have come to see the ways that I had become white (at least in the ways Jennnings describes as

---

[6] See Paul E. Lovejoy, *Transformations in Slavery: A History of Slavery in Africa*, 3rd ed. (Cambridge: Cambridge University Press, 2011); cf. Jane Ngobia and Aloys O. Ojore, "Ethnocentrism and Its Historical Manifestations," in *Ethnocentrism and Ethnic Conflict in Africa: Proceedings of the Fifth Interdisciplinary Session of the Faculty of Theology and Department of Religious Studies, Catholic University of Eastern Africa, Nairobi*, ed. Patrick Ryan (Nairobi: Catholic University of Eastern Africa, 2001), 67-99, esp. 82-83.

[7] E.g., James L. Watson, ed., *Asian and African Systems of Slavery* (Berkeley: University of California Press, 1980).

[8] See also Marla Frederick McGlathery and Traci Griffin, "'Becoming Conservative, Becoming White?': Black Evangelicals and the Para-Church Movement," in *This Side of Heaven: Race, Ethnicity, and Christian Faith*, ed. Robert J. Priest and Alvaro L. Nieves (Oxford: Oxford University Press, 2007), 145-62.

being possible for people of Color).[9] The goal here is not to demonize White people but to name the systems of marginalization that are extensions of the modern colonial project, systems that I have been assimilated into as a beneficiary and perpetuator.

Let me be as precise as possible with reference to a missiological agenda. I am the result of a more or less traditional or classical form of Christian missionary effort, the child of a mother who came to Christian faith through the labors of a (White) Pentecostal woman from Northern California who was committed to spreading the gospel among the Chinese diaspora, first in Malaysia (where I was born) and then in her homeland. Back home, after establishing some congregations for Chinese-speaking immigrants in the wider Bay Area, she sponsored my parents, among other Malaysian families, to come and pastor these churches in San Francisco and the surrounding region. My parents brought me and my three brothers to Stockton, California, in the mid-1970s to take up one of these fledgling mission communities. We were part of the first wave of what is now called reverse mission— or diaspora mission[10]—featuring non-Whites coming to Europe and North America to take up the task of Christian evangelization, usually focusing on non-White ethnic groups (like my parents working among the Chinese diaspora to California), albeit always wondering if and how they might reach Caucasian natives. We were supported by the Northern California and Nevada District of the Assemblies of God, the predominantly White, Pentecostal denomination based in Springfield, Missouri, that had sent our missionary protagonist to Malaysia decades before. Their missionary goals were—and largely remain—to evangelize the lost to the ends of the earth; to establish churches among all the peoples of every nation, tribe, and language; and to save as many souls as possible for eternal and heavenly life before the parousia. As Pentecostals, our bodies also matter at a secondary level—after all, Jesus, who is savior, is also healer of our bodies[11]—but the

[9]As set out initially in Amos Yong, *The Future of Evangelical Theology: Soundings from the Asian American Diaspora* (Downers Grove, IL: InterVarsity Press, 2014).

[10]See Chandler H. Im and Amos Yong, eds., *Global Diasporas and Mission*, Regnum Edinburgh Centenary 23 (Eugene, OR: Wipf & Stock, 2014).

[11]My book *In the Days of Caesar: Pentecostalism and Political Theology—The Cadbury Lectures 2009*, Sacra Doctrina (Grand Rapids: Eerdmans, 2010), attempts to develop the Pentecostal fivefold gospel (Jesus as savior, sanctifier, Spirit-baptizer, healer, and coming king) in the direction of a political and public theology, with missiological implications.

focus remains largely on souls and bodies as individually constituted, neither on our social interrelatedness nor on society at large (whether socially, politically, or economically configured) and certainly not on the environment and the ecosphere. The question is whether such a theological imagination, and accompanying missiology, has traction going forward.

THE END OF (COLORBLIND) THEOLOGY AND
THE END OF (MODERN) MISSION

The problem with colorblindness is that as an ecclesial, theological, and missiological posture it is not neutral but props up and sustains the White status quo. My Pentecostal church with its evangelical missiology wishes to avoid the culture wars and thus discourages stepping into what it considers the politically correct discourse of multiculturalism, but by so doing it also renders itself incapable of seeing and then questioning how the ideology of whiteness has truncated the Christian gospel.[12] For instance, to the degree that any of us are white (in Jennings's sense of whiteness), then we are no longer capable of appreciating, much less living fully into, the powerful promises of the good news—a gospel that is for both Jews and Gentiles now brought into new relationship rather than a gospel for generic human beings that requires a subordination of our ethnic-cultural particularities under a supposedly colorblind canopy. Or, while the focus on souls seems right at one level, the neglect of creational rootedness in the environment is a subtle but critical loss since now we can become socialized into Western notions of land ownership that justify colonial expansion while being bereft of the capacity to criticize theologically such theft of indigenous lands. More and more Jesus followers, however, are beginning to understand that Christian faith and commitment invite colored lenses; at the very least, the church ought to attend to the witnesses and testimonies of those who experience the world differently from those whose white skins provide them privileges that include not naming their perspectival situatedness.[13] How might the ethnoracial register help us to

---

[12]Racialization into White supremacy is ideologically conditioned; see Charles W. Mills, *The Racial Contract* (Ithaca, NY: Cornell University Press, 1997), 81-90.

[13]E.g., Anthony Reddie, *Is God Colour-Blind? Insights from Black Theology for Christian Ministry* (London: SPCK, 2010); and Sarah Shin, *Beyond Colorblind: Redeeming Our Ethnic Journey* (Downers Grove, IL: InterVarsity Press, 2017).

understand the current fading away of a (White) theological and missiological paradigm and the arrival of another?

Take for instance the postcolonial theology now widespread across the Global South and its reaction to the missionary enterprise.[14] Postcolonial theologians urge that the Christian teachings, doctrines, and ideas that missionaries brought to what is now the majority world of Asia, Africa, and Latin America were not scripturally funded as straightforwardly announced but were mixed in with (White) European and North American cultural realities, sometimes—even oftentimes(!)—fatally compromising the veracity of the gospel that was being proclaimed since such good news was for souls in the afterlife rather than transformative of lives in the present. More to the point, the voices lifted up now include those of women, the poor, and the politically marginalized of the formerly colonized societies and minorities living within the colonizer nations. These testimonies are resounding the reception of the gospel as touching all of life, not just the spiritual and not just sick and diseased bodies. Traditional theology marginalizes such postcolonial soundings by contextualizing them as mere locally relevant discourses, but postcolonial theologians counterinsist that even the historic theological tradition is similarly situational. If this platform yields postcolonial theology's concerns with economic disparity, social oppression, political injustice, and environmental well-being, then a postcolonial missiology must be focused on how the good news of Jesus Christ empowers the poor, liberates the oppressed, and extends shalom (peace and justice) across the earth.[15] To foreground these issues, however, requires intentional interrogation of the colonial legacies, including asking about how (White) Europeans and North Americans have benefited and continue to profit from the former colonies, and then charting reparative ways forward that involve transnational, transcultural, and interreligious dialogue and cooperation.

---

[14]See Mitzi J. Smith and Jayachitra Lalitha, eds., *Teaching All Nations: Interrogating the Matthean Great Commission* (Minneapolis: Fortress, 2014); cf. Kay Higuera Smith, Jayachitra Lalitha, and L. Daniel Hawk, eds., *Evangelical Postcolonial Conversations: Global Awakenings in Theology and Praxis* (Downers Grove, IL: InterVarsity Press, 2014).

[15]See my essay, "Apostolic Evangelism in the Postcolony: Opportunities and Challenges," *Mission Studies* 34, no. 2 (2017): 147-67; reprinted as chap. 9 in Amos Yong, *The Hermeneutical Spirit: Theological Interpretation and the Scriptural Imagination for the 21st Century* (Eugene, OR: Cascade Books, 2017).

Across the Western front, similarly, the emergence of the postmodern in the last half century has provided indicators that the prior modernist paradigm, including the practices of Christian mission generated out of that era, is not just under siege but disintegrating.[16] On the one (technical) side, it is not that modernity did not bring with it scientific advances, technological inventions, and medical breakthroughs, but the universal, homogenizing, and totalitarian character of modern Enlightenment rationality did not—and could not—recognize the will-to-power bent on preserving not just the presumed civilizational progressiveness but especially the economic profitability benefiting (White) European peoples. Since these modernizing economic impulses were also supported by the modern missionary endeavor, when the idolatrous power of the modern first began convulsing and then was incinerated through the two world wars, the modern Christian mission movement began to experience cracks as well. Thus, for instance, initially coming out of the middle of the twentieth century, a development aspect was attached onto the Christian missionary enterprise to plug the gap that existed between the West and majority world. However, this has either been taken over and even better achieved by secular organizations and agencies or there has been ongoing realization both that mere technical and developmental know-how itself cannot fix the injustices that perpetuate conditions of disrepair and that the classical missiological paradigm is ill equipped to address issues at these deeper levels.

On the other (spiritual) side, more recent migration from the Global South to the Euro-American West has brought alternative spiritualities into spheres dominated previously by Christian sensibilities, resulting in the fragmentation of the modern rationalist hegemony and the emergence of the postmodern smorgasbord of religious options associated with the epistemic awareness of pluralism and consciousness of difference.[17] If traditional theology has sought to dismiss postmodern voices as deconstructive of reason itself, postmodern theologians counterinsist that the main lines of the theological tradition are only established via an ecclesial will-to-power

---

[16]See, e.g., Michael W. Stroope, *Transcending Mission: The Eclipse of a Modern Tradition* (Downers Grove, IL: InterVarsity Press, 2017).

[17]For examples of Christian missional recalibration in this postmodern and pluralist context, see the essays in Scott W. Sunquist and Amos Yong, eds., *The Gospel and Pluralism Today: Reassessing Lesslie Newbigin for the 21st Century* (Downers Grove, IL: InterVarsity Press, 2015).

that silences or ignores minority traditions. Within this context, the modern mission paradigm, which both pits Christian faith against other religions and bifurcates Christian spirituality against the natural/material world, has been recognized as unsustainable. Amid this modern-postmodern fork in the road, navigating between the resistance to modernist technical rationalism on the one side and the undermining of the spiritual-natural dichotomy on the other side, some have observed the emergence of what may appear to be a via media, a technologically mediated spirituality, albeit one in and through which many electronic voices have proliferated religious options and practices. The challenge for mission in this late-modern and postmodern era is how the gospel might meaningfully signify amid the multiplicity and plurivocality of the digital and global age.

In the United States, observe also the emergence of a post-Christendom theological mentality and its impact on traditional Christian mission.[18] Articulated primarily but not only by Anabaptist theologians,[19] the post-Christendom mind realizes that the historic multicentury linking of the church and the apparatus of the state goes much deeper than the constitutional uncoupling of church and state since modernity. Instead, Christendom is conferred civilizational status, one that leads citizens of nations thus impacted to presume that their countries are worthy of patriotic allegiance equal to if not (in the worst cases) greater than their Christian commitment. Such nationalism results in a confusion that replaces the lordship of Jesus Christ with that of Caesar, and begins to establish one people group, perhaps one type of skin color (white), over others. Part of the reason that post-Christendom theologies may not be popular is that their call to the church to be the community of Jesus involves, by logical extension, also the disavowal of an uncritical nationalism, a rejection of the way in which the sacred-secular organization of the modern nation-state subordinates Christian commitments to naively considered public values, and the repudiation of any (supposedly) colorblind secularism that perpetuates a White ethnocentrism

---

[18]E.g., Amos Yong, "The Church and Mission Theology in a Post-Constantinian Era: Soundings from the Anglo-American Frontier," in *A New Day: Essays on World Christianity in Honor of Lamin Sanneh*, ed. Akintunde E. Akinade (New York: Lang, 2010), 49-61.

[19]E.g., Stuart Murray, *Post-Christendom: Church and Mission in a Strange New World* (Carlisle, UK: Paternoster, 2004); and David E. Fitch and Geoffrey Holsclaw, *Prodigal Christianity: 10 Signposts into the Missional Frontier* (San Francisco: Jossey-Bass, 2013).

against people of Color. This is the point of Jonathan Tran's call to Asian American Christians in his essay: that they act out of specifically Christian commitments governed by the lordship of Jesus that do not assume, as "model minority" Asian Americans otherwise presume, that going to Harvard is the be-all and end-all of the good (i.e., White American) life. To adjust to such a post-Christendom mission theology and praxis, however, invites reconsideration of one's fundamental sociopolitical allegiances and perhaps how our economic well-being, security, and flourishing depend on the subjugation, exploitation, and oppression of other people groups.[20] This is the task of critically analyzing whiteness, as many of the preceding essays (not just Tran's) show.

So where are we then in a postcolonial, postmodern, and post-Christendom world? If the colonial centuries served the Western nations, the postcolonial time is looking out for the rest, including the environment, and any Christian missiology that lacks such a global, ecological, and cosmic horizon is inadequate. The perspective of Indigenous peoples, as Andrea Smith's chapter above reminds us, is not that the human species owns land but that we belong to the land and to the creator of that and all land.[21] Similarly, if the modern world prioritized the mind and human rationality, the late-modern and postmodern period is more embodied in overall orientation. This means that, as Hak Joon Lee's chapter on Martin Luther King Jr.'s vision of the beloved community clearly shows, the Christian gospel will have to be holistic and therefore attentive, not just to souls or even souls-and-bodies but to how human beings, while spiritually related vertically to God, are also interrelated horizontally as social, economic, and political creatures. In fact, in light of this book, refocusing afresh on the Black church in the United States, especially as represented in the ministry of King and his compatriots over the last half century plus, begs the question of whether African American Christians in their fight for racial, social, and economic justice have not been at the vanguard of missiology of the future, after the end and

---

[20]These are mostly implicit rather than explicit in Murray, *Post-Christendom*.

[21]See also Amos Yong, "Primed for the Spirit: Creation, Redemption, and the *Missio Spiritus*," *International Review of Mission* 100, no. 2 (2011): 355-66; and Yong, "The *Missio Spiritus*: Towards a Pneumatological Missiology of Creation," in *Creation Care in Christian Mission*, ed. Kapya J. Kaoma, Regnum Edinburgh Centenary Series 29 (Oxford, UK: Regnum Books, 2015), 121-33.

demise of the modern colorblind missionary endeavor.[22] Last but not least, Lee's ensuing proposal for overcoming the binarily constructed identity politics of the present—that pits Whites versus others (non-Whites)—is also suggestive for considering, especially in North America, what a new missiology after the delinking of white Protestantism from the centers of national power might look like.[23] So, if the centuries of Christendom featured an unrivaled Christian message, a post-Christendom era will have to reckon both with many expressions of Christian spirituality and forms of Christian ministry and mission practice on the one side and with many religiosities on the other. On the former front, there is not a single white normative Christian expression but as many as may be reflected across the color spectrum. On the latter front, the rest is no longer a mass of ignorant and underdeveloped (because un-Christian and uncivilized) human beings but peoples of many tongues, tribes, and nations who have been nurtured for more than two millennia by other wisdom and religious traditions.[24]

A missionary vision built on White Euro-American social, economic, and political dominance no longer suffices in such a postcolonial, postmodern, and post-Christendom time; what is needed instead is a more pluralistic or diversified approach, one featuring more humble, multifaceted, and relational-mutual modalities of interface with others not just around the world but also here in the so-called West. Succinctly asked, can Christian theology as developed across the modern period and its associated missionary endeavors as colonially constructed survive in this postcolonial time? Alternatively queried: are we also witnessing the gradual demise of a

---

[22]E.g., Daniel White Hodge, *Homeland Insecurity: A Hip Hop Missiology for the Post–Civil Rights Context* (Downers Grove, IL: InterVarsity Press, 2018).

[23]It is not that the Black church has not been missionally engaged, but that it has not done so on the terms set by White Euro-American colonial missionary churches! Thus, for example, my "Justice Deprived, Justice Demanded: Afropentecostalisms and the Task of World Pentecostal Theology Today," *Journal of Pentecostal Theology* 15, no. 1 (2006): 127-47, makes this point precisely when read from a missiological perspective.

[24]Which is precisely where much of my prior work has been focused; e.g., Amos Yong, *Hospitality and the Other: Pentecost, Christian Practices, and the Neighbor* (Maryknoll, NY: Orbis Books, 2008); cf. also Clifton Clarke and Amos Yong, eds., *Global Renewal, Religious Pluralism, and the Great Commission: Toward a Renewal Theology of Mission and Interreligious Encounter*, Asbury Theological Seminary Series in World Christian Revitalization Movements in Pentecostal/Charismatic Studies 4 (Lexington, KY: Emeth Press, 2011); see also Oscar García-Johnson, *Spirit Outside the Gate: Decolonial Pneumatologies of the Global South* (Downers Grove, IL: InterVarsity Press, forthcoming).

colorblind theology and hence also in that respect the languishing of the Christian missionary enterprise based on that theological imagination? Put constructively, what would it take to articulate a colorful theology and equally relevant postcolonial missionary vision and praxis?

A "PERPETUAL FOREIGNER" WITNESS: PENTECOST AND MISSION FOR THE TWENTY-FIRST CENTURY

Given that we have come from a racist colonial mission history and that we are now at a moment in which many peoples, ethnicities, and voices are emerging from the underside of a racialized late modernity, where ought we to go and how might we move forward? For Protestant Christians, among the many other tasks needed (outlined in the preceding pages as well), the way forward must include—and cannot otherwise dispense with—scriptural retrieval. This involves reconsideration of both testaments; Johnny Ramírez-Johnson's and Love Sechrest's essays in this book point the way. Ramírez-Johnson in addition suggests that engaging Scripture involves not just the rational intellect but the affective and emotional dimensions that inform human cognition, and this is why overcoming the struggle against whiteness can never be merely one of arguments or words. From another perspective, any retrieval of Scripture, as Sechrest admonishes, risks reading White prejudices onto those that represent struggles in the original *Sitz im Leben* so that we might presume White biases to be scripturally underwritten when in reality the call of the gospel is to challenge all oppressive hierarchies perpetuated by majority cultures. Unless otherwise emotionally, affectively, and self-critically attuned, then, scriptural engagement may merely extend the pull of whiteness.

My own contribution in these closing pages, then, is to suggest one kind of hermeneutical posture for such scriptural reappropriation that is attentive to the power dynamics structuring marginal perspectives in relationship to centers of white socioeconomic and political power.[25] More precisely, I am suggesting what I have called elsewhere a *perpetual foreigner* hermeneutical stance, one informed by my own location as an Asian

---

[25]Here I develop ideas sketched previously in Amos Yong, "American Political Theology in a Post Age: A Perpetual Foreigner and Pentecostal Stance," in *Faith and Resistance in the Age of Trump*, ed. Miguel A. De La Torre (Maryknoll, NY: Orbis Books, 2017), 107-14.

American theologian. The Asian American experience of unending foreignness is shaped by the experience of continual liminality, one in which, on the one hand, their skin pigmentation and facial physiognomy do not allow them to experience America (the United States) as home—they are perpetually recipients of the question "Where are you from?" And, on the other hand, their Americanized accents and ways of speech also do not allow them to experience Asian countries and sites (and places of birth, for 1.5-generation Asian Americans like myself) as home. As soon as they speak, they are recognized across the Pacific Rim as being "not from here."[26] Such a constant socioeconomic and political alienness provides, I proffer, a critical diasporic, exilic, and counterimperial perspective that also subsists under much of the biblical traditions.

The reality is that much of what we call the Old Testament was forged out of the experience of exile within and out of the Babylonian empire. Post-Christendom missional perspectives cannot be comprehended so long as Christian mission feels itself sustained by political power and economic means. Instead, once we recognize that Israel's witness and mission to the nations were forged not out of the strength of the Davidic or monarchic regimes but resounded through the weakness of exile and its aftermath, then we realize that Christian mission itself might proceed from a similar posture. In fact, this was precisely the mentality of the followers of Jesus as Messiah since their apostolicity, here understood by their being sent to bear witness to Jesus, was launched not from the halls of colonial or imperial power but from marginalized statuses as "exiles of the Dispersion," as one of their foremost missionaries put it (1 Pet 1:1).[27] My main point is that such an exilic

---

[26]For historic perspective on the Chinese American experience, especially amid the nineteenth-century evangelical home missions efforts on both sides of the country (in Oregon and in the Carolinas), see Derek Chang, *Citizens of a Christian Nation: Evangelical Missions and the Problem of Race in the Nineteenth Century* (Philadelphia: University of Pennsylvania Press, 2012).

[27]For more missiological commentary on the Petrine text mentioned, see Amos Yong, "Diasporic Discipleship from West Asia Through Southeast Asia and Beyond: A Dialogue with 1 Peter," *Asia Journal of Theology* 32, no. 2 (October 2018): forthcoming. Other texts that invite the kind of missiological reading of 1 Peter include Andrew M. Mbuvi, *Temple, Exile and Identity in 1 Peter*, Library of New Testament Studies 345 (New York: T&T Clark, 2007); Travis B. Williams, *Good Works in 1 Peter: Negotiating Social Conflict and Christian Identity in the Greco-Roman World*, Wissenschaftliche Untersuchungen zum Neuen Testament 337 (Tübingen: Mohr Siebeck, 2014); and Shively T. J. Smith, *Strangers to Family: Diaspora and 1 Peter's Invention of God's Household* (Waco, TX: Baylor University Press, 2016).

and diasporic identity that transgresses conventionally ordered borders—indeed, that seeks joining based not only on modernist racial constructions but on the basis of our shared dirt-based experience as Willie Jennings especially, but also Andrew Draper, reminds us—is part and parcel of, rather than accidental to, the Christian missionary way of life. My secondary but no less important assertion is that the perpetual foreigner experience can help nurture such a missional and missiological imagination in ways unavailable to Christian identities forged at the sites of modern (Euro-American/White) sociopolitical and economic power. As such, the Asian American sojourn can contribute perspective on Christian self-understanding that promotes missional theology and practice at and from the margins.

Such marginality is more effectively elaborated as missional praxis than in terms of mission theory.[28] What I mean leaps off Andrew Draper's essay as he delineates practices of solidarity across lines of racial and ethnic differences that undermine whiteness, practices that subvert the stranglehold of modern colonialism, the European Enlightenment, and the Christendom-based Americanism undergirding the status quo of White European and North American prominence and wealth. If the blood of Jesus has indeed bridged the gap between Israel and the Gentiles, reconciling those who were once strangers to and alienated from each other (see Eph 2:12-19), then, as Johnny Ramírez-Johnson urged in his chapter, the Spirit of Jesus seeks, from that starting point, to open up awareness of and empower practices toward those modernity has labeled as different and other from us. The pathway, put in Pauline terms, is that of "humility and gentleness, with patience, bearing with one another in love," in order to strengthen "the unity of the Spirit in the bond of peace" (Eph 4:2-3).

Yet such missional practices, in order to not be limited only to the realm of interpersonal relations between believers, must extend also as apostolic practices of worship that shape ecclesial postures toward and engagements

---

[28]The following discussion of mission praxis is vastly condensed from my essay, "Many Tongues, Many Practices: Pentecost and Theology of Mission at 2010," in *Mission After Christendom: Emergent Themes in Contemporary Mission*, ed. Ogbu U. Kalu, Peter Vethanayagamony, and Edmund Kee-Fook Chia (Louisville, KY: Westminster John Knox, 2010), 43-58, 160-63; see also Terry C. Muck and Frances S. Adeney, *Christianity Encountering World Religions: The Practice of Mission in the Twenty-First Century* (Grand Rapids: Baker Academic, 2009); and David E. Fitch, *Faithful Presence: Seven Disciplines That Shape the Church for Mission* (Downers Grove, IL: Inter-Varsity Press, 2016).

with the world. Along these lines, those who understand or situate themselves on the margins of society are invited to embrace the vision of the seer of Patmos and emulate the practices he proposed for the churches of Asia minor, all of which enabled the diversity of aliens and strangers constituting these congregations and communities to resist the imperial—sociopolitical and economic—powers and rule of the Pax Romana.[29] The many peoples, tribes, and nations gathered around the throne in the apocalypse are anticipated by the faithful Jewish and Gentile messianists addressed by John and urged in the diversity of their tongues to counter the imperial forces regardless of financial or other possible gains.[30] If it is easier to be seduced by the promises of empire, as the stark warnings of the book of Revelation attest, it is more difficult to adopt a sectarian and marginal way of life not bought by the Babylonian gifts of Caesar but devoted to the promises of Christ as Lord. From this perspective, the perpetually foreign Asian American modality ought not to be allowed to slide into—be seduced by!— the *model minority* temptation that promises those of us on the margins the advantages of assimilation into the dominant status quo. Instead of being thereby domesticated, the unavoidable foreignness of the Asian American experience ought to strengthen critical resolve, not to be unpatriotic for its own sake but in order to live more faithfully into the gospel even when that demands a countercultural and costly resistance.

In the end, the perpetual foreigner comportment and its correlative practices cannot be humanly achieved despite our best intentions. Indeed, as Erin Dufault-Hunter's reflections indicate in the epilogue to follow, we are dealing not just with the weight of (modern) history and our own embeddedness and rootedness in the normalcy of a racialized whiteness, but there is also a spiritual dimension to our struggle, part and parcel of living in a

---

[29]E.g., J. Nelson Kraybill, *Apocalypse and Allegiance: Worship, Politics and Devotion in the Book of Revelation* (Grand Rapids: Brazos Press, 2010); Michael J. Gorman, *Reading Revelation Responsibly: Uncivil Worship and Witness; Following the Lamb into the New Creation* (Eugene, OR: Cascade Books, 2011); and Lynne St. Clair Darden, *Scripturalizing Revelation: An African American Postcolonial Reading of Empire* (Atlanta: SBL Press, 2015).

[30]J. Nelson Kraybill, *Imperial Cult and Commerce in John's Apocalypse*, Journal for the Study of the New Testament Supplement Series 132 (Sheffield: Sheffield Academic Press, 1996); see also Amos Yong, "Kings, Nations, and Cultures on the Way to the New Jerusalem: A Pentecostal Witness to an Apocalyptic Vision," in *The Pastor & the Kingdom: Essays in Honor of Jack W. Hayford*, ed. S. David Moore and Jonathan Huntzinger (Dallas: TKU Press, 2017), 231-51.

fallen world and captive to its principalities and powers of whiteness, in this age. Hence, any commitment to the coming reign of God in Jesus can only be a work of the Spirit of Christ poured out as at Pentecost upon all flesh.[31] The ongoing work of the Spirit of Pentecost is imperative in order that we can continue to experience its foundational miracle: that "each one heard them speaking in the native language of each" (Acts 2:6). From this Pentecost outpouring will flow the apostolic witness of mutuality and solidarity across linguistic, ethnic, and economic lines:

> All who believed were together and had all things in common; they would sell their possessions and goods and distribute the proceeds to all, as any had need. Day by day, as they spent much time together in the temple, they broke bread at home and ate their food with glad and generous hearts, praising God and having the goodwill of all the people. (Acts 2:44-47)

Beyond these daily practices of life together, apostolic mission contesting empire (the Pax Romana in the case of the first believers and whiteness in our case) speaks truth to worldly power by the Spirit: "Whether it is right in God's sight to listen to you rather than to God, you must judge; for we cannot keep from speaking about what we have seen and heard" (Acts 4:19-20). And perhaps most importantly, the apostolic priesthood and prophethood of all believers[32] extends throughout the margins so that our eating together across ethnic and cultural lines involves also our serving and governing together (Acts 6:1-6)—Jews and Hellenists in the first century and Whites and people of Color in the twenty-first century—all under the guidance of the Holy Spirit poured out on male and female, young and old, the haves and the have nots. Andrew Draper's fourth practice, that of tangible submission to non-White ecclesial leadership, is the end point of what is only intimated in the Acts narrative. Whereas the Twelve apparently attempted to reserve ultimate leadership roles for themselves, while appointing Hellenists to adjudicate specifically the issues bubbling up between

---

[31]The rest of this paragraph elaborates on the present turn to the Spirit of Pentecost, prevalent in much of my extant work but also featuring prominently in the work of other leading theologians of race: e.g., Jennings, *Christian Imagination*, 266-71; J. Kameron Carter, *Race: A Theological Account* (New York: Oxford University Press, 2008), 362-66; and Brian Bantum, *Redeeming Mulatto: A Theology of Race and Christian Hybridity* (Waco, TX: Baylor University Press, 2010), 146-59.

[32]E.g., Roger Stronstad, *The Prophethood of All Believers: A Study in Luke's Charismatic Theology*, Journal of Pentecostal Theology Supplement Series 16 (Sheffield: Sheffield Academic Press, 1999).

Greek-speaking and Hebrew-speaking members of the community, history itself has judged that it was the former, led by Stephen and Philip, who spearheaded the apostolic witness beyond the Jewish matrix. Hence, these two were the final arbiters of who was anointed by the Spirit for mission to the ends of the earth.[33]

If we are ever to overcome the heresy of whiteness, the heterodoxy of European colonialism, and the heteropraxis of American manifest destiny, then we will need to not just hear and understand but also come alongside and practice with the witness of others, especially those on the margins. At such locations in this time-between-the-times, we might be able to discern and then anticipate the eschatological revelation when we will discover that what whiteness called the margins was always the center of the whole. The Asian American contribution at this juncture is to suggest that the exilic and diasporic experience of the earliest messianists provides sites from which the Spirit can inspire the multilingual testimonies to the gospel of the reign of God that will in turn expose and expel the established conventions of this world, particularly as propagated by its imperial orders.[34] Whiteness as colonial modality can only be exploded finally by the plurivocity of the Pentecost witness. By extension, Christian mission in a postcolonial, post-Enlightenment, postmodern, and post-Christendom world can only be redeemed if carried out by eschatological peoples from every tribe, nation, and people who, by being filled with the Spirit of Pentecost, can live in multivocal mutuality and solidarity with one another in anticipation of the reign of God that is coming and will come.[35]

---

[33]Further support for such a reading of Acts 6 and following can be found in Amos Yong, *Who Is the Holy Spirit? A Walk with the Apostles* (Brewster, MA: Paraclete, 2011), part 4; my own broader scriptural and canonical missiology from a postcolonial and Pentecostal perspective can be found in Yong, *Mission After Pentecost: The Bible, the Spirit, and the Missio Dei, Mission in Global Community* (Grand Rapids: Baker Academic, 2019).

[34]Despite the theologically normative vision of the perpetual foreigner standpoint sketched here, the realities of this positionality are much more ambivalent; see, e.g., Gale A. Yee, "'She Stood in Tears Amid the Alien Corn': Ruth, the Perpetual Foreigner and Model Minority," in Randall C. Bailey, Tat-siong Benny Liew, and Fernando F. Segovia, eds., *They Were All Together in One Place: Toward Minority Biblical Criticism*, Semeia Studies 57 (Leiden and Boston: Brill, 2009), 119-40, esp. 120-24, and Szekar Wan, "Asian American Perspectives: Ambivalence of the Model Minority and Perpetual Foreigner," in Joseph A. Marchal, ed., *Studying Paul's Letters: Contemporary Perspectives and Methods* (Minneapolis: Fortress Press, 2012), 175-90.

[35]Thanks to my coeditors Love Sechrest and Johnny Ramírez-Johnson for their incisive reading of an earlier draft of this chapter. All foibles remain my own responsibility.

Epilogue

Dear Believers in Christ,

Among the US educated, and perhaps all Western culture, it is unpopular to speak of the devil, or, if we do, to make him rather small and primarily focused on wreaking havoc for individuals rather than also understood as ruling as prince of this world (e.g., Jn 14:30). This is the case regardless of the fact that we call ourselves Christians and claim to hold orthodox beliefs. I confess that I am prone to sheepishness when confronted with texts or stories of demonic activity.

So you can imagine my shock when I happened upon the following correspondence. I cannot tell you how or where it was found, as that would be indicting certain brothers and sisters when such condemnation proves—if the letter is authentic—to merely scapegoat a select few in order to excuse the many.

I am convinced of its authenticity, and I offer it to you as window into the souls of White folk.[1]

Respectfully,
Erin Dufault-Hunter
Fuller Theological Seminary

---

[1]In one of W. E. B. Du Bois's lesser-known essays, he begins with a confession of his beliefs, including belief in the devil and all his angels. The title of the work is "The Souls of White Folk," in the collection *Darkwater: Voices from Within the Veil* (New York: Harcourt, Brace, 1920; repr., Mineola, NY: Dover, 1999), 17-29.

A Letter from the Archdemon of Racialization to Her Angels in the United States: How Whiteness Secures Our Success in Overcoming the Enemy

To my faithful angels abiding in the congregations of White churches in the United States:

First, let us rejoice in the stunning if unexpected success in making certain humans White and, further, in making such whiteness a hardened category against which all other beings are measured. We have always drawn on our same basic weapons against humans: their instincts for comparison and competitiveness and their fear of scarcity. Our Master has ever brokered these sensibilities to foment chaos and division and, when especially fruitful, to justify violence against bodies and to smother alternative orderings of existence. But even he could scarcely foresee that our plot to generate a genre of humanity ex nihilo could be so enduring, hardening into a reality that now shapes the daily reality of hordes of these fools. (And who says that only our Enemy can conjure something out of nothing?!) Who could have dreamed that we could so profitably invent this entity called "White" out of a cluster of random physical characteristics, assert that these characteristics reveal ontological realities about this newly minted brand of human, use it as an excuse for pillaging and cruelty, and in the name of purity erase their unique stories—even of those who count as White!

I want you to concentrate on those who once called themselves (and some still do) "evangelicals." By and large, we have successfully gutted their sorry outposts of anything like a robust defense against the ravages of racialization. We have soothed them with lyrical but vacuous songs. We have kept them from reading portions of their handbook such as the Older Testament with its laments, demands for restitution, and communal commands to make amends. They have swallowed our version of their story as fundamentally about their own personal happiness. What genius that we severed their supposed gospel from law! How powerful our manipulation of the Enemy's claim to love each and every one of them!

Not only have we shielded them from their book's ridiculous ideas of mutual responsibility and repair. We have also kept them from seeing that even the individual repentance they value so highly meant a change of hearts and minds. We have shut their eyes to implications of "salvation" stories such as that of Zacchaeus, who foolishly offered restitution (with interest!) to those he cheated. And of course we have ingeniously focused the energy of the learned among them to mine Paul for doctrinal minutiae and spiritualize his call to share in the sufferings of fellow saints, to make peace with the Other. They mistake warm feelings of sympathy with the painstaking process of unifying across difference with another's body. Aided by their arrogance, these educated are easily misled.

One key innovation was training Whites to speak of racism as an issue, thus rendering it optional, a nice thing to address if they happen to be moved by it or have the time. In doing so, we have marvelously blinded them to the ways such language secures our victory. As part of something called "social justice," we render it tangential, and we have blinded Whites to ways racialization cannot be severed from the Enemy's claims over their political and social life. Simultaneously, this unwillingness to engage in race discredits White evangelicals.

The outcome of our strategy is that few recognize that whiteness determines their existence more than any other god. White Christians think they are free to choose whether they are going to be racialized. Thankfully, Christians seldom read sociologists. (That of course was another genius move on our part regarding theological education, to radically isolate thinking about God from any of the other disciplines.) So they do not recognize that for all their blathering about being part of the Enemy's global mission, those places where they live, worship, work, and learn more deeply correlate to race than to anything else. Give the Enemy their worship, if worship means what they do in church on Sundays. We still control their habits of heart and mind, and so they remain tethered in the narrow stall dubbed "whiteness." As we have always known, not seeing that they are so limited makes our job pitifully easy.

But there have been rumblings among some loyal to the Enemy, some who have become aware of our strategy of division, some who read their book in its entirety and comprehend that worship requires sacrifice. We cannot allow them to revere the Enemy and thus snatch their flesh out of our Master's mouth. You must entangle White evangelical Christians, ensnare them in the logic of racialization[2] so there is no escaping its

---

[2]The demonic recognizes that racialization is more pervasive and descriptive than overt prejudice denoted by the term *racism*. In explaining why they use *racialized*, Emerson and Smith note: "In

stranglehold. In this way, we force them to witness to the impossibility of the Enemy's promise that there is actually an alternative to violence and coercion, to competition and comparisons. Thankfully, we have in place certain strategies that have proven resilient among enlightened White people, and, given their gullibility and lack of creativity, freedom from your clutches seems unlikely.

Obviously, the major weakness of our approach is the exposure of its fragility, its nothingness—rooted in a phantom of difference. The most dangerous Christians comprehend race's fallacy clearly evidenced in the biological sciences, or, worse, they perceive it in the face of the Other, or, worst of all, they see it reflected in the racialized body of our Enemy Crucified. These White Christians relearn history and attend to tales of their fellow non-White Christians. They understand the weight and utter pervasiveness of racialization, comprehending that we suffocated White Western civilization's soul while crowning it with material gain.

It is at this point we must be very strategic, lest we lose our prey. You must confound their minds and emotions in a double bind. Here is what you must do: Even as they comprehend the fragility of race's logic, they must use *our* approved categories to express their solidarity with those it has devastated. They must not be allowed to imagine alternatives and certainly not enact them. Force them to recognize the burden of their whiteness, of all it has cost in blood and in testimony to their supposed beloved community. Tell them they must embrace whiteness as their primary identity because to do otherwise reveals their racism. Despite its biological fallacy, they grasp that its social effect has been real—and that it has privileged them. To speak or hope for an alternative in which whiteness—and thus racialization overall—is not determinative is to fly in the face of truth. As one of their monks

---

the post-Civil Rights United States, the racialized society is one in which intermarriage rates are low, residential separation and socioeconomic inequality are the norm, our definitions of personal identity and our choices of intimate associations reveal racial distinctiveness, and where 'we are never unaware of the race of a person with whom we interact.' In short, and this is its unchanging essence, *a racialized society is a society wherein race matters profoundly for differences in life experiences, life opportunities, and social relationships.* A racialized society can also be said to be 'a society that allocates differential economic, political, social, and even psychological rewards to groups along racial lines; lines that are socially constructed.'" Michael O. Emerson and Christian Smith, *Divided by Faith: Evangelical Religion and the Problem of Race in America* (New York: Oxford University Press, 2000), 7 (emphasis original).

observed, their impotent god refuses to change history. So insist that whiteness is them; they are whiteness. Their reality must now be lived as those benefiting from racialization. And thus whiteness continues to define and bound their existence. They cannot use language such as "postracial," as we have made sure any who sense the ethereal nature of whiteness also tend to deny the current as well as the past realities.

Stopping their reflection at just this point paralyzes them (especially the most sensitive among them, such as White males), and despite their religiosity it is easy to coax them into severing the spiritual from the physical. Get them to parrot the rhetoric of secular activism (which we know is not without its own dangers to our cause). After all, humans remain driven by base comparisons and chronic need, and these Whites desperately want to be seen as progressive, accepted as "not like those other White evangelicals." Keep them locked into the reasoning of civil rights, protest, and legislation; steer them away from Ms. Alexander or others who seek to cast us out, those who know that we demons can happily reside in cleanly swept homes made of law.[3] Crucially, hinder their spokespersons from taking into account the impoverished Whites who make up the majority of the poor in their country so privileged Whites can enact our tactic of crushing the weak, of silencing the starving.

In this way, be sure White Christians find themselves at a loss to tell their own story and without permission to do so; beyond the self-obfuscating appellation of "White," they must feel bereft of belonging. Foster under a patina of assertive protest a core misgiving that they are seen by their god. We must prevent them from developing their own strength and filling in their own story, especially a new story entangled with the Other's. Otherwise, they could become effective in fighting us; they might graciously lay aside defensiveness or incapacitating shame. If White people actually become free to robustly exploit their resources to work against racialization

---

[3]The author of a much-acclaimed book about criminal justice and race, *The New Jim Crow: Mass Incarceration in the Age of Colorblindness* (New York: New Press, 2012), Michelle Alexander left her faculty position in law at Ohio State University to teach at Union Theological Seminary. She explained on her Facebook page: "This is not simply a legal problem, or a political problem, or a policy problem. At its core, America's journey from slavery to Jim Crow to mass incarceration raises profound moral and spiritual questions about who we are, individually and collectively, who we aim to become, and what we are willing to do now."

in some settings while happily laying aside those same assets in others, we have lost the war. The Enemy seems especially pleased by this disgusting disposition, dubbed "humility" in their pitiful tradition. But gratefully, few White Christians really believe that drivel about being loved and served by their Lord; they crave attention of their fellow humans (many especially crave that of non-Whites)—and all to our advantage.

Finally, by any means necessary, block White Christians who seek to join their bodies with the bodies of the racialized other, especially in unsexy and ordinary rhythms of daily existence (if necessary, direct the enthusiastic toward the momentary and heroic). Obstruct Whites who want to enact the Enemy's call for costly attachment to the Other. I have seen the danger of such joining on multiple occasions, sometimes even among Whites unnuanced about race's logic. For example, we have recently boasted of our dominance in various police shootings, asserting our control. This is of course as it should be, for occasionally we must foment primal fear so we remain enthroned and served.

But this can be problematic, and I have seen the Enemy use this for his purposes. Recently I hovered as a Black woman told of the impact of the shootings of Philando Castile, Alton Sterling, and others. She movingly spoke about having two sons who walk to the store, about her Black husband who drives around town. As the mother spoke, I felt the dangerous forging of a connection, a rippling of empathy that progressed from one mother to another mother, from a mother to fathers, from a father to friends . . . You get the idea. We must hamper the awareness of this interconnectedness at all costs and interfere with any impulse to see White, Brown, or Yellow boys as sons of one and thus sons of all. Remember: Competition, comparison, and fear of scarcity secure their worship. If you sense Whites contemplating cooperation or if a shared humanity begins to dawn, squelch these impulses by introducing rivalry; scare them with the implications of connecting their beloveds with beloveds of those in danger. Steer them away from the perilous conviction that "this cannot happen to *our* sons" to the fearful frame: "This cannot happen to *my* son—so I will protect *mine* by steering clear of yours."

If links are forged between them, they begin to perceive the world through the others' eyes; through even one such personal connection, Whites might begin to perceive the systemic structures of racialization we have carefully contrived. Many of our plots have been thus foiled by mothers. Keep producing a culture that idealizes parenting and summarizes its purpose in cute maxims such as those perpetuated in Hallmark or Dayspring cards, lest these humans ever ponder how such practices could train them in resistance to the racialized status quo.

You have heard rumors that the Enemy will one day overthrow our Prince. Rest assured that this is mere folly. He claims that these repulsively weak creatures share a destiny of communion with him that doesn't necessitate erasure of difference or competitive striving. He claims they will be joined as one-yet-many. We know this is madness. Yet nonetheless our chokehold on White Christians loosens when Whites respond in a given moment, aware of the past but pulled into this imagined future. Whites then begin to display sensibilities we must impede at all costs: They feel the Other's pain and, even more disturbing, the Other's joys. They value the Other, displaying inexplicable affection and even cherishing the Other. They play a revolting game of "outdoing one another in love," not out of showmanship but out of self-forgetfulness. This sickening expression of friendship chips away at our fortresses, dismantles our complex system of oppression by setting off a series of interrelated, innovative practices. At all costs, Whites must not free themselves from self-centeredness and replace the Other as their center of concern. Such vulnerability to the Other proves a surprisingly vigorous weapon against which we have no defense, and, inexplicably, permeability to the Other always sets back our cause.

Overall, you have done well, my angels! Your brilliance has been the perpetuation of patterns of behavior and mechanisms of division, all the while filling White Christian mouths with hymns proclaiming their dedication to their supposed Lord! As long as we secure their bodies and decide where they can live and learn, as long as we order their relationships and determine who they welcome or wed, encourage them to believe that such singing constitutes worship. We can rest assured knowing we have White Christians' souls.

For as long as they remain defined and determined in habits of heart, mind, and body by tightly constrained categories of whiteness, as long as Whites fidget in self-absorption, as long as they utilize our prescribed options of political and social action, they serve our Master. If they break out of the boundaries of whiteness and begin to imagine alternatives like

Christian friendship, they would become free. Beware of those who recognize that the bonds of whiteness prevent them from being bound to the Enemy and all who follow him. But this appears unlikely to occur, as we have mastered their rhetoric and manacled their bodies to racialized arrangements. And those Whites who do see racialization fall all over themselves to articulate their awareness of it, usually refusing to wield their positions of relative power for any actual change. Most tellingly, they cannot imagine an alternative reality around which to organize for their future; we have captured their theological imagination—and it is shrunken and impotent. Against the Enemy's central myth, we have remade White Christian understandings of redemption, limiting their conceptions of what is possible by either ignoring the past or feeling shackled by it. This is a profound achievement. May our Master be praised and worshiped now and forevermore!

In loyalty to Lucifer,
The Archdemon of Racialization

List of Contributors

Akintunde Akinade is professor of theology at Georgetown University's Edmund E. Walsh School of Foreign Service in Qatar.

Clifton R. Clarke is associate dean for the William E. Pannell Center for African American Church Studies and associate professor of black church studies and world Christianity at Fuller Theological Seminary, Pasadena, California.

Elizabeth Conde-Frazier is academic dean and vice president of education at Esperanza College of Eastern University, St. Davids, Pennsylvania.

Andrew T. Draper is an author, speaker, scholar, and founding Senior Pastor of Urban Light Community Church.

Erin Dufault-Hunter is assistant professor of Christian ethics at Fuller Theological Seminary, Pasadena, California.

Willie James Jennings is associate professor of systematic theology and Africana studies at Yale University Divinity School, New Haven, Connecticut.

Daniel Jeyaraj is professor of world Christianity and the director of the Andrew F. Walls Centre for the Study of African and Asian Christianity at Liverpool Hope University, Liverpool, United Kingdom.

Hak Joon Lee is Lewis B. Smedes Professor of Christian Ethics at Fuller Theological Seminary, Pasadena, California.

Johnny Ramírez-Johnson is professor of anthropology and profesor del Centro Latino at Fuller Theological Seminary, Pasadena, California.

Angel D. Santiago-Vendrell is E. Stanley Jones Associate Professor of Evangelism at Asbury Theological Seminary's Dunnam School of Urban Ministries, Orlando, Florida.

Love L. Sechrest is dean of the faculty, vice president of academic affairs and associate professor of New Testament at Columbia Theological Seminary, Decatur, Georgia.

Andrea Smith is associate professor of media and cultural studies and director of graduate studies in ethnic studies at University of California Riverside, California.

Jonathan Tran is associate professor of theology and ethics in the Religion Department at Baylor University, Waco, Texas.

Amos Yong is professor of theology and mission and director of the Center for Missiological Research at Fuller Theological Seminary, Pasadena, California.

Subject Index

Scripture Index

MISSIOLOGICAL ENGAGEMENTS

Series Editors: Scott W. Sunquist,
Amos Yong, and John R. Franke

Missiological Engagements: Church, Theology, and Culture in Global Contexts charts interdisciplinary and innovative trajectories in the history, theology, and practice of Christian mission at the beginning of the third millennium.

Among its guiding questions are the following: What are the major opportunities and challenges for Christian mission in the twenty-first century? How does the missionary impulse of the gospel reframe theology and hermeneutics within a global and intercultural context? What kind of missiological thinking ought to be retrieved and reappropriated for a dynamic global Christianity? What innovations in the theology and practice of mission are needed for a renewed and revitalized Christian witness in a postmodern, postcolonial, postsecular, and post-Christian world?

Books in the series, both monographs and edited collections, will feature contributions by leading thinkers representing evangelical, Protestant, Roman Catholic, and Orthodox traditions, who work within or across the range of biblical, historical, theological, and social-scientific disciplines. Authors and editors will include the full spectrum from younger and emerging researchers to established and renowned scholars, from the Euro-American West and the Majority World, whose missiological scholarship will bridge church, academy, and society.

Missiological Engagements reflects cutting-edge trends, research, and innovations in the field that will be of relevance to theorists and practitioners in churches, academic domains, mission organizations, and NGOs, among other arenas.

Finding the Textbook You Need

The IVP Academic Textbook Selector
is an online tool for instantly finding the IVP books
suitable for over 250 courses across 24 disciplines.

ivpress.com/academic